Challenging the Grünfeld

By Edward Dearing

First published in Sweden 2005 by Quality Chess Europe AB.

ISBN 91-975243-4-4

All sales or enquiries should be directed to Quality Chess Europe
Vegagatan 18, SE-413 09 Gothenburg, Sweden
tel: +46-31-24 47 90 fax: +46-31-24 47 14
e-mail: info@qualitychessbooks.com
website: www.qualitychessbooks.com

Edited by John Shaw & Jacob Aagaard.
Typeset: Ari Ziegler
Proof reading: Danny Kristiansen
Cover Design: Carole Dunlop
Printed in The Netherlands by A-D Druk B.V.

CONTENTS

Symbols

†	Check
!	A strong move
!!	A brilliant move
!?	An interesting move
?!	A dubious move
?	A mistake
??	A blunder
+–	White has a winning position
±	White is better
⩱	White is slightly better
=	The position is equal
∞	The position is unclear
∞̲	Compensation for the sacrificed material
∓	Black is slightly better
∓	Black is better
–+	Black has a winning position
1–0	White won
½–½	The game was drawn
0–1	Black won
(x)	x'th match game
corr.	Correspondence game

Bibliography

Books:
Burgess, Emms, Gallagher & Nunn: *Nunn's Chess Openings*. Everyman, 1999.
Davies: *The Grünfeld Defence*. Everyman, 2002.
Karpov: *Beating the Grünfeld*. Batsford, 1994.
Kasparov, Speelman & Wade: *Garry Kasparov's Fighting Chess*. Batsford, 1995.
Lalic: *The Grünfeld for the Attacking Player*. Batsford, 1997.
Rowson: *Understanding the Grünfeld*. GAMBIT, 1999.
Suetin: *The Complete Grünfeld*. Batsford, 1991.
Shereshevsy & Slutsky: *Mastering the Endgame Volume 2*. Cadogan, 1992.
Stohl: *Instructive Modern Chess Masterpieces*. GAMBIT, 2001.
Yermolinsky: *The Road to Chess Improvement*. GAMBIT, 1999.

Journals & Periodicals:
British Chess Magazine.
CHESS magazine.
New In Chess Magazine.
New In Chess Yearbooks 1-71.

Electronic Resources:
Chessbase Magazine (CBM) 1–103.
Encyclopedia of Chess Openings, Volume D, Electronic Edition (2004).
Glenn Flear's monthly "Daring Defences" column at www.chesspublishing.com.
Megabase 2004.
MegaCorr 3.
Sahovski Chess Informants 1-91.
TWIC 1-530.
Ultrabase 2002.

Acknowledgements

This has been a tricky project for a number of reasons. The Modern Exchange Variation, despite having been employed regularly by the world's leading grandmasters for over two decades, has never received extensive and comprehensive coverage in any one source. An inevitable consequence of this has been the need to consult numerous magazines and journals, and basically to sift for information from a wide range of sources. In this respect *Chessbase* has proved an invaluable tool, however there was still the task of deciding which information was most relevant. Initially I envisioned this book as a smaller project, however the sheer volume of relevant games and analysis that exists on the Modern Exchange Variation is probably enough to fill a volume of ECO! Within writing two chapters my old friend Jacob Aagaard was already warning me that I was on course to more than double the agreed page count. Through a process of consultation with Jacob I trimmed certain parts that were not so important, and enhanced those areas that we thought would be of greater interest to readers. It has been a lot of work, but I am now very happy with the finished product.

In addition to there being a lot of theory for me to cover, there was also the problem that important games are played quite frequently in the 8.罝b1 variation, which meant that the book would have to be kept up-to-date after the actual writing was finished and throughout the editing and formatting process. When important games were played I tried to provide the editors (IM John Shaw and GM (elect) Jacob Aagaard) with annotated amendments to the book, however very often I was pleased, surprised and impressed to learn that they had already taken note of the games and were looking for ways to implement editorial amendments! So although I was responsible for the actual writing of this book, the final product will be very much a team effort.

Anyway, the acknowledgements:

-   First and foremost, my thanks go to Jacob Aagaard for offering me the chance to write this book, and being my main contact at Quality Chess Books. In addition to offering general advice on content, Jacob has also been very generous with his time (and criticism!) to make this project work. There was one stage when my undeniable computer illiteracy manifested itself spectacularly – by deleting all the dots in the book! Unfazed by this, Jacob simply cursed my name for five minutes, beat his head against the wall for seven, and then helped me fix the problem without complaining.
-   Secondly, I would like to thank John Shaw, for his editorial work on the book, and Ari Ziegler, for providing various articles and making suggestions on content.
-   I also wish to extend my thanks to Karl Mah, Rupesh Tailor, Max Rohrig, Seyda Duman, Ursula, Marcus, Ben Purton, and my old friend Andrew Brett, who really did an awful lot to convince me to take up the Modern Exchange Variation in the first place!

Introduction

The Background to *Challenging the Grünfeld*:

In early 1997 I sat down to do some serious work on my White opening repertoire, in preparation for the World Under-18 Championship. In general, I was happy with my openings – I had found some good lines against the King's Indian Defence, the Nimzo Indian, and most of the mainline Queen's Gambit and Slav lines – however one large hole in my opening repertoire remained: the Grünfeld.

In the past I had enjoyed mixed experiences when facing the Grünfeld. Originally I relied exclusively on the Seville Variation (1.d4 ♘f6 2.c4 g6 3.♘c3 d5 4.cxd5 ♘xd5 5.e4 ♘xc3 6.bxc3 ♗g7 7.♗c4 c5 8.♘e2 0–0 9.0–0 ♘c6 10.♗e3 ♗g4 11.f3 cxd4 12.cxd4 ♘a5 13.♗xf7 ♖xf7 14.fxg4 ♖xf1 15.♔xf1)

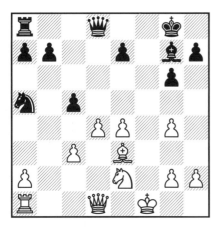

I had seen Karpov use this line to good effect in some games from his 1987 World Championship match with Kasparov, and the notion of rapidly firing out 20 moves of established theory at the board very much appealed to me. Initially my results were quite positive, however the positions I reached were highly imbalanced, and as I improved I faced more experienced opponents

who handled the Black side of the Seville Variation with understanding and precision that was quite beyond my own powers. I soon discovered that without serious study the resulting positions were simply too volatile to work out in practical play.

Subsequently I switched to the Russian System (1.d4 ♘f6 2.c4 g6 3.♘c3 d5 4.♘f3 ♗g7 5.♕b3 dxc4 6.♕xc4 0–0 7.e4)

which was popular at that time. As with the Seville Variation, my initial results were good, however I was never entirely comfortable with bringing my queen out so early. Furthermore, although I enjoyed sharp and tactical positions, I didn't much care for entering situations where I was behind in development – the potential for things backfiring was simply too high.

It was with some frustration, therefore, that I set out to discover a suitable and durable line against the Grünfeld; one that offered good winning chances but did not risk burning down the house in the process! At around this time my old friend Andrew Brett stopped by my home for some blitz chess. Andrew was in law school then, and is now an experienced lawyer.

He rarely has time to play chess, but follows the top tournaments and occasionally studies sharp mainline theory. We began playing, and I made a point of playing the Grünfeld as Black to see if I would discover anything that I disliked playing against. With a smugness befitting Andrew's lawyerly nature, he convincingly beat me three games in a row with the 8.♖b1 line.

Although I tried not to let it show, this annoyed me intensely: I was substantially higher rated and usually won at blitz too! Nevertheless, I was intrigued by how well he handled the 8.♖b1 system, and requested a crash course on its intricacies. For the next hour Andrew demonstrated the lines he knew, repeated some old games and explained which lines were currently popular or problematic for White. Needless to say, I was impressed and horrified that he knew all this, never mind the fact that he could remember it too!

Later that day I flicked through some copies of *Informant* and those *New In Chess* Yearbooks which I owned, and it quickly became clear that White scores excellently with the 8.♖b1 line. However, perhaps even more impressive than White's results was the calibre of player that employed this line: Kramnik, Khalifman, Ivanchuk, Gelfand, Yusupov, Shirov, Beliavsky, Sakaev, M.Gurevich, Bacrot and even Kasparov and Karpov have played this line as White! This line definitely held some appeal, so I set out to study it quite thoroughly. Unfortunately there were no books on it (*The Complete Grünfeld*, by Alexei Suetin, and Anatoly Karpov's *Beating the Grünfeld*, offer some limited coverage, but much of this was rather dated) so I had to pull together what I could from various issues of the *New In Chess* magazines and yearbooks, *Informant* and *Chessbase Magazine (CBM)*.

That was 1997. In 2004 I decided to play at the FIDE Chess Olympiad in Calvia, Mallorca, Spain. My preparation for the Grünfeld was a complete mess, so I again had to do some serious work on the 8.♖b1 variation, however to my disappointment there were still no books

on it! Consequently I had to go through the same arduous task of examining numerous journals and gathering notes on each line and sub-variation so that I could update my opening folder. Having gone through this process a second time, and kept detailed notes, it occurred to me that anyone else who wants to play this variation must encounter the same difficulties, which is largely why I put together this little book.

The 8.♖b1 variation (or 'The Modern Exchange Variation' as GM Bogdan Lalic dubs it in *The Grünfeld for the Attacking Player*) offers White superb winning chances, is theoretically sound, has been played by most of the best players in the world, and is much easier to play as White than to defend against as Black!

But really, what's the point?

When I decide to undertake any project I like to have a specific purpose in mind. I have written one other chess book (*Play the Sicilian Dragon*, by GAMBIT Publications) and the purpose of that book was largely to detail my experiences with the Sicilian Dragon, discussing both the strengths and weaknesses of the opening, as well as providing a detailed survey of the theory in the most popular variations. The sheer size of that project required that I use a 'tree of variations' format, with relatively little room for complete games and explanatory content. *Challenging the Grünfeld* was a project that gave me more flexibility in terms of approach. Although I wanted to provide White with a thoroughly reliable opening repertoire against the Grünfeld, I also appreciated that most people have neither the time nor the patience to wade through line after line of dense theoretical sub-variations. In light of this consideration I decided to present the book as a set of 50 annotated games between strong grandmasters, which I consider to be particularly instructive or helpful. It is my hope that the process of playing through these games will illustrate the themes, niceties and strategies of the Modern Exchange Variation in a relatively pain-free manner.

For those readers who desire more detail, or who require a more expansive knowledge of the theory surrounding the Modern Exchange Variation, this can usually be found in the 'alternatives' notes to the illustrative games. Obviously a tree format had to be used for this, and at times the theory can become rather dense, and I must apologise for this. It was my original intention to avoid dense theoretical variations wherever possible, however I approached this project on the basis that I was preparing the Modern Exchange Variation for my own use, so the level of detail included here represents the level of detail which I myself would desire from a book purporting to present a comprehensive repertoire against the Grünfeld.

The Themes and Ideas of the Modern Exchange Variation:

The opening moves of the Modern Exchange Variation proceed as follows:

1.d4 ♘f6 2.c4 g6 3.♘c3 d5 4.♘f3

4.cxd5 ♘xd5 5.e4 ♘xc3 6.bxc3 ♗g7 (6...c5 is also possible. Notably White avoids this move with the 4.♘f3 move order, although I am not sure how much difference it really makes.) 7.♘f3 is also possible, however my preference has always been to play 4.♘f3. before capturing on d5.

4...♗g7 5.cxd5 ♘xd5 6.e4 ♘xc3 7.bxc3 c5 8.♖b1!

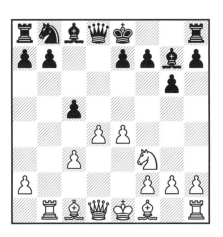

8...0–0 9.♗e2 cxd4

9...b6 is a sideline that has now become very popular at all levels on account of Black's solid yet potentially dynamic formation. In general White can obtain a small opening advantage against this system on account of his greater space and superior central control, however actually converting that slight edge to anything more is another matter entirely. In practice Black's position has proved extremely resilient and results have been good.

The 9...b6 system will be discussed in detail in Chapter 8.

9...♘c6 is perhaps Black's most logical move: the c6-knight coordinates with the g7-bishop and d8-queen to put substantial pressure on the d4-pawn. If White defends the d4-pawn with 10.♗e3, Black could try to undermine White's centre with 10...♗g4, or play 10...cxd4 11.cxd4 ♕a5†, when White must choose between 12.♕d2 ♕xd2 13.♔xd2, and 12.♗d2 ♕xa2, both of which are probably better for Black. White is therefore forced to play 10.d5!.

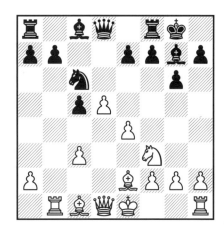

Black now has two lines:

The most obvious choice is 10...♗xc3† and this is examined in Chapter 6. Play continues 11.♗d2 ♗xd2† 12.♕xd2 and now 12...♘d4 13.♘xd4 cxd4 14.♕xd4 ♕a5† 15.♕d2 ♕xd2† 16.♔xd2 leads Black into a difficult ending. This is examined in Game 37, Kasparov – Natsis 1980.

The main alternative is 12...♘a5!? when Black attempts to hold on to the extra pawn, but in return White gains excellent attacking chances against the black king. Theory now recommends 13.h4 ♗g4! when White can choose between 14.h5!, which is the mainline and is considered in Game 38, Halkias – Lputian 2000, or 14.♘g5!?, which has scored enormously well for White and is considered in Game 39, Bacrot – Popovic 2002.

Black's primary alternative to 10...♗xc3 is 10...♘e5 which has become something of a mainline unto itself in recent years, and is considered in Chapter 7. Play continues 11.♘xe5 ♗xe5 12.♕d2! (12.♕c2?! is less accurate, but is included for illustrative purposes (Game 40). 12.♖b3!? is a relatively new idea that has hitherto scored well for White (Game 43).) 12...e6 13.f4 and now 13...♗g7 is the traditional mainline of this variation (examined in Game 41), and 13...♗c7!? is perhaps best described as the modern mainline of 9...♘c6, although perhaps this is something of a misnomer given that Khalifman – Tseitlin 1999 (Game 42) seems to have put most Grünfeld players off this line in recent years.

Occasionally Grünfeld advocates try the old 9...♕a5!? line, however nowadays this variation is considered unduly risky, if not invariably disadvantageous for Black. We will take a quick look at this system in Chapter 9, Games 48 & 49.
10.cxd4 ♕a5†

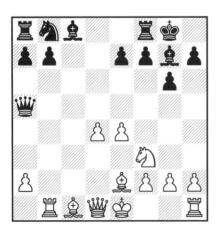

11.♗d2

In the past 11.♕d2 has enjoyed brief spells of popularity because the endgame after 11...♕xd2† 12.♗xd2 was thought to hold some dangers for Black. Nowadays Black's handling of this system has been refined to the point where White has little (if any) hope of an advantage, and consequently 11.♕d2 has fallen into widespread disuse at IM and GM level.
11..♕xa2 12.0–0

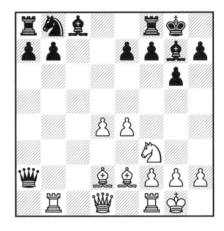

The position above represents the starting position of the mainline Modern Exchange Grünfeld. Black is a pawn up, has two connected passed pawns on the queenside, and has no visible weaknesses to speak of. Oh, and it is Black to move as well!

When one puts it in those terms I would hope it is easy for the reader to understand why I was initially somewhat sceptical of this variation. After all, where is White's compensation? This is not an easy question to answer in abstract, but I will give it a try.

The first point to note is that White is ahead in development: all of his pieces bar the f1 rook (and perhaps the d1–queen) are developed quite actively. Although neither of White's bishops can threaten anything without moving again, the point is that they are only a move away from creating a serious threat. For example, the d2–

bishop can lunge to b4 or g5, in either case hitting the e7 pawn. If White recovers his sacrificed pawn material equality will be restored, but White will retain his strong centre and formidable lead in development. The e2-bishop also enjoys hidden potential: consider the continuation 12...b6 13.♕c1 ♗b7. Now 14.♗c4! hits the black queen and puts pressure on the tender f7-pawn. Indeed at this stage White already has the option of forcing a draw via 14...♕a4 15.♗b5 ♕a2 16.♗c4, not that he would want to!

The second point to consider is Black's development. At present only Black's g7-bishop is well-placed, and even then its scope is quite restricted by the d4-pawn. Black's queen feels as though she is on the wrong side of the board, and is in the path of Black's queenside pawns[1]. Whereas White's pieces are ready to create immediate threats, Black's pieces remain undeveloped and unprepared to generate immediate counterplay.

An additional aspect to White's compensation is what Black cannot do: Black would like to play 12...♘c6, however 13.d5 ♘e5 14.♘d4 (intending 15.♗c3 and 16.♖a1 trapping the queen) is already very good for White. Black would also like to develop the c8-bishop, however at present the bishop seems to be tied to the protection of the b7-pawn[2].

A further consideration is each side's pawn structure. White enjoys a strong and mobile pawn centre that is already eager to advance with d4-d5 and e4-e5, restricting Black's forces and creating threats as they go. Black, on the other hand, will have trouble organising an effective pawn break that does not create serious weaknesses within his position. 12...a7-a5 is one mainline (Chapter 1), however this substantially weakens the b5 and b6 squares, and also does nothing to challenge White's centre or improve Black's development. 12...b7-b6 (Chapter 2) is another obvious choice, however this weakens Black's control of the queenside light squares.

One final point that I would like to mention is borrowed from Jonathan Rowson's work, *Understanding the Grünfeld*. Rowson notes that, having essentially exchanged the g8-knight for the b1–knight, Black has potentially left his kingside a little vulnerable. The problems that this exchange gives rise to are compounded by the difficulties that Black will experience in bringing his remaining minor pieces over to the kingside. Although this element doesn't really form a big part of White's compensation at this stage, I wanted to mention this observation because I had never thought of this position in those terms. I was, of course, aware that Black's kingside often comes under fire from White's minor pieces in subsequent stages of this variation, however before reading *Understanding the Grünfeld* I had never thought of Black's kingside as being 'weak' at this stage.

In conclusion, I believe that White's large lead in development, well-placed pieces and mobile pawn centre guarantee excellent compensation for the sacrificed pawn.

Recommended Repertoire:

Although this book includes fifty illustrative games (and I shudder to think how many ancillary notes, variations and sub-variations!), not all of them are strictly necessary to the repertoire which I am going to recommend. However, the games are there for a reason, and I firmly believe that a thorough knowledge of the concepts that are explored in these games will prove beneficial to those who wish to play the Modern Exchange Variation.

Chapter 1

Here we consider the variation arising after:
1.d4 ♘f6 2.c4 g6 3.♘c3 d5 4.cxd5 ♘xd5 5.e4 ♘xc3 6.bxc3 ♗g7 7.♘f3 0–0 8.♗e2 c5 9.♖b1 cxd4 10.cxd4 ♕a5† 11.♗d2 ♕xa2 12.0–0 a5!?

---

[1] However the queen does perform some useful functions on a2, in particular in terms of restricting the movement and coordination of White's forces within their own camp. We will discuss this theme in more detail as and when it occurs throughout the book.

[2] This comment is made on a purely superficial level only. In actual fact 12...♗g4! is probably Black's strongest move, and this will be considered in Chapter 4.

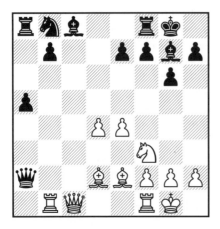

against which I am recommending 13.♗g5 a4 (13...h6 is also playable, but probably bad for Black. This is examined in Game 6) 14.♖e1! which is relatively unexplored, but has scored excellently in practice and is a favourite with GMs Boris Gelfand and Yuri Shulman, both of whom are renowned experts on the Modern Exchange Variation. This line is discussed in detail in Game 8.

Chapter 2

In Chapter 2 the line 1.d4 ♘f6 2.c4 g6 3.♘c3 d5 4.cxd5 ♘xd5 5.e4 ♘xc3 6.bxc3 ♗g7 7.♘f3 0–0 8.♗e2 c5 9.♖b1 cxd4 10.cxd4 ♕a5† 11.♗d2 ♕xa2 12.0–0 b6!? is discussed.

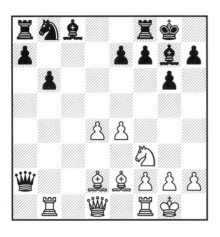

My recommendation against this line is 13.♕c1! when Black has two moves. In my opinion Black's best option is 13...♕e6!?, against which White has several dangerous options, but none which seem to guarantee a knock-out blow or even a definite advantage. My recommendation here is Chernin's 14.♖e1!?, which gives rise to unclear positions in which White enjoys enduring positional compensation and excellent practical chances (see Game 12).

The normal move is 13...♗b7, when White should play 14.♗c4 ♕a4 15.♗b5 ♕a2 16.♗c4 ♕a4 17.♗b5 ♕a2 18.♖e1 (Games 13 and 14).

Chapter 3

In this chapter we deal with one of Leko's favourite lines, 1.d4 ♘f6 2.c4 g6 3.♘c3 d5 4.cxd5 ♘xd5 5.e4 ♘xc3 6.bxc3 ♗g7 7.♘f3 c5 8.♖b1 0–0 9.♗e2 cxd4 10.cxd4 ♕a5† 11.♗d2 ♕xa2 12.0–0 ♘d7!?

which has proven quite resilient over the last few years. 13.♗b4! a5?! is shown to be good for White in Game 15, however much better is 13...♘b6, which is considered in Games 16-19.

White then has a choice: 14.♖a1!? ♕e6 15.♕b1 is considered in Game 18. White seems to have good chances in this line, however with precise play Black is able to hold the balance. Consequently it may be worth trying GM Boris

Avrukh's 15.♗d3!?, which is discussed in the notes to Game 18 and may well be promising for White. Avrukh is a respected expert on Grünfeld defence and, in particular, on the Modern Exchange Variation, so his ideas deserve consideration.

In Game 19 we examine Boris Gelfand's interpretation of the 12...♘d7 variation: 13.♗b4 ♘b6 14.h3!?. Gelfand is considered the foremost authority on the Modern Exchange Variation, and his ideas have done much to shape my understanding of how this system should be played. 14.h3 has scored excellently in practice, but unfortunately remains relatively unexplored.

Game 20 sees the Indian GM Viswanathan Anand causing GM Peter Leko some serious problems with another fresh idea: 13.♖e1!?. In the main game Leko manages to hold the balance, however the notes to move 16 take into account Stohl's recommended improvement, 16.♗d3!? which also looks promising for White.

Conclusion: You are spoilt for choice here! If I was forced to choose between these systems I think I would probably play Gelfand's 14.h3, but that is just personal preference speaking.

Chapter 4

In this chapter we deal with Black's most reliable line, 12...♗g4!.

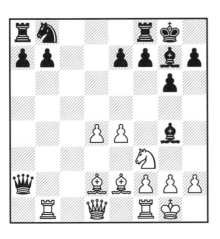

Black has been close to equality in this system for some time, however White has continuously been able find refinements that pose fresh problems. My recommendation against this system is

13.♗g5 h6 14.♗e3 (considered in Games 26-29). White has also played 13.♗g5 h6 14.♗h4, however I believe that Black has now solved his problems here (see Game 25). White has one other option in 13.♗e3 (considered in Games 30-32), which is still posing Black some problems. However I am recommending 13.♗g5 h6 14.♗e3 because it has been the choice of true experts like GM Khalifman, GM Krasenkow and, most recently, French GM Etienne Bacrot.

Chapter 5

This chapter is just a round-up of Black's dodgy sidelines, the recommendations against which are obvious (they are pretty much the only thing discussed!).

Chapter 6

In this chapter we deal with the line 1.d4 ♘f6 2.c4 g6 3.♘c3 d5 4.cxd5 ♘xd5 5.e4 ♘xc3 6.bxc3 ♗g7 7.♘f3 c5 8.♖b1 0–0 9.♗e2 ♘c6!? 10.d5 ♗xc3† 11.♗d2 ♗xd2† 12.♕xd2

and now 12...♘d4!? just leads to a bad ending for Black (see Game 37), so Black has to try

12...♘a5!? 13.h4 ♗g4, when White's best is probably 14.h5! with a dangerous kingside attack.

[Editor's note: Very recent developments suggest that 14.♘g5! is also promising (see Game 39).]

Chapter 7

This chapter deals with Black's alternative to capturing on c3, i.e. 1.d4 ♘f6 2 ♘f3 g6 3.c4 ♗g7 4 ♘c3 d5 5.cxd5 ♘xd5 6.e4 ♘xc3 7.bxc3 c5 8.♖b1 0–0 9.♗e2 ♘c6 10.d5 ♘e5!? against which I recommend following the mainline with 11.♘xe5 ♗xe5 12.♕d2! (Games 41 & 42), although those who wish to avoid all the theory have a reasonable alternative in 12.♖b3!? (Game 43).

Chapter 8

Here we deal with 1.d4 ♘f6 2.c4 g6 3 ♘f3 ♗g7 4 ♘c3 d5 5.cxd5 ♘xd5 6.e4 ♘xc3 7.bxc3 c5 8.♖b1 0–0 9.♗e2 b6,

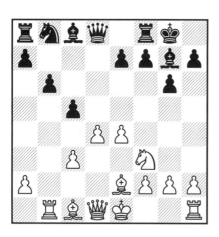

which tends to be more about ideas and understanding than long variations. Play continues 10 0–0 ♗b7 11.♕d3 and now 11...e6!?

is Game 44. Instead, 11...♗a6 12.♕e3 ♕d7 13.d5! is Game 45, and 11...♗a6 12.♕e3 ♕c8 13.d5! is Game 46, both of which are better for White on existing evidence. 11...cxd4 is considered in Game 47, however exchanging on d4 at this stage just enhances the mobility of White's pieces and leaves Black with inferior versions of the positions reached in Games 44-46.

Chapter 9

Here we just consider Black's dodgy alternatives, such as 9...♕a5, which should be met by 10.0–0!. The recommendations here are all pretty self-explanatory.

The mainline of the 8.♖b1 Grünfeld commences after 1.d4 ♘f6 2.c4 g6 3.♘c3 d5 4.cxd5 ♘xd5 5.e4 ♘xc3 6.bxc3 ♗g7 7.♘f3 0–0 8.♗e2 c5 9.♖b1 cxd4 10.cxd4 ♕a5† 11.♗d2 ♕xa2 12.0–0 with the following position:

The general ideas associated with either side's play were considered in the Introduction, and in this chapter we are going to examine one of Black's most aggressive treatments of the position, 12...a5, in greater detail.

Chapter 1: The Presumptuous 12...a5!?

Game 1
Sapis – Markowski
Koszalin 1992

1.♘f3 ♘f6 2.c4 g6 3.♘c3 d5 4.cxd5 ♘xd5 5.e4 ♘xc3 6.bxc3 ♗g7 7.d4 c5 8.♖b1 0–0 9.♗e2 cxd4 10.cxd4 ♕a5† 11.♗d2 ♕xa2 12.0–0 a5!? 13.♕c1!?

♕d1–c1 is a very common move in Grünfeld positions where Black employs the manoeuvre ♕d8-a5-a2 capturing a pawn. By placing the queen on c1 White takes immediate control of the c-file, thereby contemplating an invasion on the c7-square with ♕c1–c7, or even ♕c1–c5. On c7 the white queen would exert an unwelcome influence over Black's 7th rank, whereas on c5 she would place pressure on the e7 and a5 pawns, but would also perform the less obvious function of maintaining control of the a3-square, thereby taking another square away from the black queen. This is hardly a critical problem at this early stage, however it is not uncommon for the black queen to find herself trapped on the open board in these positions, so it is just another factor to bear in

mind. Perhaps the most important feature of the white queen's position on c1 is that she takes control of the c4-square, thereby threatening 14.♗c4 harassing the black queen. Already we can see that the black queen is critically short of squares, a4 being the only route of escape.

A further aspect to 13.♕c1, albeit only an ancillary one, is that White opens up the possibility of ♗d2-h6, forcing an exchange of dark-squared bishops and potentially weakening the black king's position. However, it should perhaps be emphasized that, notwithstanding the usefulness of the manoeuvre ♗d2-h6xg7, in general White does not want to exchange dark-squared bishops at this early stage.

Although Black's bishop undoubtedly exerts influence over the long diagonal, its power is largely superficial because 8.♖b1 cleared all targets from the long diagonal, leaving the g7-bishop striking at thin air. White's dark-squared bishop, by comparison, can come to g5 or b4, actively threatening the e7-pawn, or (albeit less commonly) can take up a position on c3 or f4, supporting the advance of White's pawn centre. One final feature of the move ♕d1–c1 to bear in mind is that it temporarily leaves the e2-bishop undefended, which means that for the time being White cannot move the d2-bishop without losing a piece.

Despite the undeniably attractive features of 13.♕c1, Black should still be okay in this line, and theory has demonstrated that White is promised more by moves such as 13.♖e1!? and 13.♗g5! which are examined in Games 5-8 of this chapter. 13.d5 is considered in Game 3, and Whites other minor alternatives are considered in Game 4.

13...♕e6 14.♗c4

This is the mainline of this variation, however it is also possible to play more slowly, e.g.

14.♗d3 ♘d7 15.♖e1 b6 16.♗c4 ♕d6 17.e5 ♕b8 18.♗g5 e6 19.♗e7 ♖e8 20.♗d6 with a clear advantage to White in Mikhalevski – Iljin, Pardubice 1996, although Black subsequently managed to dig in his heels and defend, eventually winning the game. Black's play in this example was, however, somewhat less than perfect.

14...♕xe4

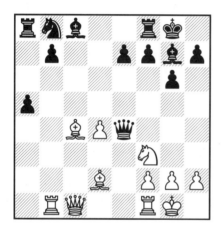

The critical move, however alternatives have also been tried.

a) 14...♕c6 has scored excellently for Black, however in practice White has always responded with 15.♗h6, thereby acquiescing in the removal of one of White's key attacking pieces. It seems far more logical, to me at least, to use the misplaced position of Black's queen as leverage for the advancement of White's central pawns, e.g. 15.d5! ♕d7 (15...♕c7 16.♗f4 ♕d8 17.♖d1±) 16.♖d1 a4 17.♕a3 when White's dominant control of the open board and extensive lead in development guarantee a clear advantage.

b) 14...♕d7 15.d5 a4 16.♕a3! ♘a6 17.♗g5 ♘c7 18.♖b6! ♖e8 19.h3!?. It is difficult for Black to unravel his pieces and gain activity here, so White simply plays a quiet move, giving the king a flight square and, perhaps more importantly, removing the possibility of Black playing ♕d7-g4, gaining time by attacking the e4 pawn. 19...♕d8 20.♖fb1± Ftacnik – Xie Jianjun, Beijing 1996.

c) 14...♕d6 15.♗f4 ♕d8 16.♕a3 (16.♗c7!? ♕e8?! (16...♕d7 looks better) 17.d5 ♗d7?! 18.♖xb7 ♕c8 19.♕b1 ♘c6 20.♕b6± Nep – Koster, Dutch Team Ch. 1995/96) 16...e6 17.d5!? (17.♗d6 ♖e8 18.♗b5 ♗d7 19.♗xd7 ♕xd7 20.♘e5±) 17...exd5 18.♗xd5 h6? 19.♖fd1 ♕f6 20.♗e5 ♕a6 21.♕b2 ♗xe5 22.♘xe5± Windhausen – Kuehnel, corr. 1991.

15.♗xf7†!?

Having sacrificed two pawns White now dives in with both feet, however it is also possible to play with more restraint, simply exploiting the exposed position of the black queen to increase White's lead in development, e.g. 15.♖e1 with the following possibilities:

a) 15...♕c6 16.♖xe7 ♗f6 (16...b5 17.♖xb5 and 16...♗f5 17.♖bxb7 are both very good for White) 17.♘e5 ♗xe7? (Bad, but Black is already in deep water, e.g. 17...♗xe5 18.dxe5 ♗e6 19.♗xe6 ♕xc1† 20.♖xc1 fxe6 21.♖cc7+–) 18.♘xc6 ♘xc6 19.♗c3 ♗f5 20.d5 ♗b4 21.♗f6 ♗e7 22.♗a1+– Bagaturov – Kalod, Brno 1994.

b) 15...♕f5 16.♖b5 ♕d7 17.♗h6 (17.♗xa5 ♘c6 18.♗b6 looks sensible and perhaps a bit better for White, however nobody has ever played it.) 17...a4 18.♖d5 ♕c6 (18...♕e8 loses in spectacular fashion to 19.♗xg7 ♔xg7 20.♖h5!! gxh5 (20...♖h8 21.♕h6† ♔g8 22.♘g5 e6 23.♘xh7+–) 21.♕g5† ♔h8 22.♖xe7 ♘d7

23.♖xe8 ♖xe8 24.♗xf7+-) 19.♘c5 ♕b6 (19...♕e8 20.♗xg7 ♔xg7 21.♖h5 transposes) 20.♖xc8+- Sjödin – Zezulkin, Stockholm 1992.

c) 15...♕g4

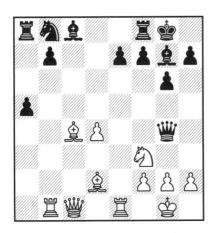

16.h3!? ♕d7 17.♘e5 ♗xe5!? (17...♕d8 18.♗g5 ♗f6 19.♗h6 ♗g7 20.♗g5 ♗f6= seems best, however 17...♕xd4 18.♗xf7† ♖xf7 (18...♔h8 19.♗c3± e.g. 19...♕d6?? 20.♘xg6† hxg6 21.♕h6 mate) 19.♕xc8†± is definitely a bad idea) 18.dxe5 ♕c6 19.♗h6 ♖d8 20.e6!? (20.♖d1! looks like an improvement, e.g. 20...♖xd1† (20...♖e8? 21.♕f4 ♗e6 22.♗b5+-) 21.♕xd1 ♘d7 22.♕d4 ♕c5 23.♕f4 ♘xe5 24.♖b5+-) 20...f6 with an unclear position in Dubinka – Blazkova, Warsaw 1996.

15...♖xf7

It is also common for Black to eschew the bishop with 15...♔h8 e.g.

a) 16.♘g5 ♕xd4 (In his annotations for *Informant 56*, Sapis mentions the line 16...♕f5 17.♕c4 intending 18.♖b5 and 19.♗e6 with the initiative. However I think White may have something which is both more concrete and more immediate in the form of 17.d5 ♘a6 18.♗e6 ♗xe6 19.♘xe6 ♖fc8 20.♘xg7! ♔xg7 21.♕a3! when the black pawns on a5, b7 and e7 are all under attack, and Black's shattered structure and exposed king give White sufficient compensation in any case.) 17.♗e6 gave White compensation

for his sacrificed pawns in Bonin – Greanias, New York Open 1992, however after 17...♘c6 it is unlikely that White has anything better than 18.♘f7† ♔g8 (18...♖xf7!? 19.♗xf7 a4 is unclear, but perhaps unduly risky on Black's part) 19.♘h6† ♔h8 20.♘f7† with a draw by perpetual check.

b) 16.♖e1 ♕f5 17.♗c4 ♘c6 18.♗h6

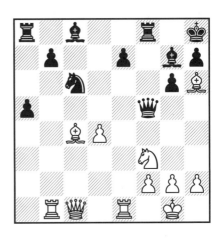

and now:

b1) 18...e6 19.♗xg7† ♔xg7 20.♕c3 (20.♖b5!? may be stronger) 20...♕f6 21.♖e3!? ♘b4 22.♖be1 ♘d5?! 23.♗xd5 exd5 was Bellmann – Rabrenovic, e-mail 2000 and now instead of 24.♖e7†, White's best was probably 24.♕c7† ♔g8 (24...♔f7 25.♖e7 ♗e6 26.♖xf7† ♗xf7 27.♕xb7±) 25.♖e8 ♗g4 26.♖xa8 ♖xa8 27.♘e5 (or 27.♕xb7 ♖f8 28.♕xd5† ♔h8 29.♖e3±/±) 27...♗e6 28.♕xb7 ♖f8 when 29.♖f1 or 29.f3 ♕f4 30.♕b6 promises White at least a slight edge.

b2) Although 18...e6 leaves Black's light-squared bishop passively trapped on c8, attempts to activate the bishop leave Black perilously underdeveloped: 18...♕f6!? 19.d5 ♗xh6 (19...♘d4 20.♘xd4 ♕xd4 21.♖xe7, and 19...♘b4 20.♗g5! ♕c3 21.♗xe7 are both better for White) 20.♕xh6 ♘b4 21.d6! (21.♘g5 ♕g7 22.♕h4 ♗f5 23.♖b3 ♖ad8 24.♖be3 ♘d5 25.♖e5 e6 26.g4 (26.♘xe6 ♗xe6 27.♖xe6 ♕b2) is very messy) 21...g5 (21...exd6 22.♘g5 ♕g7 23.♘f7†! ♔g8 (23...♖xf7 24.♖e8†+-) 24.♘xd6† ♔h8

25.♘f7† ♔g8 26.♘e5† ♔h8 27.♘xg6† with decisive advantage for White; 21...e6 22.♘e5± is good for White) 22.♕xf8†‼ ♖xf8 23.dxe7 ♕e8 24.♗f7 ♕xf7 25.e8♕† ♕xe8 26.♖xe8† ♔g7 27.♘xg5+-.

16.♕xc8† ♖f8

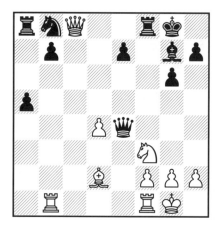

17.♕c4†

17.♕xb7?! ♕xb7 18.♖xb7 ♘c6 19.d5 ♘d4 20.♘xd4 ♗xd4 21.♖xe7 a4∓ Zpevak – Kalod, Moravia Team Championship 1996/97. As a general rule, in lines where White sacrifices the a-pawn for activity he must be careful about cashing in too early, because even if he realises a slight material gain, the black a-pawn (often supported by the hitherto inactive a8-rook) has enormous queening-potential. This is especially true where Black manages to retain his dark-squared bishop, as this guards the a1 queening-square and it is often difficult for White to orchestrate a situation where his own dark-squared bishop can oppose Black's bishop on the long diagonal.

17...e6 18.♘e5

Probably the most challenging move, although the most common continuation is 18.♖b5 ♕c6 19.♖c5 ♕a6 20.♕a2 and now 20...♘c6!? (20...♕d6 21.♖e1 looks a little better for White) 21.♕xe6† ♔h8 22.♘g5 (22.♗c3 ♖ae8 23.♕g4 ♕d3 24.♗xa5 ♘xd4 25.♘xd4 ♗xd4 26.♕xd4† ♕xd4 27.♗c3 ♕xc3 ½–½ Zpevak – Kalod, Czech

Rep. 1998. 22.d5 looks best, however 22...♖ae8 should be okay for Black) 22...♘xd4 (22...♕d3!? 23.♗e3 ♘xd4 24.♘f7† ♖xf7 25.♕xf7 ♘e2† 26.♔h1 ♖f8 27.♕e7 ♘g3† 28.hxg3 ♕xf1† was at least equal for Black in Belin – Kalod, Sydney 1999, who went on to win.) 23.♘f7† ♖xf7 24.♕xf7 ♖f8 25.♕c4 ♕xc4 26.♖xc4 b5 27.♖c7 a4 28.♗b4 ♖d8 29.♖e1 ♔g8 30.♔f1 was complex and highly unbalanced in Arkhipov – Vorobiov, Orel 1997, which eventually ended in a draw.

18...♕d5 19.♕xd5 exd5 20.♖xb7 ♗xe5 21.dxe5 ♘c6 22.e6

½–½

Instead of 22.e6 White could also have played 22.f4 however 22...♖fb8 (22...a4 appears more critical to me) 23.♖c7 (23.♖xb8†!? ♖xb8 24.♖c1) 23...♖c8 is mentioned by Sapis as leading to equality in his annotations for *Informant 56*. After 22.e6 Sapis recommends **22...♖f6** (I am not sure why Sapis believes this to be necessary, as 22...a4, 22...♘d4 and 22...♖fe8 all look as though they may be better for Black) **23.♖e1 ♖e8 24.♖d7 ♖fxe6 25.♖xe6 ♖xe6 26.♖xd5** which he assesses as equal, however after **26...a4** it seems that only Black can press for the full point.

Game 1 Conclusions: After 13.♕c1 the lines and positions which have proved the main focus of theoretical attention do not seem to trouble Black too much, provided of course that Black enters the complications with 15...♖xf7!. However, White can avoid the established theory with moves such as 14.♗d3 or 15.♖e1 in either case with a playable position in which Black will have to solve some problems without the aid of preparation. Whilst I don't believe that Black should have much to fear from either move with best play, solving complex problems over the board is rarely an easy task.

Game 2
Kramnik – Leko
Dortmund 1996

1.♘f3 ♘f6 2.c4 g6 3.♘c3 d5 4.cxd5 ♘xd5 5.e4 ♘xc3 6.bxc3 ♗g7 7.d4 c5 8.♖b1!? 0–0 9.♗e2 cxd4 10.cxd4 ♕a5† 11.♗d2 ♕xa2 12.0–0 a5!? 13.♕c1 ♗g4!

Black's last move has been Peter Leko's preference, and does much to resolve Black's problems after 13.♕c1. Perhaps disheartened by the passivity problems associated with 13...♕e6 (Game 1) Leko sought out something more active, which threatens to exchange off some pieces and liquidate into a situation where the advanced a-pawn may prove dangerous.

14.♗c4

Leko gives the line 14.♖xb7 ♖c8 15.♖c7 ♖xc7 16.♕xc7 ♗xf3 17.♗xf3 (17.♕d8†? ♗f8 18.♗h6 ♘d7! 19.♕xa8 ♖xe2–+) 17...♕xd2 18.♕b7 ♖a6 19.♕xb8† ♗f8=.

15...♕a2 16.♗c4 ♕a4 17.♖xb7!

The text is Kramnik's preference, previously White had played 17.♘g5 ♘a6 18.♘xf7 ♖xf7

19.♖xb7 ♖c8 20.♗xf7† ♔xf7 21.♗c3 as in Vaisser – Jasnikowski, Cappelle la Grande 1994, however Black could now have gained a definite advantage with 21...♕c6! 22.♕f4† ♗f5 23.exf5 ♕xb7 24.fxg6† ♔xg6∓.

In an earlier Leko game White chickened out with a draw by perpetual: 17.♗b5 ♕a2 18.♗c4 ♕a4 19.♗b5 ♕a2 20.♗c4 ♕a4 21.♗b5 ♕a2 22.♗c4 ♕a4 23.♗b5 ♕a2 24.♗c4 ½–½ Vakhidov – Leko, Yerevan 1996. This type of forced repetition is actually very common in the Modern Exchange Variation.

17...♗xf3!

Very accurate play from Leko. The natural alternative is 17...♖c8, however in his annotations for *Informant 67* Leko demonstrates that this is actually very good for White on account of 18.♗b5 ♕a2 (18...♖xc1 19.♗xa4 ♖xf1† 20.♔xf1 ♗xf3 21.gxf3 ♗xd4 22.♖xe7±) 19.♖c7 ♘a6 20.♗xa6 ♖xc7 21.♕xc7 ♗xf3 22.♗b7 ♖f8 23.♗g5! ♗e2 24.♗d5 ♕b2 25.♗xe7 ♗xf1 26.♗xf8+-.

18.gxf3

18.♗b5? ♕b3 19.gxf3 ♕xf3–+.

18...♘c6!!

18...♘a6!? is also interesting according to Leko.

19.♗b5

Forced according to Leko, who justifies his assertion with the following variations: 19.♗b3 ♕xd4 20.♗e3 ♕f6 21.♖b6 ♘d4!–+, 19.♗e3 ♘xd4 20.♗xd4 ♗xd4∓ and 19.♔g2 ♘xd4 20.♖xe7 ♕c6! with the initiative.

19...♕xb5! 20.♖xb5 ♘xd4 21.♖xa5!?

After 21.♕c5 ♘xf3† 22.♔g2 ♘xd2 23.♖e1 a4 Leko assesses the position as giving compensation for Black, who holds the initiative on account of the advancing a-pawn. Certainly the presence of the a-pawn complicates matters, however it seems hard to believe that White cannot make use of his material advantage in the next few moves to prevent the a-pawn from queening.

To this end GM Ftacnik has suggested the continuation 24.♕xe7 (dubious according to Leko) 24...a3 (24...♖fe8 25.♕c7 a3 26.♖b7 ♖f8 27.e5 a2 28.♖a1+-) 25.e5 (25.♕b4 ♘xe4!

14...♕a4 15.♗b5

15.♖xb7 ♗xf3 16.gxf3 e6?! (16...♘a6 17.♗e3 ♖fc8 is better, and looks fine for Black) 17.d5 e5?! 18.♗b5 ♕b3 19.♗e3+– 1–0 Weber – Champion, e-mail 1997.

26.♕xe4 a2∓ – Leko) 25...a2 26.♖a1 ♘c4 27.♖c5 ♖fe8 28.♖xa2!+–.

21...♘e2† 22.♔g2 ♘xc1 23.♖xc1

½–½

Game 2 Conclusions: Theory has a tendency to treat **13...♗g4!** (and this game in particular) as an antidote to White's approach with **13.♕c1**, however matters are by no means so clear. Kramnik's **17.♖xb7!** keeps Black under constant pressure (making it an excellent choice for practical play) and Ftacnik's suggestion that **24.♕xe7** (after **21.♕c5**) is good for White has still to be addressed by any sources defending the Black side.

Game 3
Lutsko – Shipov
Cherepovets 1997

1.d4 ♘f6 2.c4 g6 3.♘c3 d5 4.cxd5 ♘xd5 5.e4 ♘xc3 6.bxc3 ♗g7 7.♘f3 0–0 8.♗e2 c5 9.♖b1 cxd4 10.cxd4 ♕a5† 11.♗d2 ♕xa2 12.0–0 a5 13.d5

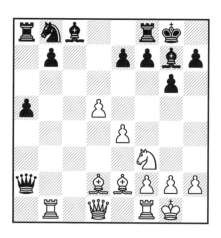

This advance has enjoyed more popularity than it deserves: although White cuts off the black queen's retreat path on the a2-g8 diagonal (which means that Black will have to take more time to remove the queen from the path of the advancing a-pawn) White achieves this at the cost of opening up the long diagonal for Black's g7 bishop, and fixing his own pawn structure in a fashion that will make it difficult to achieve the e4-e5 advance under favourable circumstances.

13...a4!?

The most principled move, and probably also Black's most aggressive continuation, however alternatives also merit consideration:

a) 13...♘a6 14.♗e3! (14.♗g5 ♘c5 15.♕d2 (neither 15.♗d3 e6! 16.♗e7 ♘xd3 17.♕xd3 exd5∞, nor 15.♗xe7 ♘xe4 16.♖c1 ♘c3 17.♖xc3 ♗xc3∓ promise White anything) 15...♕xd2 16.♘xd2 was Bartsch – Felber, e-mail 1999, and now 16...e6 17.♗e7 ♘a4 looks good for Black)

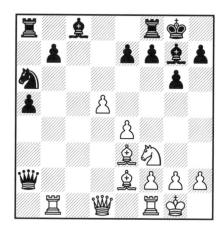

with the following possibilities:

a1) 14...e6 15.d6 ♗d7 (15...♘b4? 16.♗b5 ♖d8 17.d7 ♗xd7 18.♗xd7 intending 19. ♕a4 or 19. ♗b6 gives White a decisive advantage according to GM Chernin in his annotations for *Informant 55*) 16.♗b5! (definitely best; grabbing the b7-pawn unnecessarily complicates matters: 16.♖xb7 ♗a4 (or 16...♗c6 17.♖b6 ♘b4∞) 17.♕e1 ♘b4 with active counterplay) 16...♗xb5 (after 16...♗c6 Ftacnik, in his annotations for *CBM 31*, gives the line 17.♘d4 17...♗xe4 18.♖a1 ♕b2 19.♖xa5 with an initiative for White, however 19...♕b4 looks very strong for Black. It seems far better for White to simply play 17.♗xc6 bxc6 18.♗b6 with a slight but secure edge.) 17.♖xb5 ♕c4 18.♕b1! ♘b4 19.♖xb7 ♘a2 (19...♖fb8 20.♖c7 ♕a6 21.d7 and 19...♕c6 20.♖b6 are both good for White) 20.♖c7 ♕a4 21.e5 ♘b4 (21...♖fb8 22.♕a1±) 22.♕e4 ♕a2 23.h4 ♘d5 (23...♕d5 24.♕b1 ♖fb8 25.♖d1±) 24.♖c2± Chernin – Adorjan, Polanica Zdroj 1992.

a2) Upon 14...a4 Chernin has suggested 15.♘d4 intending 16.♖a1, however 15.♘d2!? also deserves consideration.

a3) 14...♗g4!? is also suggested by Chernin without further analysis. Developing the light-squared bishop actively at the cost of the b7-pawn is a common theme in all lines of the Modern Exchange Variation, so it probably also merits consideration in this position.

a4) 14...♘b4!? 15.♗c5 (15.♘d4 ♗d7 16.♖a1 ♕b2 17.♖b1 ♕a2 18.♖a1 ♕b2 ½–½ Parker – Mirumian, Szeged 1994) 15...♗d7 16.♗xe7 ♖fc8 17.♗xb4 axb4 ½–½ Savchenko – Vakhidov, Yerevan 1996.

b) 13...e6

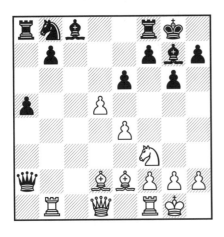

with the following possibilities:

b1) 14.♗g5 exd5 15.exd5 a4 (15...♕a3 16.d6 ♘d7 17.♗b5! ♕c5 18.♗e7 ♖e8 19.♕d3 a4 20.♖bc1 ♕b6 21.♕d5! (21.♖xc8 ♖exc8 22.♗xd7+- Leyva *Informant 60*) 21...♖a5 22.♕xf7†! 1–0 Leyva – Ramon, Havana 1994) 16.♖c1 ♕b3 17.♕d2 ♗f5

18.♗h6 ♕b2 19.♗xg7 ♕xd2 20.♘xd2 ♔xg7∓ Pelletier – Rowson, Halle 1995.

b2) 14.♗e3?! exd5 15.exd5 ♗f5 16.♖c1 (16.♖xb7 ♗e4 17.♖b5 ♖d8 18.d6 gives Black good counterplay according to Notkin in his annotations for *Informant 59*) 16...♘a6 17.♗c4 ♕b2 18.♘d4 (18.♗d4 ♗xd4 19.♘xd4 ♗d7 20.♘e6 ♖fc8∓ – Notkin) 18...♗d7 19.♘e6 fxe6 20.dxe6 ♗xe6 21.♗xe6† ♔h8 22.♕d5 was Notkin – Baikov, Russia 1993, and now 22...a4 23.♖b1 ♘c7! is slightly better for Black according to Notkin.

b3) 14.d6 and now:

b31) 14...♘c6 15.♗g5 a4 16.♗b5 ♗d7 (16...a3? 17.d7 ♗xd7 18.♕xd7 ♕xb1 19.♖xb1 a2 20.♖f1 a1♕ 21.♖xa1 ♖xa1† 22.♗f1 h6 23.♗d2 ♖d8 24.♕c7+- Cebalo – Jukic, Djakovo 1994) 17.♕d3! intending 18.♗c4 is very good for White. Bogdan Lalic gives only 17.♘d2, intending 17...a3?? 18.♗c4, which he assesses as clearly better for White, however he makes no mention of 17...h6 or 17...♖a5, both of which give Black a respectable position.

b32) 14...♗d7 Now:

b321) 15.e5 ♗c6 16.♕c1 (16.♖e1!? ♘d7 17.♗c3 – Zimmerman) 16...♗e4! 17.♖b5 ♘d7 18.♕c3 ♖fc8 19.♖a1

19...♕c2 (19...♖xc3 20.♖xa2 ♖cc8 21.♖bxa5 ♖xa5 22.♖xa5 ♗xf3 23.♗xf3 ♗xe5 24.♗xb7 ♖b8

25.♖a8 ♖xa8 26.♗xa8 ♗xd6 is equal according to Zimmerman, although obviously Black has an extra pawn so he could try and press for the full point for some time to come.) 20.♕e3 ♗xf3 21.♗d3 ♗h6 22.♗xc2 (22.♕xh6? ♕xd3 23.♗g5 ♕d4!–+) 22...♗xe3 23.♗xe3 ♗d5 24.♗b3! ♗xb3 25.♖xb3 was Zimmerman – Honfi, Budapest 1994, and now Zimmerman gives the line 25...♘xe5 26.♖xb7 ♖d8 27.♗d4 which he assesses as equal, however 27...♘c4 28.d7 ♘d6 looks clearly better for Black here.

b322) 15.♖xb7 is less openly challenging, but may ultimately be better e.g. 15...♗c6 16.♖c7 ♗xe4 17.♗c4 (17.♗g5!? may be better, although I still have confidence in Black's position) 17...♗xf3 (17...♕a3!?) 18.gxf3 (18.♕xf3 ♕xd2 19.♕xa8 (19.♖d1 ♕c2!) 19...♕xd6 20.♕xa5 ♗e5=) 18...♕b2 19.♗c1 ♕f6 20.♖e1 ♘a6

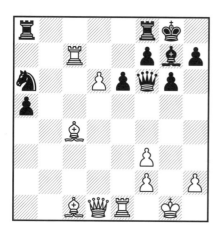

21.♖xf7!? and now 21...♖xf7 led to a nice win for White in Tratar – Shabtai, Budapest 1994 after 22.♖xe6 ♕c3 23.♖e4 ♖aa7 24.♗e3 ♖ad7 25.♗xf7† ♔xf7 26.♕d5† ♔f8 27.♕a8† 1–0. However after 21...♔xf7 it seems that the most White should have here is a draw by perpetual check e.g. 22.♖xe6 (22.♕d5 ♘b4! 23.♕b7† ♔g8 24.♖xe6 ♕a1∓) 22...♕xe6 23.♗xe6† ♔xe6 24.♕b3† ♔xd6 25.♗a3† ♘b4 26.♗xb4† axb4 27.♕xb4†=.

c) 13...♕a3

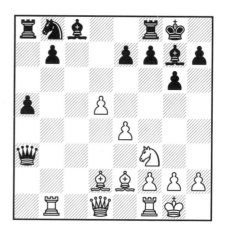

simply seems too time consuming to be justified, e.g. 14.♗e3 a4 (14...♘a6 15.♘d2 b5 (15...♕c3 16.♘c4 ♕f6 17.♘b6 ♖b8 18.♕d2± - Petursson) 16.♗xb5 ♘b4 17.♗c5! ♖b8 18.♖b3 ♕a2 19.♗c4 ♕a4 20.♗xe7+- Petursson – Henao, St. Martin Open 1993) 15.♘d4 ♕d6 16.♘b5 ♕d8 17.f4!? (White wants to build up a strong pawn centre, however this seems a little speculative. White needs to use his temporary lead in development to enhance his existing initiative, and to this end moves such as 17.♖c1 or even 17.♗d4 make more sense.) 17...a3 18.e5 ♗d7 (immediately challenging White's centre with 18...f6!? makes more sense) 19.♕b3 ♗xb5 20.♗xb5 ♕a5 21.♖a1 ♖c8 22.♗d4 ♕d2 23.♖ad1 (23.♗d3!? looks stronger, thereby avoiding Lalic's suggestion in the next note) 23...♕a5? (Lalic has pointed out that 23...♕c2!? is stronger, although after 24.♕e3 I still prefer White's position) 24.f5! with a clear advantage to White in Cebalo – Jukic, Hrvatska 1994, according to Bogdan Lalic's annotations for *Informant 62*.

d) 13...♗g4!? 14.♖xb7 ♘d7 15.♗g5 ♖fb8 16.♖xb8† ♖xb8 17.h3 ♗xf3 18.♗xf3 ♕a3 19.♗g4 ♘e5 20.♕c2 ♘xg4 21.hxg4 ♕d6 22.♕a4 ½–½ Blancke – Jasnikowski, Cuxhaven 1993.

14.♕c1

The text remains White's most common approach to this position, however of particular interest is Petursson's move 14.♗b4!? a3 (14...♖e8 15.♘d2 ♘a6 16.♗c4±)

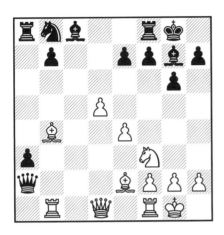

and now:

a) 15.♗xe7 ♖e8 16.♖c1!? (16.d6?! ♘c6 (16...♕xb1 17.♕xb1 a2 18.♕d3 a1♕ 19.♖xa1 ♖xa1† 20.♗f1 b6 21.♘d2!) 17.♗g5 ♖xe4 18.♗d3 ♖e6! is clearly better for Black according to GM Kozul) 16...♘d7 17.♗c4 ♕b2 18.♖c2 ♕b6 19.d6 is unclear according to Ftacnik (*Chessbase Magazine 36*).

b) 15.♗d3 b6 (Black should obviously steer clear of lines such as 15...♖e8? 16.♘d2+- and 15...♗d7 16.♗xe7 ♖e8 17.♗d6 ♗a4 18.♕c1±) 16.♗xe7 ♖e8 17.♗g5 ♗a6 18.♖xb6 ♗xd3 19.♕xd3 ♘d7 is unclear according to Petursson, who notes these variations in his annotations for *Informant 58*.

c) 15.e5!

c1) 15...♗f5 16.♖c1 (16.♖a1 ♕b2 17.♗xe7 ♖e8 18.d6 ♘c6 is unclear according to Petursson, however I would tend to prefer Black here.) 16...♖c8 (the alternative 16...♖e8 is bad on account of 17.♘d4 ♗xe5 18.♘xf5 gxf5 19.♖c2 ♕xc2! (19...♕b3 20.♖c8 ♕xb4 21.♖xe8† ♔g7 22.♕c1 ♕h4 23.g3 ♕f6 24.♕c8+-) 20.♕xc2 a2 21.♕xf5 a1♕ 22.♖xa1 ♖xa1† 23.♗f1± - Petursson. Relatively best seems 16...♕b2 17.♗xe7 ♖e8 18.♗c5 ♗xe5 19.♘xe5 ♕xe5 20.♗c4 when Petursson claims that White has sufficient compensation on account of his well-centralized bishop pair) 17.e6! and now:

c11) 17...♘a6 18.♖xc8† ♖xc8 19.♗xe7 ♘b8 (19...fxe6 20.d6 ♘c5 21.d7 ♘xd7 22.♕xd7 e5 23.♕b5±) 20.♘g5!± was Petursson – Eriksson, Malmö 1993.

c12) Obviously critical is 17...♖xc1 18.♕xc1 ♘a6 (18...♕xe2 19.♕c8† ♗f8 20.♘g5! a2 21.exf7† ♔g7 22.♗c3† ♔h6 23.♕xf8† ♔g5 24.♕h8+-) 19.exf7† ♔f8 (19...♔xf7 20.♗c4 ♕c2 21.d6† ♔e8 22.♗b5† ♔f7 23.♘g5†+-) 20.♗xa6! (Petursson mentions only 20.♗c4 which is also good, but not nearly as convincing) 20...♖xa6 (20...bxa6 21.♖e1+-) 21.♗xe7†! ♔xe7 (21...♔xf7 22.♘g5† followed by 23.♕c7 wins for White) 22.♕c7† ♗d7 23.♖e1†+-.

c2) Also logical is 15...♖d8

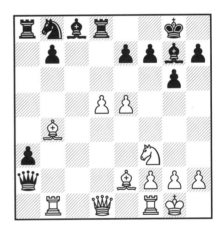

putting pressure on the d5-pawn, however Petursson is confident that White has everything under control, e.g. 16.♖c1 (16.♗xe7? ♖xd5 17.♕c1 ♗f5 18.♗c4 ♕xb1 19.♕xb1 ♗xb1 20.♖xb1 ♖d7-+) 16...♗g4 (16...♘a6 17.♗c4 ♕b2 18.♗xe7 ♖e8 19.d6 is clearly better for White according to Petursson, however 16...♗f5 is interesting, e.g. 17.♗c4 ♕b2 18.♗xe7 ♖c8 19.d6 h6 with an unclear position) 17.♗c4 ♕b2 18.♗xe7 ♖c8 (18...♖e8 19.d6± - Ftacnik) 19.d6 ♔h8 (19...♖xc4 20.♖xc4 a2 21.♖a4!) 20.♖b1! ♕c3 21.♗xf7 a2 22.♖a1 ♗xf3 23.gxf3 ♕xe5 24.♖xa2 ♖xa2 25.♗xa2±.

14...b5!

15.♖xb5

15.♗xb5 ♗a6 16.♗g5?! (16.♗xa6 ♘xa6 17.♗h6 ♖fc8 18.♕f4! looks more critical, because White is rapidly generating threats against the Black king position) 16...♖c8 17.♕e3 ♗xb5 18.♖xb5 ♕c4 19.♖bb1 a3 20.e5 a2∓ Pap – Pozsonyi, Hungary 1999.

15...♗a6 16.♗c4 ♗b2 17.♗xa2

17.♖xb2 ♕xc4 18.♕xc4 ♗xc4 19.♖a1 ♘d7 20.♖b4 ♗b3 21.♘d4 was perhaps a little better for White in Gladyszev – Belov, St Petersburg 1997, however Black could have solved his problems with 21...e6 22.dxe6 fxe6 with a roughly level position.

17...♗xc1 18.♖xb8

18.♖a5 ♗xd2 19.♘xd2 ♘d7 20.♖c1 ♗d3 21.♖xa8 ♖xa8 22.♖c7 ♖b8! 23.d6 ♗b2 24.dxe7 ♘f6 25.♖c8† ♔g7 gives black the upper hand, Shulman – Oral, Halle 1995.

18...♖fxb8 19.♖xc1 ♖b2 20.♖a1 ♖c8 21.♗e3 ♗c4!

Presumably this was Shipov's prepared improvement over 21...a3 22.h3 ♗d3 23.e5 ♖cc2 24.d6 exd6 25.exd6 ♔f8 26.♘e5 f6 27.♗e6 ♗b5 28.♗h6† ♔e8 29.♖xa3 1–0 Avrukh – Swol, Zagan 1995.

22.♗xc4 ♖xc4 23.e5 ♖cb4 24.♔f1?!

24.♘d2 a3 25.g3 a2 26.♔g2 looks better, although obviously White is still under serious pressure.

24...♖b1† 25.♖xb1 ♖xb1† 26.♔e2 ♖b5 27.d6 exd6 28.exd6 ♖d5 29.♗f4 a3 30.♘d2 a2 31.♘b3 f6 32.♘a1 ♔f7 33.f3 ♔e6 34.g4 ♖b5 35.♗e3 ♖b2† 36.♗d2 ♔xd6 37.h3 ♔e6 38.h4 h5 39.gxh5 gxh5 40.♔d3 ♔f5 41.♗c3 ♖h2 42.♔c4 ♖xh4† 43.♔b3 ♖h2 44.♘c2 ♖xc2 **0–1**

Game 3 Conclusions: Although 13.d5 was once a respectable mainline of the 12...a5 variation, it now appears that Black has several reasonable responses. Both 13...e6 and 13...♗g4!? seem to be fully playable for Black. The main text of Game 3 with 13...a4 is a more difficult question; although 14.♕c1 certainly appears to be fine for Black, Petursson's 14.♗b4!? poses more serious problems.

Game 4
Sadler – B. Lalic
England 1994

1.d4 ♘f6 2.c4 g6 3.♘c3 d5 4.cxd5 ♘xd5 5.e4 ♘xc3 6.bxc3 ♗g7 7.♘f3 c5 8.♖b1 0–0 9.♗e2 cxd4 10.cxd4 ♕a5† 11.♗d2 ♕xa2 12.0–0 a5

In this game we are going to deal with some of White's less popular alternatives to the mainlines, in particular 13.♗c3 and 13.♖a1. As theory currently stands, neither option should really trouble Black.

13.♗c3

When I first encountered 12...a5, my initial thought was to question why White does not go after the a5-pawn immediately with 13.♖a1, and indeed this does make some sense. In terms of results Black is doing fine here, but there is plenty of room for improvement on both sides of the board.

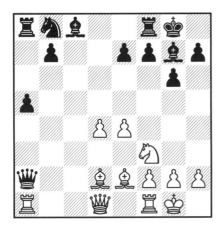

13.♖a1!? ♕b2 (the most common move, however it may be better to play 13...♕e6 14.♕c2 (in response to 14.♗d3 GM Kozul has recommended 14...♘c6! 15.d5 ♕d6!∓) [Typesetter's note: When I played on the Galician tournament circuit in 1992 I saw the talented Ukrainian IM Nedobora playing 14.♕b1. His idea was to follow up with 15.♖c1 and gain Benko-like compensation down the queenside files. It is probably not White's best plan, but it gives easy play, especially in rapid chess.] 14...♕d6?! (interestingly Kozul, in his annotations for *Informant 49*, recommended 14...♕c6! as the solution to Black's problems in this variation at the earliest stages of the 12...a5 line's inception. However, Kozul's recommendation has never been played, despite the fact that the alternatives appear less than satisfactory. Nevertheless, the position remains complicated, and there is nothing which dictates that White cannot press for an edge after something sensible such as 15.♕b1!) 15.♗xa5±

♘c6? 16.♗c7!+- Bagonyai – Chourkine, Nagykanizsa 1995) 14.♗xa5 ♘c6 15.♖b1 ♕a2 (in an earlier encounter Kalod had tried 15...♕a3!? however after 16.♗b6 (16.♗c7!? also looks strong, e.g. 16...♕a4 (16...♗g4 17.d5!) 17.d5 ♘d4 18.♘xd4 ♕xd4 19.♕xd4 ♗xd4 20.♖fd1±) 16...♗g4 17.♗c5 ♕a5 18.♖b5± he was under serious pressure: Oral – Kalod, Usti nad Labem 1996). White has now tried two moves:

a) Although it has never been played, there is certainly something to be said for 16.♗c3!? ♗e6 (16...♗g4? 17.♖a1 ♕e6 18.d5 is excellent for White, however 16...♕a3 17.♖a1 (17.♕d2!?) 17...♕xc3 18.♖xa8 ♘xd4 19.♘xd4 ♗xd4 20.♕b1 is more interesting. Although Black certainly has some compensation for the exchange, it is doubtful whether it is really enough.) 17.♖xb7 ♖fc8 (17...f5!? should be met by 18.exf5 ♗xf5 19.♖b5 intending ♖b5-c5 with an advantage for White) 18.♖b2 ♕a3 19.♕d2 ♘a5 keeps White's centre under pressure, however Black doesn't seem to have anything concrete here, and White is a pawn up.

b) 16.♗b6

16...♗g4 17.d5 (17.h3?! ♗xf3 18.♗xf3 ♗xd4 19.♗xd4 ♖ad8 20.♖xb7 ♖xd4 21.♕c1 ♕e6 22.g3 ♖c4 23.♕h6 ♘d4 gave Black excellent play in Movsesian – Oral, Litomysl 1995, and indeed Black eventually went on to win this.) 17...♘e5 18.♖e1 ♗xf3 19.gxf3 ♖fc8!? (19...♘c4!?) 20.♗d4 ♕a4 21.♕xa4 (21.♖xb7!? may be better, e.g. 21...♕xd4 (21...♘xf3† 22.♗xf3 ♗xd4 23.♕xa4 ♖xa4 24.♖xe7 ♖a2 25.♖e2 is similar) 22.♕xd4 ♘xf3† 23.♗xf3 ♗xd4 24.♖xe7 ♖e8 when the opposite coloured bishops give Black reasonable chances of holding this endgame, but White's advanced central pawns are very dangerous. If Black is going to draw this he will really have to work for it!) 21...♖xa4 22.♗e3 f5 23.f4 ♘c4 24.♖ec1 fxe4 25.♗d1 b5!! 26.♗xa4 bxa4 27.♖b4 a3 28.♖a4 ♗b2 29.♖c2 ♔f7 30.♗c1 ♘b6 31.♖xc8 ♘xa4 32.♗xb2 axb2 33.♖b8 ♔f6 34.♖b5 ♔f5 35.d6† ♔e6 36.dxe7 ♔xe7 37.♔f1 ♔d6 38.♔e1 ♔c6 39.♖b4 ♔c5 40.♖b3 ♔c4 41.♖b8 ♔d3 0–1 Pelletier – Kalod, Medellin 1996.

13...♗g4 14.♖a1

14.♖xb7 ♘c6 is clearly better for Black according to GM Bogdan Lalic, in his annotations for *Informant 60*.

14...♕e6 15.d5 ♕b6

Lalic points out the variations 15...♕xe4?? 16.♗xg7 ♔xg7 17.♖a4 ♕f5 18.♕d4† and 15...♕d6? 16.♗xg7 ♔xg7 17.e5! both with advantage to White.

16.♗xg7 ♔xg7

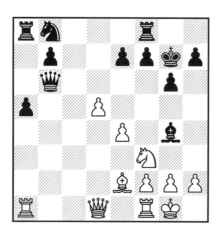

17.♖b1?!

17.♘e5! ♗xe2 18.♕xe2 ♖c8 (Lalic recommends the line 18...♕a6! 19.♕b2 f6 20.♘f3 ♘d7 which he assesses as slightly better for Black. I am by no means convinced that this is correct, but in any case White's play can be improved at an earlier stage via 19.♘c4! when Black has problems with the a5-pawn and White has options of ♕e2-b2†, followed by ♘b6, when Black has serious problems with his queenside development, and will probably have to give up at least one of his queenside pawns.) 19.♖fb1 ♕d4 20.♘f3 ♕c3 21.♕b5 ♘a6 22.h4 ♕c4 23.♕xc4 ♖xc4 24.♖xa5 ♖xe4 25.♖xb7 h6 26.d6 ½–½ Sadler – Mikhalchishin, Ischia 1994.

17...♕a7 18.♘e5!?

18.♕b3 ♘d7 19.♕xb7 ♕xb7 20.♖xb7 ♖fb8 21.♖xb8 ♖xb8∓ – Lalic.

18...♗xe2 19.♕xe2 a4! 20.♕a2 a3 21.♖fd1 ♕a4 22.♕a1

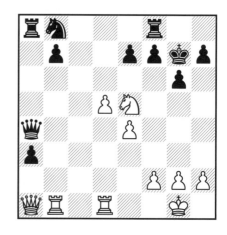

22...a2! 23.♖bc1!

Probably the only move, but White is already in serious trouble, e.g. 23.♘d7† ♔g8–+, or 23.♘g4† f6 24.♖xb7? ♕xd1† 25.♕xd1 a1♕–+.

23...f6 24.d6! exd6 25.♘c4 ♘d7 26.♘xd6 ♘c5! 27.e5?! ♘b3 28.exf6† ♔g8 29.♕e5 ♘xc1 30.♕d5† ♔h8 31.♖e1 ♘e2† 32.♔f1 a1♕ 0–1

Game 4 Conclusions: The obvious 13.♖a1!? has never proved popular, however it would be wrong to assume that this is on account of some obvious deficiency – in practice White has done well, and only Kozul's 13...♕e6 followed by 14...♕c6! appears to represent an entirely suitable defence for Black – and nobody has ever played this way! On the other hand, 13.♗c3, although a favourite with super-GM Mathew Sadler for a period, has failed to attract many followers and offers White no real chances of an advantage.

Game 5
Shipov – Najer
Russian CC, St Petersburg 1998.

1.d4 ♘f6 2.c4 g6 3.♘c3 d5 4.cxd5 ♘xd5 5.e4 ♘xc3 6.bxc3 ♗g7 7.♘f3 c5 8.♖b1 0–0 9.♗e2 cxd4 10.cxd4 ♕a5† 11.♗d2 ♕xa2 12.0–0 a5 13.♖e1!?

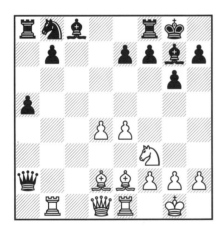

With this move White just takes a moment to protect the e2-bishop and fortify his centre, before deciding upon how to proceed with the attack.

13...♗d7!?

A relatively unusual piece deployment in these 11...♕xa2 systems, however it is by no means without merit. Black has several other ways to handle the position:

a) 13...♘c6. Now:

a1) 14.♗g5 h6 15.♗e3 ♘b4 16.♕c1 ♔h7 (16...♕c2 is complicated, but may be strong) 17.♕c5 was Wieczorek – Jasnikowski, Katowice 1993, which eventually ended in a draw. However at this particular juncture Black missed an opportunity to gain a clear advantage with 17...♘c2! e.g. 18.♗c4 ♕a3∓.

a2) 14.♗c3!? ♖d8!? (14...♗e6?! 15.♖a1 ♕b3 16.♕d2 intending 17.♖eb1 is clearly better for White. Analysts have also considered 14...♕a3 15.♕d2 ♗g4 16.♖xb7 ♖fd8 (16...♖fb8 is also logical) 17.♖a1 ♕d6 18.d5 ♗xf3 19.♗xf3 ♘e5 20.♗e2 ♖ac8! and now rather than 21.♗b2, which is recommended in *Informant 57*, simply 21.♗xa5 gives Black some problems) 15.♖a1 ♕e6 16.♗b5!

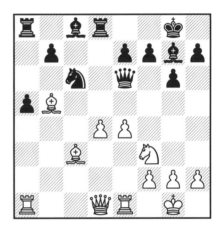

(16.d5? ♗xc3 17.dxe6 ♖xd1 18.exf7† ♔xf7 19.♖exd1 ♗xa1 20.♖xa1∓) 16...♘xd4? (16...♕d6!? keeps the position unclear according to Zezjulkin) 17.♘xd4 (17.♗xd4? ♗xd4 18.♘xd4 ♕b6 19.♖a4 e5∓) 17...♕b6 18.e5 ♖xd4 19.♕xd4 ♕xb5 20.♕d8† ♗f8 21.♖xa5+-.

b) 13...♗g4 14.♗g5 (14.♖xb7 ♗xf3 15.♗xf3 ♗xd4 is slightly better for Black according to Hachian, in his annotations for *Informant 50*) 14...♗xf3 (14...♘c6 15.d5 ♘b4 16.♗xe7 ♖fe8 17.d6 ♗d7 18.e5 b5?! 19.♘d4 ♖ab8? 20.♗xb5!+- Touzane – Martin Blanco, Linares 2000) 15.♗xf3 ♕c4

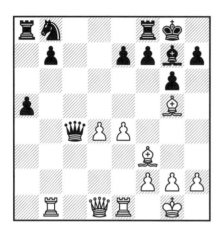

16.d5 (16.♗xe7 ♖e8 17.♖xb7 (White's last move is natural enough, but perhaps a little compliant. It seems better to play 17.♗c5 ♘d7 18.♖c1 ♕a6 19.e5 ♘xc5 20.♖xc5 a4 21.♗d5 which appears to be better for White.) 17...♘c6! is given as slightly better for Black by Hachian) 16...♕c7 17.e5 (forced according to Hachian, who only considers 17.♖c1 ♕d6 intending 18...♗e5, which he assesses as clearly better for Black. In fact White has another alternative in 17.♕c1! ♕d7 18.e5± and 17...♕xc1 18.♖exc1 is good for White, whereas 17...♖c8 18.♕xc7 ♖xc7 19.♗f4 ♖c2 20.♖xb7 ♘a6 21.♖xe7 ♗f6 22.♖b7 is very close to being clearly better for White, but the a-pawn may still complicate matters, so at this stage an assessment of unclear may be most appropriate.) 17...♗xe5 18.♖xb7!? ♕xb7 (18...♗xh2†!? 19.♔h1 ♕xb7) 19.♖xe5!? (19. d6 ♘c6 20.dxe7 ♗g7! 21.exf8♕† ♖xf8 22.♕c1! (22.♕d5? ♕b4 23.♗d2 ♕d4!∓) 22...♖c8 23.♗xc6 ♖xc6! 24.♖e8† ♗f8 25.♕a1!! ♖c8 26.♖xc8 ♕xc8 27.♕xa5 ½-½ Oratovsky – Hachian, USSR 1990).

Black has now tried two moves:

b1) 19...♕c7?! 20.♖xe7 ♕d6 21.♖e1! f6? (Hachian mentions the improvement 21...♖a7! 22.♗h6 (22.♕d4 ♘c6! 23.♕b6 ♕b4!∓) 22...♖e7! 23.♗xf8 ♔xf8 24.♖xe7 ♕xe7!? 25.d6 ♕e5 which looks balanced) 22.♖e6! ♕d7 23.d6! fxg5 24.♗xa8

♘c6 25.♗xc6 ♕xc6 26.♖e7! a4 27.d7 ♖d8 28.♕a1! 1–0 Hachian – Aleksandrov, USSR 1990.

b2) 19...♘d7 20.d6 ♕b4! 21.♖xe7 (21.dxe7? ♘xe5 22.♗xa8 ♖xa8 23.♕d8† ♔g7! is winning for Black according to Hachian, however White actually has a cute saving tactic here: 24.e8♘† ♔g8 25.♘f6† ♔g7 26.♘e8† with a perpetual check.) 21...♖ad8. Hachian's analysis ends here with the conclusion that the position is unclear. In fact White may be a little better, and the only practical example to have reached this position continued: 22.♖e4! ♕c5 23.♗e7 ♖c8 24.♗xf8 ♔xf8 25.♖e7 ♕c1 26.♔f1 ♕xd1† 27.♗xd1 ♘b6 28.♗b3 a4 29.♖xf7† ♔e8 30.♖e7† ♔f8 31.♖b7 ♖c6 32.♗xa4! ♖xd6 (32...♘xa4 33.♖b8† ♔f7 34.d7+-) 33.♗b3± Riemer – Martin, corr. 1991, however obviously Black's play can be improved at various points.

c) 13...a4 14.♗b4!? (14.♗g5 transposes to game 8, and is probably best) 14...a3?! (Both Chekhov and B.Lalic have (independently I believe) given the analysis 14...♘c6! 15.♖a1 ♕xa1 (15...♕e6!? looks acceptable, e.g. 16.d5? ♕xe4–+) 16.♕xa1 ♘xb4 with the assessment that Black is clearly better.) 15.♕c1 ♗e6 16.♖a1 ♕b3 17.♖xa3 ♖xa3 18.♕xa3 ♕xa3 19.♗xa3± Winning – Weston, Edinburgh 1996.

14.♖xb7 a4

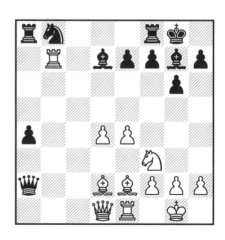

15.♗g5

Ftacnik has mentioned the line 15.♗f4 ♗c6 16.♖xe7 ♕a3 (16...♗f6? 17.♖c7 ♗xe4 18.♗c4+-) 17.♖c7 ♗xe4±. Another move which perhaps deserves consideration is 15.♕c1!? threatening 16.♗c4 trapping the black queen. Play might continue 15...♖c8 (15...♕e6 may be better, e.g. 16.♕b1 (16.♗c4 ♕c6 17.♖c7 ♕b6 18.♗d5 ♖a7 19.♖xa7 ♕xa7 is less risky, but also less potentially advantageous) 16...a3 17.d5 ♕d6 (17...a2 18.dxe6 axb1♕ 19.exf7† ♖xf7 20.♖exb1+-) 18.♗a2 ♖c8 19.♗b4 ♕f4 20.♗f1 and it looks like the a3-pawn will drop) 16.♖c7! ♖xc7 17.♕xc7 leaves Black in serious trouble, e.g. 17...h6 18.♗c4 ♕a3 19.♗d5.

15...a3

15...♕e6 16.d5 ♕d6 17.♕d2± - Ftacnik.

16.♗xe7 ♖c8 17.♕d3

17.♕b3 ♕xe2!! 18.♖xe2 a2 19.♗d6 (19.♖xa2? ♖c1†-+) 19...a1♕† 20.♖e1 ♕a4∓ - Ftacnik.

17...♗g4 18.h3

18.♖eb1 ♘c6 19.♗c5 ♗xf3 20.♗xf3 ♗xd4! 21.♗xd4 ♖d8 22.e5 ♘xd4∓.

18...♗xf3 19.♗xf3 ♘c6 20.e5 ♘xe7 21.♖xe7 ♗f8 22.♖b7

Shipov's move is strong, however Ftacnik's suggestion of 22.♗xa8 ♗xe7 23.♗b7 ♖c2 24.♕f3! threatening 25.♗d5 and 26.♕xf7† also looks very strong.

22...♖ab8

22...♖a5 23.♖eb1±.

23.♖a7 ♖d8 24.♕e3 ♕c4 25.♖d1 ♖b2?

The text loses, so a superior approach would have been 25...a2!? 26.♕d2 ♗c5 27.♕xa2 ♕xa2 28.♖xa2 ♖xd4. However even here Black faces an uncomfortable endgame, albeit one which should probably be defensible.

26.♕f4 ♖b6

26...a2 27.♕f6! ♖c8 28.d5 ♖c7 29.♖a8 ♖c8 30.e6!+-.

27.♖c1 ♕e6 28.d5 ♕f5 29.♕xf5 gxf5 30.♗h5 1-0

Game 5 Conclusions: 13.♖e1!? is an interesting and relatively unexplored alternative to White's more popular approaches. However, it would appear to be of relatively limited independent

value, because the best way for White to meet 13...a4 is with 14.♗g5! transposing to 13.♗g5! a4 14.♖e1!?, which is examined in Game 8.

Game 6
Khalifman – Dvoirys
Russian Cup final, Samara 1998

1.d4 ♘f6 2.c4 g6 3.♘c3 d5 4.♘f3 ♗g7 5.cxd5 ♘xd5 6.e4 ♘xc3 7.bxc3 c5 8.♖b1 0-0 9.♗e2 cxd4 10.cxd4 ♕a5† 11.♗d2 ♕xa2 12.0-0 a5 13.♗g5!

In my opinion this represents White's best approach to this position, and certainly the most challenging. Black has yet to find an entirely acceptable response.

13...h6?!

For some time Dvoirys harboured a preference for this provocative little move, but given that White is trying to take on e7 anyway, actually encouraging him to do so seems somewhat counter intuitive! Notwithstanding the superficial appearance of Black's approach, White must still be well-prepared in order to illustrate the deficiencies of 13...h6?!. We will come to that issue in a moment, however first I would like to take a brief look at Black's (even more) minor alternatives:

a) 13...a4 is the mainline, and this is considered in Games 7 and 8.

b) 13...♗f6!? is one of those moves that has been suggested by numerous sources, but that nobody seems to want to try. 14.♗h6 ♗g7 15.♗xg7 ♔xg7 16.d5 seems like a reasonable approach to the position for White.

c) 13...♘d7

14.e5! f6?! 15.♘d2 b5 16.♖xb5 ♗a6 17.♗c4†
♕xc4 18.♘xc4 ♗xb5 19.♕b3 ♗xc4 20.♕xc4†
♔h8 was Santa Torres – Yang Xian, Manila 1992, which was eventually drawn, however I believe White could have consolidated his advantage with something simple such as 21.exf6±.

d) 13...♕e6, protecting the e7-pawn and attacking e4, is surprisingly common, but not very good. As a general rule, when you are material up you should not retreat your active pieces from your opponent's side of the board unless provoked. For example, the presence of the black queen on a2 restricts the movement of the white queen, thereby making it more awkward for White to connect the rooks. By dropping the queen back to e6 Black not only gives White's forces more mobility within their own domain, but also gives White a target to strike at with the advancing pawns. Play has continued: 14.♖e1 (14.♕c2!? is also acceptable) 14...♘a6 (14...♕xe4 15.♗c4 ♕c6 16.♗xe7±) 15.♕a4 h6 16.♗h4 g5?! (16...♗d7) 17.♗g3± ♘b4? 18.♖xb4+– Haba – Fahnenschmidt, Bad Wiessee 1999.

e) 13...♘c6 14.d5 ♖d8 15.♗d3 ♘e5 16.♘xe5 ♗xe5 17.♗xe7 ♖d7 18.♗c5± Blasko – Toth, Hajduszoboszlo 1999.

14.♗xe7 ♖e8 15.♗d6! ♖xe4 16.♖c1

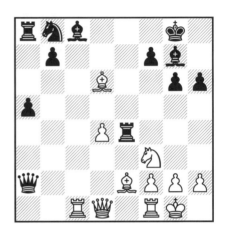

16...♗f5

The game continuation leaves Black in serious trouble, however Khalifman's annotations for *Informant* and *Chessbase Magazine* illustrate that White is in fact doing well in all continuations:

a) 16...♘c6

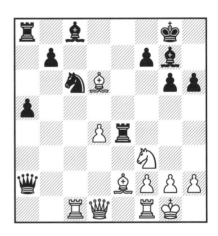

17.♗c4 ♕b2 18.♖b1 ♕c3 (18...♖xd4 19.♕e1!
♕xb1 20.♕e8† ♔h7 21.♗xf7+–) 19.♗d5 ♖xd4
20.♘xd4 ♘xd4 (20...♕xd4 21.♕xd4 (21.♕b3!?)

21...♘xd4 (21...♗xd4 22.♖fe1 ♔g7 23.♖e8±) 22.♖fe1±). Hitherto we have been following Notkin – Vorobiev, Moscow 1998 and now White should play 21.♕e1! ♕xe1 (21...♗e6 22.♗xe6 ♘xe6 23.♕xc3 ♗xc3 24.♖xb7±; 21...♗f5 22.♗xf7†!+-) 22.♖fxe1 ♗e6 23.♗xe6 ♘xe6 24.♖xb7±.

b) 16...♗e6 17.♗d3 ♘c6 (17...♗g4 18.♖e1 ♕xd6 19.♖xc8† ♔h7 20.♕a4+- h5 21.♕b5 ♔h6 22.♕xb7 1-0. Clavijo – Ramirez, Fusagasuga 1999) 18.♗xe4 ♕xd6 (18...♕xe4 19.d5±) 19.♗xc6 bxc6 20.♕a4±.

c) 16...♖e8 17.♗c4 ♕b2 18.♖b1 ♕c3 19.♕a4 ♗d7 20.♕a2 is better for White according to Notkin, and Khalifman builds on this with the continuation 20...♗e6 21.♗xe6 fxe6 22.♖fc1 ♕d3 23.♖xb7±.

d) 16...♗g4

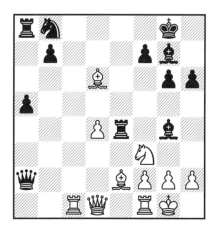

17.♗c4 ♕b2 18.h3! ♖xd4 (18...♗f5 19.♖b1 ♕c3 20.♗d5±) 19.♕e1 ♗d7 (19...♗e6 20.♗xe6 ♖xd6 21.♖c8† ♔h7 22.♗xf7+- and 19...♖xd6 20.♕e8† ♔h7 21.♗xf7 ♘c6 22.♕xa8 ♖d8 23.♗xg6†! ♔h8 24.♕xd8† ♘xd8 25.hxg4 are also very good for White) 20.♘xd4 ♕xd4 21.♗xb8 ♖xb8 22.♕xa5±.

17.♗c4 ♕b2 18.♖b1!

Previously Notkin had proposed 18.♗d5 in his Informant annotations, however Khalifman points out that Black is fine after 18...♘c6! (18...♖e8 19.♖c7± Notkin) 19.♗xe4 (19.♖b1

♖xd4) 19...♗xe4, with sufficient compensation because Black's active pieces and advancing a-pawn leave White under some pressure.

18...♕c3

18...♖xd4 19.♕a4!! ♗d7 (19...♗xb1 20.♕e8† ♔h7 21.♗xf7 ♘d7 22.♕xa8 h5 23.♗g8† ♔h6 24.♕xa5+-) 20.♖xb2 ♗xa4 21.♘xd4 ♗xd4 22.♖xb7 ♘d7 23.♖c1± - Khalifman.

19.♗d5 ♘d7

19...♘c6 20.♖xb7±.

20.♖b3

20.♖xb7 ♘f6 21.♗xf7† ♔h7 22.♗e5± is also good.

20...♖xd4

Probably better is 20...♕c8 21.♖xb7 ♕e8 22.♗xa8 ♕xa8 23.♖a3 ♗g4 24.♕d3 ♖e6 25.♗c7 ♖a6 26.♘e5± although even here White has excellent chances of gaining the full point.

21.♘xd4 ♕xd4 22.♖xb7 ♖c8

22...♗d3 23.♗xf7† ♔xf7 24.♖xd7† ♔g8 25.♕f3 and 22...♖a6 23.♕xd4 ♗xd4 24.♗a3 are both winning for White.

23.♕xd4 ♗xd4 24.h3 h5 25.♖d1 ♗f6

Necessary as 25...♗b6 26.♗b3 ♗d8 27.♗a3 (27.♗f4 ♘c5 28.♗xf7† ♔g7 29.♖a7 ♗b6±) 27...♘e5 28.♗b2 ♗e4 29.♖a7 ♗b6 30.♖e7 ♘d3 31.♖xf7 is winning for White.

26.♗b3 ♖c3

26...♖a8 27.♗a3 a4 28.♗a2 ♖d8 (28...♘e5 29.f4+-) 29.♖a7+-.

27.♗f4 ♔g7 28.♗e3 ♘e5 29.♖c1 ♖d3 30.♗c2 ♖d7 31.♖xd7 ♗xd7 32.♗d4 a4 33.♔h1 a3 34.♖a1 ♘c4 35.♗xf6† ♔xf6 36.♗d3 ♗e6 37.♗xc4 ♗xc4 38.♖xa3 ♔e5 39.♔h2 ♗d5 40.♔g3 ♔f6 41.♖a6† ♔g7 42.h4 ♗c4 43.♖d6 ♗b3 44.♔f4 ♗c4 45.♔e5 ♗f1 46.g3 ♗e2 47.♖d4 ♗f1 48.♔d6 ♔f8 49.♖b4 ♗h3 50.♖b8† ♔g7 51.♔e7 ♗e6 52.♖b6 ♗c4 53.♖f6 ♗d5 54.f4

1-0

Game 6 Conclusions: 13...h6 is doing very badly for Black! If you want to play this variation as Black, then 13...a4 is currently the move to focus on.

Game 7
Se. Ivanov – Zezulkin
Polish Championship 1994

1.♘f3 ♘f6 2.d4 g6 3.c4 ♗g7 4.♘c3 d5 5.cxd5 ♘xd5 6.e4 ♘xc3 7.bxc3 c5 8.♖b1 0–0 9.♗e2 cxd4 10.cxd4 ♕a5† 11.♗d2 ♕xa2 12.0–0 a5 13.♗g5 a4!

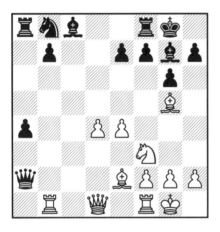

This is Black's best attempt to fight for the advantage.

14.♗xe7

Obviously the critical choice, however the subtle 14.♖e1, which is examined in Game 8, may ultimately prove superior.

14...♖e8 15.♗d6!

Alternatives promise White little:

a) 15.♗g5 ♖xe4 16.♗d3 ♖e6! 17.♕c1 ♖c6∓ - Kozul.

b) 15.♗c5 ♖xe4 16.♗d3 ♖e8 17.♖a1 ♕d5 18.♖xa4 ♖xa4 19.♕xa4 ♗d7 20.♕c2 ♗c6= Von Herman – Schnabel, OLNO 1992.

c) 15.♖a1 ♕e6 16.♗a3 ♕xe4 17.♖e1 ♗d7 18.♘e5 was agreed drawn in Dorfman – Adorjan, Polanica Zdroj 1992, and after 18...♗c6 Black has no problems whatsoever.

d) 15.♖c1 ♕e6 16.♗a3 (16.♗b4 ♕xe4 17.♖e1 ♗d7 18.♘g5 ♕f4 19.♗d2 ♕f6 20.♗c4 ♖f8 21.♘e4 ♕b6 22.d5 ♘a6 23.♗e3 ♕d8 24.♗d4 b5 25.♗xg7 ♔xg7 26.♕d4† f6 27.♗f1

♔g8 28.d6 ♖f7 29.♖e3 ♕f8 30.♕d5 ♘b4 31.♕d2 ♘a6 32.♕d5 ½–½ Sadler-Miles, Isle of Man 1995) 16...♕xe4 17.♖e1 ♗d7 18.d5 ♕f4 19.♖c4 ♕f6 20.♖c7 (20.♕d2 ♘a6 21.♖b1 b5 22.♖cc1 ♗h6 23.♕xh6 ♖xe2 24.♖e1 ♖xe1† 25.♘xe1 ♕f5 26.♖c1 b4 27.♗b2 f6∓ Vaisser – Leko, Cap d`Agde 1996) 20...♗f8! (20... b5? 21.♗xb5! ♗xb5 22.♖xe8† ♖xe8 23.♖c8+-) 21.d6!? (possibly better is 21.♗xf8 ♔xf8 22.♖xb7 a3 23.♗c4 which is unclear according to Leko) 21...♗c6 22.♕d2 ♘d7 23.♖d1 ♗g7 24.♗c4 ♖ad8 25.♘g5 ♖f8 26.♖e1 ♘e5 27.♗a2?! (after 27.♖xe5!? ♕xe5 28.♘xf7 ♕a1† 29.♗c1 ♖xf7 30.♗xf7† ♔h8 the position remains tense and highly unclear) 27...♖d7∓ Lautier – Leko, Tilburg 1996.

15...♖xe4

15...♕e6 16.e5 and 15...♗f5 16.♖a1 ♕e6 17.e5 are both better for White.

16.♖c1!?

Most commentators have assigned the text move an exclamation mark, however I am not convinced that White can prove a definite advantage after 16.♖c1. By way of alternatives, 16.♕c1!? has received some attention in the past, but is perhaps underrated by existing theory. Play has continued:

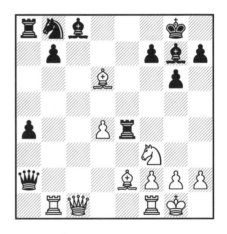

16...♗e6 17.♗d3 ♖g4 (17...♖xd4 18.♘xd4 ♗xd4 19.♖xb7 ♘d7 20.♕f4 ♗g7 21.♖xd7 ♗xd7

22.♗c4 ♕c2 23.♗d5 ♗c6 24.♕xf7† ♔h8 25.♕c7 a3 26.♗xc6 1–0 Solozhenkin – Vareille, Paris 1994) 18.h3 ♕d5 19.♕c7 ♘c6 20.hxg4 ♖c8 21.♕xb7 ♕xd6 22.♖fc1 (22.♖b6!?) 22...♗f8 23.♗e4 ♘a5 gave rise to an unclear position in Summerscale – Lerch, Cannes 1996, which Black went on to win, however it would not surprise me if White could find a way to retain his material advantage and emerge with the better chances. The game in question continued 24.♕b5?! ♖xc1† 25.♖xc1 ♘b3 26.♖d1 a3 27.d5?! ♘c5 28.♕e2?! ♗xg4 when it was clear that Black was pressing for the advantage, however it seems more logical for White to maintain a tighter watch on Black's a-pawn: 24.♕a7!? ♖xc1† 25.♖xc1 ♘b3 26.♖d1 a3 (26...♕f4!? 27.♗c6 a3 28.g5 ♘c1 29.♕a6! halts the progress of the a-pawn and puts the c1–knight under some pressure, e.g. 29...a2 (29...♗g4 30.♕c4!+–) 30.g3!) 27.g5 ♗g4?! 28.♘e5 ♗e6 29.♗b1 when White seems to have matters more under control than in the actual game. I appreciate that the situation after 24.♕a7 remains tense and unclear, however my point is simply that White's play can be improved, and it is by no means certain that Black has solved all of his problems in this sub-variation.

Let us return to the game position after 16.♖c1!?.

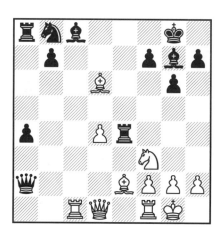

16...♘c6

This is the only move that has been played, however Black has a plethora of alternatives, analysis upon which has been published by GMs Ftacnik (in *Chessbase Magazine 60*), Chekhov (in *Chessbase Magazine 44*) and Sergey Ivanov (in *Informant 62*) respectively:

a) 16...♗e6 17.♗d3 (Chekhov believes that 17.d5!? is stronger, however this would appear to be incorrect: 17...♗xe2 18.dxe6 ♘c6 (18...♕xe6 is less accurate 19.♘g5 ♕e8 20.♕xe2 ♕xe2 21.♖c8† ♗f8 22.♖xf8† (22.♗xf8? ♘d7∓) 22...♔g7 23.♖xf7† ♔g8 (23...♔h6?? 24.h4 leads to mate) 24.♖f8†=) 19.exf7† ♔xf7 when, despite the temporarily exposed position of Black's king, White lacks the means to effectively continue the attack. Black is simply a very dangerous passed pawn up.) 17...♖xd4 (GM Sergey Ivanov pointed out the variations 17...♖g4 18.h3 and 17...♕d5 18.♗xb8 ♖xb8 19.♖c5 with a significant advantage to White in each case.) 18.♘xd4 ♗xd4

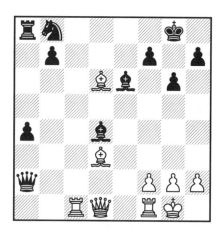

19.♗c4! ♗xc4 20.♕xd4 ♗e6 (20...b5 21.♕e4) 21.♗b4 ♘c6 (21...♘d7 22.♖c7) 22.♖xc6! bxc6 23.♗c3+– - Se. Ivanov.

b) 16...♖e8 17.♗c4 ♕b2 18.♗c5!? is given by Chekhov with the assessment that White is slightly better, one threat being 18...♗f5 19.♘g5. However Ivanov gives a more forcing solution in the form of 18.♘g5!

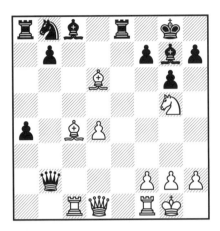

18...♗e6 19.♗xe6 fxe6 20.♕f3 ♘c6 21.♕f7†
♔h8 22.♖xc6! bxc6 23.♗e5 when White holds
both the advantage and an ongoing attack.

c) 16...♕xe2? 17.♖xc8† ♖e8 18.♕xe2+-.

d) 16...♕e6? 17.♘g5 ♕xd6 18.♖xc8† ♗f8
19.♘xe4+-.

e) 16...♗d7 17.♗c4 ♕b2 18.♗d5 (18.♖b1 ♕c3
19.♗xf7† ♔xf7 20.♘g5† ♔g8 21.♘xe4 also
appears to be very strong e.g. 21...♕xd4 22.♕xd4
♗xd4 23.♖fd1 ♘c6 24.♖xb7) 18...♖xd4 (18...♖e8
19.♘g5) 19.♘xd4 ♕xd4 20.♕f3+- - Se. Ivanov.

f) 16...♘d7

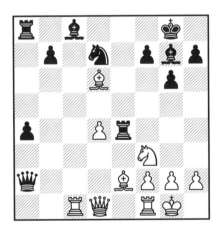

17.♗c4 ♕b2 18.♖b1 ♕c3 19.♗xf7† (19.♗d5!?
may also be good) 19...♔xf7 20.♘g5† ♔g8
21.♘xe4 ♕xd4 22.♕f3 (22.♕c2 intending

23.♕a2† looks even stronger) 22...♘f8
(22...♘f6? 23.♖b4!+- is obviously bad, and
22...♘e5 is best met by 23.♘f6† intending ♔h8?
24.♗xe5 ♕xe5 25.♖fe1+-) 23.♖fd1 is analysis by
Ivanov, with the conclusion that White holds the
initiative. I believe this may be something of an
understatement, as White appears to be clearly
better here.

g) 16...♗f5 17.♗c4 ♕b2 18.♗d5 ♖xd4 (Ftacnik's
annotations focus exclusively on the text move
however Ivanov also notes 18...♖e2 19.♖c7 and
18...♖e8 19.♘g5 in either case without assigning
an assessment, but with the obvious implication
that White holds the advantage. Ivanov also
mentions 18...♘c6!? as an interesting alternative,
but without providing any further analysis. It is by
no means clear how White should continue here.
For example, the obvious continuation 19.♗xe4
♗xe4 20.♖e1 (20.♘g5 ♗d5 21.♖c5 ♕b3 22.♕d2
(22.♕xb3 ♗xb3 23.♖b5 ♘xd4∓) 22...♘xd4∓/-+
- 22...♖d8 also looks strong.) 20...♗xf3 21.♕xf3
♘xd4 does not look the least bit promising
for White. Indeed quite the opposite - I rather
prefer Black here.) 19.♘xd4 ♕xd4 20.♗xb7
♖a7 21.♗c5 ♕d1 22.♖fxd1 ♖xb7 23.♖d8† ♗f8
24.g4! (24.♗xf8 ♘c6! may still be winning for
White, but is less clear) 24...♘d7 25.♗xf8 ♘xf8
26.gxf5 f6 27.♖cc8 ♖f7 28.fxg6 hxg6 29.♖a8±
- Ivanov.

h) 16...♗g4 17.♗c4 ♕b2

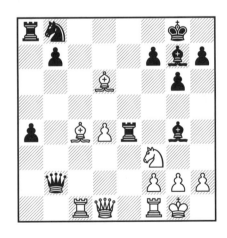

and now:

h1) Ivanov pointed out that 18.♘g5!? squanders the initiative on account of 18...♘c6!∞.

h2) 18.♗d5 goes unmentioned by any source, and may in fact prove rather strong, e.g. 18...♖e8 (18...♖xd4 19.♘xd4!+- ♗xd1 20.♖c8† ♗f8 21.♖xf8† ♔g7 22.♖xf7† ♔h6 23.♗f8† ♔h5 24.♖xh7† ♔g4 25.h3† ♔f4 26.♗d6† ♔g5 27.f4† ♔f6 28.♖f7 mate.) 19.♖b1 (19.♖c7!?) 19...♖c3 20.♖xb7 ♘d7 21.♖c7 and Black will have to invest an exchange to save his queen.

h3) 18.♕d3! is the main move:

18...♖xd4 (White is also better after 18...♖e8 19.♖b1+- and 18...♗f5 19.♘g5 (19.♗xf7†!?) 19...♕xd4 (19...♖xd4 20.♗xf7† ♔h8 21.♕xf5! gxf5 22.♖c8† ♗f8 23.♗e5 mate.) 20.♗xf7† ♔h8 21.♕xe4! ♗xe4 22.♖c8† ♗f8 23.♖xf8† ♔g7 24.♘e6†+- - Ivanov) 19.♘xd4 ♕xd4

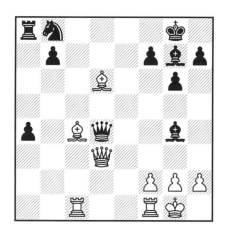

20.♕xd4 (20.♕b1!? goes unmentioned by all sources, but may be quite strong as White threatens 21.♕xb7, forking the a8-rook and the f7-pawn. It also carries the nice point that the natural 20...b6 can be met by 21.♗c5!.) 20...♖xd4 21.h3! ♗c8 (21...♗f5 22.g4 ♗e4 23.♖fe1 ♗c6 24.♖e7 is clearly better for White, and after 21...♗d7 22.♗xb8 ♖xb8 23.♖cd1 White will emerge with a decisive material advantage.) 22.♖fe1 (22.♗xf7† ♔xf7 23.♖xc8 a3 is unclear according to Ivanov, however

White is very close to winning here, e.g. 24.♖e1! g5 (24...a2? 25.♖e7† ♔f6 26.♖f8† ♔g5 27.♗f4† ♔h4 28.♖xh7 mate.) 25.♖e7† ♔g6 26.♖g8† ♔f6 27.♖f8† ♔g6 28.♗xa3 ♖xa3 29.♖xb8) 22...♘c6 23.♖e8† ♔g7 24.♖f8 ♘e5 25.♗xe5† ♗xe5 26.♖xf7†± - Ivanov.

17.♗c4 ♕b2

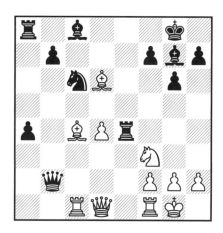

18.♖b1!?

In general White has scored well with this continuation, however with best play Black may be fine, so attention has also focused on the immediate capture on f7: 18.♗xf7†!? ♖xf7 19.♘g5† ♔g8 20.♘xe4 ♕xd4 21.♕e2 ♗f5! 22.♗c4! (22.♕a2† ♔h8 23.♘g5 h6 24.♘f7† ♔h7 25.♖fd1 ♕b2! is unclear according to Ftacnik, however if anyone is under pressure here it is White!) 22...♕b2 (Ftacnik points out the line 22...♕d5 23.♖xa4!!± intending 23...♖xa4 (Shipov played 23...♖d8 here in the game Andrews – Shipov, Internet 2000. His opponent responded with 24.♖d1 and eventually lost, however stronger may have been 24.♗c7 ♖c8 25.♗b6 taking control of d4 and holding up the b-pawn.) 24.♘f6† ♗xf6 25.♕e8† ♔g7 26.♕f8 mate.) 23.♕d3 a3! 24.♖c2! (24.♖b1? ♕xb1† 25.♕xb1 a2-+ and 24.♕d5†?! ♔h8 25.♘g5 h6 26.♘f7† ♔h7∓ are both terrible for White) 24...♕b6 (Leko pointed out the drawing combination 24...♕d4! 25.♕b3† ♔h8 26.♕xb7 ♖g8! 27.♖xc6 ♗xe4 28.♗xa3 ♗xg2!=) 25.♗xa3 ♘d4! 26.♗c5 ♕e6

27.♗xd4 ♗xe4 28.♕c4 ♗d5 29.♕d3 ♗e4 30.♕c4
½–½ Miles – Leko, Yopal 1997.

18...♕c3

18...♖xd4 19.♕e1! threatening 20.♕e8† wins
for White.

19.♗xf7† ♔xf7

Capturing the bishop is probably critical, but
practice has also witnessed 19...♔h8

20.♗d5 (20.♖c1 ♕a5 21.d5 ♘d8 22.♘g5 is
clearly better for White according to Ftacnik)
20...♖e8 21.♘g5 which gives White an attack
according to Ivanov. Practice has witnessed the
following continuations:

a) 21...♗f6 22.♘e4 (22.♗f4!? may be stronger,
intending 23.♘f7† ♔g7 24.♗h6†, forcing the
black king to g8 where it can be exposed to a
discovered check, e.g. 22...♘xd4 23.♘f7† ♔g7
24.♗h6† ♔g8 25.♘d6† ♗e6 26.♘xe8 ♖xe8
27.♕xa4) 22...♖xe4 23.♗xe4 was a little better
for White in Lindestrom – Hase, corr. 1995,
although the game was eventually drawn.

b) 21...h6 22.♗f7 ♗f5 23.♗xe8 hxg5 24.♖c1
♕xd4 25.♗xc6 bxc6 26.♗a3 ♕b6?! (26...♕xd1
27.♖fxd1 ♗e4 is more resilient, although White
is still better.) 27.♖e1 ♗d4 28.♕d2 ♖d8 29.♕xg5
♗xf2† 30.♔h1 ♗xe1 31.♖xe1 ♖d7 32.♕h6† 1–0
Haba – Goriachnik, Germany 2002.

20.♘g5† ♔g8 21.♘xe4 ♕xd4 22.♕e2!

White now threatens 23.♕a2†.

22...♗f5?

A major mistake according to Ivanov, who
also points out that 22...♕d5?? loses to 23.♘f6†!
♗xf6 24.♕e8† ♔g7 25.♕f8 mate. Ivanov instead
proposes that Black's best is 22...♗e6 after
which 23.♗c5 ♕e5 is unclear, as is 23.♖fd1 ♕c4
24.♕xc4 (24.♕f3 ♗f5!∓) 24...♗xc4 25.♗a3 b5,
although notably White could well be in serious
trouble in this last variation. Finally we must
turn our attention to 23.♖xb7 ♗c4 (by way
of alternatives, Ivanov suggests that 23...a3 is
interesting, however this seems to leave Black in
trouble after 24.♗xa3! ♗c4 (24...♖xa3 25.♘c5!
♗d5 26.♘e6+-) 25.♕f3 ♕d3 or 25...♗xf1
26.♕f7† ♔h8 27.♗b2 ♕xb2 28.♖xb2 ♗xb2
29.♘f6+-) 24.♕c2!? (Ivanov's 24.♕g4 ♗xf1
25.♕e6† ♔h8 26.♘g5 gives White a draw, e.g.
26...♗c4 (or 26...h6 27.♕xg6 hxg5 28.♕h5†
♔g8 29.♕f7†=) 27.♘f7† ♔g8 28.♘h6†=)
24...♗xf1 (24...♗d5!? 25.♘g5 ♕g4 26.f4 ♗d4†
27.♔h1 a3 may be stronger) 25.♕xc6 ♗b5 (In
his annotations for *Informant 86*, Haba mentions
the lines 25...♗a6 26.♖xg7† ♔xg7 27.h3+-, and
25...♗c4 26.h3 ♕d1† 27.♔h2 ♕d5 28.♖xg7†
♔xg7 29.♕c7† ♔h6 (Haba also mentions
29...♕f7 30.♗e5† ♔g8 31.♕d6 as winning,
perhaps missing that 31...♖a6 complicates
matters, however simply 31.♘f6† is winning for
White.) 30.♗f4† g5 31.♘xg5 ♔g6 32.♕xh7†
♔f6 33.♗d2+-) 26.♖xg7† ♔xg7 27.♕b7† ♔h6

(27...♗d7 28.♕xd7† ♔h8 29.♘g3 ♖f8 30.h3 ♕xf2† 31.♔h2 ♕f7 32.♕xa4 is better according to Haba, although even here Black remains under pressure.) 28.♗f4† g5 29.♗xg5† ♔g6 30.h4 1–0 Haba – Odeev, Bled 2002.

23.♕a2† ♔h8 24.♘g5 h6

24...♘d8 25.♖be1! ♕xd6 26.♖e8† ♗f8 27.♖xd8!+-.

25.♘f7† ♔h7 26.♖xb7 ♗e4

Ivanov points out 26...a3 27.♗xa3 ♕d3 (27...♕c3 28.♗b2! ♖xa2 29.♗xc3 ♗xc3 30.♘e5†+-) 28.♘g5†! hxg5 29.♖xg7† ♔xg7 30.♗b2†-, and 26...♕d3!? 27.♖d1 ♖e8, in either case with an obvious advantage for White.

27.♗a3!?

Best according to Ivanov, although in light of the next note 27.♕a3 may be stronger.

27...♗xg2

Ivanov awards the text an exclamation mark on the basis that 27...♗d5 is well met by 28.♕c2 (28.♕b1 may be better) however 28...♕g4 29.f3 ♘d4! looks good for Black here.

28.♗b2 ♗d5

Ivanov pointed out that 28...♕g4 loses to 29.♘g5†! hxg5 30.♖xg7† ♔h6 31.♖h7†! ♔xh7 32.♕f7† ♔h6 33.♕g7† ♔h5 34.♕h7 mate, and 28...♕d5 29.♖xd5 ♗xd5 30.♘d6 ♖g8 31.♘e8! ♘d4 32.♘f6† ♔h8 33.♘xd5 is also winning for White.

29.♗xd4 ♗xa2 30.♗xg7 ♘a5 31.♘g5† hxg5 32.♖c7 ♔g8 33.♖e1 ♗f7 34.♖ee7

1–0

Game 7 Conclusions: 14.♗xe7 is clearly very dangerous for Black, however a well prepared Grünfeld exponent should have little to fear, at least on the evidence presently available. Summerscale's 16.♕c1!? perhaps deserves more attention than it has received, although 16.♖c1 is definitely the mainline for the time being at least.

18.♖b1!? remains White's main attempt to prove an advantage in this variation, however notably the likes of Leko and Shipov are happy to defend these positions with Black. Miles

chose to avoid 18.♖b1!? in favour of capturing on f7 immediately, and Gelfand and Shulman (two seasoned exponents of the White side of this variation) steer clear of 14.♗xe7 altogether, preferring instead 14.♖e1! (examined in Game 8). It seems likely that Ivanov's original analysis (which suggests that Black should be fine in this variation) is still correct even today (8 years later), and notwithstanding Haba's recent improvements from the White perspective, Black does indeed seem to be holding his own against 14.♗xe7.

Finally, I would like to draw the reader's attention to a line which is mentioned briefly in the notes to move 16: 16...♗f5 17.♗c4 ♕b2 18.♗d5 ♘c6!?. This line has never been played and, to the best of my knowledge, has not been the subject of any published analysis. Perhaps most important though, is the fact that White does not possess a convincing or even entirely adequate response to 16...♗f5, so there is definitely room for some home analysis here!

Game 8
Shulman – Oral
Ostrava 1998

1.d4 ♘f6 2.c4 g6 3.♘c3 d5 4.cxd5 ♘xd5 5.e4 ♘xc3 6.bxc3 ♗g7 7.♘f3 c5 8.♖b1 0–0 9.♗e2 cxd4 10.cxd4 ♕a5† 11.♗d2 ♕xa2 12.0–0 a5 13.♗g5 a4 14.♖e1!

This calm waiting move presently poses Black the greatest problems in the 12...a5 variation, and is a favourite of Israeli GMs Boris Gelfand and Yuri Shulman. For the time being White simply refrains from entering any forcing variations and instead engages his last piece in the fray, indirectly supporting the e4-pawn and protecting the e2-bishop so that White can play 15.♕c1, taking control of the c-file and threatening 16.♗c4, trapping the black queen.

14...♗g4

At present it is not clear how Black should best approach this position, however 14...♗g4 develops a piece and threatens to exchange the f3-knight, so is logical enough. Alternatives have proved uncomfortable for Black:

a) In the game which originally popularised this variation Leko, defending the Black side, chose to consolidate his house with 14...♕e6!? however after 15.d5! ♕d6 (15...♕xe4 16.♗b5 ♕f5 17.♗xe7 a3 18.♗xf8 ♗xf8 19.♗c4 ♕f6 20.d6± is mentioned by Gelfand and Shulman in their annotations for *Informant 72*) 16.e5 ♗xe5 17.♘xe5 ♕xe5 18.♕d2 ♕d6 19.♗c4 ♖e8 20.♗f4 ♕d8 21.♗c3 ♘d7 22.♗b5 he found himself in a cramped position with serious dark-square weaknesses. Reacting to this Leko lashed out with 22...e5 23.dxe6 ♖xe6 24.♗c4 ♕f6 25.♕d2 but after 25...♘f8 26.♗xe6 ♘xe6 27.♗e5 White was clearly better and went on to win: Gelfand – Leko, Cap d`Agde 1996.

b) Obviously a critical test of White's 14.♖e1 strategy is 14...a3. However White would appear to be doing well: 15.♗xe7 ♖e8 16.♕c1 ♗e6 (16...♕e6? 17.♗xa3 ♕a2 18.♖a1 ♕b3 19.♗c4+- Tibensky – Kjartansson, Olomouc 2000) 17.♖xb7 ♖c8 18.♕f4± - Shulman/Gelfand.

c) 14...♗d7 was successful in its only outing after White passively played 15.♗d3 ♘c6 16.♖e2?! (16.d5!) 16...♕a3 which left Black at least equal in Notkin – Vorobiov, Moscow 1999. Instead 15.♗xe7! looks much stronger, as now 15...♖e8 can be met with 16.♕c1! threatening 17.♗c4 trapping the black queen.

d) 14...h6?! 15.♗xe7 ♖e8 16.♕c1! already

posed Black serious problems in Peredy-Ladanyi, Budapest 1997.

15.♗xe7 ♖e8

Given that Black was failing to solve his problems in this line after 15...♖e8, attention shifted briefly to the more active move 15...♖c8!?, however even here White seems to hold all the trumps:

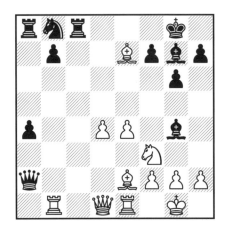

16.e5! (16.♖xb7 ♘c6 17.♗c5 a3 18.h3 ♗xf3 19.♗xf3 ♕c4 20.♗e2 ♕c3!! 21.♖b3 ♕xe1†! 22.♕xe1 a2∓ Shulman – Konguvel, Koszalin 1998) 16...♘c6 17.♗d6 a3 (17...♕d5 18.♗b5± – Krasenkow, *Chessbase Magazine 85*) 18.d5 ♘d8 19.♖a1 ♕b2 20.♘d4 (20.♘g5!? ♗f5 21.♗g4 also looks very strong) 20...♖c4 (Krasenkow points out that 20...♗d7 is convincingly answered by 21.♗f1 ♗a4 22.♕d3 ♖c3 (22...a2 23.♗a3 ♕c3 24.♕xc3 ♖xc3 25.♗b2 ♖c5 26.♖xa2 ♖xd5 27.♖ea1+-) 23.♗xa3 ♕xa1 24.♖xa1 ♖xd3 25.♗xd3 ♗xe5 26.♗b2±). So far we have been following Magai – Konguvel, Calcutta 2001, which White eventually won after 21.♘f3, however Krasenkow has pointed out that White could force a favourable ending immediately via 21.♘b3 ♖c3 (21...♖e4 22.f3 ♖e3 23.♖b1 ♕c3 24.♘a1 ♗e5 25.♖c1 ♕a5 26.♗xe5 ♖xe5 27.fxg4+-) 22.♗xg4 ♖xb3! (22...♕xb3 23.e6 ♕xd1 24.♖axd1 fxe6 25.dxe6 ♘c6 26.e7 ♔f7 27.♗d7 ♖e8 28.♗xe8† ♔xe8 29.♖a1+-)

23.♖e2 ♖d3 24.♖xb2 axb2 25.♖b1 ♖xd1†
26.♗xd1±.

16.♖a1 ♕e6 17.♗a3 ♕xe4 18.♘g5!

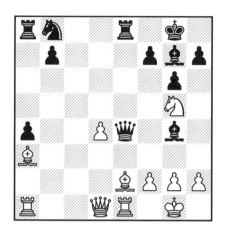

18...♕f4

Forced according to Shulman, who notes the following alternative: 18...♕xe2 19.♖xe2 ♗xe2 20.♕c2! ♘c6 (20...h6 21.♘xf7 ♔xf7 22.♖e1±) 21.♕a2 ♘xd4 22.♕xf7† ♔h8 23.♗b2 (Also interesting is 23.♖c1 ♗g4 (23...♗b5 24.♗b2!) 24.h3!? ♘e2† 25.♔h2 ♘xc1 26.♗b2 ♖g8 27.♕xb7 ♖af8 and now rather than Shulman's 28.♗xc1 which he assesses as clearly better for White, the measured 28.♕e7! would appear to be very strong indeed.) 23...♖f8. White now has a choice of three possibilities:

a) 24.♕a2!? (24...a3 25.♗xa3; 24...♗b5 25.♖d1 ♖ae8 26.h4±) b5 25.♘f7† ♖xf7 26.♕xf7 ♘f3† (26...♗c4 27.♕b7 ♖f8 looks a good deal more resilient) 27.gxf3 ♗xb2 28.♕b7! ♖e8 (28...♖g8 29.♖xa4) 29.♖e1 a3 30.♕f7 ♖a8 31.♖xe2 a2 32.♖e7 a1♕† 33.♔g2+- is given by Shulman.

b) Shulman also mentions 24.♕d5 ♘f3† 25.gxf3 ♗xb2 26.♖a2 ♖f5 (26...a3 27.♕xb7 ♗g7 28.♘e6) 27.♘f7† ♔g7 (27...♖xf7 28.♖xb2+-) 28.♘e5 ♖e8 29.♕xb7† ♔g8 30.f4 a3 31.♕b3† ♔f8 (31...♔g7 32.♖xb2 axb2 33.♕xb2±) 32.♖xa3 ♗xe5 33.fxe5 ♖g5† 34.♔h1 ♖gxe5∓.

c) However, it seems to me that the strongest move is 24.♕c7! maintaining control of the seventh rank and keeping the queen as active as possible, e.g. 24...♖ac8 (or 24...♖fc8 25.♕d7+-) 25.♕b6!.

19.♗c4!!

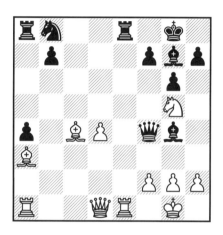

19...♘c6

Upon 19...♗e5!? Shulman provides the fantastic variation: 20.♗xf7† ♔g7 (20...♔h8 21.dxe5 ♗xd1 22.e6 ♕f6 23.♖axd1+-) 21.dxe5!! ♗xd1 (21...♕xg5 22.♕d5+-) 22.♖axd1 ♖xe5 (22...♕xg5 23.♗xe8 ♘c6 24.♖d7† ♔h8 25.♗f7 wins, and 22...♘c6 23.♖d7 ♕xg5 24.♗xe8† transposes) 23.♘e6† (23.♗b2 ♕xg5 24.♖xe5 ♕xe5 25.♗xe5† ♔xf7 26.♖d8 a3 27.♖xb8 ♖xb8 28.♗xb8 ♔e6 29.f4 b5 30.♔f2 b4 31.♔e3 also seems to be winning) 23...♖xe6 24.♗xe6 ♕c7 25.♗b2† ♔h6 26.♖d3 ♖a5 27.g4 ♖c5 28.♗d4 ♕a5 29.♖h3† ♖h5 30.♖e5 ♕xe5 31.♖xh5† ♕xh5 32.gxh5+-.

20.♘xf7! ♖xe1†

20...♗xd1 21.♘d8† ♖e6 22.♖xe6 ♔h8 23.♖e8† ♗f8 24.♘f7† ♔g7 25.♗xf8† ♔f6 26.♖e6† ♔f5 27.♗h6 ♕xd4 28.♘d6† ♔g4 29.♖e4†+-.

21.♕xe1 ♗xd4 22.♗c1! ♕f6

Black is now losing in every variation, e.g.

a) 22...♕c7 23.♖xa4 ♗xf2† (23...♖f8 24.♘h6† ♔h8 25.♘xg4 ♘e5 26.♗e3+-) 24.♔xf2 ♕b6† 25.♔g3+-.

b) 22...♗xf2† 23.♕xf2 ♕xc4 24.♘h6† ♔g7
25.♗b2† ♔xh6 26.♕h4† ♗h5 27.♕xc4+–.

c) 22...♕b8 23.♗h6+–.

**23.♘h6† ♔h8 24.♘xg4 ♗xf2† 25.♕xf2 ♕xa1
26.♕b2†
1–0**

Game 8 Conclusions: in general White seems to
be doing very well indeed with 14.♖e1!?. Black
has yet to demonstrate any method of reaching
an entirely comfortable position, however so far
there have only been a few practical games (albeit
high calibre ones!). It may be a little early to draw
any serious conclusions, other than stating that
the ball is firmly in Black's court!

Chapter 1 Conclusions:

The line with 9.♖b1 cxd4 10.cxd4 ♕a5†
11.♗d2 ♕xa2 12.0–0 a5!? leads to entertaining
and dynamic play, however this can largely be
attributed to the generous risk-factor which such
bold thrusts introduce, and if you want to defend
the Black side of this you really have to be willing
to risk playing for three results!

In general Black has scored quite well with
12...a5!?, however I believe that at present White
can seriously question the soundness of this
system with Gelfand and Shulman's 14.♖e1!?
(considered in Game 8), against which Black has
yet to demonstrate a satisfactory answer.

Chapter 2: The Logical 12...b6!?

1.d4 ♘f6 2.♘f3 g6 3.c4 ♗g7 4.♘c3 d5 5.cxd5 ♘xd5 6.e4 ♘xc3 7.bxc3 c5 8.♖b1 0–0 9.♗e2 cxd4 10.cxd4 ♕a5† 11.♗d2 ♕xa2 12.0–0 b6

In Chapter 1 we examined Black's attempts to generate immediate counterplay on the queenside with 12...a5. It was observed that Black very often falls behind in development, giving White time to whip up a dangerous initiative. In this chapter we will be examining a more prudent strategy in the form of 12...b6. This move has been played at the highest levels by the likes of Ivanchuk and Shirov, and enjoys a reputation for being both solid and reliable. Black's strategy is simply to complete development by placing both his bishops on their optimum diagonals, and then consolidate his slight material advantage in the later stages of the game. White, for his part, must act swiftly to disrupt Black's plans.

Game 9
Gelfand – Ivanchuk
Dos Hermanas 1996

1.d4 ♘f6 2.♘f3 g6 3.c4 ♗g7 4.♘c3 d5 5.cxd5 ♘xd5 6.e4 ♘xc3 7.bxc3 c5 8.♖b1 0–0 9.♗e2 cxd4 10.cxd4 ♕a5† 11.♗d2 ♕xa2 12.0–0 b6

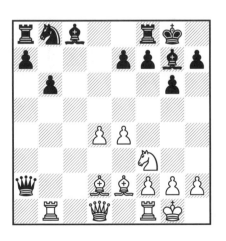

13.♗g5

A very logical approach: White attacks the e7-pawn, increasing his lead in development and temporarily disrupting Black's plans.

13...♖e8?!

This sensible-looking move has only ever been played once – in this very game by Ivanchuk! As the text will show, Gelfand convincingly demonstrates that Black cannot simply rely on solidity alone to safeguard him through these 8.♖b1 positions; active counterplay is a prerequisite if Black is to survive. To this end, Black's only challenging move is 13...♗b7, which is discussed in Game 10. The alternatives also tend to leave Black in difficulties:

a) 13...e6 14.♖a1! ♕b2 15.♕d3 (threatening 16.♖fb1, trapping the black queen) 15...♕b4 16.e5 ♗a6 17.♖xa6 ♘xa6 18.♕xa6+- Bu Xiangzhi – Gara, Budapest 1999.

b) 13...♘d7 14.♖c1 (14.♗b5!?) 14...e6 15.♗b5 (15.♖a1 ♕b2 16.♕d3 ♕b4 17.e5 f6 18.♗c1±) 15...a6 16.♗c6 (16.♖a1 ♕b2 17.♕d3 ♕b4 18.e5±) 16...♖a7 17.♕d3± Kamiljanov – Labunskiy, Moscow 1996.

c) 13...♕e6

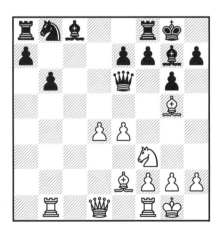

14.♖e1 ♗b7 15.♗b5 a5?! 16.d5 ♕d6 17.♘d2 ♘a6 18.♘c4 ♕c7 19.♗e3 ♘c5 20.e5 ♕d8 21.♗c6 ♗xc6 22.dxc6 ♕xd1 23.♖exd1± Sadler – Dvoirys, Oberwart 1996.

d) 13...♗a6 14.♖e1 (14.♗xa6 may be stronger: 14...♕xa6 (14...♘xa6 15.♖a1 ♕c4 16.♗xe7±) 15.♗xe7 ♖e8 16.♗d6± e.g. 16...♖xe4? 17.♘g5+-) 14...♗xe2 15.♖xe2 ♕e6 16.d5 ♕d7 17.♖a2 ♕b7?! 18.♘d4 ♖e8 19.♖c2 ♘d7 20.♘c6 ♗f6?! 21.♗f4± Del Rio Angelis – Costa, Loures 1998.

14.♗b5 ♗d7 15.♕d3 ♕a5

Alternatives:

a) 15...♖c8 is met by 16.♖fc1 when Black is no closer to solving his problems.

b) Huzman notes that 15...♕e6 16.♗c4 ♕d6 17.e5 ♕c7 18.♖fc1 leaves White with full compensation.

c) 15...h6 16.♗c4 and now:

c1) Ftacnik notes the line 16...♕a5 17.♗d5 (the adventurous, albeit entirely unnecessary, 17.e5!? has been suggested by Huzman, with following justification: 17...hxg5? 18.♗xf7† ♔xf7 19.♘xg5† ♔g8 20.♕xg6 ♕d5 (20...♕a2 21.♖be1) 21.♖fe1+- intending 22.♖e4, 23.♕h7† ♔f8 24.♖f4†, or 22.e6, with the intention of checking on f7 and swinging the rook over to the h-file to deliver mate) 17...hxg5 18.♗xa8±.

c2) 16...♕a4 17.♗d2 (Ftacnik notes the alternative 17.♖a1 ♕b4 18.♖fb1 ♕d6 19.e5 ♕c6 20.d5⯑) 17...e6 18.♖fc1 ♖d8 19.♖a1 ♕c6 20.♗a6 ♕d6 21.♗b7 is clearly better for White according to Huzman.

16.♗c4 ♘c6

a) 16...e6 17.♗d2 ♕h5 18.d5 is given by Gelfand and Huzman, with the implication that White holds the advantage.

b) 16...h6 17.e5 e6 (17...hxg5 transposes to note c to Black's 15th move, above) 18.♗d2 ♕a4 19.d5 exd5 20.♗xd5!? (20.♕xd5± looks sensible) 20...♗c6? (20...♗f5! looks better) 21.♖b4 ♕a5 22.♗xf7†+- is given by Huzman.

17.♗d2

The text is strong, however Gelfand and Huzman also note the following options:

a) 17.♖a1!? ♕b4 18.♗d2 ♕d6 19.e5 ♕c7 20.♘g5 e6 21.♖ac1!? with an initiative for White, although 21.♖fc1!? or 21.♘e4 ♘e7 are equally possible.

b) 17.♖b5 ♕a4 (17...♕a6 18.♗xf7† ♔xf7 19.♖f5† ♗xf5 20.♕xa6 ♗xe4 21.♕e2±) 18.♗b3 ♘b4 19.♗xf7† ♔xf7 20.♕c4† ♔f8 (20...e6 21.♖xb4 ♕c6 22.♕e2 ♕d6 23.♖bb1±) 21.♘e5 ♗xe5 22.dxe5 ♔g7 (22...e6 23.♖xb4 ♕c6 24.♕d3±) 23.e6 (23.♖xb4 ♕c6 is unclear according to G&H, however after 24.♕d4 ♗e6 25.♖c1 White's position looks preferable.) 23...♗xe6 24.♕d4† ♔f7 25.♖xb4 ♕d7 26.♕b2⯑ .

17...♕h5 18.♖b5 e5

18...♕g4 19.h3+-.

19.♘g5 ♘xd4?!

Alternatives:

a) 19...♘d8 20.♖d5 ♗e6 21.dxe5 ♖c8 22.f4!±.

b) 19...♖f8 20.f4!? ♘xd4 21.♖xe5 ♗xe5 22.fxe5 ♘e6 23.♘xf7+- ♘c5 (23...♗c8 24.♘h6† ♔g7 25.♖xf8 ♘xf8 26.e6+-) 24.♕d6+-.

c) Relatively best seems 19...♖e7 with the following possibilities:

c1) 20.d5 ♘d8 (20...♘d4 is met by 21.d6 after which Ftacnik suggests 21...♗xb5 22.dxe7 ♗e8 23.f4 with an initiative for White.) 21.♖bb1 ♗h6 22.♕g3 ♕g4 23.♕xg4 ♗xg4 24.f4 when White has compensation for his sacrificed material according to Gelfand and Huzman.

c2) I believe that 20.dxe5!? merits attention.

Play might continue: 20...♘xe5 21.♖xe5 ♗xe5 22.f4 ♗f6 and now G & H continue their analysis with 23.♘xf7 ♗e6 24.♗xe6 ♖xe6 25.f5 gxf5 26.exf5 ♖e2 with the assessment that the position is unclear, however 23.♗b4!? goes unmentioned by all sources, but looks as though it may be quite good, e.g. 23...♖ae8 (23...♗xg5 24.fxg5 ♖ae8 25.♖xf7!+-; 23...♖d8 24.♗xe7 ♗xe7 25.♗xf7† ♔g7 26.♗e6+-) 24.♘xf7! ♔g7 (24...♖xf7 25.♕xd7+-) 25.♗xe7 ♖xe7 26.e5+-.

20.♗xf7† ♔h8

Ftacnik notes the line 20...♔f8 21.♗b4† ♖e7 22.♖d5 ♗c6 23.♗xe7† ♔xe7 24.♕a3† ♔f6 25.♖d6†+-.

21.♗xe8 ♗xe8

21...♖xe8 22.♖d5! ♗c6 23.♖xd4 exd4 24.♕c4+-.

22.♖b2!± h6

a) 22...♕g4 23.h3 ♕d7 24.♘f3±.

b) 22...♘e2† 23.♔h1 ♘f4 24.♗xf4 exf4 25.♕d5+-.

c) 22...♗f6 23.♘e6 ♘xe6 24.♕d5 ♘c7 25.♕d6.

d) 22...♗h6 23.♘e6 ♘xe6 (23...♗xd2 24.♕xd2 ♘xe6 25.♕d5 ♘c7 26.♕b7±) 24.♕d5± (24.♗xh6 ♕xh6 25.♕d5 ♘c7 26.♕b7± is similar) intending 24...♘c7 25.♕b7.

e) 22...♖d8 23.♘f3±.

f) According to Huzman, Black's best is 22...♕e2! however after 23.♕h3 White's position remains preferable.

23.♘e6!! ♘xe6 24.♕d5 ♘c7

24...♖d8 25.♕xe6 ♕e2 26.♗xh6! ♕xb2 27.♗xg7† ♔xg7 28.♕e7† ♔f7 29.♕xd8+- - Ftacnik.

25.♕b7 ♕e2

25...♕g4 can be answered effectively with 26.♖c2!.

26.♖e1 ♕c4 27.♖c1 ♕d4

Ftacnik points out the line 27...♕e2 28.♖bc2! ♖d8 29.♗e1 ♖a6 30.♕xc7±.

28.♖bc2 ♖d8 29.♕xc7 ♔h7

29...♗a4 30.♕xd8† ♕xd8 31.♖c8 and 29...♖d7 30.♕b8 ♖d8 31.♕xa7 are both winning for White.

30.♗c3 ♕d7 31.♗e1 g5 32.♕xd7 ♖xd7 33.♖c7 1–0

Game 9 Conclusions: 13.♗g5 clearly represents a direct challenge to Black's set-up with 12...b6. However White's success in this game only embodies a model strategy against 13...♖e8?!, which has just been played once (in this game!) and has never been repeated since. Black of course has a more resilient set-up in 13...♗b7!, see next game (10).

Game 10
Gelfand – Ivanchuk
Novgorod 1996

1.d4 ♘f6 2.♘f3 g6 3.c4 ♗g7 4.♘c3 d5 5.cxd5 ♘xd5 6.e4 ♘xc3 7.bxc3 c5 8.♖b1 0–0 9.♗e2 cxd4 10.cxd4 ♕a5† 11.♗d2 ♕xa2 12.0–0 b6 13.♗g5!?

13...♗b7!

Practice has shown this to be Black's best response. Alternatives, and particularly attempts to defend the e7-pawn, tend to provide White with sufficient time to whip up an initiative.

14.♖c1!?

This move was introduced in 1996 and poses Black immediate problems: White takes complete control of the c-file, threatening 15.♖c7 or

15.♗c4, as well as 15.♗xe7. However the present theoretical state maintains that Black should be fine after 14.♖c1, which is bad news for White as the alternatives are also thought to promise little:

a) 14.♗d3 and now:

a1) 14...♕e6

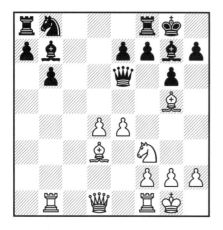

15.♖e1 ♕d6 16.♕d2 e6 gave rise to an unclear position in Miladinovic – Atalik, Vrnjacka Banja 1992, which continued 17.e5 ♕d7 18.♕f4 ♖c8 19.♗e4 ♗xe4 20.♖xe4 ♕d5 21.♖be1 ♖c3 22.♗h6 (22.♗f6 ♘d7 23.♗xg7 ♔xg7 24.♕g5 h6 25.♕e7 a5 26.♖f4 ♖f8∓, and 22.h4 ♘d7 23.h5 a5 24.hxg6 hxg6∓ are both good for Black.) 22...♖xf3! 23.gxf3 ♗xh6 24.♕xh6 ♘d7 25.♖c1 ♕b7 26.♖e3 b5 27.♖ec3 ♘b6 28.f4 ♘d5 29.♖h3 f5 30.exf6 and now GM Atalik, in his annotations for *Informant 54*, recommends 30...♘xf6! which he assesses as clearly better for Black.

a2) 14...e6 is also respectable, e.g. 15.♗e7 (15.♘e5 ♘c6 16.♗c4 ♕a3 17.♘xc6 ♗xc6 18.d5 exd5 19.exd5 ♗a4 was fine for Black in Åström – Moberg, Linköping 1996.) 15...♖c8 16.♗b4 (16.♖e1!? looks better) 16...♘c6 17.♖a1 ♕b2 18.♖b1 ♕a2 19.♖a1 ♕xa1! 20.♕xa1 ♘xb4 21.♗b1 a5 22.♕b2 ♗f8 23.♖e1 a4 24.♖e3 a3 25.♖xa3 ♖xa3 26.♕xa3 ♘a2 0–1 Grdinic – Jelen, Croatian Team Championship 1996.

b) 14.d5 e6 15.♗e7 (15.d6 ♗xe4 16.♖c1 ♘c6!? (16...♗c6 looks even stronger) 17.♗c4 ♕a5 18.♖e1 ♗xf3 19.♕xf3 ♘d4∓ Tupy – Klima, Litomysl 1997) 15...♖e8 (15...♖c8 16.♖c1 ♘d7 is also sensible) 16.d6 ♗xe4 17.♗b5 with two possibilities:

b1) 17...♘c6!? 18.♘g5 (18.♖c1 ♗xf3 19.gxf3 ♘xe7 20.♖xe8 ♖xe8 21.dxe7 ♕a3∓) 18...♗d5 19.♗xc6 (19.♖c1 ♘xe7 20.♗xe8 ♖xe8 21.dxe7 h6 22.♘h3 ♖xe7∓) 19...♗xc6 20.d7 ♖e7 21.d8♕† ♖xd8 22.♕xd8† ♖e8 23.♕c7 ♕d5 24.♕xf7† ♔h8 25.♘f3 is given as unclear by Ftacnik in his annotations for *Chessbase Magazine 63*, however I rather prefer Black after 25...♖f8!.

b2) 17...♗c6! 18.♕d3 ♕d5 19.♕xd5 exd5 20.♖fc1 (20.♖fe1 ♗xb5 21.♖xb5 ♘d7 22.♖xd5 a5∓) 20...♗xb5 21.♖xb5 a5!? (21...♗f8∓ - Ftacnik) 22.♖xd5 (22.♖xb6 a4 23.♖b7 a3 24.d7 ♘xd7 25.♖xa3 ♘e5∓) 22...a4 23.d7 ♘xd7 24.♖xd7 a3 25.♗xa3 ♖xa3∓ van Wely – Shirov, Wijk aan Zee 1998.

14...♗xe4!

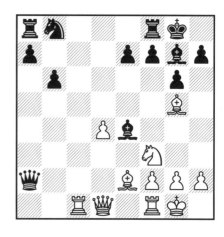

Ivanchuk accepts the challenge. Less engaging play rapidly leaves Black worse:

a) 14...e6!? 15.♖e1! and now:

a1) 15...♗xe4 16.♗c4 ♗xf3 17.♕xf3 ♕a5 18.♗e7!? with a slight edge. Instead of 18.♗e7 Chuchelov gives 18.♕xa8 ♕xg5 19.♕xa7 as leading to an advantage for White, however

I am not too sure about this after 19...♗xd4! (which goes unmentioned in Chuchelov's notes). However 19.d5!? (instead of 19.♕xa7) would appear to promise White an edge in any case.

a2) 15...♕a5!? 16.♗c4 ♘d7 (16...♘c6 17.d5 exd5 18.exd5 ♘b4 19.♗e7± -Chuchelov) 17.♕b3 ♗a6 18.♗d2! ♗xc4 19.♖xc4 ♕a6 20.♖c7 ♖ad8? (according to Chuchelov, better is 20...♘f6 21.d5 ♖ac8 22.♖xc8 ♕xc8 23.d6 ♕c6 (23...♕d7 24.♗g5! ♖c8 25.♗xf6 ♗xf6 26.e5 ♗g7 27.h4⩲) 24.e5 ♘d7 25.♖c1 ♕e4 26.♗g5⩲ when White intends 27.h4 and 28.♖c7 with compensation for the sacrificed pawn.) 21.e5! h6 was Chuchelov – Tseshkovsky, France 1996, and now rather than 22.h4 (an error brought about by time pressure), in his annotations for *Informant 68* Chuchelov proposes 22.♕b2! intending 23.♖a1 with a clear advantage to White.

b) 14...♘c6?! 15.d5 ♖fd8 was played in Galyas – Sipos, Budapest 2001, and now rather than 16.♗b5, far stronger would have been 16.dxc6! ♖xd1 17.cxb7 ♖f8 18.♗xd1+-.

15.♗xe7 ♖e8 16.♗c4 ♕a5

16...♕b2 17.♗d6 intending 18.♘e5 gives White compensation according to Gelfand and Huzman.

17.♗c5!? bxc5 18.♘g5 ♖e7!?

Gelfand and Huzman note the lines 18...♘c6 19.♗xf7† ♔h8 20.♗xe8 ♖xe8 21.♘xe4 ♖xe4 22.♖xc5 ♕b6 23.♕c2+-, and 18...♘d7 19.♗xf7† ♔h8 20.♗xe8 ♖xe8 21.♘xe4 ♖xe4 22.dxc5±.

19.♘xe4 ♘d7

Gelfand and Huzman give the lines 19...cxd4?? 20.♗d5+- and 19...♘c6 20.♗d5 ♖c8 21.♖xc5 ♕b6 22.♘d6 (22.♕a4!? looks stronger to me, e.g. 22...♖ec7 23.♘d6 ♘xd4 24.♗xf7† ♔h8 25.♖xc7+-) 22...♖cc7 23.♗xc6 ♖xc6 24.♘c8 '+-'. However this last line looks less convincing, e.g. 24...♕xc5 25.dxc5 ♖xc8 and although White is better, it seems likely that Black will win the c5-pawn, in which case White may struggle to acquire the full point.

20.dxc5 ♖d8! 21.♗d5

21.♕c2!? gives White some chances of retaining a slight edge.

21...♘f6 22.♘xf6† ♗xf6 23.♕f3 ♗g5!= 24.♖c2 ♖c7 25.♗b3 ♕b5 26.♗c4 ♕a4 27.♗b3 ♕b5 28.♗c4 ♕a4 29.♕e4 ♔f8! 30.♗d5 ♕xe4 31.♗xe4 a5 32.♖c4
½-½

Game 10 Conclusions: The strategy of challenging White's centre immediately with 13...♗b7! and 14...♘xe4! seems to offer Black excellent chances of equality, which may well account for the decline in popularity of the 13.♗g5!? line in recent years.

Game 11
S. Ernst – Nijboer
Groningen 2002

1.d4 ♘f6 2.c4 g6 3.♘c3 d5 4.cxd5 ♘xd5 5.e4 ♘xc3 6.bxc3 ♗g7 7.♘f3 c5 8.♖b1 0–0 9.♗e2 cxd4 10.cxd4 ♕a5† 11.♗d2 ♕xa2 12.0–0 b6 13.♕c1!?

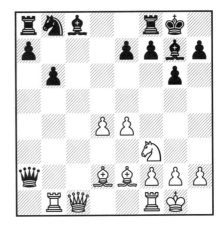

With 13.♕c1 White instigates a similar plan to the one we witnessed in Games 1 & 2 of Chapter 1. White takes control of the c-file, threatening moves such as 14.♕c7 or 14.♗c4, but at the same time cuts down the mobility of the black queen by taking control of the a3-square.

13...♕e6!?

As is the norm in this variation, making yet another move with the black queen proves highly provocative and it is not long before Black comes under fire. The modern mainline of the 12...b6-variation, 13...♗b7, will be discussed in Games 13 and 14.

14.♗c4

White's most aggressive approach, sacrificing yet another pawn for an enormous lead in development. The more restrained 14.♖e1!? is examined in Game 12.

14...♕xe4

Black pockets a second pawn, opening the e-file and exposing the black queen to further fire. However retreating the queen is hardly a solution to Black's problems, e.g. 14...♕d7 15.♘e5! ♗xe5 16.dxe5

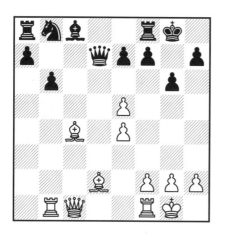

16...♗a6 (16...♘c6 17.♗h6 ♖d8 18.♗d5! ♗b7 19.e6! 1–0 was Jerabek – Sokol, corr. 1989, and 16...♗b7 17.♗h6 ♖c8 18.e6!+– was Juhnke – Soltau, Germany 1982) when White has two options:

a) 17.e6 17...fxe6 18.♗h6 ♗xc4 19.♖d1 ♗d5 (19...♕c6 20.♗xf8 ♔xf8 21.♖d4 b5 22.♕h6† ♔e8 23.♕xh7 was clearly better for White in Anton – Woldmo, corr. 1991, and 19...♕c7 20.♗xf8 ♔xf8 21.♖d4 was also much better for White in Khalifman – Komljenovic, Seville 1993) 20.♗xf8 ♔xf8 21.♕h6† ♔g8 was Sinka – Koellner, corr. 1995, and now 22.♕h3

is clearly better for White.

b) Also of interest is 17.♗h6!? ♗xc4 (17...♖c8? 18.e6 ♕d4? (18...♕xe6 19.♗xe6 ♖xc1 20.♖fxc1 fxe6 21.♖c7+–) 19.exf7† ♔h8 20.♖d1 ♕xc4 21.♕b2† 1–0 Wells – Lamb, Hastings 1988) 18.♗xf8 ♕e6 19.♕h6 ♕xe5 20.♖fc1 b5 (20...♘d7 21.♖xc4±/±) 21.♖xb5 ♗xb5 22.♗g7! f6 23.♗h8! ♔f7 24.♕xh7† ♔e8? (24...♔e6! 25.♕g8† ♔d6 26.♕d8† ♔e6 27.♕g8† ♔d6 28.♕d8† ♔e6 29.♕g8† ½–½ Vakhidov – Nadyrhanov, Tashkent 1992) 25.♕g8† 1–0 Falleiros – Schuster, corr. 1990.

15.♖e1!

Exponents of the White side have also tried 15.♗xf7†!? however it is now established that Black should be fine here: 15...♖xf7 (after 15...♔h8 both 16.♖e1 and 16.♘g5 ♕f5 17.♖b3! promise White the better chances) 16.♕xc8† ♖f8 17.♕c4† (17.♕c7 ♘c6 18.♖fe1 ♕d5 19.♖bc1 ♘xd4 20.♖xe7 ♘xf3† 21.gxf3 ♖f7 22.♖xf7 ♕xf7 23.♕d6 ♕xf3∓ Hellborg – T. Ernst, Sweden 2001.) 17...e6 when the following lines suggest that Black has excellent chances:

a) 18.♖fe1 ♕d5 19.♕xd5 (19.♖bc1 ♕xc4 20.♖xc4 ♘d7 21.♖c7 ♘f6 22.♖xe6 a5 23.♖ee7 ♗h8∓ Zaremba – Culp, e-mail 1997) 19...exd5 20.♖b5 ♘c6! (20...♖d8? 21.♗g5 ♖d7 22.♖e8† ♔f7 23.♖c8+–) 21.♖xd5 ♖fd8 22.♖xd8† ♖xd8∓ - Kouatly, *Informant 42*.

b) 18.♘g5 ♕d5 19.♕xd5 exd5∓.

c) 18.♖b5 ♕c6 19.♕b3 (19.♖c1 ♕xc4 20.♖xc4 ♘a6 21.♘g5 ♖f5!∓ – Kouatly) 19...♘a6 20.♖c1 ♕d7 21.♘e5 ♗xe5 22.♖xe5 ♘c7 23.♗h6 ♕xd4 24.♕g3! (24.♖e2?! ♖f7 25.♖xc7 ♖xc7 26.♕xe6† ♖f7 27.♕e8† ♖f8 28.♕e6† ♔h8! 29.♗c1 ♖ae8 30.♗b2 ♕xb2!–+ and 24.♗xf8 ♕xe5∓ are both good for Black according to Kouatly.) 24...♖f6! ½–½ Nemet – Kouatly, Horgen 1986. Kouatly assesses the final position as unclear, however I should imagine most players would rather be Black here.

15...♕b7

15...♕f5 16.♖b5 ♕d7 17.♘e5 ♕e8 18.♖b3 ♗b7 19.♗h6± Thomson – Gobet, Thessaloniki 1988.

16.♗b4 ♗e6!

An excellent move by Black, accepting a fracturing of the pawn structure but at the same time accelerating Black's development with the hope of consolidating the material advantage. Alternatives:

a) 16...e6 gives up the exchange but does nothing to restrain White's initiative: 17.♗xf8 ♗xf8 18.♕g5 ♗e7 19.♕f4 ♘d7 20.d5 ♘c5 21.♘g5 ♗xg5 22.♕xg5 ♗d7 23.h4+– Sandstrom – Jasnikowski, Copenhagen 1989.

b) 16...♗f6 is interesting and relatively unexplored. One fun example from a correspondence game continued: 17.♖xe7!? (17.♕h6 ♗f5? (17...♘c6! is much stronger) 18.♖xe7 ♗xe7 19.♘g5 1–0 J. Watson – Shepstone, corr. 1995) 17...♗xe7 18.♕h6 ♗xb4 (18...♖e8 19.♖e1! looks good for White) 19.♘g5 ♖d8 (19...♖e8! looks stronger, when the threat to e1 precludes White's next) 20.♖xb4! ♖d5 (Knudsen notes the following variations: 20...♘c6 21.♕xh7† ♔f8 22.♖b1+–, 20...♖d6 21.♗xf7† ♕xf7 22.♘xf7+–; 20...♖e8 21.♖b1 ♗f5 22.♕xh7† ♔f8 23.♕h8†+–, and 20...♗f5 21.♗xf7† ♕xf7 22.♘xf7 ♔xf7 23.♖xh7† ♔e8 24.♕g8† ♔e7 25.♕g7† ♔e6 26.g4+–) 21.♕xh7† ♔f8 22.h4 ♖xg5 23.hxg5 ♘c6? 24.♕h8† ♔e7 25.♕f6† ♔d7 26.d5 1–0 Sogaard – Andresen, e-mail 2000.

17.♖xe6!

The only way for White to continue the attack. Alternatives promise nothing more than equality:

a) 17.d5?! ♗xd5 18.♖xe7 ♘d7 19.♗b5 ♖fd8∓ Schoen – T. Ernst, Malmö 1988.

b) 17.♗xe6 fxe6 18.♖xe6 ♕d5 19.♖xe7 ♘c6 20.♖xg7† ♔xg7 21.♗xf8† ♖xf8 22.♕e3=.

17...fxe6 18.♘g5

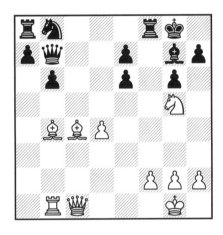

18...♘c6!

Probably best; several alternatives have been tried, however Black's position has proved difficult to defend in all instances.

a) 18...♔h8? 19.♖b3! gives White a fantastic attack:

a1) 19...♖c8 20.♖h3 ♖xc4 21.♖xh7† ♔g8 22.♕f4 ♗f6 23.♖h8† ♔g7 24.♖h7† ♔g8 25.♗xe7 ♖c1† 26.♕xc1 ♗xg5 27.♕xg5 ♕e4? (27...♔xh7 28.♕f6 ♘d7 29.♕f7† ♔h6 30.h4+–) 28.♖g7† ♔xg7 29.♕f6† ♔g8 30.♕f8† ♔h7 31.♕f7† ♔h6 32.♗f8† ♔g5 33.h4† ♔xh4 34.♕h7† ♔g5 35.♗e7† ♔f4 36.♕h4† 1–0 Touzane – Kouatly, France 1993.

a2) 19...♘d7 20.♖h3 20...h5 (20...♘f6? 21.♕b1! ♘h5 22.♖xh5 ♖f6 23.♖xh7† ♔g8 24.♕b3 ♕c6 25.♕h3!+– 1–0 Vaisser – Andrianov, USSR 1988) 21.♗xe6 ♖ac8 22.♕b1 ♗h6 23.♗d2 ♔g7 24.♖xh5 ♕c6 25.♕a1 ♕c2 26.♖xh6 ♔xh6 27.♕e1 ♕a4 28.h3 ♔g7 29.♗d5 ♕a3 30.♘e6†

♔h8 31.♘xf8 ♖xf8 32.♕e5† ♔h7 33.♗f4 ♖e8 34.♗f7 ♕a4 35.d5 1–0 Bormida – Schulze, e-mail 2001.

b) 18...♘d7 is also bad: 19.♘xe6 ♔h8 20.♘xf8 ♖xf8 (20...♘xf8 21.♕e3 gives White compensation for the sacrificed pawn, according to Dorfman.) 21.♕e3 ♖c8 22.♗e6±/± Gonzalez – Perez Moregon, Havana 1992.

c) 18...♘c6 19.♗xe6† ♔h8 20.♗xe7±.

d) 18...♘h6 19.♗xe6† ♔g7 20.d5 ♘a6 21.♗c3† ♖f6 22.h4 ♕c7 23.♕e3!? (23.♕b2 ♘c5 24.♗e5± Carillo – John, corr. 1990) 23...♘c5 24.♗e5 ♕d8 was Brenninkmeijer – Hensbergen, Bussum 1988, and now 25.♕f3! looks good for White.

19.♕e3!?

For the time being White refrains from capturing on e6, instead utilising the temporary disharmony between Black's pieces to involve the white queen in the attack. Earlier attempts in this variation had seen White plunging in immediately with 19.♘xe6 but it seems that Black has now solved his problems here. Play continues 19...♔h8 20.♗c3 (20.♗d5? ♖fc8 21.♘g5 h6∓) 20...♗f6! 21.♕h6 with the following possibilities:

a) 21...♖g8? 22.♖e1 and now:

a1) 22...♖d8? 23.♘f8! e6 (23...♖g7 24.♘xg6†+–) 24.♘xg6† ♖xg6 25.♕f8† ♖g8 26.♕xf6† ♕g7 27.d5+– Vaisser.

a2) 22...♕c8 23.♖e3! intending 24.♕h7, gives White an ongoing attack according to GM Vaisser, e.g. 23...♖g7 24.d5 ♘e5 (24...♗xc3? 25.♖xc3 ♖f7 26.♗b3! is winning for White, and 24...♘d4 25.♘xg7! ♕xc4 (25...♗xg7 26.♗xd4 ♗xd4 27.♖xe7 ♕g8 28.d6 ♗g7 29.♕h4 ♕f8 30.♕e4±) 26.♖h3 ♔g8 27.♗xd4! ♗xd4 28.♕xh7† ♔f8 29.♖f3† ♗f6 30.♘e6† ♔e8 31.g3 leaves White clearly better.) 25.♘xg7! when Black is in serious trouble:

a21) 25...♗xc4? 26.♖xe7! ♕f8 (26...♗xc3 27.♘e8!+–) 27.♘f5!+–.

a22) 25...♕xc4? 26.♖h3 ♔g8 27.♕xh7† ♔f8 28.♘e6† ♔e8 29.♕g8† ♔d7 30.♕xa8+–.

a23) 25...♘f7 26.♖xe7!!

26...♘xh6 (26...♕xc4? 27.♗xf6 ♘xh6 28.♘e6†! ♔g8 29.♖g7† ♔h8 30.♖xg6 mate.) 27.♗xf6 ♔g8! (27...♘g8? 28.♘h5† ♘xf6 29.♘xf6+–) 28.♘e6 ♘f7 29.♖c7±.

a24) 25...♘g4 26.♗xf6!! exf6 27.♕f4 ♘xe3 28.♘e6 ♘f5 29.g4 b5 30.♗f1±.

a3) 22...♖g7?! 23.g4!? (23.♘xg7±) 23...♘a5 24.♗d3 ♕c6 (24...♖f7 25.♗xg6 ♖g8 26.♗xf7 ♖xg4† 27.♔f1 ♕g2† 28.♔e2 ♕e4† 29.♕e3!+–) 25.♗a1 ♖f7 (25...♕f3!? 26.g5 ♕h5 27.♕xh5 gxh5 28.f4 ♖gg8 29.♔f2 ♗g7 30.♘xg7 ♔xg7 31.♖xe7† ♔f8 32.♖xh7+–) 26.g5 ♗g7 27.d5! ♕xd5 28.♗xg7† ♔g8 29.♗xg6 1–0 Vaisser – Pein, Budapest 1989. The notes here are based on Anatoly Vaisser's notes for *Informant 47*.

b) 21...♖f7! (Originally suggested by Vaisser in his notes for *Informant 47*, and absolutely essential if Black is going to survive in this variation.) 22.♘c5 ♕c8 23.♗xf7 ♕f5! (previously 23...bxc5 had been played, however the text is much stronger) 24.♗xg6 (24.♕c1 was tried in Ivanov – Svensson, Sweden 1999, however Sergey Ivanov pointed out that 24...♘xd4! is clearly better for Black.) 24...♕xg6 25.♕xg6 hxg6 26.♘e6 ♖c8 27.g4 ♘d8 28.♘xd8 ♖xd8 29.♖b4 ♖c8 was slightly better for Black in Agrest – Moberg, Gothenburg 1996, although the game was eventually drawn.

19...♗f6

Krasenkow points out the continuation 19...♗xd4?! 20.♕xe6† ♔g7 21.♕e4 when the e6-square appears very tender.

20.♘xe6 ♔h8 21.♕e4 ♕c8?!

Under enormous pressure Black slips up. Instead 21...♖fc8 keeps everything in order: 22.♗d5 ♕d7 23.♗d2 ♘d8! 24.♘xd8 ♕xd8 25.♗xa8 ♖xa8 when the position remains unclear according to Krasenkow. Notwithstanding that White may be able to complicate matters, one would imagine that Black should be very content with his solid king position and connected passed queenside pawns, not to mention the fact that he is still a pawn up!

22.♘xf8 ♘xb4 23.♘xg6† hxg6 24.♖xb4 ♔g7 25.♕d5?!

An error; White can consolidate his advantage with 25.g3!± according to Krasenkow. Instead White's failure to guard his back rank lets the advantage slip by giving Black time to activate and coordinate his major pieces.

25...♕e8 26.♗b5 ♖c8! 27.g3 ♕f7 28.♕e4 a5 29.♖b1 ♖d8 30.♖d1 ♕d5 31.♕e2 ♗xd4 32.♕xe7† ♕f7 33.♕xf7† ♔xf7 34.♔g2 g5 35.f4 gxf4 36.gxf4 ♗f6 37.♖xd8

½–½

Game 11 Conclusions: 14.♗c4!? embodies the most directly aggressive treatment of Black's set-up with 13...♕e6. Black needs to be well prepared in this line just to avoid being blown off

the back of the board! Notwithstanding the need for thorough preparation, Black has no need to fear or avoid the lines with 13...♕e6, because the variations that follow 14...♕xe4! appear entirely satisfactory on existing evidence.

Game 12
Chernin – C. Horvath
Hungarian Championship 1999

1.d4 ♘f6 2.c4 g6 3.♘c3 d5 4.cxd5 ♘xd5 5.e4 ♘xc3 6.bxc3 ♗g7 7.♘f3 c5 8.♖b1 0–0 9.♗e2 cxd4 10.cxd4 ♕a5† 11.♗d2 ♕xa2 12.0–0 b6 13.♕c1 ♕e6 14.♖e1!?

Originally suggested by GM Sakaev, 14.♖e1 constitutes a relatively modern interpretation of 12...b6 variation; White simply includes his final piece in the attack, indirectly protecting the e4-pawn, and waiting for Black to determine his defensive formation. Once Black is committed to a particular set-up, White's forces will be ready to adapt and exploit any weaknesses that may appear. 14.♕c2 has also been played, but can hardly be justified given that White's last move was 13.♕c1. Play has continued: 14...♕d7 15.♖fc1 ♗a6 16.♗xa6 ♘xa6 17.♕c4 ♕c8 18.♕xc8 ♖fxc8 19.♖xc8† ♖xc8 20.♖a1 ♘b8 21.♖xa7 ♘c6 22.♖d7 ½–½ Polak – Ivanchuk, Elista 1998.

14...♗b7

14...♕xe4? 15.♘g5 ♕xd4 16.♗f3 is very good for White, however 14...♗a6 makes some sense, offering an exchange of bishops and thereby alleviating Black's lagging development. White should now play 15.♖d1!? with the following possibilities:

a) 15...♕d7 16.♗h6 (16.♕a3!?) 16...♗b7 17.♗xg7 ♔xg7 18.♖b3 (18.♕e3 ♖d8 19.♗b3 e6 20.♖ed1 is perhaps a little better for White.) 18...♘a6 19.♕b2 f6 20.♘h4 ♖ad8 21.♖g3 e6 22.d5 ♘c5 23.♗g4 ♕f7 was unclear in Agrest – Gavrikov, Paide 1999, although in general Black's position seems sufficiently solid in this variation.

b) 15...♖c8 16.♕a3 ♕d7!? (16...♗c4 17.♗a4! ♘a6 18.♗f4 ♘c7 19.d5 ♕g4 20.♗e5 b5 (20...f6 21.h3! ♕h5 22.♗xc7 ♖xc7 23.♗c6 ♖ac8 24.♖ec1 ♗e2 25.♘d4+- - Krasenkow) 21.♗xg7 bxa4? (21...♔xg7 22.♘e5±) 22.♗a1 1–0 Kostin – Loginov, Loosdorf 1993) 17.♗f4 (17.♗a4!? b5 18.♗b3 ♗b7 19.♗f4 is an interesting idea.) 17...♗c4 18.d5 b5 19.♘e5 ♗xe5 20.♗xe5 a5 21.♗a1 a4 (21...b4!?) with two examples:

b1) 22.h3!? ♕d8 23.♗e2 ♗xe2?! 24.♖xe2!? (24.♕b2! f6 25.♕xe2±) 24...♘d7?! 25.♖xb5± Weber – Cuno, corr. 1999.

b2) 22.♕g3 ♕d8 23.♗g4 ♘d7 24.♕c3 f6 25.♕h3 ♖c7 26.♗e6† ♔g7 27.e5±/± Lambert - Bernal, e-mail 2001.

15.♗b5

The text move is an attempt by White to take control of (or at least pressurise) the c6 and d7-squares, the idea being to pave the way for White's advancing central pawns. Also of interest is the immediate attack on the black queen with 15.♗c4, e.g. 15...♕d7 16.♗h6 ♖c8 (16...♘c6 17.♗xg7 ♔xg7 18.♗b5 (18.d5 ♘a5 19.♗b5 ♕d6 20.♕b2† ♔g8 gave White some compensation in Eriksson – Moberg, Sweden 2000.) 18...♕c8?! 19.d5 ♘a5 20.♕b2† ♔g8 was Eriksson – T. Ernst, Skara 2002, and now Krasenkow, in his annotations for *Chessbase Magazine 91*, suggests that 21.♕d2!? intending ♕d2-h6, or e4-e5 and d5-d5, would have been very strong for White.) 17.♗xg7 ♔xg7 18.d5 ♘a6 19.♕b2† f6 and now 20.♗xa6 ♗xa6 21.♘d4 was better for White in Eriksson – Moberg, Sweden 2004, however 20.♗b5! looks even stronger, e.g. 20...♕d8 (20...♕d6 21.e5±) 21.♗xa6 ♗xa6 22.♘d4 ♕d7 23.♘e6† ♔h8 24.♕a3 ♗c4 25.♕e3±.

15...♘a6 16.♗f4

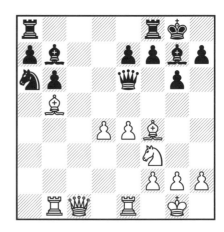

Although White has nothing by way of an immediate knock-out blow in this position, his advantage lies in the fact that he can gradually improve the position of his pieces by building up on the a6-knight (and, indirectly, the a7-pawn), taking control of the c-file, pressurising the e7-pawn, etc. At some opportune moment White may choose to advance the central pawns, further restricting Black's pieces. Black, by comparison, faces an arduous task. Although Black's army is relatively well developed, they coordinate poorly. There are no major targets to latch onto, and a constructive plan is not immediately obvious. A further point to note is that although the bishops can be seen as putting pressure on White's centre, another perspective observes that the bishops are simply restricted by White's central pawn phalanx.

16...♕c8 17.♕e3 ♕d8 18.♖bc1 ♖c8 19.♖xc8 ♕xc8 20.♖c1 ♕a8 21.♕a3 ♘b8 22.d5± a6 23.♗a4 b5 24.♗b3 ♘d7

24...♖e8 25.♖c7 ♗f8 26.♘g5+- - Krasenkow, *Chessbase Magazine 70.*

25.♕xe7 ♕d8 26.♕xd8 ♖xd8 27.♖c7 ♗a8 28.d6 h6 29.e5! ♗xf3 30.e6 ♗g4

After 30...fxe6 Krasenkow notes the following concluding combination: 31.♗xe6† ♔f8 (31...♔h7 32.gxf3 ♘f8 33.♗h3 ♔g8 34.♖a7) 32.♗xd7 (32.gxf3 ♔e8) 32...♗d5 33.♗d2! g5 34.♖c8 ♗f6 35.♗a5+-.

31.e7 ♖e8 32.h3 ♗e6 33.♗xe6 fxe6 34.♖xd7 a5 35.♖c7 a4 36.d7 ♔f7

1–0

Game 12 Conclusions: GM Alex Chernin has a tendency to excel in his handling of middlegame positions in the 8.♖b1 Grünfeld, and his ideas have frequently shaped the subsequent development of many lines. Clearly it is far too early to be drawing any definite conclusions on the comparative worth (or correctness) of 14.♖e1!?, however I will say that I believe we will be seeing a lot more of this move. Although Black clearly did badly in this game, there were numerous points at which play could have deviated, and I have a feeling that future practice will focus more on 14...♗a6. The game Agrest – Gavrikov, Paide 1999, in particular, posed White some problems that were not entirely resolved, so this may be a good place to start looking for an appropriate defence for Black.

Game 13
Solozhenkin – Beshukov
Russian Championship, Elista 1996

1.d4 ♘f6 2.c4 g6 3.♘c3 d5 4.cxd5 ♘xd5 5.e4 ♘xc3 6.bxc3 ♗g7 7.♘f3 c5 8.♖b1 0–0 9.♗e2 cxd4 10.cxd4 ♕a5† 11.♗d2 ♕xa2 12.0–0 b6 13.♕c1 ♗b7!?

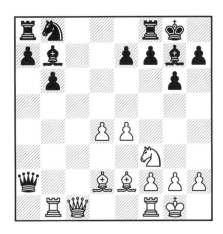

Certainly a more principled approach than 13...♕e6, albeit one that gives White the option of forcing a draw immediately.

14.♗c4 ♕a4 15.♗b5 ♕a2 16.♗c4 ♕a4 17.♗b5 ♕a2 18.♖e1

It is very common for White to insert this little repetition in order to gain a couple of moves on the clock. It is a good idea in practical play, but a nightmare for writers because it means each game, although covering the same variations, has a different move number!

18...♖c8 19.♕d1 ♕c2

17.../19...e6 will be covered in Game 14. In addition to the text 19...♘c6!? has also been tried from time to time. Play continues 20.♖e2 with the following possibilities:

a) 20...a6 21.♗a4 b5 22.♗b3 ♕a3 23.♖e3 ♕d6 24.e5 ♕d8 25.d5 ♘a5 26.♗xa5 ♕xa5 27.♕d4 is some analysis by Sergey Ivanov (included in his annotations for *Informant 49*) who concludes that White has compensation for his sacrificed material. However perhaps White has something stronger in the form of 22.♖a1 ♕e6 (22...♕b2 23.♗e1 forces Black to concede his queen) 23.d5 ♕d6 24.dxc6 ♗xc6 25.♗b3 ♗xa1 26.♕xa1 when Black has a rook and two connect passed pawns for the two pieces, but White's active minor pieces guarantee a substantial advantage, especially given the weak dark-squares surrounding the black king.

b) 20...♕a3 was played in Hultin – Cadarso, Spain 1993 (without the earlier repetition), but was promptly refuted by 21.d5!+– when the knight cannot move on account of 22.♗b4 winning the black queen.

c) 20...e6 21.d5 exd5 22.♗e1! ♕a3 23.exd5 ♖d8 24.dxc6+– was Wells – Pribyl, Germany 1989, e.g. 24...♖xd1 25.cxb7.

20.♕e2 ♘c6

The immediate retreat with 20...♕c7!? is also playable, e.g. 21.♖bc1 (21.♖ec1 ♕d8 22.♖xc8 ♗xc8 23.♗f4 ♗d7 24.♖c1 a6 25.♗c4 e6 26.d5 b5 27.♗b3 a5 28.dxe6 fxe6 29.♘g5 ♕f6 30.♕f3 occurred in Agrest – Krzywicki, Bielsko Biala 1990, and is given in *Informant 49* with the conclusion that White has compensation for his sacrificed material. The text is stronger.) 21...♕d8 22.♖xc8 with the following possibilities:

a) 22...♗xc8

a1) 23.♖c1 ♗d7 (23...♗g4 24.h3 ♗xf3 25.♕xf3 ♘d7 26.e5 ♘f8 27.♗b4 a6 28.♗c4 e6 29.♗e7± Peredy – Dolgener, Hungary 1998) 24.e5 (24.♗f4 transposes to Agrest -Krzywicki, above) 24...♗xb5 25.♕xb5 ♘d7 26.♖c6 ♘f8 27.♗g5∞ A. Shneider – T. Ernst, Reykjavik 1994.

a2) 23.♗c4!? a5 24.♘g5 e6 25.d5 h6 26.dxe6 hxg5 27.exf7† ♔f8 28.e5 ♖a7 29.e6 gave White compensation for his sacrificed piece in Sherbakov – Konguvel, Calcutta 1996, according to Komarov (*Informant 66*).

That encounter continued: 29...♘c6 30.♗c1 ♗f6 (30...♗c3 31.♗a3† ♗b4 32.♗xb4† axb4 33.♕e4+–) 31.♕e4 ♘e7 and now 32.♕f3! looks strong, e.g. 32...♘f5 (32...♔g7 33.♕xf6† ♔xf6 34.♗b2† ♔f5 35.♖e5† ♔f4 36.g3† ♔g4 37.♗e2† ♔h3 38.♖xg5 with 39.♗f1 mate to follow.) 33.♗a3† ♗e7 (33...♖e7 34.♖d1 ♕c7 35.♕c6!!+–) 34.♖d1 ♕c7 35.♕h3! ♘h4 36.♕c3 and it seems that mate is unstoppable, e.g. 36...♗xe6 37.♗b2 ♔xf7 38.♕g7† ♔e8 39.♕h8† ♔f7 (39...♗f8 40.♗b5†) 40.♗xe6† ♔xe6 41.♕g8† ♔f5 42.♕d5† ♔g4 43.♕d4† ♕f4 44.h3† ♔f5 45.♕d5†.

b) 22...♕xc8 23.♖c1 (23.♗g5!? a6 24.♗c4 b5 25.♗a2 ♕d7 26.♘e5! looked good for White in Pein – Varley, British Championship 1989. The game continued: 26...♗xe5 27.dxe5 ♕e8

(27...♞c6 28.e6 fxe6 29.♕g4↑) 28.♕g4 ♞c6 29.♕h4 ♞b4? (Black had to try 29...♞xe5 30.♗xe7 ♕d7 intending 31...♕d2 to take away the h6-square from the white queen.) 30.♗b3 ♖c8? 31.♗xe7 ♖c3 32.♗xf7† ♕xf7 33.♗xb4 ♖d3 34.♗d6 ♖d2 1–0) 23...♕d8 24.♗f4

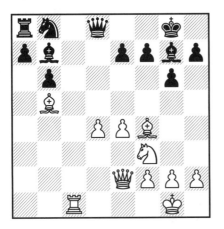

with the following possibilities:

b1) 24...a6 25.♗a4 and now:

b11) 25...b5 26.♗b3 ♞c6 meets with the jaw-dropping counter strike 27.♗xf7†! ♚xf7 28.♕a2† ♚e8 (28...e6 29.♞g5† ♕xg5 (29...♚e8 30.♖xc6!+-) 30.♗xg5 ♗xd4 31.♕d2!± - Se. Ivanov) 29.♕g8† ♚d7 (29...♗f8 30.d5! (30.♕xh7 also appears strong) 30...♖c8 31.♗h6! ♚d7 32.dxc6† ♖xc6 33.♞e5†+-) 30.♕xg7 ♕f8 31.♕xf8 ♖xf8 32.d5 ♞a5 33.♞e5† ♚d8 34.♗h6± - Se. Ivanov (Informant 49).

b12) 25...♞d7 26.♖c7 (Ivanov rejects 26.♗xd7 ♕xd7 27.♖c7 on the basis of 27...♕b5! when White has some back rank problems. However 28.♕c2! seems to keep everything covered, and appears to be better for White.) 26...b5 27.♗b3 e5 28.♗xf7†! ♚xf7 29.♗xe5, gives White a strong attack according to Ivanov (Informant 49).

b13) 25...e6 26.♖c7 ♗c8 27.♕c4 ♗d7 (27...♞d7 28.♗c6 ♖b8 29.♗xd7 ♗xd7 30.♖xd7+-) 28.♗xd7 ♞xd7 29.♕c6

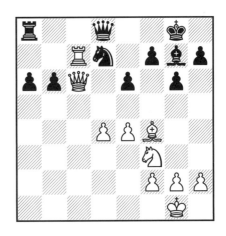

29...♞f8 (note that the trick 29...♞c5 fails to 30.♗g5 f6 31.♗d2!+-) 30.♞g5 (30.h4!? clearing a space for the king on h2, and preparing ♞g5 and/or ♕b6, is also interesting.) 30...♕xd4 (30...♕e8 31.♕xe8 ♖xe8 32.♞xf7 intending 33.♞d6 leaves Black in trouble. Note that the d4-pawn is immune from capture on account of 32...♗xd4? 33.♞h6† ♚h8 34.e5! with 35.♗g5-f6 (mate) to follow.) 31.g3 ♖d8 32.♖xf7 gave White a strong attack in Se. Ivanov – Beshukov, USSR 1990.

b2) 24...a5 was tried in Khalifman – Dvoirys, Leningrad 1990, which continued 25.♞g5?! (Ftacnik awards 25.♞g5 an exclamation mark, however Khalifman and Nesis (Informant 51) consider the move to be dubious, recommending instead 25.♖c7! ♗a6 (25...♗c8 26.♗c4! ♞a6 27.♗xf7†!) 26.♕c4! h6 27.♞e5!±) 25...♗a6 26.♕a2 e6 27.♗xa6 ♖xa6 28.♞xf7! and now 28...♕f6! is Black's best, after which Khalifman and Nesis maintain that White has nothing more than a draw: 29.♞e5 (29.♗e5 ♕xf7 30.♖c7 ♖c8! leaves Black with a decisive advantage, and 29.♞h6† ♚xh6 30.♗xh6 g5! is unclear.) 29...♕xf4 30.♕xe6† ♚h8 31.♞f7†=.

21.♗d3!

The natural move here is 21.♖ec1 however this promises little on account of 21...♕a2 22.♗c4 ♞xd4! 23.♞xd4 ♖xc4 24.♕xc4 ♕xd2 as in De

Boer – Rytshagov, Amsterdam Open 1995, when Rytshagov (in his notes for *Informant 64*) proposes that White's best is 25.♘f3! with an unclear position.

21...♕a2

22.♖a1

Currently White's most popular treatment of this line, however the older move 22.♗c4 also deserves attention: 22.♗c4 ♕a4 (22...♕a3 23.♗xf7† ♔xf7 24.♕c4†∞) 23.♗b3! (23.♗b5 ♕c2 (23...♕a2 24.♗c4=) 24.♗d3 ½–½ Khalifman – Oll, Parnu 1996. Trying to trap Black's queen with 23.♖a1 backfires horribly to 23...♕c2 24.♖a2? ♘xd4! 25.♖xc2 ♘xe2† 26.♖xe2 ♖xc4 27.♖xc4 ♗a6–+) 23...♕a6 24.♕e3 when White has to consider three responses:

a) 24...♖f8 25.♖a1 ♘a5?! (25...♗b5 26.♖eb1 ♕h5 27.h3! e6!? gives White compensation for his sacrificed material according to Komarov (*Informant 66*).) 26.♖eb1 ♖ac8? (26...♘xb3? 27.♕xb3 ♕e2 28.♖e1 is winning for White. Komarov mentions the lines 26...♗c6 27.♗b4 ♖ae8 28.d5 ♗d7 (28...♗xa1 29.♖xa1 ♗d7 30.♕h6 and 28...♗b5 29.♗xa5 bxa5 30.♘d4 are both decisively advantageous to White.) 29.e5↑ and 26...♖ab8 27.♗b4!±) 27.♗d1!+– Komarov – Liss, Paris 1996.

b) 24...e6!? 25.d5 exd5 26.exd5 ♘a5 is unclear according to Shirov (*Informant 65*).

c) 24...♘a5 25.♗xf7† ♔xf7 26.♘g5† ♔g8! (26...♔e8 27.♕h3!, ♗xd4 28.♕xh7 b5 (28...♖c6? 29.♗b4 ♗c5 30.♖ed1) 29.♗xa5 ♕f6 30.♖ed1!± Poluljahov – Tseshkovsky, Krasnodar 1996) 27.♕h3 h6 was Lautier – Shirov, Belgrade Invest 1995, and now Shirov, in his annotations for *Informant 65*, proposes that instead of 28.♕e6† (which seems to give White only a draw with best play) White can keep some chances alive with 28.♘e6!. Black now has two options:

c1) 28...g5 29.f4 ♘c4 30.♗c3 gives White an attack, one plan being 30...b5 31.♘xg7 ♔xg7 32.fxg5 ♖ab8?! (32...♕b6! looks more resilient) 33.d5† ♔g8 34.gxh6 ♕b6† 35.♔h1 ♔h7 36.♖xb5 ♕xb5 37.♕f5† ♔xh6 38.♕e6† ♔h5 39.g4† ♔h4 40.♖g1+–.

c2) 28...h5 29.♕g3

and now 29...♔f7?! is bad on account of 30.♘f4! (30.♘xg7!? ♔xg7 31.♕e5† ♔f7 32.d5 b5 33.♗xa5 ♕xa5 34.♕e6† ♔f8 35.♕xg6 ♕c3 36.d6 (36.♕xh5!?) 36...exd6 (36...♕f6 37.dxe7† ♔xe7 38.♕h7† ♕f7 39.♖xb5 ♖c7 40.♕h6±) 37.♕xd6† ♔g8∞) 30...♖c6 (30...b5 31.♗xa5 ♗xd4 32.♖xb5±) 31.d5 ♖f6 32.♗c3 ♖xf4 (32...♗h6 33.♗xf6 ♗xf4 34.♕xf4 exf6 35.e5 ♕d3 36.e6† ♔g8 37.d6+–) 33.♕xf4† ♔g8 34.♗xg7 ♔xg7 35.♕e5† ♔h6 36.♕xe7±, so Black should try 29...♔h7! when 30.♕g5 ♔g8 31.d5 ♘c4 32.♖a1 (32.♗f4!? may be a way to keep some pieces on the board and maintain White's initiative.) 32...♕b5 33.♘xg7 ♘xd2 34.♘e6 ♕b4 is unclear (Shirov).

22...♕b2

22...♕b3? 23.♖eb1 ♕e6 24.d5+-.

23.♖a4!?

Originally suggested by Khalifman, this aesthetically pleasing rook move enjoys the dual virtues of protecting d4 and preparing 24.♖ea1, thereby enhancing White's pressure on the a-file. Note that 23.♖eb1? is bad on account of 23...♘xd4!-+.

23...♕b3

Ftacnik notes the line 23...b5 24.♖xb5 a6 25.♗d3±.

24.♖ea1 ♘d8

24...♘a5? 25.♖xa5 (Chekhov assesses 25.♗xa5 bxa5 26.♖xa5 as clearly better for White, and Solozhenkin also notes 25.♖b4 ♕e6 26.♖xa5 bxa5 27.♖xb7±) 25...bxa5 26.♖b1 ♕a2 27.♖xb7 a4 28.h4 a3 29.♔h2±.

Ftacnik points out the line 24...a5? 25.♖1a3! ♕b2 26.♖a2 ♕b3 27.♖4a3 ♕e6 28.d5±.

25.♖4a3

25.♖xa7 ♖xa7 (25...♘c6 26.♖xa8 ♖xa8 27.♖b1±) 26.♖xa7 ♕b2 (26...♖a8!?) 27.d5 ♖a8 28.♖xa8 ♗xa8 29.♗e3± - Chekhov.

25...♕e6

25...♕b2? 26.♖1a2 ♖c1† 27.♗xc1 ♕xc1† 28.♕f1+-.

26.♖xa7 ♖xa7?

26...♕d6 27.♗e3 ♘c6 is slightly better for White according to Solozhenkin, in his annotations for *Informant 68*.

27.♖xa7

27...♕d6

In a subsequent game Black tried 27...♖a8 28.♖xa8 ♗xa8 29.h3 (29.♗f4!? ♕d7 (29...♘c6? 30.d5 ♕f6 31.♗e3 ♕a1† 32.♕f1±) 30.d5 ♘b7±) 29...♕a2 30.♔h2 ♕b2 (30...♘e6 31.♗c4 ♕c2 32.♗xe6 fxe6 33.♕b5 ♕c6 34.♕b3±) 31.d5 ♘b7 (31...e6 32.♗c4 b5? 33.♖xb5 exd5 34.exd5 ♗xd5 35.♕e8† ♗f8 36.♕xd8 ♗xf3 37.♘h6 ♕e5† 38.♔g1 ♕a1† 39.♗f1 ♕a8 40.♕xf8† ♕xf8 41.♗xf8+-) 32.♕e3 ♘c5 33.♕f4! h6 was Polak – Kalod, Olomouc 1998, and now instead of 34.♗c4, White's best would appear to be 34.♕b8† ♔h7 35.♖xa8 ♘xd3 36.♕e8 ♘xf2 (36...♘e5 37.♗e3 ♘xf3† 38.gxf3 ♕f6±) 37.♕xe7 ♕f6±.

The comments to this note are based on Ftacnik's annotations in *CBM 67*.

28.♗e3 e6 29.h4 ♖c7

In his annotations for *CBM 56*, Solozhenkin notes the lines 29...♖a8 30.♖xa8 ♗xa8 31.♕a2 ♕b8 (31...♘b7 32.♕a7) 32.d5±/±, and 29...h5 30.♕b2! intending ♘f3-d2-c4, with an advantage.

30.♖a4

The text is good, but perhaps even stronger is 30.♕b2! ♗f8 (30...♗c8 31.♖a4± - Ftacnik) 31.♕d2! with 32.♗f4 to follow -Solozhenkin.
30...♘c6 31.♕b2 ♘e7 32.♖b4 ♘c8 33.♕d2 ♗f8 34.♖b3 ♕c6 35.h5 ♕a4

On 35...gxh5? Solozhenkin intended 36.♖b5! with the nice point that 36...♘d6 37.♖g5†! ♗g7 38.d5 is very good for White.
36.♖b2 ♘d6 37.♗f4! ♘c4

37...♕a5!? 38.hxg6 hxg6 39.♕e2± may be better – Ftacnik.
38.♗xc4 ♖xc4 39.♖xb6 ♗xe4 40.♖b8!+- ♕a1† 41.♔h2 ♕a6 42.♘g5 ♗f5 43.♘xh7 ♖c8 44.♘f6† ♔h8 45.♖xc8 ♕xc8 46.♗e5
1–0
White intends 47.♕g5 with an irresistible attack.

Game 13 Conclusions: Black's plan of 18...♖c8 and 19...♕c2 does not cut the mustard. Engaging in these prolonged manoeuvres for the ultimate purpose of simply retreating the queen to c7 is unjustifiably time consuming and allows White to engineer a strong positional bind. Black is under pressure in several avenues of this variation, and Khalifman's excellent discovery 23.♖a4!? could well be the last nail in the coffin. If Black is going to play the lines with 13...♗b7 then 19…e6 (examined in Game 14) seems like the way forward.

Game 14
Ivanchuk – Svidler
Linares 1998

1.d4 ♘f6 2.c4 g6 3.♘c3 d5 4.cxd5 ♘xd5 5.e4 ♘xc3 6.bxc3 ♗g7 7.♘f3 c5 8.♖b1 0–0 9.♗e2 cxd4 10.cxd4 ♕a5† 11.♗d2 ♕xa2 12.0–0 b6 13.♕c1 ♗b7 14.♗c4 ♕a4 15.♗b5 ♕a2 16.♗c4 ♕a4 17.♗b5 ♕a2 18.♖e1
The text seems best, as the alternatives promise little:
a) 18.♖b2 ♕e6 19.♖e1 ♖c8 20.♖c2 was Brenninkmeijer – van Heste, Amsterdam 1988, and now Ftacnik recommends 20...♘d7! with equality.

b) 18.♕e1?! ♕c2 19.d5 ♗a6∓ Yusupov – Korchnoi, Reykjavik 1988.
c) 18.d5 ♖c8 19.♕d1 ♘a6! 20.♗g5 ♘c5∞.
18...♖c8 19.♕d1 e6!

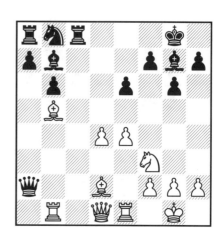

This is Black's most solid treatment of the 12...b6 positions. Rather than rushing around with the queen, or developing the b8-knight into a dangerous world, Black first stabilises the position in the centre so that White will not be able to advance the d-pawn without conceding an exchange of pawns, and thereby weakening his central pawn presence.
20.h4!?

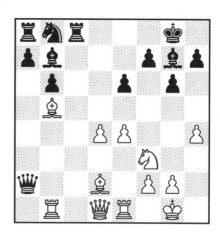

The text was originally GM Komarov's interpretation of this position, although much recognition for establishing the move's stature should also be attributed to Ivanchuk for his impressive win in the main game. Before 20.h4 became the latest word practice focused on 20.♕e2 and 20.♗a4, and there is nothing to dictate that these traditional moves are in any respect inferior to the text. Let's take a look at each of them in turn:

a) 20.♕e2 ♘c6 (20...♗a6 21.♖ec1! intending 24.♖a1±) 21.♕e3 (21.♖a1 ♕b2 22.♖eb1 ♘xd4!), and now:

a1) 21...♖d8 22.♖a1 ♕b2 with two options:

a11) 23.♗xc6 ♗xc6 24.♗c3 was played in Epishin – Tseitlin, USSR 1988, and now White gained a clear advantage after 24...♕b3?! 25.♖eb1 ♕c2 26.♘d2! ♗h6 27.♕xh6 ♕xc3 28.♘f3 f6 29.♖c1 ♕b2 30.♕f4!±. However, GM Epishin, in his annotations for *Informant 46* maintains that Black can establish equal chances via the more accurate continuation: 24...♕b5! 25.d5 ♗xc3 26.♕xc3 ♗d7! 27.♘e5 exd5 28.exd5 f6!=.

a12) 23.♖eb1 ♕c2 24.♖c1 (24.♘e1 ♘xd4 25.♘xc2 ♘xc2 and 24.♗d3 ♘xd4 25.♗xc2 ♘xc2 are both unclear according to Epishin (*Informant 46*).) 24...♘xd4 (24...♕b2? 25.♖ab1 ♕a2 26.♗c4 ♕a4 27.♖a1+- - T. Ernst) 25.♘xd4 (25.♖xc2 ♘xc2 26.♕f4 ♘xa1 27.♘g5 ♖f8 28.♗b4 ♘b3 is unclear according to Epishin.) 25...♕xe4

(The position is now clearly better for Black according to Epishin, however matters are by no means so clear cut.) 26.♘c6! ♕xe3 27.♗xe3 ♗xc6 28.♗xc6 ♗xa1 29.♗xa8 ♗b2 30.♖b1 ♖xa8 31.♖xb2 ♖d8 was Sakaev – T. Ernst, Gausdal 1992, which was eventually drawn in 131 moves. GM Curt Hansen assesses this position as slightly better for White.

a2) 21...♘a5 22.♕f4 (intending 23.♘g5) 22...♗c6 23.♗a6 ♖d8 24.♕h4 ♘b3? 25.♗c4 ♗a4 26.♗h6 ♕c2 (26...♗h8 27.♕e7+- - Konikowski) 27.♗xg7 ♔xg7 28.♗xb3 ♗xb3 was Beroun – Hybl, corr. 1994, and now 29.d5 led to an advantage for White, however the immediate 29.♖bc1!? looks very strong indeed, e.g. 29...♕b2 30.♘g5! h6 31.♘xf7 ♖f8 32.♘xh6+-.

a3) 21...e5 22.d5 ♘d4 (22...♘a5?! 23.♕g5∞ - Khalifman, *Informant 45*) 23.♘xd4 exd4 24.♕f4 ♗f8 25.♖a1

25...♕c2 (25...♕b2 26.♗d3!? (26.♖eb1 ♕c2=) 26...♕b3 27.♕f3!∞ - Khalifman) 26.♗d7! ♖c5 (26...♖d8 27.♖ac1 intending 27.♖c7 gives White a substantial advantage.) 27.♗b4 d3 (27...♖c4 28.♗xf8 ♖xf8 29.♖xa7±) 28.♗xc5 ♗xc5 29.♖ec1 ♕b2 30.♗d1 a5! 31.♖ab1 ♕c3 (31...♕c2 32.♖bc1 ♕b3 33.♗c6!±) 32.♗b5 a4 33.♖xd3± Khalifman – Epishin, Vilnius 1988.

b) 20.♗a4

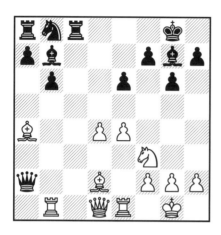

Black now has the following possibilities:

b1) Chekhov notes the line 20...♕c4 21.♖c1 (21.♗f4!?, taking the c7-square away from the black queen, seems logical to me. Play might continue 21...♘c6 (21...♕c3 22.♗d6!? contemplates something like 23.♖e3 ♕c4 24.♘e5, or 23.♖e2-c2 perhaps.) 22.♗b5 ♕a2 23.♕d3 when Black's queen would appear to be in trouble. Relatively best now seems 23...a6 24.♗c4 (24.♖a1 ♕b2 25.♖eb1 axb5 26.♖xa8 ♕xb1† 27.♕xb1 ♖xa8∞) 24...♕a4 25.♖a1 ♕b4 26.♖eb1 ♕e7 27.♖xb6±/±) 21...♕a6 22.♖xc8† ♗xc8 23.♕c2 ♗d7 24.♖c1! with the implication that White is better, however 24...b5 25.♗b3 ♘c6 (or possibly 25...♕b7) may be acceptable for Black.

b2) 20...♘c6 21.♗b3 ♕a3! (21...♕a6?! 22.d5 exd5 23.exd5 ♘a5 24.♗xa5 ♕xa5 25.♖e7±) 22.d5 exd5 23.exd5! (This is much more promising than 23.♗xd5, e.g. 23...♕e7 24.♗g5 ♗f6 25.♗xf6 ½–½ Alterman – Rytshagov, Komotini 1992. In *Informant 56* GM Boris Alterman observes that White has compensation for his sacrificed material after 25...♕xf6 26.e5 ♕e7 27.e6 f6 28.♕a4 however it is doubtful that White has anything more tangible.).

Black's most popular response is now 23...♘d4, however two other moves also deserve a brief mention:

b21) Firstly, Zlender notes the line 23...♘a5 24.♗xa5 bxa5 (24...♕xa5 25.♖e7 ♖ab8 26.♘g5! ♗f6 27.♖xf7!±) 25.d6 (25.♘g5!? ♕d6 26.♕f3 ♕f6 27.♕g3! looks like a sensible idea, as White can meet 27...h6 28.♘e4 ♕e5 with 29.♘d6! ♕xg3 30.hxg3 ♖c7 31.♘e8! intending 32.d6 and either 33.♖e1–e7 (pressurising f7) or even 33.♗xf7† intending 33...♔xf7 34.♖e7† followed by 35.♘xg7. Note that 31...♖d7 is bad on account of 32.♗a4!.) 25...♗xf3 26.gxf3 (26.♕xf3 ♕xd6 27.♗d5 ♖ab8 28.♕xf7† ♔h8 29.♖xb8 ♕xb8 gives both sides problems: for White the a-pawns may prove troublesome, whereas for Black it may be difficult to activate all of his major pieces without leaving the king vulnerable.) 26...♖f8 27.♖e4 (27.♖e3!?) 27...♖ad8 28.d7 ♕c5 29.♗a4 with compensation for the sacrificed material, although this all looks a bit sketchy to me! I'll be sticking with my 25.♘g5 move thank you very much!

b22) The second move to consider is 23...♘e7. There has only ever been one outing with this move (and that was in a correspondence game) so it is a little early to draw any conclusions. The encounter in question continued: 24.♗f4!? ♗c3 (a bit optimistic perhaps) 25.d6! ♗xe1

26.♗xf7†!! ♔xf7 27.♕xe1 ♕a2 28.♖a1 ♕xa1 (28...♕d5 29.♕xe7† ♔g8 30.♖e1) 29.♘g5† ♔g8 30.♕xa1 ♘d5 31.♗e5 ♖c6 32.♗h8 ♘c3 33.♗xc3 ♖xd6 34.h4 1–0 Pinasco – Lukin, corr. 2000.

b23) 23...♘d4 24.♘xd4 ♗xd4 25.♖e4! (25.♕g4 ♗c3! 26.♗c1 ♕b4 27.♖e4 ♕b5 28.♕d1 ♖e8 29.♖xe8† ♕xe8 30.♗b2 ♗xb2 31.♖xb2 ♕e5 32.♖e2 ♕d6 33.♕d4 a5∓ Khenkin – van Wely, France 2000)

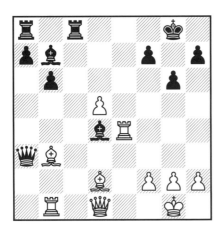

25...♕c5 (25...♗f6 26.♗b4 ♕a6 27.♕f3±; 25...♗c3!? 26.♗g5 ♕d6 (26...♖e8? 27.♖xe8† ♖xe8 28.d6! ♖e1† 29.♕xe1 ♗xe1 30.d7+- - Zlender) 27.♖e7 ♖c7 28.♖xc7 ♕xc7 29.d6 ♕c6 30.♕f3 ♕xf3 31.gxf3 ♔g7?! 32.♖c1 was possibly a bit better for White in Zlender – Tarnowiecki, corr. 1995, however I doubt White had much, if anything, around move 30.) 26.♗e1! (guarding f2) 26...♗f6 (26...♗g7 27.♗b4 ♕b5 28.♖e7 ♕xb4 29.d6!↑ - Chekhov; 26...♗c3? 27.♖c1! ♕a5 28.♖xc3 ♖xc3 29.♖c4+- - Chernin, *Informant 59*) 27.♕f3 ♔g7 (27...♖xd5?? 28.♗xd5 ♕xd5 29.♖e8†+- - Chekhov) 28.♖f4 ♕d6 (28...♕e7 29.♗b4 ♕e5 30.♖e1 ♕b2 31.♗e7!+- - Chernin) 29.♗b4 ♕d8?! (according to Chernin better was 29...♖c5 30.♗xc5 bxc5 although notably White remains clearly better) 30.♗d2! earned White a clear advantage, which was subsequently converted to the full point in Chernin – Dvoirys, Podolsk 1993. White's last devious retreat set up the threat of 31.♖xf6 ♕xf6 32.♗h6† winning the black queen. In order to deal with this threat Black had to play 30...g5, which conceded a decisive weakening of the kingside.

b3) 20...♘a6!

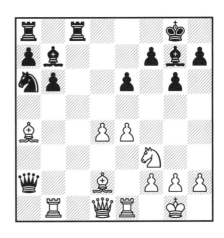

21.h4 ♕a3 22.h5 ♕f8 23.♗f4!? (23.♕e2! intending 24.♗b5 is better according to GM Komarov (*Informant 65*). After the text it is doubtful that White holds any advantage.) 23...♖d8 24.♕d2 (Some sources indicate that Kramnik included the repetition 24.♗g5 ♖d6 25.♗f4 ♖dd8 while others indicate that Kramnik played ♕d2 immediately.) 24...♖ac8 25.hxg6 hxg6 26.♕e3 ♖c4 (26...♘b4!?) 27.♗b5 ♖b4 28.♕e2 ♖xb1 29.♖xb1 ♘b8 30.♖d1 ♕b4 31.♗g5 ♖c8 32.d5 exd5 33.exd5 a6 34.♗e8 ♕f8 35.♗a4 b5 36.♗b3 with an excellent position for Black in Kramnik – Bacrot, Paris 1995, although White eventually won this encounter.

20...h5!?

This last move leaves a significant hole on g5, and seems somewhat counterintuitive to the extent that it justifies White's own advance of the h-pawn without in any respect enhancing Black's position. Notwithstanding the obvious drawbacks of 20...h5, alternatives have hitherto promised little:

a) 20...♘c6? 21.♖e2! (21.♗c3 ♕a3 is unclear according to Ftacnik) 21...a6 (Komarov points out that 21...♘xd4 22.♘xd4 ♗xd4 23.♗b4, and 21...♕a3 22.d5 exd5 23.exd5 intending 24.♗b4, both yield White a decisive advantage.) 22.♗a4 b5 23.♖a1 ♕b2 24.♗e1 ♕xe2 25.♕xe2 bxa4

26.♗xa4 was clearly better for White in Komarov – Mrdja, Verona 1996.

b) Ftacnik notes the line 20...a6!? 21.♗d3 ♘d7 22.h5 ♕a3 23.♕e2 ♕e7±.

c) 20...♕c2 21.♕e2 ♘c6 22.d5!? (22.♕e3 ♘a5 23.h5 ♕c7∞) 22...exd5 23.exd5 ♘d4 24.♘xd4 ♗xd4 25.d6 ♗c6! is unclear according to Komarov (*Informant 65*).

21.♕e2 ♘c6 22.♗c4 ♕a4?!

According to Ftacnik (*Chessbase Magazine*) better is 22...♕a3!

23.d5 exd5 24.exd5 ♘d4 25.♘xd4 ♗xd4 26.♗b3∞.

23.♖a1 ♕c2 24.♗d3 ♕b2

24...♕b3 25.♖eb1+-.

25.♖a4! b5

Ivanchuk (*Informant 72*) notes the line 25...♕b3 26.♖ea1! with advantage to White, e.g. 26...♖d8? 27.♖1a3 ♕b2 28.♖a2 ♕b3 29.♗c2+-. Ftacnik noted that 25...♘xd4 26.♘xd4 ♗xd4 27.♖b1 is also good for White.

26.♗xb5 ♖d8

Ivanchuk notes the line 26...a5?! 27.d5! exd5 28.exd5 ♘b4 29.d6 ♗xf3 30.gxf3 ♖c2 (30...♖d8 31.d7 ♘c2 32.♖xa5 ♖xa5 33.♗xa5 ♘xe1 34.♕xb2+-) 31.♕e4! with advantage to White, and Ftacnik points out that 26...♘xd4 27.♘xd4 ♗xd4 28.♖b4! ♕xd2 29.♕xd2 ♗c3 30.♕d7! ♗xb4 31.♖b1+-.

27.♗g5 ♕xe2 28.♗xe2 ♖d7 29.♖b1

The dust has settled and White enjoys a comfortable advantage in the ensuing transition between the queenless-middlegame and endgame stages. Ivanchuk's technique in establishing and converting a decisive advantage is highly instructive.

29...♘d8

This may appear passive, however Black is already in serious trouble, e.g.

a) 29...a5 30.♗b5 ♖xd4 (30...♖c8 31.♖ba1±) 31.♗xc6+- - Ivanchuk.

b) 29...♖c8 30.d5 exd5 31.exd5 ♘e5 32.♘xe5 ♗xe5 33.♖xa7± - Ivanchuk.

c) 29...f6 30.♗e3 a5 31.♗b5± - Ftacnik.

d) 29...♘e7 30.♘e5! ♗xe5 (30...♗xe4 31.♘xd7 ♗xb1 32.♗xe7+-) 31.dxe5± - Ftacnik.

30.♗d3 f5

Ivanchuk points out that 30...a6 allows White to penetrate the Black camp with 31.♖b6 ♖c7 32.♖d6!±. More resilient is 30...♗c6!? however even here White has everything covered: 31.♖ab4! a5 32.♖b8 f6 33.♗d2 ♖da7 (33...♖xb8 34.♖xb8 a4 35.♗a5+-) 34.d5 exd5 35.exd5 ♗xd5 36.♗xg6±.

31.d5! fxe4

31...exd5? 32.exf5 gxf5 33.♗xf5+-.

32.♗xe4 ♗xd5

32...♔h7 33.dxe6 ♗xe4 34.♖xe4, and 32...♔f7? 33.♗xd8 ♖axd8 34.dxe6† ♔xe6 35.♗xb7 both yield White a decisive advantage according to Ftacnik.

33.&xg6 &b7 34.&xb7 &xb7 35.&e3 a5 36.&xh5 &c6

Perhaps more challenging is Ftacnik's 36...&b3!? when White must play with some accuracy to maintain winning chances, e.g. 37.&a3 (37.&g4 &d6 38.&g6 a4 39.&d4 &a5 40.g4 &e5 41.&xb3 axb3 42.&xg7† &xg7 43.&d4 &c4 44.f4 b2 45.&xb2 &xb2 46.fxe5 &d3 47.g5 &xe5 48.&f2±) 37...a4 38.&d4 &xd4 39.&xd4 &d8 40.&e3±.

37.&g4 &xf3 38.&xg7†! &xg7 39.&xf3 &b8?

39...a4 40.&xb7 &b8 gives Black more in the way of drawing chances, however White is clearly better in any case.

40.&f4 &d8 41.&xb7 a4 42.&e5† &g8 43.h5 &d1† 44.&h2 &e1 45.f4! &xe5 46.fxe5 a3 47.&c8 &f7 48.h6 a2 49.&xe6†! &xe6 50.h7 a1&51.h8& &d5 52.&g8† &e4 53.&g6† &d5 54.&f7† &e4 55.&g6† &d5 56.&f7† &e4 57.e6 &h8† 58.&g3 1–0

Game 14 Conclusions: Black's strategy with 19...e6 seems like a very tenable system, and should be treated with respect. The immense flexibility in both sides' set-ups makes it difficult to provide concrete conclusions as to which side is better in these lines, however in general White seems to score well, and Black certainly has some problems to solve in order to make this line entirely fire-proof.

Conclusions on 12...b6!?:

I have a great deal of respect for the 12...b6 systems: they have proved resilient and reliable at even the highest levels, and have stood the test of time in the face of stern opposition. If White is to demonstrate an advantage here he will have to play very accurately indeed, and at present no established path to an edge is evident.

In Game 9 Gelfand meets 12...b6 with 13.&g5!?. Ivanchuk reacts passively, defending the e7-pawn with 13...&e8?!, and lives to regret it as the Israeli super-GM dishes out some convincing punishment.

Game 10 is less enjoyable from White's perspective, as Ivanchuk improves over his earlier play with 13...&b7! reaching an entirely satisfactory position after 14.&c1!? &xe4!. This really marked the beginning of the end of White's experiments with 13.&g5, as it quickly became clear that other routes to an advantage must be sought out.

In Game 11 White attempted a more subtle approach with 13.&c1!? intending 14.&c4, however Black managed to hold the balance with 13...&e6! 14.&c4 &xe4!. White manages to generate a dangerous attack in this system, however objectively Black's resources are sufficient to weather the storm, so it seems that 14.&c4 is also insufficient for a genuine edge, although no doubt many players will be attracted to this line on account of White's excellent practical chances of success.

In Game 12 GM Chernin, a respected expert on the 8.&b1 system, reinvigorates 14.&e1!?, a relatively unexplored sideline in which White forgoes an immediate assault in preference of longer-term exploitation of White's positional compensation. Although Chernin scores a convincing victory, Black's play was less than exemplary, and in particular the game Agrest – Gavrikov, Paide 1999 (considered in the notes to Black's 14th move) represents a more mature handling of the Black pieces. In general the positions after 14.&e1!? are so unexplored that one can only realistically describe them as unclear (sorry, I know that is not especially helpful!). However I will say that I have confidence in White's position and would be happier to play the White side than to defend with the Black bits.

Games 13 & 14 deal with the lines where Black forgoes 13.&c1!? &e6 in favour of 13...&b7!?. In both games this gives White time to coordinate his major forces and establish lasting positional compensation, and consequently I much prefer White's chances here. In my opinion, if Black is going to play 12.b6, then 13...&e6 is definitely the most resilient set-up.

Chapter 3: The Chameleon 12...♘d7!?

1.d4 ♘f6 2.c4 g6 3.♘c3 d5 4.cxd5 ♘xd5 5.e4 ♘xc3 6.bxc3 ♗g7 7.♘f3 c5 8.♖b1 0-0 9.♗e2 cxd4 10.cxd4 ♕a5† 11.♗d2 ♕xa2 12.0-0 ♘d7!?

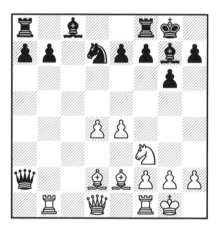

A very logical approach, and one that has found favour with GMs Leko and Tseitlin. If we cast our minds back to Chapter 1 (12...a5) it will be recalled that Black's problems were largely associated with lagging development, which meant that Black struggled to contain White's expansive initiative as the middlegame developed. The developments in Chapter 2 (12...b6) represent a logical progression from Chapter 1: Black recognises that his position is not quite as solid as first appearances may suggest, and instead spends a couple of moves developing his queenside forces. Black is, after all, a pawn up - so what's the rush? However, throughout Chapter 2 a few other defects in Black's position became clear:

- Firstly, after 12...b6 13.♕c1, it is clear that Black will have to deal with the threat of 14.♗c4 (and possibly also ♕c1-c7 - hitting b7 and e7 simultaneously - at some point) and that

Black's last move has done little to anticipate this threat.

- Secondly, and perhaps more importantly, although the light-squared bishop appears well placed on b7, very often it actually proves quite inactive. Although Black's b7-bishop exerts some pressure on White's centre, that is really all it achieves. Overall the b7-bishop (And, for that matter, the g7-bishop also!) frequently found itself restricted by the white pawn centre. This, of itself, perhaps provides some indication that the light-squared bishop may be better developed somewhere on the c8-h3 diagonal. The obvious position would be g4 (although ideas involving f7-f5, fracturing White's centre, expand Black's options), however at move 12 this would leave the b7 pawn unprotected (as it turns out, this is not such a problem, and consequently 12...♗g4 is the subject of Chapter 4).

- Finally, in both the 12...a5 and the 12...b6 variations, there exists a problem of what to do with the b8-knight. Very often developing it to c6 simply serves to spur on the expansion of White's centre with d4-d5. In practical play it is not uncommon for Black to develop the knight to a6, however it frequently becomes stranded there because the b4 and c5 squares are unavailable, and the retreat to c7 invariably proves pointless. That only leaves d7, however in this case there is a danger that the knight's presence will obstruct the retreat avenue of the black queen (e.g. ♕a2-e6-d7).

This short analysis provides us with a backdrop to the justifications surrounding 12...♘d7:

- Black acknowledges the impetus for rapid development, and so develops the b8-knight immediately.

- By placing the knight on d7 Black anticipates two of White's principle methods of attack: 13.♗g5 can simply be met by 13...♘f6, answering 14.e5 with 14...♘d5, when Black appears to have everything covered; alternatively, should White employ the plan with 13.♕c1, intending 14.♗c4, Black can take control of the c4-square with 13...♘b6, when the b7-pawn is guarded and the light-squared bishop is free to develop to g4, with an excellent position.

- Finally, by developing the b8-knight now, and not delaying a couple of moves, Black is able to reposition the knight more actively without incurring too much risk of the black queen's retreat path being obstructed.

Game 15
Petursson – T. Ernst
Reykjavik 1995

1.d4 ♘f6 2.c4 g6 3.♘c3 d5 4.cxd5 ♘xd5 5.e4 ♘xc3 6.bxc3 ♗g7 7.♘f3 c5 8.♖b1 0–0 9.♗e2 cxd4 10.cxd4 ♕a5† 11.♗d2 ♕xa2 12.0–0 ♘d7!? 13.♗b4!

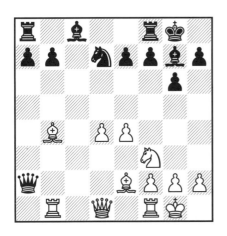

With 13.♗g5 and 13.♕c1 appearing relatively ineffectual, White finds another way to pressurise the e7-pawn, in the process taking the a3-square away from the black queen.

13...a5!?

In the early days of 12...♘d7 this thrust enjoyed a brief period of popularity, however it is now generally regarded as an inferior option.

Alternatives:

a) The mainline is 13...♘b6 and this will be examined in Games 16–18.

b) Protecting e7 directly with 13...♕e6 has also been played several times, however White's resources should prove sufficient to guarantee an edge. 14.♖e1 (14.♕c2 ♘f6 (or 14...♘b6 15.d5 ♕d7 16.♖fd1±) 15.♘e5! intending 16.♗c4, both look comfortably better for White.) 14...a6 (14...♘b6 15.♗b5! (taking the d7-square away from the black queen) 15...♗d7 16.d5 ♕g4 17.h3 ♕h5 18.♗xd7 ♘xd7 19.♗xe7± Lopepe – Monetti, corr. 1991; 14...♕xe4 15.♗c4 ♕c6 (15...♕f4 16.♗xe7± ♖e8? 17.g3+-) 16.♖c1 ♕b6 17.♗xe7±/+-) 15.♕c2 (Now that b6 is unguarded, perhaps 15.e5 makes some sense, e.g. 15...♘b6 16.♗xe7 ♕xe7 17.♖xb6 ♗e6 18.♗d3 ♗d5 19.♗e4±.)

15...♖e8?! (15...b5!?) 16.♗c4 ♕g4 17.h3 ♕f4 18.e5± J. Watson – Keatinge Clay, San Francisco 1999.

c) 13...♖e8 14.♗b5!? (14.♕d3 ♘b6 15.♖a1 ♕e6 16.♖a5!±) 14...♕e6 (14...a6 15.♖a1 ♕b2 16.♕e1± White intends to trap the black queen with the really cute manoeuvre 17.♗c4 and 18.♖a2.) 15.e5 ♕d5 16.♕d3 b6 17.♖fc1 ♖b8 18.♗c4 ♕a8 19.♗xf7† ♔xf7 20.♘g5† ♔g8 21.♕b3† 1–0 Tratar – Kosmac, Bled 1992.

14.♖a1!

14.♗xe7 is less accurate on account of 14...♖e8 15.♖a1 (15.♗d6 ♖xe4 16.♗d3 ♖e6∞ - Ftacnik, *Chessbase Magazine 26*) 15...♕e6 16.♗a3 ♕xe4 17.♗c4 ♕f5 18.♖b1 ♘f8 19.♖b5 ♕f4 20.g3 ♕f6 (20...♕c7!? 21.♖c5 ♕d8) 21.♘e5 was Wells – I.Gurevich, Lloyds Bank Masters 1994, and now 21...♗e6 gives Black a good position with no problems.

14...♕e6 15.♕c2

a) 15.♗d3 b6 16.♗a3 ♗a6 17.♗xa6 ♖xa6 18.♕e2 ♖aa8 19.♖ac1 ♖fc8 20.d5 ♕f6 21.e5 ♘xe5 22.♘xe5 ♖xc1 23.♖xc1 ♕xe5∓/-+ Etchegaray – Leko, Oviedo 1993.

b) 15.e5 ♘b6 16.♘g5

16...♕f5 (16...♕d7 may be better) 17.♗xe7 ♖e8 18.♗d3 (18.g4 ♕f4 19.♘h3 ♕h6 20.♗c5 ♘d7 is better for Black, however 18.♗c5!? ♘d7 19.f4 looks like an interesting idea, e.g. 19...♘xc5 20.g4 ♕d7 21.dxc5.) 18...♕f4 19.g3 ♕xd4 is given by Ftacnik with the assessment that the position is unclear. However, this must be wrong as 20.♗xg6! looks winning for White, e.g. 20...♕xd1 21.♗xf7† ♔h8 22.♖fxd1 when the e7-bishop is immune from capture on account of 22...♖xe7 23.♖d8† ♗f8 24.♖xf8† ♔g7 25.♖g8† ♔h6 26.♖b1+-.

15...♘f6

15...♘c6 16.♕xc6 (16.♕b1! looks stronger, when White can follow up with 17.♖c1, with a

powerful build-up on the queenside.) 16...bxc6 17.♖xa5 ♖xa5 18.♗xa5 was a bit better for White in Beck – Hummel, Austria 1997, on account of the weak c6-pawn. Ftacnik points out that 15...b6? is bad because of 16.♗c4±.

16.♘e5!

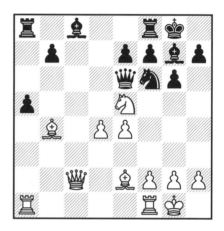

Petursson's excellent novelty suddenly pushes Black against the ropes. With 16.♘e5 White guards e4, removes the c6, d7 and g4 flight squares from the black queen, and prepares 17.♗c4 enhancing the pressure on f7. Alternatives have failed to guarantee White an advantage:

a) 16.♗d3 ♘h5! 17.♗c4 (17.♖fd1 ♘f4 18.♗f1 (18.♗c4 ♕g4 19.♗f1 ♘h3† 20.♔h1 ♕xe4!) 18...b6 19.d5 ♕g4 20.♘d4 (20.♖a2 ♗a6!) 20...♗a6 21.f3 ♕g5 22.♗xa6 (22.♗c3 ♗e2! 23.♘xe2 ♘h3† 24.♔h1 ♘f2† 25.♔g1 ♘h3†=) 22...axb4 23.g3! b3! gave Black a clear advantage in Brenninkmeijer – van Mil, Netherlands 1991. The notes here are based on Ftacnik's notes for *Chessbase Magazine 26*) 17...♕d7 18.♖fd1 (18.♖xa5 ♖xa5 19.♗xa5 ♘f4 gives Black counterplay according to Krasenkow.) 18...♘f4 19.♘e5 ♗xe5 20.dxe5 ♕g4 21.f3 ♕g5 22.♖xa5 (22.♗xa5!?) 22...♖xa5 23.♗xa5 ♕xe5 and now 24.♗b4 gave White compensation for his sacrificed pawn in Sadler – Krasenkow, Hastings 1993, but nothing more (Krasenkow, *Chessbase Magazine 40*).

b) 16.e5 ♘d5 17.♗xa5 ♗d7= - Ftacnik.

16...♘d7

16...b5 17.♖xa5 ♖xa5 18.♗xa5 ♗b7

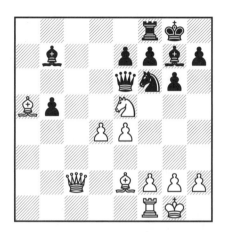

19.♗d3 (19.f3!? ♘d7 20.f4±) 19...♖c8
(19...♘d7!? 20.♘f3 ♖a8 21.♗b4 ♕b6 22.♗xe7
♗xd4 23.♘xd4 ♕xd4 24.♗xb5?! (24.♖d1!?)
24...♕e5 ½–½ Aubel – van Egmond, Holland
1996) 20.♕b1 was slightly better for White
in Nedobora – Krasenkova, Moscow 1994:
Petursson, *Informant 64*.
**17.♘f3 ♘f6 18.♘e5 ♘d7 19.♗c4! ♕f6 20.f4!
♕b6**

20...♘xe5 21.fxe5 ♕b6 22.♗c5 ♕d8 23.♕b3±
- Ftacnik, *CBM 47*.
21.♗xe7 ♗xe5

It seems irrational to surrender control of the
dark-squares with White's bishop so venomously
poised on e7, however Petursson demonstrates
that Ernst's decision was justified by the following
continuation: 21...♘xe5 22.fxe5 ♕xd4† 23.♔h1
b5 24.♗d5 ♗e6 (24...♗d7 25.♗xf8 ♖xf8 26.♖xa5
gives White a clear advantage on account of the
enduring weakness of the f7-pawn.) 25.♗xf8
♖xf8 26.♗xe6 fxe6 27.♖xf8† ♗xf8 28.♖xa5±.
22.fxe5 ♕xd4† 23.♔h1 ♘xe5 24.♗d5!±

If one examines the comparative influence of
the f8-rook and the d5-bishop, it is quite clear
that the bishop is a monster! White should be in
no hurry to cash in one of his best chips, and this
supposition is borne out by Ftacnik's observation

that 24.♗xf8 ♕xc4 25.♕b2 ♕e6 gives rise to an
unclear position.
24...♗g4

24...♖e8 25.♗c5 ♕d3 26.♗xf7†+-.
25.♗c5

The obvious 25.♗xf8 was also good according
to Petursson, however White just can't bring
himself to part with that dark-squared bishop!
25...♕d3 26.♕b2 ♘d7

On 26...♖fe8 both 27.♗d4 and 27.♗d6 give
White a decisive advantage.

27.♗xf8

27.♗d4 ♗e6 28.♗h8 f6 29.♗xe6† ♔xh8
30.♖ad1 ♕xe4 31.♗xd7±.
**27...♖xf8 28.h3 ♗h5 29.♕f2 ♔g7 30.♖xa5 f5!
31.♕b2† ♘f6**

31...♖f6 32.♖fa1 fxe4 33.♕xb7 ♖d6
34.♗xe4+-.
32.♖c1?!

An unfortunate slip; Petursson points out that
White could have decided things with 32.♖aa1!.
32...♔h6 (32...fxe4 33.♕xb7† ♔h6 34.♗e7 ♖e8
35.♕xf6 ♕xd5 36.♖a7 ♕e5 37.♕f7 and 32...b6
33.♕e5 ♖e8 34.♖a7† ♔h6 35.♕f4† should also
be winning for White.) 33.♕c1† g5 34.♖xf5+-,
whereas Ftacnik notes that 32.♕xb7† ♔h6 33.♖fa1
was also strong.
32...♔h6! 33.♖a3

Or 33.♕xb7!? ♘xe4 34.♖a7.

33...♕e2 34.♕xe2?

A time trouble error. Instead 34.♕xb7 ♘xe4 (34...fxe4 35.♕e7 and 34...f4 35.♕e7 ♘d7 36.♖g1 f3 37.g4! are both winning for White.) 35.♖a7 ♘f2† 36.♔h2 ♕e5† 37.g3 f4 38.♕xh7† ♔g5 39.h4† ♔g4 40.♕d7† ♖f5 41.♖c4 should have proved decisive.

34...♗xe2 35.♖xb7 fxe4 36.♔g1 ♗d3 37.♗a6 ♗xa6 38.♖xa6 ♘h5 39.♖e1?

39.♖e6! ♘g3 40.♖c7+-.

39...♖e8 40.♔f2

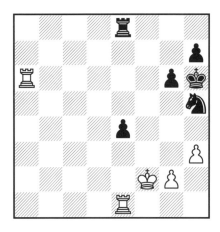

40...♔g5?

40...♘f4! was better.

41.g4 ♘f4 42.♔g3 ♘d3 43.h4† ♔h6 44.♖a7 g5 45.♖b1?

45.♖h1!

45...gxh4† 46.♔xh4 ♘f4! 47.♖bb7 ♘g6† 48.♔g3 ♘f8 49.♖e7 ♖b8? 50.♖xe4 ♖b3† 51.♔f2 ♘g6 52.♖a5 ♖b7 53.♖e3 ♔g7 54.♔g3 ♖c7 55.♖ea3 ♔h6 56.♖a7 ♖c1! 57.♖f3 ♖g1† 58.♔h3 ♖h1† 59.♔g3 ♖g1† 60.♔h3 ♖h1† 61.♔g2 ♖b1! 62.♖fa3 ♔g5? 63.♖xh7!+- ♖b4 64.♔h3 ♘f4† 65.♔g3 ♘e2† 66.♔f2 ♘d4 67.♖g7† ♔f4 68.♔g2 ♖b2† 69.♔h3 ♘e6 70.f7† ♔g5 71.♖f5† ♔g6 72.♖a6 ♖e2 73.♖b5 ♖e1 74.♖bb6 ♔f6 75.♖xe6† ♖xe6 76.♖xe6† ♔xe6 77.♔h4 ♔f6 78.♔h5

1–0

Game 15 Conclusions: At present it would appear that the combination of 12...♘d7 and 13...a5!? is simply asking too much of Black's position. Petursson's excellent discovery 16.♘e5! currently poses advocates of this line serious problems.

Game 16
Yakovich – Kazak
USSR 1990

1.d4 ♘f6 2.c4 g6 3.♘c3 d5 4.♘f3 ♗g7 5.cxd5 ♘xd5 6.e4 ♘xc3 7.bxc3 c5 8.♖b1 0–0 9.♗e2 cxd4 10.cxd4 ♕a5† 11.♗d2 ♕xa2 12 0–0 ♘d7 13.♗b4 ♘b6!

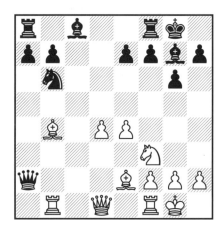

Introduced by GM Gavrikov in 1988, 13...♘b6 is Black's most reliable option, and the move which maintains consistency with the strategy discussed in the introductory paragraphs of this chapter.

14.♘e5

White's most direct approach. 14.♖a1 is considered in Game 18, and Gelfand's pet move 14.h3!? will be considered in Game 19. Other moves have generally proved ineffectual against Black's solid set-up:

a) After 14.♕d3!? Black has two respectable options:

a1) 14...♖e8!? 15.♘g5!? (15.♖a1 ♕e6 16.♖a5 may be an edge.) 15...♗e6 (15...♗xd4!?) 16.d5

♗d7 17.♕f3 f5! 18.♗d3! (Gavrikov notes the variations 18.exf5?! ♗xf5∓ 19.g4? ♗xb1 20.♕f7† ♔h8 21.♘c3 ♖g8 22.♕xe7 h6–+, and 18.♘c3?! h6! 19.♗xg7 ♔xg7 20.♘e6† (20.♕c3†? ♔g8 21.♕h3 ♕xe2 22.♕xh6 ♕h5–+) 20...♗xe6 21.dxe6 ♕xe6 22.exf5∓) 18...♗f6 was Khalifman – Gavrikov, USSR Championship 1988, and now Gavrikov, in his annotations for *Informant 46*, suggests that White's best is 19.♕g3!? fxe4 20.♗xe4! (20.♘xe4 ♘xd5 (20...♕xd5? 21.♗xf6† exf6 22.♗xg6+-) 21.♘xf6† ♘xf6 22.♗xg6 hxg6 23.♕xg6† ♔h8∓) 20...♕e2! 21.♖fe1 ♕g4 22.♕xg4 ♗xg4 23.♘e6 when White has compensation for his sacrificed material.

a2) 14...♗e6!

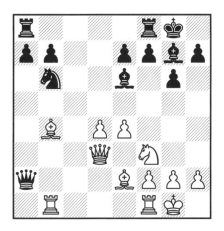

15.♖a1 (15.d5?? ♘xd5! 16.exd5 ♗f5–+ Tukmakov – Gavrikov, Moscow 1989) 15...♕c4! (15...♕b3 16.♗xe7 (16.♕d2!? ♘c4 (16...♖fc8 looks equal) 17.♗xc4 ♕xc4 was B. Martin – Mansoor, Manila 1992, and now 18.♖fc1 might be an edge for White.) 16...♖fe8·17.♗c5 ♘a4 18.♕xb3 ♗xb3 19.♗b5 ♘xc5 20.♗xe8 ♖xe8 21.♖a3 was Se. Ivanov – Novik, USSR 1989, and now Sergey Ivanov, in his annotations for *Informant 48*, gives the continuation 21...♗c4! 22.dxc5 ♗xf1 23.♔xf1 with equality.) 16.♗xe7 ♕xd3 17.♗xd3 ♖fe8 18.♗c5 ♗c4 19.♗xc4 ♘xc4 20.♖fc1 b6! 21.♖xc4 (21.♗b4? b5∓) 21...bxc5 22.dxc5 ♖xe4= - Gavrikov, *Informant 47*.

b) 14.♗xe7 ♖e8 15.♖a1 (15.♗c5 ♖xe4 (15...♘d7!? - Gavrikov) 16.♗d3 ♖e8 17.♖a1 ♕b2 18.♖b1 ♕a2= - Gavrikov, *Informant 46*) 15...♕e6 16.♗c5 ♕xe4! (16...♘d7?! 17.♗b4! ♕xe4 18.♗c4 ♕f5 19.♖a5! ♕f6 20.♘g5 ♖e6 21.♘xe6 fxe6 22.d5 ♘b6 23.♗b3 exd5 24.♖xd5 ♗e6 25.♖d6 1–0 Bu Xiangzhi – Meiser, Budapest 1999) 17.♘e5 ♗xe5 18.♗f3 ♗xh2† 19.♔xh2 ♕f4† 20.♔g1 ♘d7 21.♗xa7 ♘f6 22.♕c1 ♕f5 23.♖e1 ♖xe1† 24.♕xe1 ♕f4 25.d5 gave White compensation in Vaisser – Kozul, Ptuj 1989: Gavrikov, *Informant 47*.

c) 14.♗b5 ♗d7 15.♗xd7 ♘xd7 16.♗xe7 ♖fe8= Gavrikov.

14...♕e6!?

This logical retreat has fallen into disuse in recent years, as attention has shifted to the more aggressive line with 14...f6, which is examined in Game 17. In addition to these possibilities Black also has a few other options:

a) 14...♗xe5?! 15.dxe5 ♕e6 16.♕d4 ♗d7 (16...♖e8 17.f4 ♕d7 18.♕e3 ♖d8 19.♖bd1 ♕c7 20.♖xd8† ♕xd8 21.f5+- Sakaev – Cotton, Singapore 1990) 17.f4 f6 (17...♘a4!? 18.f5 (Acquiescing in an immediate queen exchange seems somewhat premature to me; the alternatives 18.♔h1 and 18.♖fd1 both look very good for White.) 18...♕b6 19.♕xb6 ♘xb6 20.f6± -Alterman & Vaisman, *Informant 48*.

Alternatively 17...♗c6!? 18.f5 ♕d7 is unclear according to Lagunov (*Informant 48*), and now 19.♕e3 ♖fd8 was De Boer – Hotting, corr. 1994, after which White had a strong continuation in 20.♖bd1! ♕e8 (20...♕c7 21.f6 exf6 (on 21...♕xe5 22.♗xe7 wins) 22.exf6 ♔h8 23.♕h6 ♖g8 24.♖d3+-) 21.♖xd8 ♖xd8 22.e6±) 18.exf6 (Alterman and Vaisman give the line 18.♗c5 fxe5 19.fxe5 ♖xf1† 20.♗xf1 ♔g7!! 21.♗xb6 axb6 22.♖xb6 ♗c6 23.♗c4 ♖a4!=, however 21.♗xb6 looks neither forced nor logical. Indeed given the precarious queenside piece arrangement (a8-rook defends a7-pawn, which defends b6-knight, whose movement is restricted because it presently defends the a7-pawn on the g1–a7 diagonal) White's most logical treatment of the position would appear to be 21.♖a1! with a considerable advantage.) 18...♕xf6 19.♕e3!± Alterman – Rogozenko, USSR 1989.

b) 14...♗d7 15.♘xd7 (15.♕d3!?) 15...♘xd7 16.♗b5 (16.e5!? looks like a good try for an edge) 16...♖fd8 (16...♖f6 17.♗xe7 (17.♕f3!?±) 17...♘xe4 18.♕d3 ♕d5 19.♗xf8 ♖xf8 20.♗c4 ♕xd4 21.♖xd4 ♗xd4 22.♖xb7± Nilsson – Danek, corr. 1990) 17.♗xe7 ♖e8 18.♗c5 ♘xc5 and now 19.♗xe8 ♘xe4 gave White less than nothing in Cosma -Nestorovic, Belgrade 1995, and Tesic – Marinkovic, Nis 1995 (both of which ended in draws where White was probably pleased to escape with half a point), so perhaps White should try 19.dxc5!? ♖ec8 20.♖c1 although I doubt White really has much (if anything) here.

c) 14...♗e6 15.♗xe7 (15.♖a1 ♖fe8 16.♗c5 ♗xe5! 17.dxe5 ♗c4 18.♗xc4 ♕xc4= Khalifman – Kindermann, Berlin 1989).

Black now has the following options:

c1) 15...♖fe8 and now:

c11) 16.♗c5 ♖ed8? (16...♘d7 17.♘xd7 ♗xd7 18.e5 ♗c6 19.♗f3 ♗xf3 20.♕xf3 b6 21.♗d6± -Komarov,D *Informant 48*) 17.f4 f5 18.♗xb6 axb6 19.♖xb6 ♗xe5 (19...♕a7 20.♖xe6! ♖xd4 21.♖e8† ♖xe8 22.♕b3†+-) 20.fxe5 fxe4 21.♖xb7 ♖a4 (21...♕d5 22.♖e7±; 21...♗c4 22.♗xc4† ♕xc4 23.♖ff7+-) 22.♕c1! ♖axd4 23.♖e7!

gave White a decisive advantage in Komarov – Gauglitz, Kecskemet 1989.

c12) 16.♗h4 g5?! (16...f6 or 16...♖ec8 looks more sensible) 17.♗g3! (17.♗xg5 f6 18.♖a1 ♕b3? (18...♕b2! 19.♘d3 (19.♗h5 looks more to the point) 19...♕xd4 20.♗e3 ♕xe4∞ -Novik, *Informant 49*) 19.♕d2 ♖ac8 20.♗d1 ♕c3 21.♗xc3 ♖xc3 22.♗d2+- Se. Ivanov – Novik, USSR 1990) 17...♖ad8 18.♗b5 ♖f8 was Sakaev – Novik, Sochi 1990, and now Novik proposes 19.♕h5! f6 (19...♖xd4 20.♘f3±) 20.d5 fxe5 21.dxe6 ♕xe6 22.♕xg5 with a clear advantage to White.

c2) 15...♖fc8

16.♘d3 (16.f4!? f6 (16...♖c2 17.♖f2! ♖d2 18.♕e1±) 17.♘d3 f5 18.d5! ♗f7 19.♘b4 ♕a4 20.e5± Se. Ivanov, *Informant 50*) 16...♗c4 17.♖e1 ♗xd4 (Sergey Ivanov notes the variations 17...♘a4 18.♖a1 ♘c3 19.♖xa2 ♘xd1 20.♖c2 ♗xd3 21.♖xd3 ♖xc2 22.♗xc2 ♘c3 23.d5 and 17...♕a4 18.♘c5 ♕xd1 19.♖bxd1 ♗xe2 20.♖xe2, in both cases with a clear advantage to White.) 18.♘b4 ♗xe2 19.♕xd4 ♕c4 (19...♕e6 20.♗g5! ♗c4 (20...♖c4 21.♕d2 ♖xe4 22.f3 ♖e5 23.♗f4±) 21.♖bd1 ♖e8 22.f4↑ – Se. Ivanov) and now rather than 20.♕e3?! as in Se. Ivanov – Zdrojewski, Leningrad 1990, Se. Ivanov has suggested 20.♕b2 ♕e6! (20...♗g4 21.♗f6) 21.♗f6 ♘a4 (21...♘c4 22.♕d4; 21...♗c4 22.♗h8 f6 23.♗xf6±/± Bauld – Fabrizi, corr. 1998) 22.♕a1 when White holds the initiative.

15.f4 f5 16.♗c5!

16...fxe4

Yakovich notes the line 16...♕f6 17.♕b3† ♔h8 18.♕a3!+-. Alternatively 16...♔h8 17.♗xb6!? axb6 18.♗c4 ♕d6 (18...♕f6 19.♘f7†! ♖xf7 20.e5 ♕c6 21.♗xf7 e6 22.d5+- -Yakovich, *Informant 50*) 19.♘f7† ♖xf7 20.e5! ♕d7 21.♗xf7 e6 22.♗xe6 ♕xe6 23.d5 ♕e7 24.♔h1 ♕c7 25.♕b3 appeared to be substantially better for White in Yakovich – Lhagvasuren, Cheliabinsk 1990, although Black later managed to complicate things and draw.

17.♗xb6 ♗xe5 18.dxe5 axb6 19.♕d4 ♕c6 20.♖fc1! ♕d7!

20...♖a4? 21.♕d1! ♕d7 22.♖xc8! gave White a decisive advantage in Se. Ivanov – Maslov, USSR 1989.

21.♕xb6 ♕d2

Sergey Ivanov, in his annotations for *Informant 48*, notes that 21...♖xf4?! 22.♖d1 gives White an attack, however matters remain somewhat unclear after both 22...♕a4 and 22...♕f5. Ivanov also suggests that Black's best may be 21...♖d8 with an unclear position, however in this case I rather prefer White after a regrouping move such as 22.♕e3! when White's chances seem preferable.

22.♗c4† ♔h8 23.e6! ♖a3!

Black is under serious pressure; Yakovich notes the following alternatives:

a) 23...♕xf4 24.♖f1 ♕h6 25.♖xf8† ♕xf8 26.♖f1 ♕e8 27.♕d4† ♔g8 28.♖f7+-.

b) 23...♕a5 24.♕d4† ♔g8 25.♕xe4+-.

c) 23...♕d6 24.♕xd6 exd6 25.♖b6 ♔g7 26.♖xd6 ♔f6 27.♖e1+-.

However in this last variation I am not sure that things are as easy as Yakovich suggests, e.g. 27...♔e7! 28.♖d4 ♖xf4 and it is by no means clear that White holds any advantage whatsoever.

24.♔h1 ♖d8

Yakovich notes the lines 24...♕d6? 25.♕xd6 exd6 26.e7 ♖e8 27.♗b5+- and 24...♖c3 25.♖d1 with an attack.

25.f5?!

An unfortunately slip; Yakovich shows that White could have consolidated his initiative into an advantage with 25.♗b3! ♖a6 26.♕c7! (26.♕c5 ♖ad6!) 26...♕d6 27.♕c3† ♔g8 28.♖d1 ♕b6 29.♖xd8† ♕xd8 30.♖d1 ♕f8 31.♕e5±.

25...gxf5 26.♕c5 ♕d6 27.♕xf5 ♖d3!= 28.♕xe4 ♖d1† 29.♖xd1 ♕xd1† 30.♕e1

½-½

Game 16 Conclusions: Whatever popularity 14...♕e6!? once enjoyed seems to have dwindled in recent years, however the notes to Game 16 do not reveal any absolute reason why this line should be bad for Black. Improvements for Black are noted at moves 21 and 23, and it is consequently by no means clear that White was genuinely better in this game. However, notwithstanding that Black's play can be improved upon, in general Black's position after 14...♕e6!? simply feels quite passive, whereas White's formation exudes energy. I suspect that White should therefore be better after 14...♕e6!?, although I have yet to work out exactly how to achieve this end!

Game 17
Shirov – Leko
Dortmund 1998

1.d4 ♘f6 2.c4 g6 3.♘c3 d5 4.cxd5 ♘xd5 5.e4 ♘xc3 6.bxc3 ♗g7 7.♘f3 c5 8.♖b1 0–0 9.♗e2 cxd4 10.cxd4 ♕a5† 11.♗d2 ♕xa2 12.0–0 ♘d7 13.♗b4 ♘b6 14.♘e5 f6!

Leko's preference is Black's most dangerous response: Black gains time by driving the white knight back, and then uses this tempo to orchestrate an immediate counter strike against White's centre.

15.♘d3

Shirov fails to prove any advantage with this move, however the alternatives are not stunning, and only the relatively unexplored 15.♖a1 seems to hold any promise:

a) 15.♘c4 ♘xc4 16.♖a1 ♘b2! (16...♕b2 17.♗xc4† ♔h8 18.♖b1!+- – Lagunow, *Informant 50*) 17.♖xa2 ♘xd1 18.♗c4† ♔h8 19.♖xd1 ♖d8

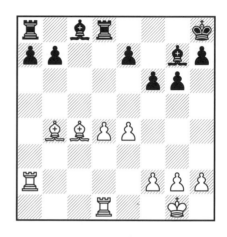

20.♗xe7 (20.f3 e6 21.♗c5 ♗d7 (21...a6!? looks sensible, e.g. 22.♗b6 ♖d6 23.♗c5 ♖d8=) 22.♗xa7 ♖dc8 23.♗c5 b5 24.♗b3 ♖xa2 25.♗xa2 ♗f8 26.♗xf8 ♖xf8 27.♖c1 ♖a8 28.♗b3 ♖a3 29.♖b1 ♔g7 30.♗d1 ♖d3 31.♗e2 ♖xd4 32.♗xb5 ½–½ Flumbort – Ferrari, Murek 1998) 20...♖e8 21.♗c5 ♖xe4 22.♖xa7 ♖xa7 23.♗xa7 ♗f8!. An excellent move: Black will place the bishop on d6, where it can blockade the d-pawn and remain active simultaneously. White has now tried three options:

a1) 24.f3 can be met by 24...♖e7!? (or 24...♖e3 25.d5 ♖c3 26.♗b5 ♖b3! 27.♗e8 ♗d6 28.♗f7 ♗d7= -Lagunow, *Informant 50*) 25.♗c5 ♖c7 26.♗xf8 ♖xc4= – Ftacnik, *Chessbase Magazine 50*.

a2) 24.♗d5 ♖e2 25.♖c1 ♖b2 26.f3 ♗f5 27.g4 ♗c2 28.♗c5 ♗xc5 29.dxc5 ♗d3 30.c6 ½–½ Burn – W. Taylor, corr. 1996.

a3) 24.g3 ♗d6 25.♔g2 (25.♗d5 ♖e7 26.♖c1 ♗h3= – Ftacnik) 25...♔g7 26.♗d5 ♖e7 27.♗b6 ♗e6 28.♗f3 (28.♗xe6 ♖xe6 29.♖b1 ♖e7= – Ftacnik) 28...h5 and Black was very close to equality in Se. Ivanov – Daniliuk, Elista 1995. The game was drawn in 56 moves.

b) 15.♖a1 ♕e6 (15...♕b2?? 16.♘d3 ♕xd4 17.♗c5+- Agrest – Karasev, St Petersburg 1992) 16.♘d3 (16.♗g4 f5 17.exf5 gxf5 18.♗f3 ♖d8 19.♖e1 ♗e5! 20.♖xe5 ♕xe5 21.dxe5 ♖xd1† 22.♖xd1 ♔f7 was at least equal for Black in Neverov – Malisauskas, Podolsk 1989.) 16...♕f7!?

(16...♕xe4?! appears to be bad on account of 17.♗f3 ♕f5 18.♖e1 ♖e8 19.♗c5 ♗d7 20.♗xb7 ♖ab8 21.♖xa7± Agrest – Maslov, USSR 1990, however immediately striking out at White's centre with 16...f5 may be a decent idea.) 17.♗c5 ♗d7 18.♕b1 f5 19.e5 ♗c6 20.♘b4 ♗e4 21.♗d3 ♗xd3 (21...♘c4!? may be better) 22.♘xd3 ♗h6?! 23.e6! ♕xe6 24.♖e1 ♕c8?! 25.♕b3† ♔h8 26.♗xe7 ♖e8 27.♕f7 ♗g7 28.♘e5+- Poecksteiner – Danek, Aschach 1993. Obviously 15.♖a1 deserves further consideration.

c) 15.♘f3 ♕f7! 16.♕c1!? ♗d7 17.♕a3 ♖fc8 18.♗xe7 ♖e8

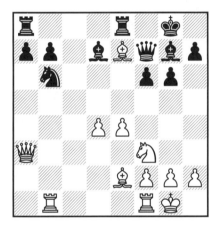

19.♗c5 (19.♗d6! ♖xe4 20.♖xb6 ♖xe2 21.♖xb7 a5 with unclear play.) 19...♖xe4 20.♖xb6! (20.♗xb6 ♖xe2 and 20.♗d3 ♖ee8 are both clearly better for Black according to Lagunow, although I doubt Black is really much better in the latter variation.) 20...♖xe2 21.♖xb7 a5 22.♕d3 ♖ee8! 23.d5 was Shevelev – Lagunow, USSR 1989. In his annotations for *Informant 48* Lagunow suggests that instead of 23...ab8? Black should now have played 23...♖ec8! 24.♖a7 (24.♗a3 ♗f5! 25.♕b3 a4 26.♕b5 ♗d3–+) 24...♖xa7 25.♗xa7 a4∓.

15...♕f7 16.d5

GM Peter Leko, in *Informant 73*, proposes that 16.♘c5!? would give White compensation for his sacrificed material. The only practical example

with this move turned out well for White, but Black's play can be improved: 16...♖d8 (the immediate 16...f5!? intending 17.e5 (17. exf5 ♗xf5 is good for Black.) 17...♖d8 looks promising.

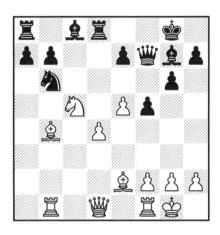

Black currently threatens 18...♗xe5, and if the white queen moves then d4 is left unprotected. Perhaps the most important factor of all is that Black has established a firm grip on the d5-square, thereby robbing White's position of its inherent dynamism.) 17.♗a5 (17.d5 f5!) 17...f5 18.♖b4 ♔h8?! (18...fxe4 19.♘xe4 ♔h8 20.♕d2 ♗f5 looks comfortable for Black.) 19.♕a1! (now the b6-knight is under siege) 19...♖b8 20.e5 ♘d5 21.♗xd8 ♘xb4 22.♖b1 ♘c6 23.♗c7 ♖a8 24.♕a4 e6 25.♗d6± Chloupek – P. David, Vysehrad 1990.

16...f5 17.♘c5?

A serious error according to Leko, albeit one that had been played before. In *Informant 73* Leko notes the alternatives 17.f3 ♘c4 18.♕c1 b5 19.♗c3 a6 20.♘c5 ♘d6, and 17.f4!? ♘c4! (17...fxe4 18.♘e5 gives White compensation for his sacrificed pawns according to Leko, however 18...♕f6 contemplating moves such as ♖f8-d8 or g6-g5 looks decidedly awkward for White.) 18.♕c1 b5, in either case with an unclear position.

17...fxe4!

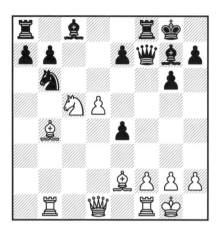

This was Leko's prepared improvement, after which it becomes quite clear that White has absolutely no advantage, and should perhaps even be thinking about equalising. Previous play had seen 17...♖d8 18.f3 e6 19.d6 ♗e5 20.d7 ♗xd7 21.♘xb7 ♖db8 22.f4 ♖xb7 23.fxe5∞ Bazhin – Daniliuk, Alekhine Open 1992.

18.d6 ♖d8! 19.♘xe4

19.d7 ♗xd7 20.♘xb7 ♖f8∓ - Ftacnik.

19...♗f5 20.♗d3

20.♘g5? ♕f6 21.♕b3† e6∓ - Leko.

20...♗xe4 21.♗xe4 exd6

22.f4?

Another error according to Leko, albeit one that is difficult to condemn given that White is already under pressure to prove compensation. The alternatives are also unattractive:

a) Ftacnik notes the line 22.♗xd6 ♔h8! (22...♕e6 23.♖xb6! ♕xe4 24.♕b3† ♔h8 25.♖b4 ♕c6∓) 23.♕d3 ♕f6 24.♖fd1 ♗f8–+.

b) Leko also considers 22.♗a5 d5 23.♗f3 ♖d6 24.♗xb6 axb6 25.♕d3 to be slightly better for Black.

22...d5 23.♗c2

23.♗d3 ♘c4 24.f5 ♘e3 25.fxg6 ♕xf1†! 26.♕xf1 ♘xf1 27.gxh7† ♔h8–+.

23...♘c4 24.♖b3

24.f5 ♘e3 25.fxg6 ♕xf1† 26.♕xf1 ♘xf1 27.gxh7† ♔h8 28.♔xf1 ♖d7∓.

24...a5 25.♗a3

25.f5 axb4 26.fxg6 ♕c7–+.

25...d4!∓/–+

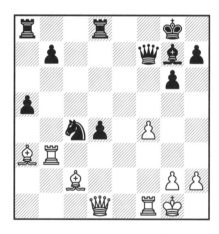

26.f5 ♘e3 27.♕f3 ♖d7!?

Good, but Leko also notes the line 27...♘xf1 28.♔xf1 (28.♕xf1 a4 29.♖b1 ♕c7 and 28.♖xb7 ♘d2 29.♕c6 ♖ac8 30.♕a6 ♕c4 both leave Black with a decisive advantage according to Ftacnik.) 28...♖d7 29.♗e4 ♖ad8–+.

28.♕h3

28.♖xe3 dxe3 29.fxg6 ♕xf3 30.gxh7† ♔h8 31.♖xf3 ♖d2–+.

28...d3!–+ 29.♗xd3 ♘xf1 30.fxg6 ♗d4† 31.♔h1 ♕f2

0–1

Game 17 Conclusions: A fantastic game by Leko, and a vivid demonstration of the dynamic potential inherent in Black's position. At present White is struggling to prove an edge after 14.♞e5 f6! in the established lines, although perhaps the relatively unexplored 15.♖a1!? offers a glimmer of hope. In any case, Leko's play in this game is enough to put me off 14.♞e5 for the time being!

Game 18
Se. Ivanov – Tseitlin
St Petersburg 1999

1.d4 ♞f6 2.c4 g6 3.♞c3 d5 4.cxd5 ♞xd5 5.e4 ♞xc3 6.bxc3 ♝g7 7.♞f3 c5 8.♖b1 0–0 9.♝e2 cxd4 10.cxd4 ♛a5† 11.♝d2 ♛xa2 12.0–0 ♞d7 13.♝b4 ♞b6 14.♖a1!?

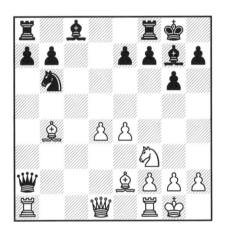

Given that it is very common for Black to retreat the queen unprovoked, it seems counterintuitive to spend a move driving the old girl back to the safety of her own camp. However, White's justification is rather specific to this position: the precarious position of the b6-knight has the potential to give Black some queenside development problems. With the rook on a1 controlling the a-file, its a8-counterpart is tied to the protection of the a7-pawn. If the a7-pawn were to drop then the b6-knight and the b7-pawn would suddenly become

very vulnerable indeed. A further aspect of this reasoning is that Black cannot play a7-a6 without removing the protection of the b6-knight, making a7 a permanent weakness in some respects. An additional point to consider is that in many of the examples we have looked at so far White has had some trouble finding an active posting for the f1–rook. Having placed the b1–rook on a1, White then has the aesthetically pleasing option of playing ♖a1–a5 (ordinarily Black would just kick the rook back with b7-b6, however here the b6-knight obstructs this response) and then following up with ♖fa1, doubling on the a-file, when the f1–rook has discovered a very useful posting indeed. A final justification for White's approach is that, frankly, progress with direct approaches such as 14.♞e5 have thus far proved rather ineffectual!

14...♛e6 15.♛b1!

This seems like the most logical option, however alternatives are also of interest:

a) 15.♝d3!? with the following possibilities:

a1) 15...♝d7 16.♖a5 was seen in Schulz – Kamlah, corr. 1993, and now 16...♞c4!? 17.♝xc4 (17.d5? ♛b6–+) 17...♛xc4 18.♝xe7 ♖fe8 19.♞e5 ♛c7 is unclear.

a2) 15...♝d7 16.♖a5 ♛d8 17.h3 ♞d7 18.♛a1 ♞b8 19.♝c3 (19.♖xa7 ♖xa7 20.♛xa7 ♞c6=) 19...♞c6 20.♖a3 e6 21.♝c4 b6 22.♖d1 ♝b7 23.d5 ♝xc3 24.♖xc3 exd5 25.♝xd5 ♛e8 26.♛c1 ♞a5 27.♛h6 ♛a4 28.♝b3 ♛xe4 29.♖e1 1–0 S.B. Hansen – Vanheste, Lyngby 1989.

a3) 15...♞c4 16.d5 ♛b6 17.♝xe7 ♞b2 was Glavina Rossi – Darcyl, Buenos Aires 1990, and now 18.♛c2 ♞xd3 (18...♖e8 19.♝c5±) 19.♝xf8 ♝xa1 20.♛xd3 is clearly better for White.

a4) 15...f6!? 16.♖c1 (16.♝c5!? ♝d7 17.♛b1±, and 16.♖a5!? both merit consideration) 16...♖d8 17.♖c7 ♖d7 18.♖c5 ♛f7 19.♛e2 e5 20.♖fc1! ♔h8?! 21.dxe5 ♛b3 22.♝c3 (22.exf6!? ♝xf6 23.♝c3+–) 22...fxe5 23.♖xe5 h6 24.♛e3 ♔h7 25.♖b5 ♛a3 26.♖a5 ♛b3 27.♝xg7 ♔xg7 28.♞e5 ♖e7 29.♖b1 ♛c3 30.♖c5 ♛a3 31.♛d4 ♔h7 32.♖a1 ♛b3 33.♖b5 ♛e6 34.f4 ♖b8 35.♖xa7 ♞d7 36.♞xg6 ♛c6 37.♞xe7 1–0 Avrukh – Spiropoulos, Athens 2003.

b) Although it has never been played T.Behl and U.Kaeser (hereinafter 'B&K') analyse 15.♕c2

in *Informant 68*. Their analysis runs: 15.♕c2!? ♗d7 (15...♕c6?! 16.♕xc6 bxc6 17.♗xe7 ♖e8 18.♗c5 ♘d7 19.♖xa7 ♖xa7 20.♗xa7 ♖xe4∓. B&K also claim that 15...♕d7 is a strong move that gives rise to an unclear position, however I don't see why. Given that it embodies Black's thematic pawn-break in this chapter, I would imagine that 15...f5 is also worth considering.) 16.♖fb1 ♖fc8 (16...♖ac8 17.♗c5!±) 17.♗c5 ♗e8! 18.♘g5 ♕d7 19.♗b5 when they claim that White has compensation for his sacrificed pawn. However I suspect this may be nonsense: 19...♕xd4! just looks good for Black.

15...♗d7

a) 15...♖e8 16.♖a5 ♗d7 17.♖c1!? (17.♘e5 looks better) 17...♖ec8 18.♗c3? ♘a4! 19.d5 ♕b6 20.♕xb6 ♘xb6∓ Matisson – Z. Szabo, e-mail 1999.

b) 15...f5 and now:

b1) 16.♖a5!? ♕f7 (16...fxe4 17.♘g5 ♕f6?! (17...♕d7!) was J. Horvath – Deak, Hungary 1992, and now instead of the natural recapture 18.♘xe4, White had a much stronger resource in 18.♕b3† ♔h8 19.♖e5! when Black is in serious trouble. Alternatively 16...♕xe4 17.♗d3 gives White good compensation and definite attacking chances.) 17.e5 (Fixing the pawn structure in this

manner seems somewhat compliant on White's part. Instead the alternative 17.♗d1!? intending 18.♗b3 and 19.♘e5/g5, looks strong, as does 17.♘e5 ♕f6 18.♗c5, e.g. 18...♗e6 19.♕b4! ♖fe8 20.♖fa1±.) 17...h6 (17...♗h6!?) 18.♖c1 ♖d8 19.♗c5 ♘d5 20.♖xa7 (20.♗c4 ♗e6 21.♕xb7 looks more critical) 20...♖xa7 21.♗xa7 e6 22.♗b6 was better for White in Cebalo – Kozul, Zadar 1995, although Black went on to win.

b2) 16.e5

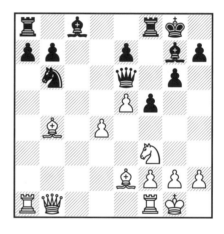

16...♗h6 (16...h6 17.♖a5 ♖d8 18.♖c1 ♔h7 19.♗d1 ♕f7 20.♖c7 ♘d5 21.♗b3± Rogozenko – Berndt, Germany 1996) 17.d5 (17.♗c5!?±) 17...♘xd5 18.♗c4 b5! (18...♖d8 19.♖d1 ♕c6?! (19...♕f7!?±) 20.♕b3 e6 21.♗d6 b5 22.♗xb5 ♕b7 23.♕c4 ♗d7 24.♗a6 ♕c6 25.♕h4±/+- Cebalo – Sale, Bled 1995) 19.♘d4 bxc4? (Obviously Kozul intended to sacrifice his queen, however it strikes me that things really aren't that desperate yet. For example, Black could try 19...♕f7 20.♘xb5 ♗e6 21.♘d4±.) 20.♘xe6 ♗xe6 21.♖a6 ♔f7 22.♗a3 ♖fb8 23.♕c2 ♖c8 24.♖d1 c3 25.g3 ♖c7 26.♖d3 ♗d2 27.♖xe6 ♔xe6 28.♕b3+- Cebalo – Kozul, Slovakian Team Championship 1994.

c) 15...♕d7? 16.♗c5! is winning for White.

16.♖a5!

Originally suggested by Khalifman, this pleasing rook venture takes control of the fifth rank, preparing actions in the centre, whilst at the same time contemplating the possibility of doubling on the a-file and ganging up on Black's a7-pawn.

16...♘c8?!

This move prepares a reshuffling of Black's frontline, bringing the queen to b6, and reposting the c8-knight on d6. It is a nice idea, but inevitably time consuming and perhaps a shade artificial, so White should be able to demonstrate an advantage. Black's alternatives must also be considered:

a) 16...♗c6 17.♗d3! (Daniliuk (in *Informant* 56) notes the continuations 17.d5 ♗xd5 18.exd5 (18.♖xd5? ♘xd5 19.♗c4 ♘c3 20.♕b3 ♕b6−+) 18...♕xe2 19.♖e1 ♕c4 20.♖e4 ♕c8 21.♗xe7 ♖e8 22.d6 ♕c6∓, 17.♘e5 ♖fd8 18.♗g4 ♕f6 19.♗c5 ♕f4∞, and 17.♘g5 ♕f6 18.d5 ♗xd5 19.exd5 ♕xg5 20.d6 e5 21.f4 ♕h6∓) 17...♕d7 18.d5 ♗a4 19.♗c5!.

At this juncture GM Dimitri Komarov has analysed three possibilities:

a1) 19...♗c3 20.♗b5! ♗xb5 21.♖xb5 ♖fc8 22.♗xb6 axb6 23.♖xb6 is clearly better for White on account of the weak b7-pawn.

a2) 19...♘c8 20.♗d4 (20.♕a2 b6 21.♖xa4 bxc5 22.♖a5!? ♕d6 (22...♘b6 23.♖xc5 ♖fc8 24.♗b5±) 23.♖c1 ♘b6 24.♖axc5 ♖fc8 25.♖c6 ♖xc6 26.♖xc6±) 20...♗xd4 (20...♘b6 21.♕b4!) 21.♘xd4 b6 22.♖a6∞.

a3) 19...♖fc8 20.♕b4 e6 21.♗d4!? exd5 22.♗xg7 ♔xg7 (22...dxe4 23.♗a1 ♕xd3 24.♕b2+−) 23.♕d4† f6 (23...♔g8 24.exd5 ♗c2 25.♘e5 ♕d6 26.♗xc2 ♖xc2 27.♘g4 'with an attack' according to Daniliuk, in *Informant* 65, although White would appear to be winning here.) 24.e5 ♕e7 and now 25.♖e1 ♗e8 26.h4 gave White compensation for his sacrificed pawns in Sherbakov – Daniliuk, Russian Championship, Elista 1995, and Sherbakov did indeed go on to win. However, at move 25 White may have a more immediate resource in the form of 25.♖xa4!? ♘xa4 26.♖e1! ♖c7 (26...♘c5?? 27.exf6† ♕xf6 28.♖e7†−) 27.♕xa4 when I believe White should be better, but it would be prudent not to underestimate the trouble that Black's queenside pawns may pose as the game progresses.

b) 16...f6?! 17.♗c5 ♗h6 18.d5 ♕f7 19.♕b3 ♗f4 20.♖fa1± Pankratov – Kliatskin, corr. 1994.

c) 16...♖fc8 17.d5 (17.♘e5!?) 17...♕f6 18.e5

18...♕f5 (18...♕f4 19.♗d2 ♕g4 20.h3 ♕f5 21.♗d3 ♕h5 22.e6! ♗e8 23.d6! ♖c5 24.♕xb6! ♖xa5 25.♕xa5+− Kulvietis – Scholbach, e-mail 1999) 19.♗d3 ♕h5 20.e6 ♗e8 21.d6 1–0 Enev – van Dusen, e-mail 1997.

d) 16...♗a4 17.♗c5 (17.♖c1!? ♖fc8 18.♖xc8† ♕xc8 (18...♖xc8 19.♗c5! (19.♖xa7?! ♗c2) 19...♗c6 20.♗d3±) 19.♗c5±) 17...♖fc8 18.d5 ♕d7 19.♕b4 ♕e8 20.♘d4 ♗d7 21.♗d1 ♘c4

22.♖xa7 ♖xa7 23.♗xa7 ♘d6 24.♗b3 ♘xe4 25.♘e6 fxe6 26.♕xe4 ♖c3 27.♖b1 ♕c8 28.♗e3 ♔h8 29.dxe6 ♗b5 30.♕b4 ♗a6 ½–½ Kipper – Lautier, Germany 1998.

17.d5!

17.♘e5 ♗e8! 18.♗a3 (18.♖d1 ♘d6 19.f4 ♕c8 ½–½ Huzman – Tseitlin, Tel Aviv 1999; 18.♗c4 ♕b6! - Ftacnik) 18...b5! 19.♗xb5 ♗xe5 20.♗xe8 (20.dxe5 ♖b8 21.♕d3?! ♕xe5–+ - Khalifman, *Informant 52*) and now rather than 20...♕c7?! 21.♖c5 ♗d6 22.♗a4! ♗xc5 23.dxc5⩲ as in Khalifman – Kozul, Bled 1991, Khalifman suggests that Black should play 20...♗xd4! 21.♕b7 (Ftacnik's suggestion of 21.♗a4!?, which he assesses as offering White compensation for his sacrificed pawn, may be better.) 21...♘b6 22.♗b5 with equality.

17...♕b6 18.e5

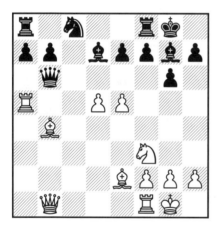

18...a6

An earlier encounter in this variation continued 18...♗f5 19.♕b3 a6 20.♕a3 ♗g4 (After 20...♖e8 21.♖c1 looks better for White, however Gelfand and Atlas (hereinafter 'G&A'), annotating for *Informant 58*, suggest that 21.♖c5!? (intending 22.♗a5) is strong. This is probably true, however I am curious as to whether 21...♘d6!? works, e.g. 22.♗a5 (22.exd6 exd6 23.♖cc1 ♖xe2∓) 22...♘b5 23.♗xb6 ♘xa3 24.♖fc1 ♗g4 when White's advanced centre is suddenly under pressure.)

21.♖e1 ♖e8 22.♖c5! (22.h3?! ♗xf3 23.♗xf3 ♘a7 gives Black counterplay according to G&A.) 22...♕d8?! (Passive play from Black. Better was 22...♗xf3 23.♗xf3 ♘a7 24.♗a5 ♘b5 25.♗xb6 ♘xa3

which looks a little better for White after, e.g. 26.♗g4!? taking control of the c8-square.) 23.h3 b6 (23...♗f5 can be met by 24.♘d4 ♗xe5 (24...b6 25.♘xf5 bxc5 26.♗a5) 25.♘xf5 gxf5 26.♗b5 -G&A) 24.♖cc1 ♗xf3 25.♗xf3 a5 26.♗d2 ♖a7 (26...b5?! allows 27.d6! with 28.♗c6 to follow) 27.♕a4 ♖f8 (27...♕d7 28.♕a2! when the attempt to exchange a pair of rooks with 28...♖c7 leaves White better after 29.♗g4 ♕d8 30.♖xc7 ♕xc7 31.f4) 28.♗f4 (28.♕c6!?± has also been suggested as strong) 28...b5?! (28...♖c7 29.d6 ♖xc1 30.♖xc1 exd6 31.exd6±) 29.♕xb5 a4 30.♗g4 ♖a5 (30...♖a8 31.♗xc8 ♖xc8 32.♖xc8 ♕xc8 33.♕xa4±) 31.♕b4 ♕b6 32.♕c4 ♘a7 33.♗d2+- Gelfand – Kozul, Biel 1993.

19.♕e4 ♘a7

In over-the-board chess the text is employed almost without exception, however there have been numerous correspondence games with 19...♗f5, after which an obvious route to an advantage is still to present itself. The following have been tried:

a) 20.♕h4 f6!

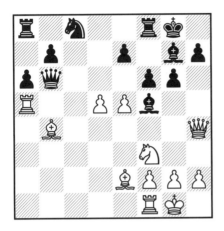

looks very comfortable for Black. Behl and Kaeser analyse 20.♕h4 in *Informant 68*, but consider only 20...♕d8?! 21.♖d1 when they claim that White has compensation, which is true, but a more accurate assessment would be that White holds a definite advantage.

b) 20.♕f4 ♞a7 (20...f6!? looks sensible) 21.♖fa1 ♖ac8 is given as equal by Behl and Kaeser, but I would take that with a pinch of salt to say the least.

c) 20.♕c4 f6 (20...♞a7!? 21.♖fa1 ♖fc8 22.♕h4∞) 21.♖fa1 fxe5 22.d6† e6 was played in Westerlund – Aldobasic, corr. 1999, and now rather than 23.d7 ♞d6 which passed any advantage in the position to Black, White should probably have tried 23.♖d1 ♕d8 (23...♖d8 24.d7 ♞a7 25.♞xe5 keeps Black under pressure, e.g. 25...♞b5 26.g4!? ♗xe5 27.gxf5 gxf5 28.♗c5! ♕c6 29.♗f3! ♕xf3 30.♕xe6† ♔h8 31.♕xe5† ♔g8 32.♕e6† ♔g7 33.♗d4†±) 24.♞xe5 ♞b6 25.♕b3∞.

20.♖fa1?!

A very natural move on White's part, but there is a very sensible line of argument which maintains that now that White has established pawns on e5 and d5, and Black has relieved the pressure on the a-pawn by playing a7-a6, the a5-rook no longer has anything to achieve on the a-file. The logical progression from this is that the f1–rook

is essentially misplaced on a1, which means that White's 20th move is in fact inaccurate. So what should White play instead? Well, it seems that White's best option is simply to accept that the a5-rook has achieved everything it needed to, and simply retreat the rook to the back rank, and then re-route it to more pressing duties: 20.♖aa1 ♞b5 (Krasenkow notes the lines 20...♖fe8 21.♗a5 ♕b2 22.♞d4 (22.♖fb1 ♗f5) 22...♗f5 23.♕e3 ♖ec8 24.f4±, and 20...♞b5? 21.♗a5 ♕c5 22.♖fc1+-) 21.♕h4

Black has now tried two moves:

a) 21...♖fe8 22.♗xe7 ♞c3 23.♗c4 ♖ac8 24.d6 h6 25.♖fe1 (25.♗f6!? ♗xf6 26.♗xf7† ♔xf7 27.♕xf6†+- - Krasenkow) 25...g5 26.♗xg5 ♖xc4 27.♕xc4 ♖c8 was Magai – Holmsten, Elista Olympiad 1998, and now Krasenkow points out that 28.♗e3! is winning for White.

b) 21...♖fc8!? 22.♖fe1!? (22.♕xe7!?) 22...♞c3 23.♗xc3 ♖xc3 24.♖ab1! ♕c5? (A serious mistake according to Pankratov, who provides the following annotations: 24...♕c7! 25.♞g5 h6 (25...♕xe5!?) 26.♞e4! g5 27.♕h5 ♖a3 (27...♖c2 28.♗d3 is unclear according to Pankratov, although I would rather be White here. 27...♗f5 28.♞xc3 ♕xc3 29.♖bc1, and 27...♕xe5 28.♞xc3 ♕xc3 29.♗g4 ♗xg4 30.♕xg4 are both substantially better for White.) 28.d6 'with advantage to White' (Pankratov). However, Pankratov goes on to note that Jonathan Tait has suggested that Black is fine after 28...exd6. No further analysis is supplied however a sensible continuation would seem to be 29.♘f6† (29.♘xd6 ♗e6 30.♖xb7 ♕c3 looks fine for Black) 29...♔f8 30.♗c4!? (30.♘d5 ♕c5 31.♘b6 ♖d8 32.♘c4∞) 30...♗e6! (Alternatives seem to lose control of the position, e.g. 30...♕xc4?? 31.♘xd7† ♔g8 32.♘b6+-, however 30...♗f5!? deserves attention: 31.♗d5! (31.♖bc1 ♗g6!) 31...♗g6 (31...♗xb1 32.exd6+-) 32.♕xg6!! fxg6 33.exd6 ♗xf6 34.dxc7 ♖c8 35.♖xb7 ♖c3 36.♖b6 ♔g7=) 31.♘h7† ♔g8 32.♘f6† and it would appear that White has nothing better than a draw by repetition.) 25.♘g5 ♗f5 26.♕xh7† ♔f8 27.♖bd1 (27.e6!? f6 28.♘f7 ♕xd5 (28...♗xb1? 29.♘h6!+-) 29.♘h8!, (Pankratov)) 27...♖d8?! (According to Pankratov, better is 27...♕b4!? 28.e6 fxe6 29.♘xe6† (29.♗f3!?; 29.g4!?) 29...♗xe6 30.dxe6 ♕f4 31.♕xg6 ♕f6 32.♕e4 with a substantial advantage to White.) 28.e6! f6 29.g4+- 1–0 Pankratov – Leko, e-mail 1999. As Pankratov's analysis shows, White's attack should prove decisive: 29...fxg5 (29...♗c2 30.♘f7 g5 31.♕h5 ♗xd1 32.♘h6+-) 30.gxf5 gxf5 (30...♖xd5 31.♖xd5 ♕xd5 32.♕xg6 ♔g8 33.f6+-) 31.♗h5! ♖c2 32.♕xf5† ♔g8 (32...♗f6 33.♖f1 with 34.♕g6 to follow) 33.♗f7† ♔f8 34.♗g6†.

20...♖ac8

a) 20...♖fe8 21.♗c5 (21.♕f4 and 21.♕h4!? both offer White compensation according to Behl and Kaeser, *Informant 68*.) 21...♕c7 22.♕e3 ♘b5 23.♗b6 ♕b8 24.h4 gives White an initiative according to Hungarian IM Yuri Zimmerman.

b) 20...♗f5 21.♕h4!?∞ - Behl & Kaeser, *Informant 68*.

21.♗xe7

Practice has also seen 21.♗xa6!? when 21...♗f5 22.♕e1 bxa6 23.♖xa6 ♕b7 24.♖xa7 ♕xd5 25.♖d1 ♕c4 26.♖xe7

½–½ was Aberbach – Geider, e-mail 1997, however this game may have been settled prematurely as Black still has some work to do in the final position.

21...♖fe8

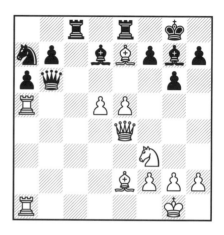

Black has given back his extra pawn but activated his pieces. The white a5 rook is placed extremely awkwardly. Still, the d5 and e5 pawns cause Black some trouble.

22.♗g5 ♘b5

22...♗f5 23.♕f4 (23.♕e3 ♕xe3 24.♗xe3 ♗xe5 25.♘xe5 ♖xe5 26.♗xa6 bxa6 27.♗xa7 ♗e6=) 23...♖c2 24.♕a4 was Zimmerman – Behl, Budapest 1996, and now Behl & Kaeser observe that Black's most accurate continuation is 24...♘c6! 25.dxc6 ♖xe2 26.♗e3 ♕xc6 27.♕xc6 bxc6 28.♖xa6=.

23.♗f1

23.♗e3 ♕d6!.

23...♕c7 24.♕h4?!

A definite inaccuracy, which allows Black to implement an important exchange sacrifice on e5. Krasenkow instead observes that a better approach would be 24.♗f4! ♘c3 25.♕e3 ♗b5!? when he points out that White's a5-rook is entirely misplaced. If I may build on this assessment, I would add that the rook's poor placing is emphasised by the fact that White also cannot use the a1–rook because it is currently tied to the protection of the a5-rook. However things aren't all bad here, and after something sensible such as 26.d6 ♕d7 27.♗xb5 ♘xb5 28.♖e1 White's advanced pawns give him some chances for an advantage.

24...♖xe5! 25.♘xe5 ♕xe5 26.♗h6

After 26.♖d1 Black can respond with 26...♖c2, which gives Black compensation according to Krasenkow, however 26...♘c3! looks even stronger.

26...♕xd5 27.♗xg7 ♔xg7 28.♖e1 ♖e8

½–½

Game 18 Conclusions: 14.♖a1!? currently appears to be a promising line for White, and can give rise to positions in which Black is subjected to prolonged manoeuvring in relatively limited space. In the mainline with 14...♕e6 15.♕b1 ♗d7 16.♖a5! Black was under pressure after 16...♘c8, and 20.♖aa1 (as in Pankratov – Leko, e-mail 1999) would have made it very difficult for Black to hold the balance (although if Pankratov's analysis of 30...♗f5!? is correct then perhaps White has no more than a draw here). In terms of promising alternatives for White, the sideline 15.♗d3!? remains relatively unexplored, and was recently used to powerful effect by Grünfeld expert GM Boris Avrukh, so this could be a potentially fruitful area to look for new ideas.

Game 19
Gelfand – Tseitlin
Tel Aviv 1999

1.d4 ♘f6 2 ♘f3 g6 3.c4 ♗g7 4 ♘c3 d5 5.cxd5 ♘xd5 6.e4 ♘xc3 7.bxc3 c5 8.♖b1 0–0 9.♗e2 cxd4 10.cxd4 ♕a5† 11.♗d2 ♕xa2 12 0–0 ♘d7 13.♗b4 ♘b6 14.h3!?

This little move has so far been a big success. However, although results have been positive, I doubt that what we shall examine here represents a permanent challenge to Black's set-up. It is true that 14.h3 prevents Black playing 14...♗g4 (thereby exchanging pieces and diminishing White's attacking chances), but note that in the other games which we examined in this chapter, it was very rare that Black was able to successfully implement this manoeuvre in any case. In the games in which Black succeeded in the opening,

it was invariably by means other than this exchanging manoeuvre, and most frequently it was through careful and measured development, combined with a timely counter-strike in the centre.

14...♗d7

14...f5!? promises Black counterplay according to GM Igor Stohl, in his excellent work *Instructive Modern Chess Masterpieces*.

15.♖a1 ♕e6 16.♗d3

16...f6?

It transpires that this is simply too slow, however Black does have a range of legitimate alternatives:

a) 16...♖fc8? does nothing to discourage White's expansive central dominance: 17.d5 ♘xd5 (17...♕f6 18.e5 ♕f4 19.♗d2+-) 18.exd5 ♕xd5 19.♖a5±/+- Wells – Beaumont, Edinburgh 1989.

b) 16...♗e8!? This clears a path of retreat for the black queen, however I can't help but feel that voluntarily disrupting the coordination of Black's rooks must be wrong. Play has continued: 17.♖e1 (17.♖a5!?) 17...♕d7 18.♖a5 ♕d8 19.♕b3 ♗c6 20.d5 ♗d7 21.e5±/± Wells – Kindermann, Germany 1989.

c) On the evidence available (which, I must emphasise, is quite limited) Black's best appears to be 16...♘c4!?

17.♖b1 (17.d5 ♕b6 18.♗xe7 is unclear according to Gelfand (*Informant 75*). Play might continue 18...♕b2!? 19.♕d2 ♖fe8∞. The only other game that has featured 16...♘c4 continued 17.♘g5 ♕c6 (17...♕b6 18.♗c5±) 18.♗xe7 (18.♕b3!?) 18...♖fe8 19.d5 ♕c8 20.♖c1 b5 21.d6 ♕c5 22.♘f3 and now instead of 22...♕a3?!, as in De Figueiredo – Lamarche Rodriguez, corr. 2000, Black should have played 22...♖ec8!? with a marginally preferable position.) 17...b5 18.d5 ♕f6 (18...♕a6!?) 19.♗xc4 bxc4 20.e5 ♕f5!? (20...♕f4 21.♗xe7 is unclear according to Gelfand, however after 21...♖fe8 White can play 22.♗d6 intending 23.♖b7 with the superior chances.) 21.♗xe7 ♖fc8 22.♖b7 c3 23.♕d4 (23.♗d6!? c2 24.♕d2 is similar, but may have the virtue of saving a move on 23.♕d4) 23...c2 24.♕e3 h5 25.♗d6 ♖c4 26.♘d4 ♗h6 27.♘xf5 ♗xe3 28.♘e7† ♔g7 29.♗a3 (29. fxe3!? c1♕ 30.♖xc1 ♖xc1† 31.♔h2∞ leaves White with some very advanced central pawns as compensation for the exchange.) 29...♗c5 30.♗b2 ♗xe7 (30...♖d8!? 31.e6† ♔f8!) 31.♖xd7 ♖b8 32.♗c1 ♗c5 33.e6 ♔f6? (33...a5) 34.♖e1! g5 35.e7 ♖d4 36.♗b2 ♖e8 37.♖c7 1–0 Handke – Tseitlin, Biel 1999.

17.♗c5!

17.♕e2 ♖fc8 18.♖a5 ♘c4 19.♖c5 b5 was fine for Black in Meissner – Gaerts, Germany 1992.

17...♖fc8

An inaccuracy according to Gelfand, who notes the following variations:

a) 17...♕f7 18.♕b1 (Krasenkow, in *Chessbase Magazine 71*, notes that 18.d5 is met by 18... f5!) 18...♘a4 19.♕xb7 ♘xc5 20.dxc5±.

b) 17...♘c8 18.♕b1 b6 19.♖c1 ♘d6 20.d5 ♕f7 21.♗xd6 exd6 22.♖c7±.

18.d5

18.♕b1 is met by 18...♘a4 according to Gelfand, who also proposes 18.♖a5!? as an interesting alternative.

18...♕f7   19.♗xb6   axb6   20.♖xa8   ♖xa8 21.♕b3±

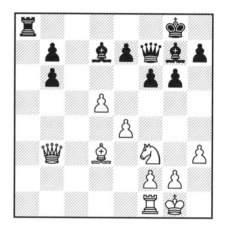

21...♕e8

Krasenkow notes the lines 21...e6 22.♗c4 and 21...f5 22.♕xb6 (22.e5 ♗a4 23.♕a2 (23.♕b4!?± looks sensible to me) 23...♕e8 24.♖a1 ♖a5∞) 22...fxe4 23.♕xb7 ♕e8 24.♗xe4±.

22.♕xb6

22.♖b1 b5 23.♗xb5 ♗xb5 24.♕xb5 ♕xb5 25.♖xb5 ♖a4 and White is slightly better according to Gelfand.

22...♖a3 23.♗c4 ♖a4

There are two other moves that White had to consider:

a) 23...♗xh3 24.gxh3 ♖xf3 25.d6† (25.♕e6† ♔h8 26.d6+– is simpler) 25...♔h8 (25...♔f8 26.♖d1) 26.♗b5 ♕b8 (26...♖b3 27.♗xe8 ♖xb6

28.d7 ♖d6 29.♖c1+-) 27.dxe7 (27.♔g2+-)
27...♖g3† 28.♔h2 ♖c3† 29.♔g2 ♖c8 30.♖d1+-.

b) 23...♕c8 24.d6† (24.♗b5 allows
24...♗xh3!, however 24.♗b3± keeps everything
under control.) 24...e6 25.♖c1+-. These notes
are based on Boris Gelfand's observations in
Informant 75.

24.♗b3!

Fantastic play! Gelfand sacrifices the e4-
pawn in order to gain enough time to capture
the b7-pawn and swing the f1–rook into the
attack. The game is now decided in convincing
fashion.

24...♖xe4

24...♖a8 25.♖c1.

25.♕xb7+- ♔f8

25...♖e2 26.♖a1 ♗c8 27.d6†.

26.♖c1 ♖e2

26...♕d8 27.d6 (27.♖c7 also wins) 27...♖e2
28.♖c7 ♔e8 29.♖xd7!.

**27.♖c7 ♖b2 28.d6 exd6 29.♖xd7! ♖xb3
30.♕c7 ♖b8 31.♖xg7**
1–0

Game 19 Conclusions: Well, it is a little hard to
draw any solid conclusions at this stage, as there
have only been a couple of games with 14.h3!?.
However, thus far results have been good for
White, and Black has yet to demonstrate a path
to equality. A further point in favour of 14.h3
is that it was super-GM Boris Gelfand handling
the White pieces, and given his undeniable
expertise in the 8.♖b1 variation we should
perhaps pay special attention to this little
move. In terms of finding improvements for
Black, the best bet is probably GM Igor Stohl's
recommendation 14...f5!? although as yet there
are no practical examples with this move.

Game 20
Anand – Leko
Linares 2000

1.d4 ♘f6 2 ♘f3 g6 3.c4 ♗g7 4 ♘c3 d5 5.cxd5
♘xd5 6.e4 ♘xc3 7.bxc3 c5 8.♖b1 0–0 9.♗e2
cxd4 10.cxd4 ♕a5† 11.♗d2 ♕xa2 12 0–0
♘d7!? 13.♖e1!?

Not a new move, but probably not one that
Leko was expecting. I can still recall when Anand
first began playing 1.d4 against elite opposition.
There seemed to be a fresh and creative vitality
to his handling of 1.d4 systems, and very often
he infused established openings with new ideas
in the earliest stages of the game. This particular
game was no exception, with Anand setting
Leko exacting problems right from the outset.
Although Leko had faced 13.♖e1 before, there
was little (if any) established theory on the move,
and in any case the true potential of White's piece
deployment was still to be realised.

13...♘b6 14.♖a1!?

Having deviated from the mainlines, Anand
now departs from precedent entirely. An earlier
Leko game in this variation had continued:
14.h3 ♗d7 15.♖a1 ♕e6 16.♗d3 ♖fd8 17.♕e2
♗e8 18.♗e3 ♕d7 19.♖a5 ♘a4 20.♕d2 a6 when
Black had no problems: ½–½ Chernin – Leko,
Hungarian Championship 1997.

14...♕b2!

Leko chooses the best move; it would have
been easy (and inaccurate) to have continued in
the spirit of the 12...♘d7 mainlines, retreating
the queen to e6. However after 14...♕e6 15.♕b1!
GM Igor Stohl observes that we have reached a

position similar to the line 12...♘d7 13.♗b4 ♘b6 14.♖a1 ♕e6 15.♕b1, the difference being that White's f1–rook is placed more actively on e1, supporting the central pawns and defending the e2-bishop so that White can play d4-d5 rapidly. After 15...♗d7 (15...f5?! 16.♘g5 ♕f6 17.e5± - Stohl) 16.d5 or 16.♖a5!?, Stohl prefers White's chances.

15.h3!

Another prophylactic measure, anticipating a potential ♗c8-g4, which would allow Black to simplify the position and put pressure on White's d-pawn.

15...f5!?

This risky venture invigorates the position, defining the character of the middlegame and setting White concrete problems. Leko has apparently commented that he had actually analysed this position before he played it in this game (presumably after his encounter with Chernin). However Stohl is critical of Leko's choice, and instead recommends 15...♗d7!? after which White has two options:

a) In *Chessbase Magazine 76* Krasenkow suggested 16.♗a5!?

(16...♖ac8 is interesting, however 16...♗b5 17.♖b1 ♗xe2 18.♖xe2 ♕a3 19.♗b4 is clearly better for White.) 17.♕d3 (17.♗d3? runs into 17...♗xd4) which he assesses as yielding White compensation for his sacrificed pawn.

b) 16.♗d3 is Stohl's recommendation; his analysis continues: 16...♖fc8 17.♖e2 ♗b5 18.♗a5 (18.♖b1?! ♗a4! 19.♕e1 ♕a3 is slightly better for Black, however 18.♗g5!? is not considered, and may be worth a look, e.g. 18...♕b4 19.♗xe7 ♕xe7 20.♗xb5 a6∞) 18...♕xa1 19.♕xa1 ♗xd3 with compensation for the sacrificed queen (although in actual fact, on a purely point-based system, material is level) the point being that 20.♖e3 is met by 20...♗h6!. It seems that White should therefore try 20.♖e1 ♘c4 21.♗b4 when Black's queenside pawns will inevitably prove dangerous, but I feel that White's chances should be preferred.

16.♖b1

Given that the black queen is presently short of retreat routes, there is some logic to keeping her where she is for the time being. A correspondence game in this line continued 16.♗d3!? (best - Stohl)

with the intention of following up with 17.♕d3, 18.♖eb1, or 17.♗d3 and 18.♖e2, in either case with a view to trapping the black queen. Krasenkow's analysis continues 16...♖fc8

16...fxe4 (Knudsen analyses 16...♗d7 17.exf5 (17.♖e2 fxe4 (17...♗xd4 18.♖b1 ♗a4 19.♕e1 ♕a3 20.♖xb6! ♕xd3 (20...♗xb6 21.♗c4† ♔h8 22.♗b4+-) 21.♖b4±) 18.♗a5 ♕xa1 19.♕xa1 exd3?!

(This seems inaccurate: if Black is going to defend this position then it makes more sense to disrupt White's kingside structure with 19...exf3!, when the position remains tense, although I rather prefer the side with the queen!) 20.♖xe7 when White holds the initiative.) 17...♗xf5 18.♗xf5 ♖xf5 19.♖xe7 when the rook's presence on e7 causes Black some discomfort.) 17.♗xe4 ♕b5 18.♖a5 (awarded an exclamation mark by Stohl, although 18.♕c2!? contemplating ♖eb1 or ♕a2† seems strong) 18...♕e8 (18...♕c4 19.♖c5 (Stohl suggests 19.♗c2!? presumably with the idea of bringing the bishop to the a2-g8 diagonal. I agree with the sentiment, however I think that 19.♗b1 may be better as 19.♗c2 ♖xf3!? has the potential to complicate matters.) 19...♕f7 20.♖c7! gives White excellent compensation according to Stohl, who provides the following sample variation: 20...♗f6 (20...♘d5 21.♗xd5 ♕xd5 22.♖exe7±) 21.♘g5!, ♗xg5 22.♗xg5 ♕xf2† 23.♔h2 e6? 24.♖xh7!+-) 19.♗b4 ♗f6 20.♗c5 ♔h8 21.♕b3± Noomen – Corti, e-mail 2000. Finally, it should be noted that Krasenkow has observed that 16.e5 ♗e6 promises White little.

16...♕a2 17.♕c1?!

White now threatens 18.♖xb6 and 19.♗c4†, winning Black's queen. However this is just a trick, and ultimately White's strategy proves ineffectual. Stohl observed that 17.♗d3 fxe4 18.♗xe4 ♕f7 is unclear, a particularly important defect in White's position is that the rook is far less active on b1 than it had been on a1. Relatively best was 17.♖a1 ♕b2 (17...♕e6 18.♘g5± - Stohl) 18.♗d3, transposing to the note to 16.♗d3 discussed above.

17...♔h8

The natural and obvious choice, but not Black's only move. Stohl observes the following variations:

a) 17...♗e6!? 18.♖a1 (18.♘g5 ♖fc8∓; 18.d5? ♖ac8–+) 18...♖fc8 19.♗c3 ♕b3 20.♖a3 ♖xc3 21.♕xc3 ♕xc3 22.♖xc3 fxe4 23.♘e5∞.

b) 17...♕f7?! 18.♘g5 ♕f6 19.e5 ♕c6 20.♕a3!, when White has good attacking chances, e.g. 20...h6 21.♖ec1 ♕a4 22.♗c4† ♔h8

23.♘f7† ♔h7 24.♕xa4 ♘xa4 25.♗b4±.

18.♖a1 ♕g8! 19.♗a5

a) 19.♗d3 ♗e6! 20.exf5 (20.d5? ♖fc8 ...fe4∓) 20...♗xf5 21.♗xf5 ♖xf5 22.♖xe7 ♖f7= - Stohl.

b) 19.e5 ♗e6 is fine for Black - Krasenkow.

19...fxe4

19...♗e6 20.♖xb6 axb6 21.♖xa8 ♖xa8 22.♗d3⩲.

20.♗xb6 exf3 21.♗xf3 ♗xh3

21...♖xf3 22.gxf3 ♗xh3 23.♖xa7 ♖xa7 24.♗xa7± ♕d5?! 25.♖xe7 ♕xf3 26.♖e8† ♗f8 27.♕g5 - Stohl.

22.♖xa7

a) 22.gxh3? ♖xf3–+;

b) 22.♗xa7 ♗e6! (22...♖xf3 23.gxf3 ♕d5 24.♕e3 ♖f8 25.♗c5±) 23.♗c7 ♗d5 24.♗xd5 ♕xd5 25.♖xe7 ♖xa7 26.♖xa7 ♕xd4 27.♖a3 ♕xf2† 28.♔h2 ♕d4 when Black has good counterplay and the probable result is a draw - Stohl.

c) 22.♗xb7 ♖ab8 23.♖xa7 ♖xb7! 24.♖xb7 ♕d5= - Krasenkow.

22...♗xg2!

23.♔xg2!

The only move that maintains the balance. Krasenkow notes the alternatives 23.♗xg2? ♖xa7 24.♗xa7 ♕a2!∓ and 23.♖xa8 ♗xf3 24.♖xf8 ♕xf8∓ when White is under some pressure.

23...♕b3 24.♕d1 ♕xb6 25.♖xb7 ♕f6 26.♖exe7 ♖a1! 27.♖xg7!

The only move. 27.♕e2? ♕h4 28.♖f7 ♕h1†
29.♔g3 ♖g1† 30.♔f4 ♕h4† 31.♔g4 ♗h6†, and
27.♕xa1? ♕xf3† 28.♔h2 ♕xf2† 29.♔h1 ♕h4†
30.♔g1 ♗xd4† both win for Black.

**27...♖xd1 28.♖xh7† ♔g8 29.♗d5† ♖f7
30.♖bxf7 ♕g5† 31.♔h3 ♕xd5 32.♖hg7†
½–½**

Game 20 Conclusions: As with 14.h3 (Game 19),
it is difficult to draw any concrete conclusions
on 13.♖e1!? because there has been very little
practical experience with the move. However
Anand clearly had enough faith in the move to
play it against Leko and, in my opinion at least,
White had some chances to be better with Stohl's
recommendation 16.♗d3!?.

Conclusions on 12...♘d7!?:

13.♗b4! a5 (Game 15) seems to be difficult
for Black on account of 14.♖a1! ♕e6 15.♕c2
♘f6 16.♘e5! when White's activity can quickly
become overwhelming. In Game 16 Black tried
14.♘e5 ♕e6!? and although he may have had
chances to hold the balance in the game, in
general Black's set-up seems unduly passive and I
wouldn't be surprised if White can forcibly secure

an advantage. Far more impressive was Leko's
play as Black in Game 17, and at present 14.♘e5
f6! appears entirely satisfactory for Black.

Game 18 sees White putting Black under
serious pressure with 14.♖a1!? ♕e6 15.♕b1,
however ultimately Black seems to be just
about holding on here (see Pankratov – Leko, e-
mail 1999). If I were to play this line, I would
be quite tempted to try Avrukh's 15.♗d3!?,
which is relatively unexplored and seems quite
promising.

In Game 19 we see Gelfand making another
significant contribution to the theory of the
Modern Exchange Variation with 14.h3!?.
There has not been much practical experience
with this move to date, however results
have been encouraging, and Black has yet
to demonstrate a suitable path to equality.

Finally, Game 20 once again sees Leko defending
the Black side of the 12...♘d7 Grünfeld, but
this time he is facing Anand, who introduces a
relatively fresh interpretation of this system with
13.♖e1!?. Leko defends actively and gives a truly
impressive performance, however it seems that
White could have secured some advantage with
GM Igor Stohl's recommendation 16.♗d3!?.

Chapter 4: The Reliable Recipe 12...♗g4!

1.d4 ♘f6 2.c4 g6 3.♘c3 d5 4.cxd5 ♘xd5 5.e4 ♘xc3 6.bxc3 ♗g7 7.♘f3 c5 8.♖b1 0–0 9.♗e2 cxd4 10.cxd4 ♕a5† 11.♗d2 ♕xa2 12.0–0 ♗g4!

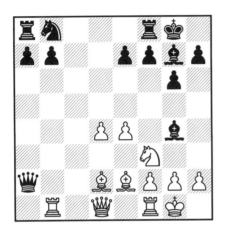

At present 12...♗g4 represents Black's most popular defence against the 8.♖b1 variation, and arguably also the most reliable one. By playing 12...♗g4 Black leaves the b7-pawn undefended, but acknowledges that rapid development and counterplay against White's centre is more important than retaining a material advantage. Indeed, if we cast our minds back to Chapters 1–3, it was very rare indeed that Black's b-pawn proved itself to be of much consequence; where Black's queenside pawns posed a threat it was more often because Black's a-pawn was given an opportunity to run.

Game 21
Johannessen – Nakamura
Bermuda 2002

1.d4 ♘f6 2.c4 g6 3.♘c3 d5 4.cxd5 ♘xd5 5.e4 ♘xc3 6.bxc3 ♗g7 7.♘f3 c5 8.♖b1 0–0 9.♗e2

cxd4 10.cxd4 ♕a5† 11.♗d2 ♕xa2 12.0–0 ♗g4! 13.♗g5!

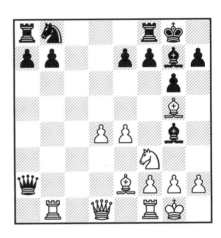

White's most principled approach is to go after the e7-pawn. Alternatives (other than 13.♗e3!? which is examined in Games 30-33) promise White nothing:

a) 13.♖xb7 ♗xf3 14.♗xf3 ♗xd4 is know to be fine for Black, e.g. 15.e5!? (15.♗b4 ♖d8 16.♕c1 e5 is at least equal for Black. 15.♗h6? ♖d8 16.♖xe7 ♘c6–+) 15...♘a6 16.♖xe7 ♖ad8 gives Black excellent counterplay.

b) 13.d5 ♘d7 14.♖xb7 ♖fb8! 15.♕b1 ♕xb1 16.♖fxb1 ♖xb7 17.♖xb7 ♘c5! 18.♖xe7 ♗f8 19.♖c7 (19.♖xf7?! ♘xe4!∓ - Se. Ivanov) was Se. Ivanov – Lukin, Russia 1992, and now Sergey Ivanov, in *Informant 54*, suggests that Black should have played 19...♗d6 20.♖c6 ♘xe4 21.♗e3 (21.♘g5 ♘xd2 22.♗xg4 ♖d8 is equal according to Sakaev and Lukin.) 21...♗d7 22.♖a6 ♗c8 23.♖xa7 ♖xa7 24.♗xa7 ♗b7 25.♗c4 ♘c3=.
13...♕e6?!

This passive retreat is inaccurate on two counts. Firstly, although 13...♕e6 removes the black queen from the danger zone, it wasn't actually in any immediate danger. Retreating the queen from a2-removes its positive functions (e.g. tying the white queen to the protection of the e2-bishop, restricting the movement of White's pieces within their own camp, etc.), while at the same time costing Black time and inconvenience in the regrouping process. Secondly, the purpose of 13...♕e6 seems to be to defend the e7-pawn, which is entirely unnecessary. As Game 22 will illustrate, capturing on e7 even when provoked by 13...h6 does not yield White any advantage.

a) 13...h6 is the mainline, and this will be examined in Games 22-29.

b) 13...a5 14.♖xb7 a4 15.♗xe7 ♖c8 16.h3 ♗xf3 17.♗xf3 ♘c6 18.e5 ♘xe7 19.♖xe7± Peralta – Gamarra Caceres, Asuncion 1999.

c) 13...♗f6 14.♗xf6 (14.♗e3 ♘c6 15.♖xb7 ♖ab8 16.♖xb8 ♖xb8 17.h3 ♗d7 18.d5 ♘e5 19.♗f4 ♕b2 20.♕c1 ♖b7 21.♖xb2 ♖xb2 22.♗xe5 ♖xe2 23.♗xf6 exf6 24.♖a1 ♖xe4 25.♖xa7 ♗f5 26.d6± Gelfand – Ivanchuk, Cap d'Agde 1998) 14...exf6 15.♖xb7 ♘c6 16.d5 ♗xf3 17.gxf3 (17.♗xf3!?) 17...♖fd8 18.♖e1 a5 19.♖c7 ♘b4 20.♗c4 ♕b2 21.d6 ♖f8 22.f4 a4 23.♖e2 a3 24.♔g2 ♖fb8 25.♗xf7† ♔h8 26.♖xb2 axb2 27.♕d4 1–0 Agrest – Moingt, Bastia 1998.

d) 13...♖d8

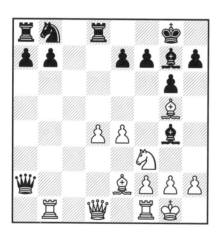

14.d5 ♖d7 15.♗b5 ♖c7 (15...♘c6? 16.♕a4 ♕xa4 17.♗xa4+-) 16.♖e1 ♘a6 (Shipov notes the lines 16...a6 17.♗a4 ♗xf3 18.gxf3± and

16...♗xf3!? 17.♕xf3 ♘d7 (17...a6? 18.♗e8; 17...♘a6?! 18.e5±) 18.♗xe7 ♘e5 19.♕a3 ♕xa3 20.♗xa3 a6 when Black will follow up with b7-b5 with some counterplay.) 17.e5 ♖c5 (17...♗xf3 18.♕xf3 ♗xe5? 19.♗xa6 bxa6 20.d6+-) 18.♗xa6 bxa6 (Both 18...♖xd5? 19.♕xd5! ♕xd5 20.♗xb7 ♕d8 21.♖ed1! ♕e8 22.♗xa8 ♕xa8 23.♗xe7 and 18...♕xa6 19.♗xe7 leave White substantially better.) 19.♕d4! ♖c4 20.♕e3± Shipov – Dvoirys, Berlin 1996. The comments here are based on Shipov's notes for *Informant 67*.

14.h3!?

The text is strong, and would be my own preference in this position, however two other moves also merit consideration:

a) 14.d5 ♕xe4 (14...♕d7 15.♕b3 b6 16.♕a3± - Sakaev, *Informant 47*).

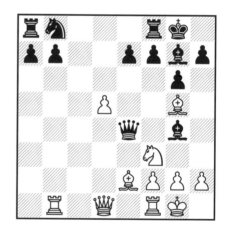

White has now tried two options:

a1) 15.♖xb7 is generally considered inaccurate. Play continues 15...♗e6! (15...h6!? is also interesting, e.g. 16.♖xe7 (16.♗xe7 ♖e8 17.♗d6 (17.h3 ♗h5) 17...♕xe2 18.♕xe2 ♖xe2 19.♗xb8 a5∓, or 16.♗e3 a5 17.♕d2 ♖c8!∓) 16...♕b4 17.♕d2 a5!= Avrukh) 16.♖b5! (16.♗xe7 ♗xd5 17.♗d3 ♕g4∓) 16...♗f5! 17.♖e1 (According to Azmaiparashvili, in his annotations for *Informant 68*, better is 17.♘d2!? ♕e5 18.♘c4! ♕c7 19.d6 exd6 20.♘xd6 with compensation.) and now Garcia Ilundain – Azmaiparashvili, Pamplona

1996 continued 17...a5! 18.♗f1 (18.♘d2 ♛d4 19.♗xe7 ♖c8 20.d6 a4 21.♗f3 ♖a7∞ - Avrukh) 18...♛c2 19.♛xc2 ♗xc2

20.♗xe7 with unclear complications that were eventually resolved in Black's favour. However Boris Avrukh believes that White's play can be improved via 20.♖xe7! a4 21.♗c4! a3 22.♗a2 h6 23.♗f4 g5 24.♗g3 when White may well be a little better.

a2) 15.♛d2!? f6?! (better is 15...a5 16.♖xb7 f6 17.♗e3 when White maintains good compensation according to Sakaev and Lukin, *Informant 47*) 16.♗e3 a5 17.♖fc1! ♖c8 18.h3 ♗d7 19.♖xc8† ♗xc8 20.♗d3 ♛a4 (20...♛xd5 21.♖c1 ♛d7 22.♗c4† ♔h8 23.♗e6! ♛xe6 24.♛d8† ♛g8 25.♖xc8+- Sakaev) 21.♗c5 ♛d7 22.♛e2 ♗f8 23.♗c4± Sakaev – Bukhman, Leningrad 1989.

b) 14.♖e1!? h6 (14...♛xe4!? 15.♗d3 ♛d5 16.♗xe7! ♗xf3 17.gxf3 ♘c6 18.♗e4 ♛d7 19.♗xf8 ♖xf8± - San Segundo) 15.♗h4 15...♛xe4 16.♗d3 ♛f4 (16...♛xd4?! 17.♘xd4 ♗xd1 18.♗xe7 ♗a4 19.♗xf8±) 17.♗xe7 ♖e8 (17...♘c6 18.♗xf8 ♘xd4 19.♗xg7 ♘xf3† 20.gxf3 ♗xf3 21.♛xf3!? ♛xf3 22.♖e3 ♛g4† 23.♖g3 ♛h5 24.♗f6±) 18.d5 ♘d7 (18...♗xf3 19.♛xf3 ♛xf3 20.gxf3 and 18...♘e5 19.♖b4! ♗xf3 20.♖xf4 ♗xd1 21.♖xe5 ♘d7 22.♖e1 both give White compensation for his sacrificed pawn.) 19.♖b4! ♗xf3 20.gxf3

♛b8? (20...♛c7 21.d6=) 21.d6! ♗c3 22.♗xg6! ♗xb4 23.♛d5 ♖f8 24.♖e4 ♘f6 25.♗xf6 ♛xd6 26.♗h7† 1–0 San Segundo – Alonso, Malaga 1999. The comments here are based on GM San Segundo's annotations for *Informant 75*.

c) 14.♖xb7 ♛xe4 15.♖xe7 ♛d5 is fine for Black according to Avrukh, *Chessbase Magazine 57.*

14...♗xf3 15.♗xf3 ♛d7 16.d5!

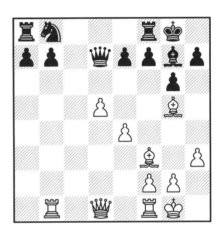

It is very important to advance the d-pawn first in order to deny the knight access to the c6-square. 16.e5 ♘c6 is already awkward for White in the sense that 17.d5 now cannot be played without conceding the e5-pawn.

16...♘a6

This turns out badly for Black, however satisfactory alternatives are not obvious:

a) 16...b6? 17.e5! f6 18.d6 fxg5 19.♗xa8 ♘a6 20.dxe7 ♛xe7 21.♖e1+- Al Ashhab – Mohsen, Tanta 1997.

b) Krasenkow notes that 16...♗e5 is met by 17.♗g4 when White will follow up with 18.f4, establishing a powerful centre.

c) Relatively best was 16...a5 according to Krasenkow, the idea being to simply push the a-pawn down the board and interfere with White's piece coordination.

17.♛e2 ♘c5 18.e5! ♖ae8?!

18...♖fe8 may have been better.

19.♖fd1 f6?! 20.♗e3 ♖c8

20...b6 21.♗xc5 bxc5 22.♕c4! fxe5 23.d6†
♔h8 24.♖b7 is better for White according to
Krasenkow in *Chessbase Magazine 88*.

21.d6! b6

21...fxe5 22.♗xc5 ♖xc5 23.♕a2† ♔h8
24.♕xa7 ♖c4 25.♖xb7, and 21...exd6 22.♕a2†
♔h8 23.♕xa7 are both terrible for Black.

22.♗xc5 ♖xc5 23.e6

Look at those lads go!

23...♕c8

Krasenkow notes that 23...♕d8 24.dxe7 ♕xe7
25.♖d7 ♕e8 26.♖xa7 ♖e5 27.♕c4, intending
♖xb6 and/or ♕c7, is also losing.

**24.dxe7 ♖e8 25.♖d8! ♖xd8 26.exd8♕† ♕xd8
27.e7 ♕e8 28.♕e6† ♔h8 29.♖d1 ♖c8 30.♕xc8!
♕xc8 31.♖d8†**

1–0

A beautifully controlled game by Johannessen,
and a vivid demonstration of how to handle
positions where Black prematurely retreats the
queen to e6.

Game 21 Conclusions: 13...♕e6?! is solid but
passive. Provided White keeps his head and plays
sensible chess there should not be too much
trouble proving an advantage.

Game 22
Kramnik – Kasparov
Novgorod 1994

1 ♘f3 ♘f6 2.c4 g6 3.♘c3 d5 4.cxd5 ♘xd5 5.e4
♘xc3 6.bxc3 c5 7.d4 ♗g7 8.♖b1 0–0 9.♗e2
cxd4 10.cxd4 ♕a5† 11.♗d2 ♕xa2 12 0–0 ♗g4!
13.♗g5 h6!

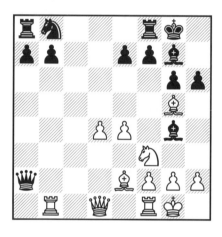

Practice has demonstrated this to be Black's
most reliable response.

14.♗xe7?!

As Kasparov convincingly demonstrates, the
immediate capture on e7 secures White no
advantage whatsoever. White in fact has two
stronger alternatives in 14.♗h4 (considered
in Games 23-25) and 14.♗e3 (considered in
Games 26-29).

14...♖e8 15.♖xb7 ♘c6!

Probably best, although alternatives have
also been considered. In his annotations for
Informant 61 Kramnik notes the variations
15...♗c8? 16.♖c7± and 15...♕e6 16.e5!±, the
point being 16...♖xe7 17.d5 ♗xf3 18.♗xf3 ♕xe5
19.♖xe7 ♕xe7 20.d6+–. However 15...♘d7!? is
a more feasible option: 16.♗b4 (16.♗c5 ♖xe4∓)
16...♖xe4 17.♖e1 ♗xf3 18.♗xf3 ♖xd4∓ Hultin
– T. Ernst, Gausdal Troll Masters 1991.

16.♗c5 ♖xe4 17.♗d3 ♖xd4!

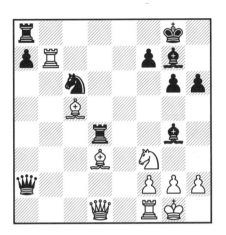

A strong novelty by Kasparov which resolves Black's difficulties in this variation. 17...♖f4? 18.♕c1! is clearly better for White according to Kramnik, however previous play had focussed on 17...♖ee8 18.♗b5 ♖ec8 (Kramnik notes that after 18...♕d5 White can maintain a strong initiative with: 19.♕a4!? ♗xf3 20.gxf3 ♖ac8 (20...♘xd4? 21.♗xd4 ♕xb7 22.♗xe8 ♗xd4 23.♗c6 and 20...♖e6 21.♗c4 ♕xf3 22.♗xe6 fxe6 23.♕d1 are both good for White) 21.♗c4!?.) 19.♕d3 (19.♕a4!?) 19...♗e6 20.♖e1 ♗d5 as in Manso – Sanchez Almeyra, San Sebastian 1993, is unclear according to Ftacnik, *CBM 43*.

18.♗xd4 ♘xd4= 19.♗e4?!

19.♕b1 ♕xb1 20.♖fxb1 ♘xf3† 21.gxf3 ♗xf3 22.♖b8† ♖xb8 23.♖xb8† ♗f8 24.♗c4 g5 (24... a5 25.♖b6 g5 26.♖f6 ♗h5 27.♖a6 ♔g7 28.♖xa5 ½–½ Elbilia – Nataf, Bermuda 1999) 25.♖c8 a5 26.♗c7 ♗h5 27.♖a7 ♗b4= - Kramnik.

19...♖d8 20.♕b1 ♘e2†!?

According to Kramnik Black could have resolved the tactical issues immediately with 20...♕xb1 21.♖fxb1 ♘e2† 22.♔f1 ♘c3 23.♖b8 ♖f8!=.

21.♔h1 ♕c4 22.♗xg6!?

22.♖b4 ♕e6 23.♖b8 ♖xb8 24.♕xb8† ♔h7 gives Black sufficient compensation for the exchange according to Kramnik, and Ftacnik notes that 22.♖b8 ♖xb8 23.♕xb8† ♔h7 24.♘d2 ♕d4 gives rise to an unclear position.

22...♘c3!

22...fxg6? 23.♕xg6 gives White a strong attack.

23.♗xf7†

This leads to a draw, however Ftacnik suggested that Kramnik's play could have been improved via 23.♕e1! with the following possibilities:

a) 23...♖f8? 24.♗xf7†! ♖xf7 25.♕e8† ♖f8 (25...♗f8 26.♕xf7† ♕xf7 27.♖xf7 ♔xf7 28.♘e5†+-) 26.♕g6 ♕xf1† 27.♘g1+-.

b) 23...fxg6 24.♖xg7† ♔xg7 25.♕e7† ♕f7 (25...♔g8 26.♕xd8† ♗g7 27.♖e1+-) 26.♕xd8 ♗xf3 (26...♕xf3 27.♕d4† ♔g8 28.♖b1!+-) 27.♕d4† ♔h7 28.♕xc3 ♗d5 29.f4+-.

c) Relatively best is 23...♗e6! when Black retains compensation.

23...♕xf7 24.♖xf7 ♘xb1 25.♖xa7 ♘c3 26.h3 ½–½

26...♗f5 is equal.

Game 22 Conclusions: 13...h6! is entirely justified as 14.♗xe7?! promises White nothing after 14...♖e8 15.♖xb7 ♘c6! 16.♗c5 ♖xe4 17.♗d3 ♖xd4!, when Black obtains excellent compensation for the exchange.

Game 23
Anand – Illescas Cordoba
Madrid 1998

1.d4 ♘f6 2.♘f3 g6 3.c4 ♗g7 4.♘c3 d5 5.cxd5 ♘xd5 6.e4 ♘xc3 7.bxc3 c5 8.♖b1 0–0 9.♗e2 cxd4 10.cxd4 ♕a5† 11.♗d2 ♕xa2 12 0–0 ♗g4 13.♗g5 h6 14.♗h4

If White is not going to take on e7 then this is the most obvious retreat, maintaining some pressure on e7 and perhaps rerouting the bishop to g3, where it can support the advance of White's central pawns and pressurise the c7 and b8-squares. However, 14.♗h4 only became popular after Anand's success in this game. Prior to that 14.♗e3 was White's main choice, the argument being that the pawn on h6 is a weakening of Black's kingside. The lines with 14.♗e3 are considered in Games 26-29.

A further point to consider at this juncture is that the notion that 13...h6 helps White is also open to question, and for this reason 13.♗e3!? (thereby preserving the option of a subsequent ♗e3-g5, perhaps to harass a rook on d8) has enjoyed various spells of popularity.

14...♖d8

A natural move which places pressure on the d4-pawn. Black's main alternatives are 14...g5!? (considered in Game 24) and 14...a5 (considered in Game 25). Black also has a host of minor alternatives:

a) Jonathan Rowson, in his excellent text *Understanding the Grünfeld*, suggests that 14...♕e6 has a lot to be said for it. In actual fact I doubt it has much to be said for it, but White still must play accurately to prove an advantage. 15.h3 (15.e5!? ♕d7 (15...♖d8!?) 16.d5! ♗xf3 17.♗xf3 ♖xe5 18.d6 is given by Ivan Sokolov in *Informant 73* as clearly better for White, however Rowson asserts (correctly it would seem) that Black is fine here.) 15...♗xf3 16.♗xf3 ♕d7 17.d5

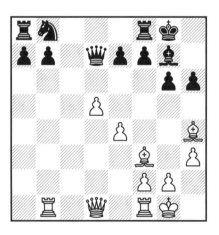

There are now two lines that must be considered:

a1) 17...♗e5 18.♗g4 (Also of interest is 18.♕d2!? g5 19.♗g3 ♗xg3 20.fxg3 ♕d6 21.h4!? f6 22.e5 ♕xe5 23.♖xb7 ♕d6 24.♕d3 f5 25.♖e1 (25.hxg5!±) 25...e5 26.♗g4 ♕a6 (26...e4

27.♖xe4! fxe4 28.♕xe4+-) 27.♕b1 gxh4 28.♖xe5 ♘d7 29.♗xf5 ♖ab8 30.♖e7 ♖xf5 31.♖xb8† ♘xb8 32.♕xf5 ♕b6† 33.♔h1 1–0 Sokolin – Ady, New York 1999) 18...♕d6 19.♖xb7 g5 20.♗g3 ♗xg3 21.fxg3

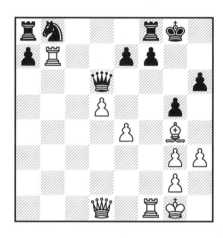

21...a5? (21...♘a6 22.♕c2 (Rowson noted that 22.♖d7?! ♕b6† 23.♔h2 ♘c5 24.♖xe7? ♕d6 traps the marauding White rook.) 22...♘c5 23.e5 ♕xd5 24.♖xe7±) 22.♕f3 ♘a6 23.♖d7! (Rowson mentions only 23.♗h5; the text is stronger.) and now P. Adams – Gibbs, corr. 1999 concluded 23...♕c5†?! 24.♔h2 ♘b8 25.♖d8! 1–0, whereas 23...♕b6† 24.♔h2 ♖a7 25.♖xa7 ♕xa7 26.♗e6 ♕d4 27.♗xf7† ♔g7 28.♕h5 1–0 was Gilles – Paul, e-mail 2000. Rowson has since suggested (in the August 2001 issue of *British Chess Magazine*) that 23...♕f6 may be stronger. This may be true, but I still prefer White after 24.♕e3 (24.♕xf6 is very close to being good, but remains unclear: 24...exf6 25.♖xf6 ♘c5 26.♖e7! a4 (26...♖fe8 27.♖c7 ♘xe4 28.♖fxf7+-) 27.♗h5 a3 28.♗xf7† ♔h8 (28...♔g7 29.e5!) 29.♖xh6† ♔g7 30.♖g6† ♔h7 (30...♔h8? 31.♗g8+-) 31.♖f6 ♔h8 and now it is not clear whether White has anything better than a perpetual, e.g. 32.d6 a2 33.♗xa2 ♖xf6 34.e5 ♖ff8 35.♗c4 (35.♗f7 ♖a1† 36.♔h2 g4!! 37.hxg4 ♘e4–+) 35...♖a1† 36.♔h2 and White's advanced pawns are dangerous, but, well...he is a rook down!) 24...♕e5 25.♔h2! (25.♖f5 ♕a1† 26.♔h2

♖ac8 intending 27...♖c1 may pose White some problems.) 25...a4 (25...♖ac8 26.♕b6+-) 26.♖f5 ♕b2 (26...♕a1 27.♕b6+-) 27.♖xe7 (27.♖b7!? ♕g7 28.♗h5+-) 27...a3 28.e5+-.

a2) 17...♘a6

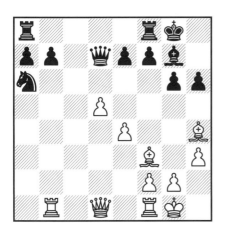

18.♗g4! (18.♕e2 ♘c5?! (18...♗e5 is better according to Rowson) 19.e5 e6 20.♖fd1 exd5 21.♗xd5 ♕f5 22.♗e7 ♖fc8 (22...♘a4 23.♗xf8 ♘c3 24.♕d3 ♕xd3 25.♖xd3 ♘xb1 26.♗xg7 ♔xg7 27.♖xb7 ♖e8 28.f4± - Stohl) 23.♕e3 ♘a4 24.e6 gave White an initiative in Komljenovic – Sanchez Almeyra, San Sebastian 1993, according to Stohl) 18...f5 19.exf5 gxf5 20.♗f3 ♘c5 21.♖e1 ♗f6 22.♗g3 ♖ac8 23.d6!? (23.♗f4 ♔h7 24.♕d2±) 23...e6 (23...exd6 24.♗xd6 (24.♗d5†!? ♔h7 25.♗f4 intending 26.♕h5 deserves consideration) 24...♖fd8 25.♗xb7! ♘xb7 26.♕d5† ♕f7 27.♕xf7† ♔xf7 28.♖xb7† ♔g8 (28...♔g6 29.♖e6±) 29.♗f4±) and now rather than 24.♕d2?! as in Halkias – Gustafsson, Hengelo 1999, White should have played 24.♖xe6!!±, e.g. 24...♘xe6 25.♖xb7 ♕e8 (25...♕d8 26.♗d5+-; 25...♘c7 26.♖xa7±) 26.d7±.

b) 14...♗f6?! 15.♗xf6 (15.♗g3 ♘c6 16.d5 ♗xf3 17.♗xf3 (17.gxf3 ♘d4 guarantees Black sufficient counterplay) 17...♘e5 18.♖xb7 a5= Lautier, *Chessbase Magazine 68*) 15...exf6 16.♖xb7 ♘c6 17.h3 ♗xf3 18.♗xf3 ♕c4 19.d5 ♘e5 20.♕d2!

♘xf3†?! (20...a5 21.♖c1 ♕d3 22.♕xd3 ♘xd3 23.♖c3 ♘e5 24.♗e2 is slightly better for White according to Lautier, and Ftacnik noted that 20...♔g7 21.♖c1 ♕a4 22.♕e3 ♖fb8 is also slightly better for White.) 21.gxf3 ♖c8 22.♕b2!± f5? (22...♕xh3? runs into 23.♕xf6, and 22...♔g7 23.♔g2 ♖b8 24.♖xb8 ♕xb8 25.♖xb8 ♖xb8 26.♖a1 ♖b7 27.♖a6 g5 28.f4 gxf4 29.♔f3 is clearly better for White) 23.e5

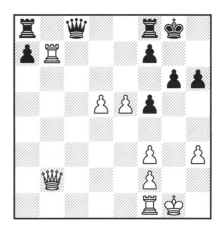

23...♕c4 24.♖d1 ♖ad8 25.d6 ♕f4 26.♕c3 a5 27.♖e1 (27.♕xa5 ♕xf3 28.♕d5 ♕xd5 29.♖xd5 ♖fe8± - Ftacnik) 27...♖b8 28.♖xb8 ♖xb8 29.d7 ♖d8 30.e6! ♕g5† (30...fxe6 31.♕c6+-) 31.♔f1 ♕e7 32.♕c6 ♔h7 33.♕c7 ♔g7 34.♕xd8 1–0 Lautier – Svidler, Tilburg 1998.

c) 14...e6!? is a natural enough move that has attracted little interest. Play might continue: 15.♖xb7 g5 16.♗g3 ♖d8 and now the only moves that have been played are 17.h3 and 17.♗c7, both of which drop the d4-pawn. Better is 17.d5, or 17.♖c7!? e.g. 17...a5 (17...♗xf3 18.♗xf3 ♗xd4 (18...♖xd4 19.♖c8† ♔h7 20.e5!+-) 19.e5+-) 18.♖c2 ♕a4 (18...♕a3 19.♘e5!) 19.♖c8±.

d) 14...b6 15.h3 ♗xf3 (15...♗d7 16.♖a1 ♕e6 17.♕d3±) 16.♗xf3 ♘d7 17.♗xe7± - Ftacnik.

e) 14...♘c6 15.d5

with the following possibilities:

e1) 15...♗xf3 16.♗xf3 ♘e5 17.♖xb7?! (17.♗xe7± may be stronger) 17...g5 (17...e6!)

18.♗g3 e6 19.♗h5 ♕a6 20.♖b4 (20.♕b1!?) 20...♖ad8 21.f4 gxf4 22.♗xf4 ♘d3 23.♖b3 ♘xf4 24.♖xf4 ♕a4?? (24...f5!) 25.♖g4+- ♔h8 26.♖xg7 ♕xe4 27.♖xf7 1–0 Dearing – Walker, Docklands Open 2000.

e2) 15...♘e5 16.♗xe7 ♖fe8 17.♖xb7 a5 18.♖e1 ♘xf3† 19.♗xf3 ♗c8 20.♖c7 ♗e5 21.d6 ♕e6 22.♕a4 ♗a6 23.♖d1 ♖eb8 24.♖c5 ♖b3 25.♖xe5 1–0 Kordts – Just, Fuerth 2000.

e3) 15...♖fd8 16.♖xb7 g5 17.♗g3 e6 (17... f5 18.♖c7!? fxe4 19.♖xc6 exf3 20.♗c4 ♕a3 21.♖e1 ♔h8 and now 22.♖e3?? ♕xe3 0–1 was Kozak – Kaufman, Olomouc 1999, so White should probably have played 22.♗e5!±) 18.♕c1!? (18.♗c7!?) 18...♘a5 (18...exd5!) 19.♖xf7!!

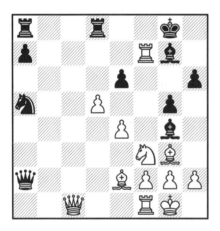

19...♕xe2 (19...♔xf7 20.♕c7† ♔g8 21.♗e5 ♗h8 22.♘xg5 hxg5 23.♗xg4+-) 20.♖xg7† ♔xg7 21.♕c7† ♔g6 22.♘e5† ♔f6 23.♕f7 mate. 1–0 Karason – Kjartansson, Reykjavik 2003.

15.d5 g5 16.♗g3 b6?!

This preserves Black's material advantage for the time being, but weakens Black on the light-squares and does nothing to generate counterplay or challenge White's central dominance. 16... e6!? 17.♗c7 ♖d7 (17...♖e8 18.d6 ♘d7 19.♖xb7 ♖ec8±) 18.d6 ♘a6 19.♗b5 ♖xc7 20.dxc7 ♘xc7 21.♕d7 is unclear according to Ftacnik. By way of improvement over the game Anand recommends 16...♘d7 17.♖xb7 (17.♖e1 ♘c5 (17...♗xf3

18.♗xf3 ♘e5 19.♖xb7 ♕a3∞) 18.♘xg5 ♗xe2 19.♖xe2 ♕a4∓) 17...♘c5 18.♖xe7 (18.♖b4 a5) 18...♗f6 19.♖c7 (19.♖xf7 ♔xf7 20.♘xg5†∞) 19...♘xe4 20.♗c4 ♕a5 which he assesses as unclear.

17.♖e1! ♗xf3

This turns out badly for Black, however it is clear that White is already comfortably in the driving seat:

a) 17...e6 18.♘xg5 ♗xe2 19.♖xe2 ♕a5 20.♘f3 (20.♘xf7!? ♔xf7 21.dxe6† ♔e8 22.♕b3±) 20... exd5 21.exd5 ♘c6 22.♖d2± - Ftacnik.

b) 17...♗c3? 18.♘e5! ♗xe1 (18...♗xe2 19.♖xe2 ♕a6 20.♖e3 ♗xe5 21.♖xe5 ♘d7 22.♗c3 b5± - Bellman) 19.♘xg4 ♗c3 20.♘xh6† ♔g7 21.♘f5† ♔f8 22.♗f1!± 1–0 Bellmann – Kratz, corr. 2000.

c) 17...♘d7 18.♘xg5! ♗xe2 19.♖xe2 ♕c4 20.♘f3± - Anand.

18.♗xf3 ♘d7 19.e5±/±

19...♖ac8 20.e6! fxe6

20...♘f6 21.exf7† ♔xf7 22.d6 exd6 23.♖a1 ♕c2 24.♖xa7†± - Anand.

21.♖xe6 ♘f6

Black concedes the e7-pawn, however attempts to preserve Black's material advantage quickly lead to catastrophe: Ftacnik notes the lines 21...♗f6 22.♖e2 (22.d6! Anand) 22...♕c4 23.d6 e6 24.♖xe6 ♗c5 25.♖e7± and 21...♕a3 22.d6 ♗f6 23.dxe7 ♗xe7 24.♗d6! ♗xd6 25.♖xd6+-. Anand points out that 21...&f8 22.&e2! &c4 23.d6 gives White a decisive advantage.

22.&xe7! &c2

22...&xd5 23.&e8†! (23.&e2 &a5 24.&d2 &c5 25.&e2 &h8 26.&bd1 is better for White according to Anand) 23...&f8 (23...&xe8 24.&xd5†+-) and now rather than 24.&xd5† &xd5 25.&xc8 &xd1† 26.&xd1 &f7 (intending 27...&c5) which Anand assesses as slightly better for White, Ftacnik proposes 24.&b5! &c3 25.&xd8 &xd8 26.&xd8 &a1† 27.&d1 &xd1† 28.&xd1 &xd1 29.&b8+-.

23.d6!±

23...&xd1† 24.&xd1 a5 25.h3! a4 26.&c7! &h8

Anand observes that 26...a3 27.&dc1! &b8 28.&a7 cuts out any counterplay that Black has based on advancing the a-pawn, and Ftacnik consolidates the assessment that White is winning by providing the following variation: 26...b5 27.&b1 (27.&xc8 &xc8 28.d7 &xd7 29.&xd7 b4 30.&d5†±) 27...&b8 28.d7 b4 29.&a7 &b5 30.&c6 &c5 31.&c7 &xd7 32.&xd7 &xd7 33.&d6 &d5 34.&xd7 a3 35.&xg7† &xg7 36.&xb4+-.

27.&dc1! &b8 28.&a7+- &d7

28...b5 29.d7 &xd7 30.&xb8 &xb8 31.&b1 &f8 32.&xb5 a3 33.&a8 &d6 34.&d5+- - Ftacnik.

29.&cc7 a3 30.&d5! b5 31.&xd7 &xd7 32.&xd7 b4 33.&b3 &a8 34.&b7 1–0

Anand demonstrates that White is winning with the following line: 34... a2 35.&xa2 &xa2 36.d7 &a1† 37.&h2 &f6 38.d8&† &xd8 39.&e5†.

Game 23 Conclusions: 14...&d8 is not as bad as many commentators have suggested, and notably Anand assesses the line with 16...&d7 as leading to unclear complications. Notwithstanding the fact that there are some unresolved issues here, I think we should take heed of GM practice: although this game was one of the first to deal with 14.&h4 (having been played in 1998), nobody has played 14...&d8 since, which seems to suggest that, even with improvements over Black's play in our illustrative game, White should be better in this line.

Game 24
Shulman – Votava
Pardubice 1999

1.d4 &f6 2.c4 g6 3.&c3 d5 4.cxd5 &xd5 5.e4 &xc3 6.bxc3 &g7 7.&f3 c5 8.&b1 0–0 9.&e2 cxd4 10.cxd4 &a5† 11.&d2 &xa2 12.0–0 &g4 13.&g5 h6 14.&h4 g5 15.&g3 &c6

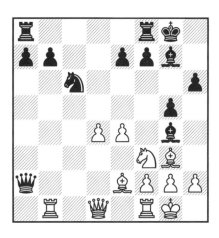

With 15...&c6 Black lashes out at White's centre immediately, however provoking White into advancing his powerful pawn centre is a highly risky strategy.

16.d5 ⅾad8!

Obvious but also best; the alternatives have proved favourable for White in practice:

a) 16...♘a5 17.ⅾe1 (17.e5 b6 18.ⅾa1 ♕b2 (18...♕b3 19.♕d4 ♗f5 20.♘d2 ♕c2 21.♗a6 ♕c7 22.f4 ♕d7 23.fxg5 hxg5 was at least slightly better for White in Dobrin – Haika, e-mail 2000) 19.ⅾb1 ♕a2 20.ⅾb4 ♗h5 was a bit better for White in Sapis – Touzane, Legnica 1994.)

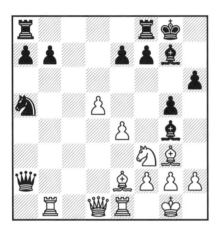

17...♗c3 (17...ⅾfc8 18.♘e5 ♗xe2 19.ⅾxe2 ♕a3 was Surender – Kulczycki, e-mail 2001, and now instead of 20.♘g4 h5, which was good for Black, White could have maintained a slight edge with 20.ⅾe3 ♗c3 21.ⅾxc3 ♕xc3 22.ⅾc1 ♕b4 23.♕f3) 18.♘e5! ♗xe5 (18...♗xe1 19.♘xg4 ♗c3 20.♘xh6† ♚h7 21.♘f5 is unclear, but perhaps a little better for White.) 19.♗xe5 ♗xe2 20.ⅾxe2 ♕c4 21.ⅾe3 f6 22.♗c3 b6 23.♕h5 ♚g7 24.h4 ⅾh8 25.e5 1–0 Jakubowski – Janaszak, Poland 2001.

b) 16...♗xf3 17.♗xf3 ♘d4 18.ⅾxb7 e6 19.♗h5 exd5 20.♗d6 (20.ⅾd7!?±) 20...dxe4 21.♗xf8 ⅾxf8 22.♕b1 ♘e2† 23.♗xe2 ♕xe2 as in Kuemin – Lupulescu, Patras 2001, was certainly better for White at this stage, although Black actually went on to win.

c) 16...ⅾfd8 17.ⅾxb7 e6 18.♕c1!? transposes to Karason – Kjartansson, Reykjavik 2003, which was considered in Game 23 under the notes to Black's 14th move alternatives.

17.ⅾxb7 f5!

This was originally suggested by GM Alex Chernin in *Informant 56* as an improvement over his game with GM Jozsef Horvath. That earlier encounter continued 17...e6 18.♗c7! exd5 19.♗xd8 dxe4 20.♗e7 (20.♗c7!?±) 20...ⅾe8 (Ftacnik suggests that 20...♘xe7 21.ⅾxe7 (21.♘d4!?) 21...exf3 22.♗xf3 ♗xf3 23.♕xf3 a5! may be an improvement, when Black has definite counterplay) and now instead of 21.♗c5 (as in Chernin – J. Horvath, Hungarian Championship 1992) Chernin suggests that he should have played 21.♗b5! exf3 22.♗xc6 fxg2 23.♗xe8! ♗xd1 24.ⅾxd1 ♕e2 25.ⅾbd7! ♗e5 26.♗c5+–.

18.ⅾc7!

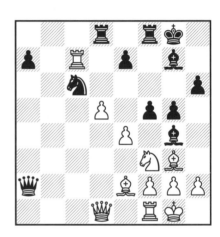

The text would appear to be White's best, however alternatives have also been tried:

a) 18.♗c7 fxe4! 19.♗xd8 exf3 20.gxf3 ♘xd8∓ - Se. Ivanov, *Informant 75*.

b) 18.♗d3 fxe4 (18...♘d4!?) 19.♗xe4 ♗f5 20.♕b1 ♕xb1 21.ⅾxb1 ♗xb1 22.dxc6 ♗e4= - Se. Ivanov, *Informant 75*.

c) In *Understanding the Grünfeld*, Jonathan Rowson suggests that 18.dxc6 is best, when 18...ⅾxd1 19.♗xd1 ♕a6 20.exf5 ♕xc6 21.ⅾxa7 ♗xf5 22.ⅾxe7 gives White "a slight but enduring advantage". However Black's play can be improved by the obvious 21...♕c5, protecting the e7-pawn, when f5 will be rounded up in any case. Alternatively Seipel – Ivanon, corr. 2000 continued 21...♗f6!? 22.♗b3† ♔g7 23.♖e1?! ♗xf5 (23...♗xf3!?) 24.♗e5 ♕c5 25.♗xf6† ♔xf6 with a good position for Black. Instead the Greek GM Stelios Halkias has tried 20.♗b3† ♔h8 21.exf5 when 21...♗xf3 22.gxf3 ♕xc6 23.♖xe7 ♕xf3 24.♗c2 h5 25.♗e4 ♕c3 was Halkias – Fontaine, Greece 1999. The game eventually ended in a draw, although it was by no means clear that White's compensation was sufficient at this stage.

d) 18.♕e1 ♗xf3 19.♗xf3 ♘d4 20.♗h5 (20.exf5 ♘xf3† 21.gxf3 ♕xd5 22.♖xa7 ♖xf5= –A.Chernin, *Informant 56*) and now rather than 20...f4, as in Se. Ivanov – Pierrot, Cappelle la Grande 1999, Sergey Ivanov suggests in *Informant 75* that Black's best is 20...♘c2! 21.♕e2 f4 22.♗xf4 ♖xf4 (22...gxf4?! 23.♖xe7!) 23.g3 ♖ff8 24.♖c1 (It may be better to play 24.♖xe7 ♕a4 25.♕d3 ♘d4 26.♖b1 ♖d7 27.♖e8 (27.♘d1!?) 27...♕a5 28.♖xf8† ♔xf8 29.♖b8† ♔e7 30.♖e8† ♔d6 31.f4 gxf4 32.gxf4 ♔e7 33.e5† ♗xe5!? 34.♕g6† (34. fxe5!? ♕xe5 35.♕g6† ♔xd5∞) 34...♕c5 35.♖xe7 ♕e1† 36.♔g2 ♕d2† 37.♔h3 ♕xf4 38.♕g1 ½–½ Jenkinson – Juradowitch, corr. 1999. Although Black managed to hold things together here, I wouldn't be surprised if White had a significant improvement somewhere.) 24...♖c8 25.♗g4 ♖c3 (25...♕c4!?) 26.♖xe7 ♘e3!∓.

18...fxe4 19.♖xc6 exf3 20.♗c4!

20.gxf3 ♗h3 (20...♗h5!? may be better) 21.♗c4 ♕a3 22.♖e1 ♔h8 is a line given by Shulman and Kapengut, the conclusion being that White's chances of an advantage are less clear than those obtained under the game continuation.

20...♕a3!

20...♕b2 21.♖e1 e6 22.d6±.

21.♖e1 ♔h8

21...♔h7 22.d6 exd6 23.♗xd6 (23.♖c7 ♖fe8 24.♖xe8 ♖xe8 25.♗xd6†) 23...♖xd6 24.♖xd6 fxg2 25.♕d3† ♕xd3 26.♗xd3† ♔h8 27.♔xg2± - Shulman & Kapengut.

22.♖xh6†!? ♗xh6 23.♕d4† ♗g7

Also bad is 23...♖f6, e.g. 24.♗e5 ♗g7 25.♗xf6!? (Shulman and Kapengut give 25.♕xg4 ♕b4 26.♖d1 (26.♖c1!?± may be stronger) 26...♗f7

27.d6 as their main recommendation, when they assert that it is difficult for Black to defend against White's threats. This may be so, but I am more concerned about simply 27...♖xe5 when White is a rook down and the f7-rook is immune from capture because the c4-bishop is pinned to White's queen, and 28.♕h5† ♖h7 just seems to be losing for White.) 25...♗xf6 26.♕xg4 ♕c3 27.♕e4 fxg2? 28.♖e3+-.

24.♕xg4 ♖c8 25.♕h3† ♔g8 26.♕e6† ♔h8 27.♕h3† ♔g8 28.♕e6† ♔h8 29.d6 ♖xc4

30.dxe7?

An unfortunate error that lets the full point slip from White's grasp. Undeniably superior was 30.♗e5! threatening 31.♕h6† and 32.♕xg7 mate. Black must then fight to save his neck: 30...♔h7 (Alternatively 30...♗xe5 31.♕xe5† ♔h7 32.♕xe7† ♔g8 33.♕xg5† ♔h8 34.♕e5† ♔h7 35.♕h5† ♔g8 36.♕d5† sees White recovering the rook he invested earlier, and heading for an endgame where an extra pawn and the open position of the black king should yield excellent prospects.) 31.♗xg7 ♔xg7 32.♕xe7†! ♔f7 33.♕xg5† ♔h7 34.♕h5† ♔g7 35.♕e5† ♔g8 (35...♔h7 36.d7 ♕f8 37.♕h5† ♔g8 38.♕g5† ♖g7 39.♕d5†+-) 36.♕e8† ♔g7 37.d7 when, despite being a rook down, White's advantage appears decisive. After the text White's winning chances are minimal.

30...♖c1! 31.♕h3† ♔g8 32.♕e6† ♔h8

33.exf8♕†

33.e8♕?! ♖xe8 34.♕xe8† ♔h7 35.♕e4†
♔h8=.

33...♗xf8 34.gxf3

34.♗e5† ♔h7 35.♕f7† ♔h6 36.♕f6† ♔h7=.

**34...♖xe1† 35.♕xe1 ♕xf3 36.♕e5† ♔g8
37.♕xg5† ♔f7 38.♕a5 ♕d1† 39.♔g2 ♕d4
40.h4 ♗g7 41.f3 ♕b6 42.♕a2†?! ♗e7= 43.♕d5
a6 44.h5 ♕e6 45.♕d2 ♔f7 46.♗f4 ♗e5 47.♗g5
♗f6 48.♗e3 ♕e5 49.♕a2† ♕e6 50.♕a3 ♕c4
51.♕d6 ♕b5 52.♕c7† ♗e7 53.♕f4† ♗f6
54.♕c7† ♗e7 55.♕f4† ♗f6 56.h6 ♕e2† 57.♗f2
♕e5 58.♕c4† ♔g6 59.♕xa6 ♔xh6 60.♗h4
♔g7 61.♗xf6† ♕xf6 ½–½**

Game 24 Conclusions: Black can put up a tough
defence with 14.♗h4 g5 15.♗g3 ♘c6 16.d5
♖ad8! 17.♖xb7 f5!, however it seems that with
exact play White can secure an advantage via
18.♖c7! fxe4 19.♖xc6 exf3 20.♗c4! when Black
is definitely forced onto the defensive.

Game 25
C. Horvath – Groszpeter
Hungary 2000

**1.d4 ♘f6 2.c4 g6 3.♘c3 d5 4.cxd5 ♘xd5 5.e4
♘xc3 6.bxc3 ♗g7 7.♘f3 c5 8.♖b1 0–0 9.♗e2
cxd4 10.cxd4 ♕a5† 11.♗d2 ♕xa2 12.0–0 ♗g4
13.♗g5 h6 14.♗h4 a5!?**

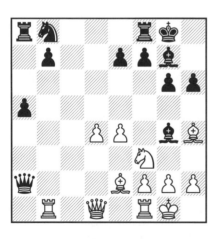

This early pawn lunge echoes the themes that
we considered in Chapter 1, however in this
position Black is better developed: the g4-bishop
is ready to trade on f3 at an opportune moment,
and the inclusion of the pawn move h7-h6 gives
the black king a little more breathing room, and
introduces the possibility of g6-g5, discontinuing
the h4-bishop's pressure on e7.

15.♖xb7 g5 16.♗g3 a4 17.♖c7!

Black has scored exceedingly well with
14...a5, and only this subtle move has had any
real success in this variation. The main alternative
is 17.h4!? however this has been heavily explored
and has yet to reveal a true challenge to Black's
set-up:

After 17.h4 Black has three options, of which
only the third seems to guarantee full equality:

a) 17...gxh4 18.♗xh4 e5 19.d5±.

b) 17...a3 18.hxg5 hxg5 with two possibilities:

b1) 19.♖b5 ♘c6 (19...f6 20.♕d3 ♖c8 21.♖fb1
♘d7 22.♗d1±) 20.♖xg5 ♗xf3 21.gxf3! ♕b2
22.♗c4!

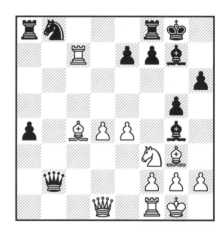

Black now has a choice of three moves, all of
which merit consideration:

b11) Ivan Sokolov observes that 22...a2!? is
bad on account of 23...♕xa1 24.♖xa1 ♘xd4
25.♔g2, however Ftacnik pointed out that
Black can achieve equality with 23.♕a1 ♕c2
24.♗d5 (24.d5 f6 25.♖c1 ♕xc1† 26.♕xc1 a1♕

27.dxc6† ♔h7–+) 24...♖fc8 25.♗e6!! (25.♗xc6
♖xc6 26.♖xg7† ♔xg7 27.d5† ♖f6 28.♗e5 ♕e2
29.♕d1 ♕xd1 30.♖xd1 ♗g6 31.♗xf6 ♗xf6∓)
25...♔f8 26.♖xg7 fxe6 27.d5 exd5 28.exd5 ♘d4
29.♕xd4 a1♕ 30.♖xa1 ♖xa1† 31.♔xa1 ♕c1†
32.♕xc1 ♖xc1† 33.♔g2 ♖xg7=.

b12) Instead of 22...a2 Ivan Sokolov proposes
that Black's best is 22...♕xd4! when 23.♕c1
(23.♕xd4 ♘xd4 24.♔g2 e6!∓) 23...♖a5 24.♖g4!
(24.♗d5 e6 25.♕xc6 exd5 26.♗e5 ♕xe5 27.♖xe5
♗xe5 28.f4!=) 24...♘e5! 25.♖xg7† ♔xg7
26.♕g5† ♘g6 27.♕xa5 ♕xc4 28.♕xa3 e5=.

b13) The only move that has been tested in
practice is 22...♖fd8, after which play continued
23.f4! ♖xd4! (23...♕xd4 24.♕g4 ♔f8 25.e5±)
24.♗xf7†!!

This sacrifice is absolutely essential if White is
to fight for the advantage. Instead 24.♕g4? ♖xc4
25.e5 ♕xe5 26.fxe5 ♖xg4 27.♖xg4 a2 28.♖a1 f5
promises White nothing but trouble.

Returning to the position after 24.♗xf7†!!,
play continued 24...♔xf7 25.♕h5† ♔g8
(25...♔f8 26.♖f5† ♗f6 27.♕h8† ♔f7 28.♕xa8+-)
26.e5 ♕b3 27.♕g6 ♕f7 28.♕xc6 ♖ad8, which
was Lautier – I. Sokolov, Malmö 1998. Now,
instead of 29.♕a6?!, Ftacnik proposes that
Lautier should have tried 29.f5!? a2 (29...♖d1
30.♖xd1 ♖xd1† 31.♔h2 a2 32.♕a8† ♔h7 33
e6+-) 30.f6 ♖d1 31.♖xg7† ♕xg7 32.♕c4† e6

(32...♕f7 33.♕g4†+-) 33.♕xe6† ♔h7 34.♕xa2
♖xf1† 35.♔xf1 ♕g6 when White retains a clear
advantage.

b2) 19.♖c7!

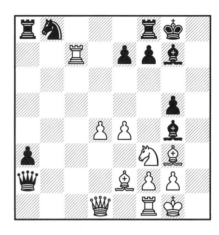

With this move Gelfand takes control of the
c-file threatening 20.♗c4, or 20.♖c2 hitting the
black queen and defending the e2-bishop, so that
White can follow up with 21.♘xg5, winning
a pawn and leaving Black's kingside under
serious pressure. Three moves have now been
considered:

b21) 19...♘d7 20.e5! (an excellent move, at
once circumventing the influence and mobility of
both the d7-knight and the g7-bishop) 20...♕b2
(20...♖fc8 21.♗c4 ♕xc4 (21...♕b2 22.♗xf7†
♔h8 23.♖xc8† ♖xc8 24.♕d3±) 22.♖xc4 ♖xc4
23.♕b3 ♖aa4 24.♘xg5±) 21.♖c2 ♕b3 22.♘xg5
a2! 23.♖xa2 ♕xd1 24.♖xd1 ♖xa2 25.♗xg4
♘b6±.

b22) 19...♕b2 20.♖c2 ♕b6 (In his annotations
for Chessbase Magazine Gelfand explains that
during the game he thought the critical test
of White's idea to be 20...♕b3 21.♘xg5 a2
22.♖xa2 ♕xd1 23.♖xd1 ♖xa2 24.♗xg4±. White
has a bishop and two pawns for the exchange,
and can consider plans to create an advantage
by advancing the d-pawn or using the activity
of the minor pieces to create pressure against the
black king. Black, for his part, should attempt

to simplify the position by exchanging a pair of rooks, thereby reducing White's initiative.) 21.♘xg5 ♕xd4 (21...♗xe2 22.♕xe2 ♘d7 23.e5 ♖a4 24.e6 is clearly better for White, and 21... a2? 22.♖xa2 ♖xa2 23.♗xg4 ♗xd4 24.♗e6! fxe6 25.♕h5 ♖fxf2 26.♕g6† is winning) 22.♕xd4 ♗xd4 23.♗xg4 a2 24.♖xa2 ♖xa2 25.♘e6 ♘c6 26.♘xf8 ♔xf8♭. This endgame gives Black reasonable drawing chances, however White has the bishop pair and an extra pawn, so there is plenty of potential to make Black suffer!

b23) 19...♘a6? 20.♖xe7 ♕b2 21.♘c4 ♕b4 (21...♗f6 22.♖xf7 ♖xf7 23.e5! ♗e7 24.♗xf7† ♔xf7 25.♘g5†, and 21...a2 22.♖xf7 ♖xf7 23.♗xf7† ♔xf7 24.♘xg5† are both losing for Black) 22.♗xf7† ♔h8 (22...♖xf7 23.♖xf7 ♗xd4 24.♗e5!! ♗xe5 25.♕d5+-) 23.♖d7!!

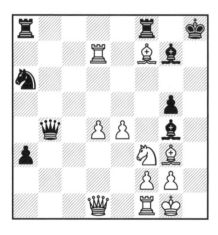

23...♗xd7 (23...♗f6 24.♗d5 24...♗xd7 25.♘xg5 is losing for Black, as is 23...♕b5 24.♖d5! and 23...a2 24.♗xa2 ♖xf3 (24...♗xd7 25.♘xg5) 25.gxf3 ♗xd7 26.♔g2 ♗xd4 27.♖h1† ♔g7 28.♗e5†) 24.♘xg5 ♕b6 25.♗e6! ♕xe6 26.♘xe6 ♗xe6 27.♗e5 was clearly better for White, if not winning, in Gelfand – Shirov, Poland 1998. The comments to this game are based on Gelfand and Huzman's annotations for *Informant 73* and *Chessbase Magazine 67*.

c) 17...♘c6! 18.hxg5 hxg5 19.d5 (19.e5?! ♖ad8 leaves d4 weak) 19...♗xf3 20.♗xf3 ♘d4

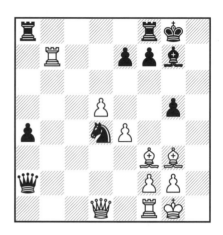

21.d6 (Krasenkow notes the variations 21.♗g4 a3 22.♖xe7 ♕b2∓, and 21.e5?! ♘xf3† (21...♕c4!? 22.♖xe7 a3 has the potential to be quite dangerous for White) 22.♕xf3 a3 23.♖xe7 ♕b2! 24.♕e3 a2 25.♖a7 ♖xa7 26.♕xa7 ♖c8! 27.e6 fxe6 28.♕d7 ♖f8 29.♕xe6† ♔h7 30.♕h3† ♔g6–+) 21...e5 22.d7? (22.♖e7 is met by 22...♕b2 intending 23...a3, however Stohl (in *Chessbase Magazine 69*) suggests that 22.♗g4! may be an improvement, e.g. 23...a3 (22...♕c4 23.♕c1 ♕xc1 24.♖xc1 a3 25.♖a1↑) 23.♕c1 ♕c2 24.♕xg5 ♕xe4 25.♖e7 a2! 26.♗xe5 ♕xe5 27.♖xe5 a1♕ 28.♖xa1 ♖xa1† 29.♔h2 f6 30.♕g6 fxe5 31.♗e6† ♘xe6 32.♕xe6† ♔h7 33.♕h3† ♗h6 34.♕d3† ♔g7 35.♕c3! with a probable draw as Black will not be able to hold onto his e-pawn) 22...♕e6 23.♗g4 ♕c6 24.♖b1 (24.♕b1 a3 25.♖c1 a2–+) 24...♕xe4 25.♖e1 ♕d5 was Shipov – I. Sokolov, Hastings 1999, and now White played 26.♗f5! seizing control of the important f5-square (otherwise Black would have played f7-f5 himself). Nevertheless, White's position is at least slightly worse at this stage and Black went on to win a powerful game.

Before returning to the present game, note that 17.♖xe7? ♘c6 is good for Black because the d4-pawn drops.

Returning to the position after 17.♖c7, we can see that White is attempting to implement a similar idea to the one introduced by Boris

Gelfand after 17.h4 a3 18.hxg5 hxg5 19.♖c7, but with the important refinement that Black is prevented from playing 17...♘c6.

Nevertheless, although Black loses the chance to pressurise White's centre with 17...♘c6, White in turn loses the opportunity to immediately undermine Black's kingside with the h2-h4xg5 ideas. These plans can still be implemented but are less effective where Black has an extra move with which to organise his defences.

17...♕b2!

This is definitely Black's best; the alternatives have invariably left Black in difficulties:

a) 17...a3 18.h3 ♗h5 19.♗c4 ♕b2 20.♗d5

20...♖a5? (20...♗xf3 transposes to the game, however Krasenkow suggested that 20...♖a6 may be better, as this would enhance Black's control of the c6-square, and possibly provide Black with a subsequent opportunity to develop the b8-knight on c6.) 21.♖b7 ♖b5 22.♖xe7 ♖c8 (Krasenkow notes the important point that if Black's rook had been developed to a6 instead of a5, Black would now be able to play 22...♘c6 immediately, without the need for 22...♖c8.) 23.♖a7 ♘c6 24.♗xc6 ♖xc6 25.♖a8† ♔h7 26.d5 was Vera – Herrera, Las Tunas 2001, and now 26...♖cb6? gave Black a lost position after 27.♘xg5† ♔g6 28.♘f3 ♔h7 29.d6, however Krasenkow (in *Chessbase Magazine 83*) proposes

that Black can fight on with 26...♖c3 27.♘xg5† (27.d6 ♗xf3 28.gxf3 ♖b8) 27...♔g6 28.♘f3 ♗xf3 29.gxf3 ♖bb3 when the position remains tense and complicated.

b) 17...♕b3 18.♕xb3 axb3 19.♖b1 b2 (19...♖c8 20.♖xc8† ♗xc8 21.h3! is slightly better for White according to Sherbakov, on account of the weak b3-pawn.) 20.♖xb2 ♖a1† 21.♗f1 ♗xf3 22.gxf3 ♗xd4 23.♖b5 ♖a2 24.♗c4 ♖b2 25.♖f5 ♖b4 26.♔g2±/± Sherbakov – Vokarev, Novgorod Open 1999. White's bishop pair and superior king position provide an enduring initiative and the b8-knight has yet to establish a way to enter the game.

18.♗c4

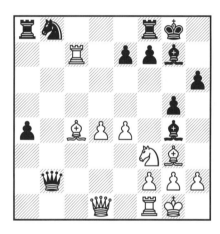

18...a3

The text is very forcing, however Black has also managed to establish equality with 18...♘d7 e.g. 19.♗d5 ♖ad8 (19...♖ac8!? 20.♕xa4 (20.♖b7 ♕a3) 20...♘b6 21.♕b3 ♕xb3 22.♗xb3 ♗xf3 23.gxf3 ♖xc7 24.♗xc7 ♖xd4= - Krasenkow) 20.♕xa4 (20.♖b7 ♗xf3 21.♖xb2 ♗xd1 22.♖xd1 e6 23.♗c6 ♘c5 gives Black counterplay) 20...♗xf3 21.gxf3 (Krasenkow notes that 21.♖xd7?! ♖xd7 22.♕xd7 ♗e2 23.♖e1 e6 24.♗b7 ♗xd4 leaves White in trouble as the f2-square is weak and the b7-bishop is a little short of squares.) 21...♕xd4 22.♕xd4 ♗xd4 23.♖d1 e5 24.♔g2 ♘f6= Solozhenkin – Tseitlin, 15th ECC Final 1999. Finally, note that winning a pawn with 18...♗xf3 19.♕xf3 ♖xd4 20.♖d1 gives White a strong initiative because of the activity of all his pieces.

19.♗d5

19.♖xe7? allows 19...♘c6, developing Black's last piece and hitting the e7-rook and the vulnerable d4-pawn.

19...♗xf3! 20.gxf3

The text is forced as 20.♕xf3? would have allowed 20...a2, when White will have to forfeit material in order to prevent Black gaining a second queen.

20...♖a6 21.♖b7 ♕xd4 22.♕xd4

22.♕b3? a2 and 22.♕c2?! e6 both appear preferable for Black.

22...♗xd4 23.♗xb8 a2 24.♗xa2 ♖xa2

½–½

Game 25 Conclusions: The variations discussed in Game 25 illustrate the 14.♗h4 variation at its most complicated. The lines here are dangerous for both sides, however it seems that at present best play should lead to a draw. The critical points to remember are 14...a5!? 15.♖xb7 g5 16.♗g3 a4 and now 17.h4 should be met by 17...♘c6!, whereas the more modern 17.♖c7! should be met by 17...♕b2!, followed by a rapid advance of the a-pawn. It seems that in 14...a5! Black has discovered a solution to his problems against 14.♗h4 for the time being, and it is therefore quite likely that this line is responsible for the diminished popularity of the 14.♗h4 system.

Game 26
Se. Ivanov – Polovodin
St Petersburg 1997

1.d4 ♘f6 2.c4 g6 3.♘c3 d5 4.cxd5 ♘xd5 5.e4 ♘xc3 6.bxc3 ♗g7 7.♘f3 c5 8.♖b1 0–0 9.♗e2 cxd4 10.cxd4 ♕a5† 11.♗d2 ♕xa2 12.0–0 ♗g4 13.♗g5 h6 14.♗e3!?

When the theory surrounding 12...♗g4 started developing this surprising retreat rapidly emerged as White's main challenge to Black's set-up. White's idea is that, by provoking h7-h6,

Black's kingside has been weakened, and White may be able to win a vital tempo at a later stage with ♕c1/d2, coordinating with the e3-bishop to threaten the h6-pawn. Initially Black faced some serious problems in this line, however eventually solutions were found and attention switched to 14.♗h4!? and the notion of omitting 13.♗g5 entirely in favour of 13.♗e3!? even gained some popularity. At the present time 14.♗e3 seems to be back in vogue, and Black is once again searching for a suitable route to equality.

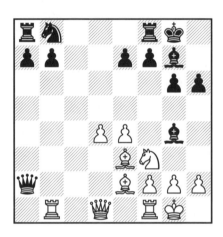

14...b6

14...♘c6 is the mainline, and this is examined in Games 27-29. The text experienced a brief surge of popularity in the early nineties, but is now considered insufficiently challenging.

15.♕d3!?

Alternatives have proved less successful for White:

a) 15.h3 ♗xf3 16.♗xf3 e5! 17.d5 (17.dxe5 ♘c6) 17...♘d7 was fine for Black in M. Gurevich – Ivanchuk, Manila 1990.

b) 15.♖a1 ♕b2 (15...♕e6?! 16.h3 ♗xf3 17.♗xf3 ♘d7 18.e5 ♖ad8 19.♕b1 a5 20.♕b5 was clearly better for White in Solozhenkin – Polovodin, Russia 1992, according to Solozhenkin (*Informant 54*)) 16.♖b1 (In *Informant 54* Solozhenkin notes the line 16.♕d3 ♕b4 17.h3 ♗d7 18.♖fb1 ♕d6 19.♕d2 when White holds the initiative.) 16...♕a2 17.♖a1 ♕b2 18.♕d3 ♕b4 19.♖fb1 ♕d6

20.e5 (20.h3 ♗xf3 21.♗xf3 e5 22.d5 ♘c6! 23.♕d2 ♘d4∓) 20...♕d7! 21.♕d2?! (21.♕e4 ♗f5 22.♕xa8 ♘c6 23.♕xf8† ♗xf8 is clearly better for Black, however 21.♖xb6! ♘c6 22.♖b5 ♖ab8 would have kept things balanced.) 21...♘c6! gave Black an excellent position in Vaisser – Khenkin, Tel Aviv 1992. The comments here are based on Khenkin's annotations for *Informant 55*.

15...♘d7

a) 15...♖c8 16.h3 ♗xf3 17.♗xf3 e5 18.d5∞ - Se. Ivanov.

b) 15...♗xf3 16.♗xf3 e5 17.d5 (17.♖a1 ♕e6 18.d5 also gives White sufficient compensation) 17...♕a6 18.♕d2∞ - Se. Ivanov.

c) 15...♖d8!? 16.♖fc1 ♘d7 17.♖a1 (17.♕a6 ♕xa6 18.♗xa6∞ - Se. Ivanov) 17...♕e6 is unclear according to Ftacnik.

d) 15...♘c6 16.♖a1 ♕e6 17.d5 ♘b4 18.dxe6 ♘xd3 19.♗xd3 ♗xa1 20.♖xa1 ♗xf3 21.gxf3 fxe6 22.e5± - Ftacnik.

16.h3 ♗xf3 17.♗xf3

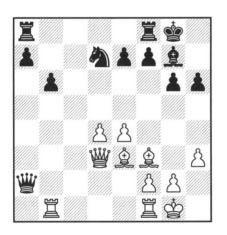

17...e5?!

Sergey Ivanov considers the text to be inaccurate, and instead proposes that Black should try 17...♖fd8 18.♕b5 (18.♖a1 ♕e6 19.♕b5 is similar according to Ftacnik) 18...a6 19.♕b4 when the position remains unclear, but White has compensation that is typical of many positions in the 8.♖b1 lines.

18.♖a1!

The immediate 18.d5 allows 18...♘c5! 19.♕b5 ♕a4 20.♗xc5 ♕xb5 21.♖xb5 bxc5 22.♖xc5 ♖fc8 23.♖xc8† ♖xc8 24.♖a1 ♖c7 which was fine for Black in Trisic – Leko, Dortmund 1992.

18...♕e6 19.d5 ♕d6

19...♕e7 20.♖fc1 ♘c5 21.♗xc5 bxc5 22.d6 is better for White according to Se. Ivanov.

20.♖fc1

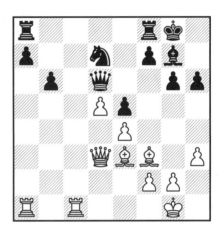

20...♘c5

The text allows White to recover his sacrificed pawn with a definite positional advantage, however White was threatening an invasion on the c-file via 21.♖c6, and Ftacnik notes the following variations, which illustrate that it is by no means easy for Black to wrest control of the c-file: 20...♖fc8 21.♖xc8† ♖xc8 22.♖xa7, or 20...♖fd8!? 21.♖c6 ♕b8 22.♕c4. In either case White remains very much in control of the position and retains a definite edge.

21.♗xc5 bxc5 22.♖a6 ♕d7 23.♖xc5± h5

23...♖fc8? 24.♗g4+−.

24.♗d1!

An excellent move. The bishop was achieving nothing on f3, so Ivanov redirects it to the c6-square via a4. Once the light-squared bishop reaches c6 not only will it dislodge the a8-rook, weakening Black's protection of the a7-pawn, but it will also support the advance of White's d-pawn.

24...♖fc8 25.♗a4 ♕d8 26.♖xc8!? ♖xc8 27.d6!

27.♖xa7?! ♕b6 complicates matters unnecessarily.

27...♕g5 28.g3 h4 29.d7 ♖d8 30.♖xa7 hxg3 31.fxg3 ♕c1† 32.♔g2 ♕b2† 33.♕c2! ♕d4

33...♕xc2†? 34.♗xc2 ♗f6 35.h4 ♔f8 36.♔h3 ♔e7 37.♗a4+-. White will advance the kingside pawns, creating a second weakness for Black to deal with.

34.♖c7 ♗f6 35.h4 ♔g7 36.♖c8 ♕e3 37.♗c6 g5!? 38.hxg5 ♗xg5 39.♕d1 ♗e7 40.♕g4† ♕g5 41.♕xg5† ♗xg5 42.♔f3 ♗e7 43.♔e3 ♔f6 44.♔d3 ♗e6 45.♔c4 ♗g5 46.♔b5 ♗e7 47.♔b6 ♗d2 48.♗a4 ♗e1 49.g4 ♗d2 50.♔c5 ♗e3† 51 ♔d5 ♗d4?

This loses; after 51...♗f4 52 ♗b5 (52.♖c3 ♖h8!) 52...♗h2! White remains clearly better of course, but Black would have some chances of holding on.

52 ♗b5 ♗b2 53.♖c2 ♗d4 54.♖h2 ♖g8 55.♖h7 ♗b6 56.g5! ♗a5 57 ♗a4 ♗c7 58 ♔c6 ♗d8 59 ♔b7 ♗a5 60 ♗c6 ♖xg5 61.♖h8+- f5 62.♖e8† ♔d6 63.♖a8 ♗c7 64 ♗a4!

1–0

Black resigned as 64...fxe4 65.♖a6† ♔e7 66 ♔xc7 decides matters beyond any point of contention.

Game 26 Conclusions: After 14.♗e3!? Black cannot afford to take time out to consolidate his material lead with 14...b6. Such indulgences weaken the queenside light-squares irreparably and also give White time to generate a powerful initiative via, e.g. 15.♕d3!? ♘d7 16.h3 ♗xf3 17.♗xf3. If Black is going to secure appropriate counterplay in this variation then he has no choice but to accelerate his development and immediately enhance the pressure on White's pawn centre. This strategy is examined in our next game.

Game 27
Khalifman – Leko
Linares 2000

1.d4 ♘f6 2 ♘f3 g6 3.c4 ♗g7 4 ♘c3 d5 5.cxd5 ♘xd5 6.e4 ♘xc3 7.bxc3 c5 8.♖b1 0–0 9.♗e2

cxd4 10.cxd4 ♕a5† 11.♗d2 ♕xa2 12 0–0 ♗g4 13.♗g5 h6 14.♗e3 ♘c6!

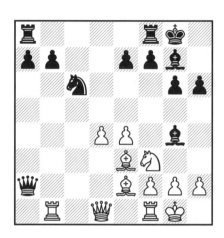

15.d5!

This is definitely White's most challenging approach. The alternatives should not give Black too many problems:

a) Rowson notes that 15.h3 is bad on account of 15...♗xf3 16.♗xf3 ♗xd4! 17.♗xd4 ♖fd8 when 18.♖a1 ♕c4 19.♖a4 ♘b4 ensures that Black will recover his piece with a pawn or two extra in the bank.

b) 15.♖xb7 is more tricky, but can be neutralized with careful play. 15...♖ab8 16.♖xb8 ♖xb8 17.h3 ♗d7! 18.d5 (18.♗d3 ♘b4 19.♕b1 a5 20.♕xa2 ♘xa2 21.♗d2 ♘b4 22.♖b1 e6 23.♘e5 ♗e8 24.♗f1 ♗f8 25.d5 exd5 26.exd5 ♖c8 27.♘c4 ♘xd5 28.♗xa5 ½–½ gave Black no problems in San Segundo Carrillo – Azmaiparashvili, Madrid 1996) 18...♘e5! 19.♗f4 (19.♘xe5 ♗xe5 20.f4 (20.♗xh6 gives Black full compensation for the pawn according to Gelfand, e.g. 20...♗a4 (20...a5!?⩲) 21.♕e1 ♗b2 22.♗d3∞) 20...♗b2! 21.fxe5 (21.♗f3 ♗b5 22.♖e1 ♗c3 23.♗c1 ♗a4 24.♖xb2 ♗xd1 25.♗xc3 ♗xf3 26.gxf3∓ -Bandza, *Informant* 69) 21...♖xe2 22.♖f2 ♖xf2 23.♗xf2 ♕c4! 24.♗xa7 ♕xe4 25.♕d4 ♕xd4† 26.♗xd4 ♗b5 ½–½ Bandza – Berggreen, corr. 1996) 19...♕b2! 20.♕c1 g5!=. This excellent move enables Black to equalise completely by seizing control of the dark squares. 21.♗xe5 ♗xe5 22.♘xe5 ♕xe5 23.♕a1 ♖b2 24.♕xa7 ♖xe2 25.♕xd7 ♖xe4 26.♖d1 ♔g7 27.g3 h5 28.d6 ♖e1† ½–½ Gelfand – J. Polgar, Novgorod 1996.

15...♘e5

15...♘a5 is considered in Game 28, and 15...♗xf3 in Game 29. However Black does have two other obvious moves that should at least be considered:

a) 15...♖ad8 16.♖xb7 e6 17.♖c7! exd5? 18.♖xc6 ♗xf3 19.gxf3 dxe4 20.♕c2 ♕xc2 21.♖xc2 exf3 22.♗xf3+- Haba – Novotny, Czech Republic 1997.

b) 15...♖fd8 16.♖xb7 e6 17.♖c7 ♗xf3 18.♗xf3! (18.gxf3 ♘b4 19.♗c4 ♕b2 20.♖xa7 ♖xa7 21.♗xa7 exd5 22.exd5 ♕e5 23.♕b3 ♘xd5 (23...♕g5† 24.♔h1 ♕f4!? intending 25...♗e5 may be better) 24.♖d1 ♕g5† 25.♔f1 ♘f4 26.♖xd8† ♕xd8 27.♗xf7† ♔h7 was fine for Black in van Wely – Ivanchuk, Frankfurt 2000) 18...♘e5 19.d6 ♗f8 20.♗c5 ♕a5 (20...a5!?) 21.♗e2 ♖ac8 22.♕a1 ♕xa1 23.♖xa1 ♖xc7 24.dxc7 ♖c8 25.♗xf8 ♔xf8 26.♖c1 ♔e7 27.♗a6 ♔d7 28.♖d1† 1–0 Bacrot – McShane, Biel 2004.

16.♖xb7

16.♖e1 ♗xf3 17.gxf3 g5!? 18.♖xb7 ♘g6 19.♕b1 ♕xb1 20.♖exb1 a5 21.♖1b3 ♗e5! 22.♖a3 ♗d6 23.♖a4 ♗b4 saw Black holding his own in Haba – Votava, Czech Championship 1999.

16...e6

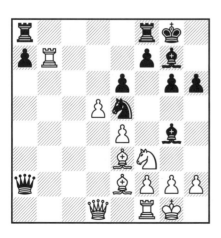

17.d6

There is presently some debate as to whether White should play d5-d6 immediately, or delay this advance for a move in favour of 17.♖e1. On balance I prefer Khalifman's move order in the main game because 17.♖e1 ♗xf3 18.gxf3 allows Black to interpose 18...exd5! 19.exd5 (19.♕xd5 ♕c2 looks fine for Black) before playing 19...♖fd8. This leaves White's d-pawn significantly weaker and allows the following continuation 20.d6

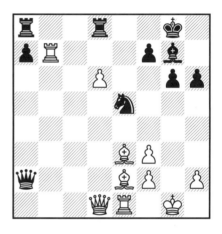

20...♕a5 (20...♕a3!? - Krasenkow) 21.♖f1 ♕a2 22.f4 ♖xd6! 23.♕xd6 ♕xe2 24.♕d1 ♘f3† 25.♔g2 ♘h4† 26.♔h3 (This represents the critical difference from the main game: with the e-pawns on e4 and e6 White could have played ♔g3, however now 26.♔g3 is met by 26...♘f5†) 26...♕a6 27.♖d7 Thus far we have been following San Segundo – Illescas Cordoba, Cala Mendia, Mallorca 2001. In that game 27...♗f6 was played, however Krasenkow (in *Chessbase Magazine 88*) asserts that this is inaccurate on account of 28.♖d6! (28.♖e1?! was the move actually played). By way of improvement Krasenkow suggests 27...♘f5 28.♕d3 ♕xd3 29.♖xd3 a5 with equality.

17...♖fd8

17...♘xf3† 18.gxf3 ♗h3 19.♖e1 ♖fb8 (19...♗c3 20.♕b1! ♕xb1 21.♖exb1±/± Browne – Grey, San Francisco 1996) 20.♕b1 ♕xb1

21.♖exb1 ♖xb7 22.♖xb7 a5 23.f4 ♗f6 24.e5± Binelli – Kunzmann, e-mail 1999.

18.♖e1 ♗xf3

The established mainline, and a universal preference at GM level, however alternatives have also been tried:

a) 18...♕a5? runs into 19.♖b5! ♕c3 20.♖c5 ♕b2 21.♘xe5 ♗xe5 22.♗xg4 ♗xd6 23.♕c1 1–0 Biriukov – Rogovoi, White Nights 1999.

b) 18...♘c4 seems playable, and brought Black rapid equality in its only outing: 19.♗c5 (19.♗f4!? or 19.♗xc4 ♕xc4 20.e5 ♕a6 21.♖b4 ♗xf3 22.♕xf3 ♗xe5 23.♖b7 f5 24.d7 may be a more promising try for the advantage.) 19...♗xf3 20.gxf3 ♘xd6 (20...♕a5!?) 21.♗xd6 ♗e5 22.♕c1 ♗xd6 23.♗c4 ½–½ Jianu – Zhigalko, Artek 2000.

19.gxf3

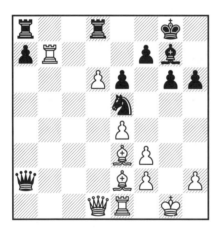

19...♕a5!?

In the present position Black faces the problem of anticipating and countering White's plan of 20.f4 and 21.e5, which would shut in the dark-squared bishop on g7 and solidify the advanced position of White's d-pawn. The text move, originally introduced by GM Illescas Cordoba and subsequently employed with effect by Kasparov, takes advantage of the undefended position of the e1–rook and threatens to meet 20.f4 with 20...♖xd6, when suddenly White is in trouble.

Notwithstanding the critical nature of 19...♕a5, White should also be aware of 19...♕a3 which is similar to the text in that it anticipates 20.f4 by attacking the d6-pawn, but fails tactically to 20.f4! (20.d7 ♕e7 21.♗b5 ♕h4= Gelfand – Ivanchuk, Manila 1990) 20...♖xd6 21.♕c1!!

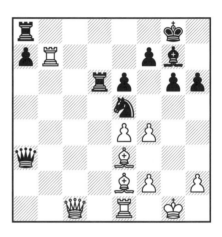

21...♕xc1 22.♖xc1 when Black's knight is trapped in the middle of the board! 22...♘c6 (Gelfand notes the lines 22...♖d7 23.♖b3+-, 22...♘d7?? 23.e5 ♖d5 24.♗f3+- and 22...♘d3 23.♖cc7 a5 (23...♖f8 24.e5 ♖d5 25.♖xa7±) 24.♖xf7 ♗h8 25.♖fe7+-) 23.e5 ♘d4 (23...♘a5 24.exd6 ♘xb7 25.♗f3 ♖d8 26.♗xb7+-) 24.♖cc7!! ♘xe2† 25.♔f1 ♖dd8 (25...♖a6 26.♖xf7 ♗f8 27.♔xe2± - Ftacnik) 26.♖xf7 ♗f8? (26...♗h8 27.♔xe2 a5 28.♖h7 ♖db8 29.♖xb8† ♖xb8 30.♖e7 ♖a8 31.♖xe6 ♔f7 32.♖c6 a4 33.♗d4± - Gelfand, *Informant 66*) 27.♔xe2 ♖db8 28.♖xb8 ♖xb8 29.♖f6! ♖e8 (29...a5 30.♖xg6† ♔f7 31.♖f6† and 29...♔g7 30.♖xe6 ♖b2† 31.♔d3 a5 32.f5! are both losing for Black) 30.♖xg6† ♔h7 31.♖f6 gave White a decisive advantage in Gelfand - Kamsky, Dos Hermanas 1996.

20.♖f1!

The only move to challenge Black's defence. Of the alternatives, 20.♗d2 ♕a2 21.♗e3 ♕a5 22.♗d2 ♕a2 23.♗e3 ½–½ was Lautier – Illescas Cordoba, Hoogovens 1997, and the advance 20.d7? just loses material to the obvious 20...♖xd7 21.♖xd7 ♘xd7∓. 20.♖b5? is also bad on account of 20...♘xf3†! when White drops the exchange and should be lost.

20...♗f8

Another accurate move from Black, first played by Kasparov in his encounter with Kramnik at Linares 1998. For some time this retreat was thought to represent the solution to Black's problems in this line, however now this assessment is very much in question. Black's alternatives have proved consistently unsatisfactory:

a) After 20...♕a3 White can utilise Gelfand's idea (discussed above) via 21.f4! ♖xd6 22.♕c1 (22.♕b1!? ♘c6 (22...♘d7 23.e5 ♖b6 24.♗xb6 ♘xb6 25.♕e4±) 23.♖xf7 ♔xf7 24.♕b7† ♘e7 25.♕xa8± - Pelletier, *Informant 72*) 22...♕a2 (22...♕xc1 23.♖xc1 ♘c6 24.e5±) 23.♗b5!

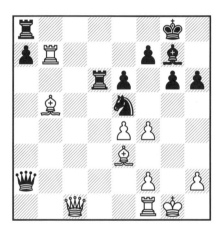

and now 23...♘c6? (23...♘f3† 24.♔g2 ♘h4† 25.♔h3 e5! 26.♕c4 ♕xc4 27.♗xc4 exf4 28.♖xf7 ♔h7 29.♗xf4 ♖f6 30.♖xf6 ♗xf6 31.e5± - Pelletier. In concurring with this view Ftacnik notes the lines 23...♘g4 24.♕c7 ♖f8 25.♕xd6+- and 23...♖b6 24.♗xb6 ♘f3† 25.♔g2 axb6 26.♕c7±) 24.♖xc6 ♖c8 (24...♕e2 25.e5+-) 25.♗d5! 1–0 was Pelletier – Jelen, Dresden 1998, e.g. 25...♖xc1 26.♗xa2+-.

b) 20...g5 21.f4 gxf4 (21...♘g6? 22.f5! exf5 23.♕b3 ♘e5 24.♖b5+-) 22.♗xf4 ♖ab8 (22...♕a3 23.d7±) 23.♖xb8 ♖xb8 24.♕c1!± - Avrukh, *Chessbase Magazine 64*.

c) 20...♖d7 21.♖xd7 ♘xd7 22.♕c1!± - Ftacnik.

d) 20...♕a2 21.f4 ♖xd6 doesn't quite work in view of 22.♕xd6 ♕xe2 23.♕d1 ♘f3† 24.♔g2 ♘h4† 25.♔g3! ♕a6 26.♕d7 ♖f8 27.♖c1 ♕e2 28.♕d1!+- - Krasenkow.

21.d7!

Kasparov points out that 21.♖b5? is bad on account of 21...♕a2, e.g. 22.♖xe5? ♗xd6 23.♖b5 ♗xh2† 24.♔xh2 ♖xd1 25.♗xd1 ♕c4–+ (*Informant 72*).

21...♕a2!

A clever move, renewing the threat to White's d-pawn by utilising the relatively vulnerable position of the e2-bishop.

22.♗b5

22.♖e1 ♕a5! 23.♖f1 ♕a2 24.♖e1 ½-½, Jo. Eriksson - Ziegler, Swedish Ch. 1999.

22...a6

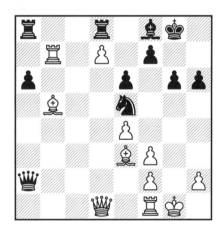

23.♗a4!

This excellent novelty was introduced in an earlier game by GM Petr Haba, which makes it all the more surprising that Leko was willing to defend this position against Khalifman. The earlier encounter Kramnik-Kasparov, Linares 1998 had continued 23.♗d4 ♗g7 24.♗xe5 when a draw was agreed because 24...♗xe5 25.♗c6 a5 26.♖b5 ♖a6 27.♖xe5 ♖xc6 28.♕a1 leads to dead equality. In his annotations for *Informant 72*

Kasparov also notes the line 23.f4 axb5 24.fxe5 ♕a6 25.♖c7 b4 which he assesses as unclear.

23...♘xf3† 24.♔g2

24.♕xf3 ♕xa4 25.♖d1 ♕c6 26.♖b6 ♕c7 27.e5 ♖xd7! 28.♖xd7 ♕xd7 29.♕xa8 ♕d1† 30.♔g2 ♕g4†= - Kasparov.

24...♘e5

Alternatives:

a) The original game which rejuvenated this variation for White continued 24...♘h4† 25.♔h3!

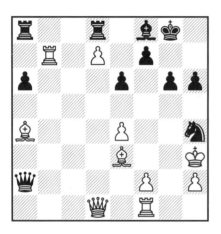

(This is the real improvement that Haba introduced. In his *Informant* annotations Kasparov had only considered 25.♔h1 ♕c4 26.f3 ♗e7 27.♗b6 ♖f8 which he assessed as unclear. Interestingly this position was subsequently tested in a computer match and proved difficult for Black. That game continued: 28.♖c7 ♕b4 29.♖c6 ♕b2 30.♖f2 ♕a3 31.♖c4 ♖ab8 32.♗c7 ♖b2 33.♖xb2 ♕xb2 34.♖c2 ♕a3 35.♖d2 ♕xf3† 36.♕xf3 ♘xf3 37.d8♕ ♖xd8 38.♖xd8† ♗xd8 39.♗xd8 Gambit Tiger 1.0 – Junior 6.0, Spain 2001, and White eventually managed to grind out a win.) 25...♕c4 (Ftacnik suggested that 25...g5!? may be better) 26.f3 ♗e7?! (26...g5 27.♖f2 ♕c3!? needs further investigation. Black seems to hold his ground: 28.♗d4 ♕a3 29.♗b6 ♘g6 30.♗xd8 ♘f4† 31.♔g3 ♖xd8⩱ - Ftacnik) 27.♖f2 ♕c3 (27...e5 28.♗b3 ♕c6 29.♗d5 ♕d6

30.f4±) 28.♕d4! ♕a5? 29.♗xh6 ♗f8 30.♗xf8 ♖xf8 31.♔xh4 ♔h7 32.♔h3 1–0 Haba – Skytte, Cappelle la Grande 2000.

b) 24...♘g5 25.♕c2 ♕a3 26.♖d1 e5 27.♗c6 ♕e7 28.♖b3 ♖ab8 29.♖xb8 ♖xb8 30.♕c3 ♗g7 31.♗c5 ♕f6 32.♗d6± Pelletier – Stohl, Mitropa Cup 1998.

25.♗b6 ♕c4 26.♕d4!

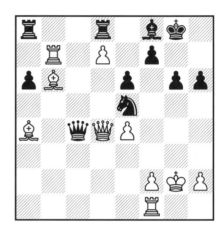

26...♕xd4

Ftacnik notes that 26...♕e2 is bad on account of 27.♕xe5 ♕g4† 28.♕g3 ♕xe4† 29.♕f3 ♕xa4 30.♖c1+-.

27.♗xd4 ♘d3

Defending the knight with 27...♗g7 is also bad: 28.♗b6 ♖f8 29.♖d1 ♗f6 30.♗c7! ♔g7 (30...g5 31.d8♕ ♖fxd8 32.♖xd8† ♖xd8 33.♗xd8 ♗xd8 34.♖b8+-) 31.♖b4! g5 32.♖bd4!+- - Krasenkow. White now threatens 29.♗b6, 29.♗f6 or even 29.♖b3, attacking both the a8-rook and the d3-knight. Needless to say, Black is in trouble!

28.♗c6

Now White has a lot of threats!

28...♘c5 29.♖c7! ♗d6 30.♗xc5! ♗xc7 31.♗xa8 ♖xa8 32.♗e7!+- ♖d8

32...f5 33.♖c1 ♔f7 34.♖xc7 ♔xe7 35.♖c8, and 32...♖d8 33.♖c1! ♗xe7 34.♖c8† are both winning for White.

33.♖d1 f5 34.♗xd8 ♗xd8 35.exf5 gxf5 36.♖d6

♔f7 37.♖xa6 ♔e7 38.♔g3 ♗c7†
38...♔xd7 39.♖a7† ♔d6 40.♖h7+-.
39.♔h4 ♔xd7
39...♗xh2 40.♖xe6† ♔xd7 41.♖xh6+-.
40.♖a7! ♔c6 41.♖xc7† ♔xc7 42.♔h5 e5
42...♔d6 43.♔xh6 ♔e7 44.♔g6+-.
**43.♔xh6 ♔d6 44.♔g5 ♔e6 45.h4 f4 46.h5 f3
47.♔g4**
1–0

Game 27 Conclusions: Black is currently facing
some very real problems in the mainline after
13.♗g5 h6 14.♗e3 ♘c6 15.d5 ♘e5 16.♖xb7 e6
17.d6 ♖fd8 18.♖e1 ♗xf3 19.gxf3 ♕a5!? 20.♖f1!
♗f8 21.d7! ♕a2! 22.♗b5 a6 23.♗a4!. At present
this seems at least slightly preferable for White. If
Black is looking for an improvement in this line
then perhaps the relatively unexplored 18...♘c4
could set White some fresh problems, but aside
from that Black may have to look to 15...♘a5!?
(Game 28) or 15... ♗xf3 (Game 29).

Game 28
Kramnik – Anand
Dos Hermanas 1996

1.♘f3 g6 2.d4 ♘f6 3.c4 ♗g7 4.♘c3 d5 5.cxd5
♘xd5 6.e4 ♘xc3 7.bxc3 c5 8.♖b1 0–0 9.♗e2
cxd4 10.cxd4 ♕a5† 11.♗d2 ♕xa2 12.0–0 ♗g4
13.♗g5 h6 14.♗e3 ♘c6 15.d5 ♘a5

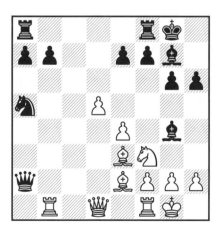

By moving the knight to a5 Black relinquishes
some control of the centre, but hopes to
compensate for this by hanging onto the b7-
pawn and keeping the a5-knight out of the line
of fire. As we shall see, these aspirations will prove
misguided.
16.♗c5!
For a period 16.♖b4 (threatening 17.♖a4)
was popular, however Anand eventually solved
Black's problems in this variation after 16...♗xf3!
17.♗xf3 ♘c4 18.♗d4 ♘d2 19.♖b2 ♘xf3†
20.♕xf3 ♕a6 21.♗xg7 ♔xg7 22.♕c3† ♔g8
23.♕c7 ♕d6!

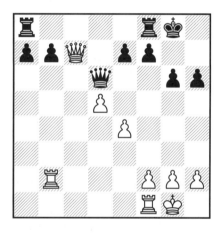

24.♖xb7 (24.♕xd6 exd6 25.♖xb7 a5 gives
Black sufficient compensation according to
Ftacnik.) 24...♕xc7 25.♖xc7 a5 26.♖a1 (26.♖xe7
♖fb8!) 26...♖fb8 27.h4 a4 28.♔h2, Kamsky
– Anand, Las Palmas 1995, and now Anand, in
his *Informant* annotations, suggests that Black's
best approach to this position is 28...a3! 29.♖xe7
(29.♖c3 a2 30.♖c2 ♖b4=) 29...a2 30.d6 ♔f8
31.♖c7 ♖b1 32.♖xa2 ♖xa2 33.♖c8† ♔g7 34.d7
♖d1 35.d8♕ ♖xd8 36.♖xd8 ♖xf2=.
16...♗f6
This move attempts to protect e7, but in fact
only serves to provoke White. In fact some
Grünfeld players have decided that increasing
Black's activity is the key to this position, and
instead have actually provoked the capture on

e7 with 16...b6. Black has tried the following alternatives:

a) 16...b6!? has not received much attention, but certainly appears respectable. Play continues 17.♗xe7 ♖fe8 18.d6.

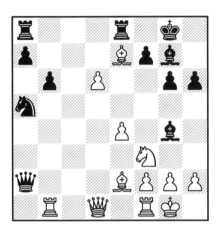

Black now has a choice of two moves:

a1) 18...♕e6?! 19.h3 ♗xf3 20.♗xf3 ♘c6 21.e5 ♘xe7 22.♗xa8 ♖xa8 23.dxe7 ♕xe7 24.f4 ♖d8 25.♕b3 (25.♕g4!? g5 26.♖be1 may be better - Krasenkow) 25...g5 26.fxg5 hxg5 27.♖f5 ♗xe5 28.♖e1! ♗d4† was Sasikiran – Summerscale, Torquay 2002, and now rather than 29.♔f1?!, Krasenkow proposes 29.♔h2! ♕d6† (29...♕xe1? 30.♕xf7† ♔h8 31.♕h5† ♔g8 32.♕xg5† ♗g7 33.♕xd8†+-) 30.♔h1 ♕g6 31.♖ef1 with a clear advantage to White, e.g. 31...♖d7 32.♕b5±/+-.

a2) 18...♘c6 19.♗b5 ♘xe7 20.♗xe8 ♖xe8 21.dxe7 ♕a3 22.♖e1 ♕xe7 23.h3 ♗e6 24.♕a4 ♕d7 25.♕a6 ♖d8 was Bunzmann – van Wely, Germany 2001, and now 26.e5± looks best, although White has a lot of work ahead of him.

b) 16...♗xf3 17.♗xf3 ♖fe8 18.♖e1 b6 (18...♗e5 19.♖e2 ♕c4 20.♖c2 ♕a4 21.♗xe7!±) 19.♖e2 ♕c4 20.♖c2 ♕a4 (20...♕a6 21.♖e2 ♕b7 22.♗b4 ♕d7 23.♗xa5 bxa5 24.♗b5+-) 21.♗xe7! ♘c4 22.d6 ♗f8 (22...♘e5 23.♖c7 ♘xf3† 24.♕xf3 ♖ec8 25.♕d1!+-) 23.e5 ♖ab8 (23...♗xe7 24.♗xa8 ♗xd6 25.♖xc4 ♕xc4 26.♗d5, and 23...♖ac8

24.d7 ♗xe7 25.dxe8♕† ♖xe8 26.♖a1 are both winning for White) 24.♖a1 ♘a3 25.♖d2 ♕xd1† 26.♖dxd1 1–0 Sherbakov – Vorontsov, Kurgan 1995. The comments here are based on Ftacnik's annotations for *Chessbase Magazine 49*.

17.e5! ♗xe5

17...♗xf3 18.♗xf3 ♗xe5 19.♗xe7±.

18.♖b4!

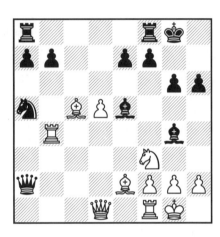

Previous practice had focussed on 18.h3, however the text is considerably stronger.

18...♗xf3

18...♖fd8 19.♖xg4 ♖xd5 20.♖a4!+- - Kramnik, *Informant 63*.

19.♗xf3 ♖ae8

Alternatives:

a) 19...♗f6? 20.♖a4 ♕b3 21.♖xa5 ♕xd1 22.♖xd1 b6 23.d6!± 23...♖ac8 (23...bxa5 24.dxe7 ♖fc8 25.♗xa8 ♖xa8 26.♖d7+-) 24.d7 ♖cd8 25.♗xe7! ♗xe7 26.♖xa7 ♖b8 (26...♗c5 27.♖e1 f5 28.♗d5† ♔g7 29.♖e8+-) 27.♖e1 ♗d8 (27...♗f6 28.♗d5 b5 29.♖e8! ♖bxe8 30.dxe8♕ ♖xe8 31.♗xf7†+-) 28.♖e8 b5 29.♖a8 ♖xa8 30.♗xa8 b4 31.♗d5 ♔g7 32.♔f1 1–0 Kramnik – Timman, Novgorod 1995.

b) 19...♖ac8 20.♗xe7 ♖fe8 21.d6±.

20.♗e3!

20.♖a4? ♕b3 21.♖xa5 ♕xd1 22.♖xd1 b6 23.♖xa7 bxc5∓.

20...♘c4

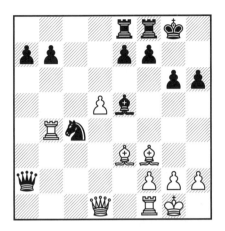

With this last move Anand departs from his earlier game with Kramnik in the same variation.

a) 20...b6 21.♗xh6 ♗g7± - Kramnik, *Informant 63.*

b) 20...♗g7? 21.♖a4 ♕b2 22.♖xa5+- - Ftacnik.

c) 20...♗c3 21.♖a4! ♕b2 (21...♕b3 22.♗xh6 ♕xd1 (22...b5 23.♖xb3 ♘xb3 24.♖a3) 23.♖xd1 b5 24.♖a3 ♗b4 25.♖a2±) 22.♕d3 b5 (22...♕b3 23.♖xa5+-) 23.♗c1 bxa4! 24.♗xb2 ♗xb2 was Kramnik – Anand, Riga 1995, and now rather than 25.d6?, which served only to squander White's advantage after 25...♗f6!, Kramnik proposes that White should play 25.♕d2 ♘c4 26.♕c2 ♖c8 27.♗e2 ♘e3 (27...a3 28.♗xc4 ♗e5 29.d6+-) 28.♕xb2 ♘xf1 29.♔xf1 when White holds a decisive advantage. The notes here are based on Kramnik's annotations for *Informant 63.*

21.♗xh6 ♘d6 22.♗xf8

The text delivered White a convincing victory in this game, however it is by no means clear that White is better with best play. This view is confirmed by the fact that Gelfand, a renowned expert in the 8.♖b1 variation, subsequently eschewed Kramnik's approach in this game in favour of an aggressive line of immediate play on the kingside. The game to which I

am referring continued: 22.h4!? ♖c8 (22...♗g7 23.♗xg7 ♔xg7 24.♕d4† ♔h7 25.h5 gives White an attack.) 23.h5 ♕c2!? (23...♖c4 24.♖xc4 ♕xc4 25.♗xf8 ♔xf8 26.hxg6 fxg6 27.♖e1±) 24.hxg6 ♕xd1 (24...fxg6 25.♗g4) 25.♖xd1 f5 (25...fxg6 26.♗g4 ♗f5 27.♗xf5 gxf5 and 25...♗g7 26.gxf7† ♖xf7 27.♗e3 both leave White slightly better according to Gelfand.) 26.♗xf8 ♔xf8

27.♖a4 b5?! (Better was 27...a6 28.g4 ♖c3 29.♔g2 ♔g7 when the position remains unclear despite White's extra exchange.) 28.♖xa7 b4 29.♖b1 ♖b8 (29...b3 30.g7† ♔xg7 31.♖xb3±) 30.♖b3 ♖c3 (30...♘b5 31.g7†) 31.♖c7± Gelfand – Macieja, Portoroz 2001. The notes here are based on Gelfand's annotations for *Chessbase Magazine 85*, and although he asserts that White is clearly better here, the position remains very difficult for both sides. This observation was confirmed to some extent by the fact that Gelfand was ultimately unable to convert his advantage: the game ended in a 118 move draw.

22...♖xf8

22...♔xf8 was tried in Agrest – Hellers, Stockholm 1996, however rather than 23.♖a4 ♕b2 24.♖xa7 ♖c8 25.♕a4 b5 26.♕a3 ♕xa3 27.♖xa3 b4 28.♖b3 ♖c3 29.h3 ♘b5 30.♖fb1 ♘d4 ½–½, White could have tried a similar strategy to the one employed by Kramnik in the main game.

23.h4!

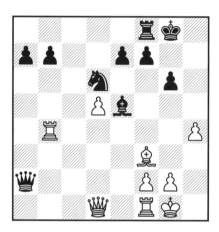

Although White is slightly ahead on material this is essentially useless unless that material can be made to exert a definite influence on Black's position. At present Black's pawn structure supports his minor pieces (and vice versa) and is almost impregnable. In order to change this White must attempt to open some lines on the kingside and create some avenues of influence for the rooks.

23...♖c8

23...b5 24.♖g4 gives White an attack according to Kramnik, *Informant 66*.

24.♗e4

24.h5 is premature because it can be met by 24...g5!, keeping the kingside closed.

24...♕a5

The text works out badly for Black; by way of alternatives Kramnik notes the following lines:

a) 24...♖c4 25.♗b1 ♕a5 26.♖xc4 ♘xc4 27.h5 with a kingside attack.

b) 24...b5!? is an interesting idea according to Bologan, *Chessbase Magazine 53*.

c) 24...a5 25.♗b1 ♕a3 26.♖g4 gives White familiar pressure on the kingside.

d) 24...♖c3!? may be best, e.g. 25.♖a4 ♕d2 26.♕g4 (26.♕f3!?) 26...b5 27.♖xa7 ♖c4 (27...♗d4 28.♖xg6! ♗xa7 29.♗f5† ♔f8 30.♗xc8 b4 31.♗f5+-) 28.♖xe7 ♖f6 29.♖e6 fxe6 30.♕xg6†

♗g7 31.♕xe6† ♔h8! is unclear.

25.♖a4 ♕b5

25...♕c7 26.♗d3 b5 27.♖g4±.

26.♗b1± ♖c5

26...♖c4 27.♖xc4 ♕xc4 28.g3±.

27.♗d3 ♕d7 28.♖xa7± ♖xd5 29.♖a8† ♔g7 30.h5! ♖d4

30...♘f5 31.hxg6 fxg6 32.♕e2 is clearly better for White according to Bologan, however 30...g5! limits White to a slight advantage according to Kramnik.

31.♕e2 ♗f6 32.hxg6 fxg6 33.♗b1

Another idea would be to play 33.♗c2 intending to exchange a pair of rooks with 34.♖d1, which is also clearly better for White.

33...♕g4 34.♕a2

A time trouble induced error; better was 34.♕xg4 ♖xg4 35.♗a2±.

34...♘c4 35.♕b3 b5 36.♖e1! ♖d2? 37.♖a2! ♖d5 38.♗e4 ♖e5 39.♖ae2 ♕h4 40.g3 ♕h6 41.♕d3+- ♘d6 42.♗d5 ♖xe2 43.♕xe2 ♕h3 44.♗e6 ♕h8 45.♕f3 ♕b8

46.♔g2?

This makes things more complicated. White could have maintained his decisive advantage with 46.♖e2! b4 (46...♕b7 47.♗d5) 47.♖a2.

46...b4 47.♖h1 ♕b7! 48.♗d5 ♕b5 49.g4 ♘f7 50.♗b3 ♘h6 51.♖e1 ♕g5 52.♖e4 ♘f5 53. ♕d1! ♘h4† 54.♔h3 ♕c5 55.♕e2 g5 56.♕c4

♕xc4 57.♖xc4 ♗c3 58.♖c5 ♘f3 59.♔g3 ♘e5 60.♖b5 ♗d2 61.f3 ♗c3 62.f4 gxf4† 63.♔xf4 ♘f7 64.♖d5 ♗b2 65.♔f5 ♗f6 66.♖d1 ♘g5 67.♖d3 ♘f7 68.♖d7 ♘d6† 69.♔f4 ♘f7 70.♖b7 ♗e5† 71.♔e3 ♗d6 72.♔e4 ♘g5† 73.♔f5 ♘f3 74.♗d5 ♘h4† 75.♔g5 ♘g6 76.♖a7 ♘f8 77.♔f5 ♗c5 78.♖b7 ♗d6 79.g5 ♘g6 80.♖a7 ♘f8 81.♗b3 ♘g6 82.♖a8 ♘f8 83.♔g4 ♗c7 84.♔h5 ♗d6 85.♖c8 ♗e5 86.♖c5 ♘g6 87.♖c8 ♘f8 88.♖c1 ♗c3 89.♖f1 e6 90.♖d1 ♔f7 91.♖d8 ♘g6 92.♖d7† ♔e8 93.♗a4 ♘e5 94.♖b7 ♔f8 95.g6 ♘d3 96.♔h6 ♘c5 97.♖b8† ♔e7 98.♗c2 ♘d7 99.♖b7 ♔d6 100.g7 ♗xg7† 101.♔xg7
1–0

Unless otherwise indicated, the comments to this game are based on Kramnik's annotations for *Informant 66*.

Game 28 Conclusions: 13.♗g5 h6 14.♗e3 ♘c6 15.d5 ♘a5 is certainly a resilient system. On the evidence available it seems that White should be able to obtain slightly better chances with accurate play, however very often this requires aggressive tactical variations which give rise to volatile and highly imbalanced positions where both sides have their chances.

Game 29
Krasenkow – Svidler
Rubinstein Memorial Poland 2000

1.d4 ♘f6 2.c4 g6 3.♘c3 d5 4.cxd5 ♘xd5 5.e4 ♘xc3 6.bxc3 ♗g7 7.♘f3 c5 8.♖b1 0–0 9.♗e2 cxd4 10.cxd4 ♕a5† 11.♗d2 ♕xa2 12.0–0 ♗g4 13.♗g5 h6 14.♗e3 ♘c6 15.d5 ♗xf3!?

At present this seems to be Black's most reliable method of dealing with 14.♗e3.

16.gxf3!

A move born out of desperation as much as inspiration. For some time White struggled to nibble out an edge with the more obvious 16.♗xf3, but it would appear that White's resources in this line have been fully exhausted.

Play should continue 16...♘e5 and now:

a) 17.♗c5 ♗f6 18.♖xb7 ♖fb8 19.♕b1 (19.♗xe7 ♖xb7 20.♗xf6 ♖e8 21.♕c1 ♕b2! is fine for Black – Rowson.) 19...♕xb1 20.♖fxb1 ♖xb7 21.♖xb7 ♖c8 22.♗e3 a5 23.♖a7 (23.♗xh6 g5) 23...♗g5!? (In this line the h6 pawn actually proves useful for Black.) 24.♗xg5 hxg5 25.h3 ♔f8 26.♖xa5 ♖c1† 27.♔h2 ♖c2 28.♔g1 ♖c1† 29.♔h2 ♖c2 30.♔g1 ½–½ was Bunzmann – Leko, Hamburg 1999.

b) 17.♖xb7 a5

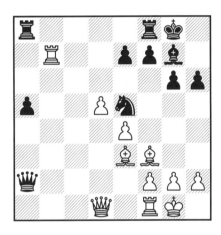

18.♖xe7 (18.♗c5 ♖fb8 19.♖xb8† ♖xb8 20.♗xe7 a4 21.d6 ♕e6! 22.♕xa4 ♘xf3† 23.gxf3 ♕h3! 24.♕a5 ♕xf3 25.♕d5 (25.♗h4 ♕xe4 26.♗g3 avoids the perpetual and gives White some chances to play for the full point, albeit not many.) 25...♕g4† ½–½ van Wely – Svidler, Biel 2000.) 18...a4 19.♗d4 ♘xf3† 20.gxf3 ♗xd4 21.♕xd4 a3 22.d6 ♕e2 23.♔g2 a2 24.♖a1 ♕f1† 25.♔g3 ♕g1† 26.♔h3 ♕f1† 27.♔g3 ½–½ Kramnik – Svidler, Korchnoi Birthday Tournament, Zurich 2001.

Once it became clear that 16.♗xf3 had been neutralized, attention switched to the only other option available: 16.gxf3. Fortunately, recapturing with the pawn is not as bad as it looks, and leads to highly unbalanced positions which actually score well for White in practice.

16...♘d4

Alternatives:

a) 16...♖fd8 17.♖xb7 e6 18.♖c7 ♘a5 19.♖c2 (It looks more challenging to play 19.d6!?

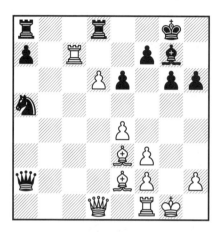

19...♗e5 20.♖c2 ♕b3 (20...♕a3 21.d7) 21.♗xh6 ♖xd6 22.♕c1 when White has some pressure (because of Black's king position, the poorly placed a5-knight, and control of the c-file) and can contemplate implementing the thematic f3-f4 and e4-e5 advance.) 19...♕b3 20.♖c5 ♕a3 21.♕d3 ½–½ Ruck – Zaja, Austria 2002.

b) 16...♘a5!? has been used with success in a few correspondence games, but White's handling of the position in each case was somewhat questionable, so I have decided to omit them entirely and simply suggest that I believe White's most logical plan here is to play 17.f4 and 18.e5, shutting down the g7-bishop. Thereafter it makes sense to activate the e2 bishop (ideally by placing it on f3 or e4), but care should be taken to ensure that Black cannot cause too many problems with a timely ♘a5-c4.

17.♗d3

17.♗xd4!? ♗xd4 18.♕xd4 ♕xe2 19.♔g2 ♕a6 should be okay for Black - Krasenkow.

17...♕a3!?

Alternatives:

a) Krasenkow notes the line 17...b6!? 18.♖b4 e5 as deserving of consideration. Play might then continue 19.f4 ♕a3 20.♖a4 ♕b3 21.♔g2!?±. It is

also worth noting that 21.♗xd4 ♕xd1 22.♖xd1 exd4 23.e5 g5! is fine for Black, however 21.fxe5 ♕xd1 22.♖xd1 ♘f3† 23.♔g2 ♘xe5 24.♗b5± is also interesting.

b) 17...a5 18.f4 b5 19.♔h1!? (The text sets in motion an imaginative kingside attack, however a more reserved approach would be 19.♗xd4 ♗xd4 20.♗xb5 when White appears to be slightly better, but the opposite coloured bishops could make it difficult to achieve more.) 19...♖fc8 (Advancing the queenside pawns with 19...b4 or 19...a4 also makes sense, especially as they are half way there already!) 20.f5 ♕a4 21.♕d2 ♘f3 22.♕e2 ♘e5

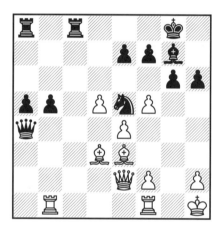

23.fxg6 ♘xd3!? (This initiates a volatile series of combinations; it would have been safer to play 23...fxg6 24.♖a1 (24.♖xb5 ♘xd3 25.♕xd3 ♕c4 is fine for Black) 24...♕b3 25.♗xb5 ♖c2 26.♕d1 ♖b2, when Black has no problems.) 24.gxf7† ♔f8? (This turns out very badly for Black. In *Chessbase Magazine 86* GM Krasenkow analyses this position in considerable depth and concludes that Black has a playable position after 24...♔h7, 24...♔h8 and even 24...♔xf7. In each case Krasenkow asserts that White has no way to forcibly establish an advantage, and consequently the position should be regarded as unclear). 25.♕g4! ♘e5 (Krasenkow notes that 25...h5 is bad on account of 26.♕f5! ♕c2 (26...♘e5 27.♖g1 ♘g4 28.♕h7 ♔xf7 29.♕xh5†,

26...♘c5 27.f3, and 26...♕c4 27.♖g1 ♕c3 28.♗h6 e6 29.♖xg7 exf5 30.♖h7† ♕g7 31.♖xg7 ♔e7 32.exf5 all guarantee White a definite, if not decisive, advantage.) 27.♕h7 ♔xf7 28.♗d4 ♖g8 29.♖g1 e5 30.dxe6† ♔xe6 31.♕f5† ♔e7 32.♕g5† when White is winning.) 26.♕f5 ♘xf7 27.♖g1 ♗f6 28.♖g6 ♗g5 29.♗xg5 hxg5 30.♖xg5 ♕d4 31.♖bg1 ♕h8 32.e5 e6 33.dxe6 ♖c7 34.♖h5! ♕xe5 35.♖g8†! ♔e7 36.♕xf7† ♔d6 37.♖xe5 ♖xg8 38.♕xg8 1–0 Agrest – Bacrot, Leon 2001.

18.f4 ♕d6 19.♖xb7 ♖fb8 20.♕b1 ♘f3† 21.♔g2 ♘h4† 22.♔h1

22...g5?

Speculative play from Svidler. This kingside lunge undermines White's centre to a degree, but does so at an unjustifiable cost to the safety of the black king. Furthermore, it may have simply been unnecessary. Admittedly taking action on the queenside with 22...a5 23.♖c1 looks better for White, but Krasenkow notes that it would have made more sense to hit White's centre at its head with 22...e6! 23.♗xa7 (23.dxe6 fxe6 24.♖d1 ♖xb7 25.♕xb7 may be a better try for the advantage, however I would be tempted to try 23.♗c4 with the idea of establishing a powerful bishop on d5 if Black plays 23...exd5, or (if Black hesitates) advancing the e- and d-pawns, or exchanging on e6 and attempting to exploit Black's weakness on the light squares.) 23...♖xb7 24.♕xb7 ♖d8 gives Black a 'satisfactory position' according to Krasenkow, whereas I believe White is a little better.

23.♖g1!

23...gxf4

23...♘f3? 24.♖g3 gxf4?? 25.♗c5+−.

24.♗c5 ♕e5 25.♗d4?!

The text move is aesthetically pleasing, however Krasenkow points out that he could have generated a decisive initiative via 25.♗xe7 ♘g6 (25...♘f3 26.♗f6! and 25...♖xb7 26.♕xb7 ♖b8 27.♗f6! are both terrible for Black) 26.d6 ♖e8 27.♗b5 ♖xe7 28.dxe7 ♘xe7 29.♗c4!+−.

25...♖xb7

25...♕xd4 26.♖xb8† ♖xb8 27.♕xb8† ♔h7 28.♕b1±.

26.♕xb7 ♕xd4 27.♕xa8† ♔h7 28.♗b1 ♕e5

28...♕xf2 29.e5† ♘g6 30.d6! exd6 31.♗xg6† fxg6 32.♕e4 ♔h8 33.exd6+− − Krasenkow.

29.♕e8 ♘f3 30.♖c1?!

30.♖d1! ♘xh2 (30...♔g6 31.d6! exd6 32.♖xd6†!) 31.♕xf7 ♘g4 32.♔g2 ♘f6 33.♖g1!+−.

30...♔g6!? 31.♖c6† ♗f6 32.♕g8† ♔h5 33.♕xf7† ♔h4 34.♕g6??

34.♕h7! ♕g5 35.♖c1 ♔h3 36.♕f5† ♕xf5 37.exf5 ♘xh2 38.♖c4 f3 39.♔g1+−.

34...♗g5!

After this move it is suddenly the white monarch who is in danger!

35.♔g2 ♘d4 36.f3 ♕b8?

36...♘xc6 37.♕xc6 ♗f6 38.♕c2 would have led to a draw.

37.e5!

37...♕xe5

37...♕b2† 38.♗c2 ♕b4 39.♕d3+–.

38.♕e4 ♘xc6??

38...♕xe4 39.♗xe4 ♘b5 would have still been difficult for White.

39.dxc6 ♗f6 40.c7! ♕xc7 41.♕e1†

1–0

41...♔g5 42.h4† ♔h5 43.♕e6 gives White a forced mate on the light squares, despite the fact that Black is two pawns up with a move in hand! Unless indicated otherwise, the comments to this game are based on Krasenkow's annotations for *CBM 79*. Krasenkow is an excellent commentator, and I find his annotations both instructive and entertaining, so it is definitely worth checking out his full commentary on the Krasenkow – Svidler and Agrest – Bacrot games considered here.

Game 29 Conclusions: At present 13.♗g5 h6 14.♗e3 ♘c6 15.d5 ♗xf3!? would appear to represent Black's most solid and reliable defence in this line. White certainly has nothing after 16.♗xf3, and although results have been good with 16.gxf3!?, the resulting positions are often unclear and double-edged. Nevertheless, if White

is to assert an edge in this line then 16.gxf3 is a necessary evil, and if Black wishes to assert full equality then an appropriate antidote must be discovered.

Game 30
Mozetic – Leko
Tilburg 1993

1.d4 ♘f6 2.c4 g6 3.♘c3 d5 4.cxd5 ♘xd5 5.e4 ♘xc3 6.bxc3 ♗g7 7.♘f3 c5 8.♖b1 0–0 9.♗e2 cxd4 10.cxd4 ♕a5† 11.♗d2 ♕xa2 12.0–0 ♗g4 13.♗e3

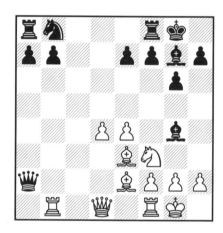

This line bears an obvious similarity to 13.♗g5 h6 14.♗e3, the only difference being the inclusion of the move 13...h6. In that line White argues that 13...h6 weakens Black's kingside, however in this variation White reasons that h7-h6 is hardly a major weakening, and that it would be better to preserve control of the g5-square in case a subsequent ♗e3-g5 would be beneficial.

13...b6

When the 12...♗g4 variation first became popular 13...b6 was a popular reply to 13.♗e3 (in the same way that 14...b6 was a frequent reply to 13.♗g5 h6 14.♗e3), however moving the b-pawn weakens Black on the light squares and does nothing to challenge White's powerful centre. Aside from the mainline (13...♘c6) which is considered in Games 31 & 32, there is one other alternative of which White should be aware: 13...&c8 14.&xb7 &d7 (14...e6 15.h3 &xf3 16.&xf3±)

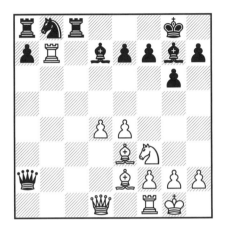

15.&d3 &c6 16.&b1 &a4 17.&e1 &d7 (17...&c2 18.&xc2 &xc2 19.&b7±) 18.&a5 &b6 19.&a1 &b3 20.&a6 &c7 (20...&c2 21.&b7 &d8 22.&xa7±) 21.&fb1 &c2 (21...&c3 22.&xa4 &xa4 23.&xa4+-) 22.&c1 &b2 23.&cb1 &c2 24.&c1 &b2 25.&xc7 &xa1† 26.&c1 &b2 (26...&a2? 27.&b7 &d8 28.&xa7) 27.&b7 &d8 28.&xa7± Khalifman – Orlov, St Petersburg 1997. The notes here are based on Ftacnik's comments in *Chessbase Magazine 58*.

14.&d3!?

This move works out well for White in the main game, however there is a serious alternative in 14.&a1, after which Black has tried two lines of defence:

a) 14...&e6 15.h3 &xf3 (15...&h5 16.e5!?, intending 17.g4, is clearly better for White.) 16.&xf3 a5?! (The text facilitates the manoeuvre 17...&a6-b4, however in *Informant 52* Chernin suggests that 16...&d7 may have been better, although 17.e5 &ad8 18.&b1! a5 19.&b5! with 20.&fc1–c6, 20.&d5 or 20.&g4 to follow, gives White strong compensation.) 17.e5 &a7 18.&b1!± &d7 (18...&a6 19.d5! &xe5 20.&xb6 &aa8 21.d6 &fb8 22.&xa8 &xb6 23.&xb6+-)

19.&xb6 &a6 20.&b2 &d8 21.&b5! e6 22.&fb1 (intending 23.&b7 &a7 24.d5+-) 22...a4 23.&xa4 &xa4 24.&xa4+- Chernin – Gorjatschkin, Neu Isenburg 1991.

b) 14...&b2 15.h3 &xf3 16.&xf3 e5 17.d5 &d7 18.&e2!? (18.&a4 &c5 19.&xc5 bxc5 20.d6 &b4 21.&a6 &b6 22.&e2 &fd8 23.&fd1= Gelfand – Kamsky, Tilburg 1992) 18...&b4 19.&b1! &d6 (19...&xb1 20.&fxb1 &fc8 21.&a6 &cb8 (21...&c7 22.d6) 22.&b5∞ - Vera) 20.&c1 &c5 (20...&fc8 21.&xc8† &xc8 22.&xa7±) 21.&xc5! bxc5 22.&a6 &b8 was Vera – Henao, Cuba 1993, and now Vera, in *Informant 58*, suggests that White should play 23.&b5! &b7 24.&d3 with a small but definite advantage for White.

14...&xf3

Alternatives:

a) 14...&d8 15.&fc1! &d7 16.&a1 &e6 17.&g5!

17...&xe2 18.&xe2 &d6 (Ftacnik notes that 18...&f6? 19.e5 &f5 20.g4 traps the black queen, and Chernin gives the line 18...&b3!? 19.&ab1 &a4 20.&f3!, when White has the initiative as compensation for the sacrificed pawn.) 19.&a2! e6 20.e5! &xe5 (Chernin notes that 20...&d5 21.&xd5 exd5 22.e6 fxe6 (22...&f6 23.exf7† &h8 24.&c7) 23.&xe6 &dc8 24.&xc8† &xc8 25.&xa7 should be winning for White, whilst 20...&e7 21.&c7, intending &e4, is clearly better for White.)

21.dxe5 &xe5 22.h4! &g7 (22...&xa1 23.&xa1 e5 (23...&d5 24.&c7 &f8 (24...&d7 25.&xd7 &xd7 26.&e4±) 25.&d4±) 24.&e4±) 23.&ab1 &d5 24.&e2 h6 25.&d1 &b7 26.&f3 &f6 27.&c4 e5 28.h5!±/± Chernin – C. Horvath, Hungarian Championship 1992.

b) 14...&c8? 15.h3 &xf3 16.&xf3 e5 17.&a1 &e6 (17...&c2 18.&fc1 gives White a decisive advantage, as did 17...&c4 18.&fc1! &e6 19.&g4, in Botsari – Licina, Hradec Kralove 1992) 18.&g4+-.

15.&xf3 e5 16.&a1

The text is probably best, although also of interest was 16.d5 &a6! 17.&d2 &d7 18.&e2 &a3 (18...&b7!?∞ -Novik) as in Sakaev – Novik, Moscow Open 1992, and now Novik, in *Informant 56*, proposes 19.&fc1! when White has compensation for his sacrificed pawn.

16...&e6 17.d5 &d6 18.&b5!

18.&fc1 &d8 19.&b5 &d7∞ - Novik, *Informant 56*.

18...&d7

18...&d7 19.&e2! &b7 20.&fc1±.

19.&c6!

19...&e7

19...&xc6 20.dxc6 &c5 (20...&f6 21.c7 (21.&fc1! intending 22.c7 and 23.&b6 is clearly better for White according to Pavlovic.) 21...h5 22.&fc1 &d7 23.&e2 a5 24.&b5± - Ftacnik) 21.&xc5 bxc5 22.&g4! f5 23.&e2! &fc8

24.&c4† &f8? (24...&h8±) 25.&fb1!+- Pavlovic – Zygouris, Hania 1993.

20.&g4 &c5

Mozetic notes the line 20...&f6 21.d6 &d8 22.&h3 &h5 23.g3 &f6 (23...&f4 24.gxf4 exf4 25.&d2 &xa1 (25...&h4 26.&a3!) 26.&xa1±) 24.&c7 &g7 (24...&g5 25.&xd8 &xd8 26.&fc1 intending 27.d7 and 28.&c8 is clearly better for White.) 25.&fd1 &g5 (25...&e6 26.&xe6 fxe6 27.&xa7±) 26.&xd8 &xd8 27.d7 intending &dc1–c8 with a clear advantage to White.

21.d6 &b7

21...&h4 22.&xc5 bxc5 (if 22...&xg4 then 23.&xb6 wins) 23.&e2!? intending 24.&c4 is clearly better for White according to Peter Leko.

22.&c7 &xc7 23.dxc7 &xe4

23...f5 24.&xc5 bxc5 25.&e2 &fc8 (25...&ac8 26.&xa7) 26.&c4† &f8 27.&d5+-.

24.&ac1 f5

24...&d6 25.&fd1 f5 26.&e2 &f7 27.&d7 &ac8 28.&c4 f4 29.&d2 a5 30.&e6+-.

25.&e2 &f7 26.&a6 &ac8 27.&fd1± &e7 28.f3 f4

Black could also have tried 28...&c5, however this would have run into 29.&xc5! bxc5 30.&xc5† &e6 (30...&f7 31.&d7† &f6 32.&xf8+-) 31.&d6† &e7 (31...&f7 32.&d7†) 32.&d8† when White is winning in any case.

29.&xb6 axb6 30.fxe4 &f6 31.&c6!+- &fe8 32.&dd6 &xc7 33.&e6† &f7 34.&xf6† &g7 35.&xg6† hxg6 36.&xc7†

1–0

The comments to this game are based on Mozetic's annotations for *Informant 59*, unless otherwise indicated.

Game 30 Conclusions: As with Game 26, Black cannot really afford to play moves such as 13...b6. Not only does this fail to challenge White's central dominance, it also substantially weakens the queenside light squares (a point which is of particular importance with the light-squared bishop fulfilling other duties on g4) and gives White time to mobilise his forces and rapidly generate an initiative.

Game 31
Kramnik – Topalov
Linares 1998

1.♘f3 ♘f6 2.c4 c5 3.♘c3 d5 4.cxd5 ♘xd5 5.d4
♘xc3 6.bxc3 g6 7.e4 ♗g7 8.♖b1 0–0 9.♗e2
cxd4 10.cxd4 ♕a5† 11.♗d2 ♕xa2 12 0–0 ♗g4
13.♗e3 ♘c6

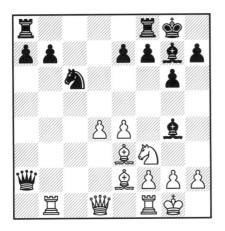

14.d5

14.♖xb7 has been used with success by Ivanchuk,
but Black should not have anything to worry about,
e.g. 14...♖ab8 15.♖xb8 (15.♖c7 ♖fc8 16.♖xc8†
♖xc8 17.h3 (17.d5 ♘e5=) 17...♗xf3 18.♗xf3 ♖d8
transposes to 15.♖xb8. This move order was used
in Chernin – Stohl, Hungary 1998, considered
below with the move number adjusted.) 15...♖xb8
16.h3 ♗xf3! (This highlights an important
difference between the 13.♗e3 and the 13.♗g5
h6 14.♗e3 lines. In the 13.♗g5 variation Black's
best response was 16...♗d7, however in this line
♗d7 is less accurate because 17.d5 ♘e5 18.♗f4
♕b2 19.♕c1 cannot be met by 19...g5, as it can
when the pawn is on h6.) 17.♗xf3 ♖d8 18.d5
♘e5 19.♕c1 (19.♗g5 ♗f6 20.♗xf6 exf6 21.♕d4
♖b8 22.♗d1 ♖b2 23.♗a4 a5 24.♗e8 ♖b1 25.♖xb1
♕xb1† 26.♔h2 ♕b8 0–1 Chernin – Stohl,
Hungary 1998.) 19...♘c4! 20.♗g5 ♖e8! 21.♖e1
(21.♗g4 ♕a4! 22.♗h6 ♗xh6 23.♕xh6 ♘e5=) 21...
e6! 22.♖e2 ♕b3 23.dxe6 ♖xe6= Khalifman – Stohl,

Germany 1997. The comments here are based on
Igor Stohl's annotations for *Informant 71*.
14...♗xf3

This is probably Black's most popular treatment
of the 13.♗e3 line, however Black also has the
usual alternatives. 14...♘a5 is considered in
Game 32, and the following options must also be
considered:

a) 14...♘e5 15.♖xb7 (15.♖e1!? has only been
played a couple of times, but with success on each
occasion:
15...♗xf3 16.gxf3 ♖fd8 (16...♖fc8 17.♖xb7 ♕a3
18.♗g5 f6 19.♗c1 ♕d6 20.♕a4 ♖c7 21.♖a3±
Sharavdorj – Serpik, USA 2004) 17.♖b4
(threatening 18.♗a4 and 19.♗d4, trapping the
black queen) 17...b5 18.♖xb5 e6 19.d6 ♘c4
20.♗xc4 ♕xc4 21.♖c5 ♕b4 22.e5 h6 23.♕e2
♕b7 24.♖ec1 ♖ac8 25.♖xc8 ♖xc8 26.♖xc8† ♕xc8
27.♕b5± Shabalov – Owens, Chicago 2002)
15...e6 (15...♖fb8 16.♖xe7 ♖b2 17.♗d4 ♖xe2
18.♗xe5 ♗xf3 19.gxf3 ♗xe5 20.♖xe5± - Ftacnik)
16.d6 and now:

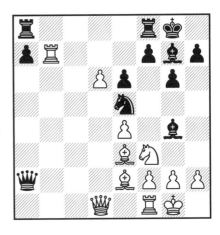

a1) 16...♗xf3 17.gxf3 would be more acceptable
if the pawn were on h6, because Black could
play ...g5, to some extent securing the position
of the knight on e5. However, now White can
obtain a clear advantage by playing 18.f4 and
19.e5 shutting in the g7-bishop and securing the
position of the d6-pawn.

a2) 16...♘xf3† 17.gxf3 ♗h3 18.♖e1 ♕a5?! (Roberto G. Alvarez notes the line 18...e5 19.♕a1 ♕xa1 20.♖xa1 ♖fb8 21.♖bxa7 ♖xa7 22.♗xa7 ♖b2 23.♗f1± , but suggests that 18...♖fb8!? may be better.) 19.♖b5!? ♕d8 20.♗g5 f6 21.♗e3 f5 22.♕d2 fxe4 23.♗g5 e3 24.fxe3 ♗f6 25.e4± Rodriguez – Zenker, corr. 2001.

a3) 16...♖fd8 is the normal move in the line with 13.♗g5 h6 14.♗e3, however here White can make use of the g5-square to play 17.♗g5! ♗xf3 18.gxf3 f6 (18...♖xd6? 19.♕xd6 ♕xe2 20.♖b8†+- -Illescas Cordoba) 19.♗e3 ♗f8 20.d7± ♖xd7? 21.♖xd7 ♘xd7 22.♕xd7 ♕xe2 23.♖c1! ♗xf3 24.♕xe6† ♔h8 25.♗d4+- San Segundo – De la Villa Garcia, Mondariz 1997.

b) 14...♖fd8 was once used with success by Tseshkovsky against Sakaev, but White's play can be improved in various places and nobody has been tempted to try this line since.

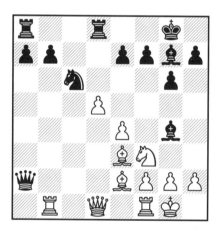

Play continued 15.♖xb7 e6 16.♖c7 (An obvious try is 16.♗g5!? f6 (16...♖d6!? 17.♗f4±) 17.♕c1! when 17...exd5 (17...fxg5 18.♗c4 ♕a4 19.♗b3! ♘d4 20.♕xg5 is clearly better for White, and 17...♕xe2 18.♕xc6± fxg5? 19.♕c7 is actually winning.) 18.♗xf6! ♗xf6 19.♕xc6 intending 20.♕c7 looks fantastic for White.) 16...♗xf3! (16...♘e5 17.♖c2! ♕a4 18.♘xe5 ♗xe2 19.♕xe2 ♗xe5 20.dxe6 ♕xe4 21.exf7† ♔xf7 22.♖c4 ♕d5± - Sakaev, *Informant 70*) and now 17.gxf3 was Sakaev

– Tseshkovsky, Yugoslavia 1997, which gave rise to equal chances, but perhaps 17.♗xf3 ♘e5 18.d6 is a better try, the obvious analogy being the recent game Bacrot – McShane, Biel 2004, considered in the notes to Game 27.

15.♗xf3 ♘e5

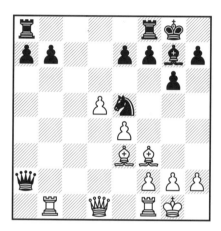

The universal choice in this position, but 15...♘a5 is also possible of course.

16.♗e2!

The text is the only move that has managed to really challenge Black's defences, however those defending the Black side should be aware of two other continuations:

a) 16.♖xb7 a5! (16...e6!? has been used with some success by Azmaiparashvili, however White has always responded with 17.dxe6 ♕xe6 18.♖xa7 when White will have 4 pawns versus 3 on the kingside, but will struggle to acquire the full point. Instead Illescas Cordoba, in *Informant 71*, points out that 17.♕e2! is clearly better for White. Alternatively 16...♘xf3† 17.♕xf3 a5 18.♗c5 ♕c4 19.♗xe7 ♖fb8 20.♖xb8† ♖xb8 21.d6 was clearly better for White in Moiseenko – Khaetsky, Kharkov 2000. Finally, Ftacnik proposed 16...♕a3 without further analysis, but with the assessment that Black has counterplay.) 17.♖xe7 a4 18.♗d4 (Ftacnik notes the lines 18.♕e2 ♕xe2 19.♗xe2 a3 20.f4 a2 21.fxe5 a1♕ 22.♖xa1 ♖xa1† 23.♔f2 f5 is unclear and 18.♗f4

♕b2! 19.♗xe5 ♗xe5 20.♕e2 a3 wins for Black.) 18...♘xf3† 19.gxf3 ♗xd4 20.♕xd4 a3 was Bacrot – Illescas Cordoba, Pamplona 1998, and now 21.♔g2 ♕b2 was equal according to Illescas Cordoba (*Informant 71*), however Ftacnik has since suggested that White may be able to gain an edge with 21.♖a1 (21.f4 ♕b2 22.♕xb2 axb2 23.♖b7 ♖fb8 24.♖xb8† ♖xb8 25.♖b1 ♔f8 is slightly better for White according to Ftacnik, but I don't believe Black should have any problems drawing this.) 21...♕b2 22.♕e5 ♕xe5 (22...f6? 23.♕c7+-) 23.♖xe5 a2 24.d6 ♖fb8 25.♔g2 ♖b1 26.♖xa2 ♖xa2 27.d7 ♖d1 28.♖e8† ♔g7 29.d8♕ ♖xd8 30.♖xd8 when obviously Black should have good drawing chances, but White can still press a little.

b) 16.♗c5 ♗f6 17.♖xb7 ♖fb8 18.♗xe7 (18.♖xb8† ♖xb8 19.d6 ♕a5 20.♕d5 ♘d7!? 21.♗e3 ♕xd5 22.exd5 exd6 23.♗xa7 is equal according to Makarychev, and 18.♖xe7 ♗xe7 19.♗xe7 ♖b7 20.d6 ♕e6 is also fine for Black according to Azmaiparashvili.) 18...♖xb7 19.♗xf6 ♖e8 20.h4?! (20.♕c1 ♕b2 21.♕f4 ♖b6 22.♔h1 a5 is dangerous for White, but 20.g3!? deserves attention according to Azmaiparashvili.) 20...♕a3 21.♗xe5 ♖xe5 22.♕d4 ♕b2 23.♕c4 ♖e8 24.♕c6 ♕b5 was good for Black in Krasenkow – Azmaiparashvili, Yerevan 1996.

16...♘c4 17.♗g5

17...♘d6
Provocative play by Topalov, however the alternatives are hardly tame:

a) 17...♖fe8 18.♖xb7 ♘d6 19.♖b4 a5 20.♖a4 ♕b2 21.♗c1! (21.♕d3?! ♖ab8 22.♗c1 (22.♖xa5 ♕e5=) 22...♕c3!= Huzman – Alterman, Israel 1998) 21...♕b6 (21...♕b7 22.f4 ♗b2 23.♗e3 f5 24.e5 ♘e4 25.♗d4 ♘c3 26.♗xc3 ♗xc3 27.g4 ♗b4 28.gxf5 gxf5 29.♔h1± Jelen – Sebenik, Bled 1999) 22.♗e3 ♕b2 23.♗c1 (23.f4 intending 24.e5 looks like a better try for the advantage.) 23...♕b6 24.♕d3 ♖eb8 25.♗g5 ♖b7 26.♖c1 ♕b2 27.♖c5 h6 28.♗d2 ♕b3 29.♕c2 ♕b1† 30.♗f1 ♕xc2 31.♖xc2 ♖b1 32.g3 ½–½ Sakaev – Notkin, Russian Championship, Elista 1996. Black managed to hold his own in this game, however I suspect that White was better around move 21, and 17...♖e8 has not been repeated at GM level since.

b) 17...♖fb8!?

18.♗xc4 (18.♗xe7 runs into 18...♘d2) 18...♕xc4 19.♗xe7 (Krasenkow suggested 19.♕f3!? freeing up the f1–rook so that it can occupy the c-file next move.) 19...b5 20.♖c1 (Better is 20.♕f3 however after 20...♕c3 Krasenkow believes that Black should be okay despite the advanced position of White's d-pawn.) 20...♕xe4 21.♖e1 (21.d6 ♗f8 22.♖e1 ♕f4) 21...♕f5 22.d6 ♗f6 23.♗xf6 ♕xf6 24.♕d5

罝d8 25.d7 Black had the better practical chances in Comas Fabrego – McShane, Istanbul 2003, although with best play the position is probably objectively equal.

18.♗xe7!

An important novelty from Kramnik; previously White had managed to gain an edge with 18.♗d3 in Gelfand – Illescas Cordoba, Dos Hermanas 1997, however Black's play could have been improved. The text is critical.

18...♘xe4 19.♗f3!

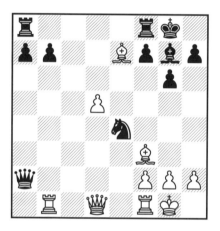

An excellent move, after which Kramnik brings considerable pressure to bear on Black's position. Note that 19.♗xf8 was bad because of 19...♘c3! 20.♗xg7 ♘xd1 21.罝fxd1 ♕xe2∓. 19.罝b4 and 19.♗c4 ♕xc4 20.罝b4 were also possible, but neither promises White even a hint of an advantage.

19...♘d2

Kramnik, in his annotations for *Informant 72*, notes the lines 19...♘c3 20.♕b3 ♕xb3 21.罝xb3 罝fe8 22.d6, and 19...罝fe8 20.d6 in either case with advantage to White.

20.♕e2!

20.♗xf8?! ♔xf8! 21.罝xb7 (21.♕e2 罝e8) 21...♘xf1 22.♕xf1= squanders the initiative.

20...罝fe8

20...♕xb1 21.罝xb1 ♘xb1 22.d6 is clearly better for White according to Kramnik, however Ftacnik notes that 20...♘xf3† 21.♕xf3 罝fb8

22.d6 b6 23.♕e4 (23.罝fe1 or 23.♕c6 may be better.) 23...f5 24.♕f3 ♕e6 25.罝fe1 ♕d7 26.♕d5† ♔h8 gives rise to an unclear position. Kramnik also suggests 20...罝fb8!? as an interesting move that may merit consideration, although after 21.罝fd1 White's chances look slightly preferable.

21.d6 ♘xf3†

The alternatives 21...♕a5 22.♗xb7 ♘xb1 (22...罝ab8 23.罝b5) 23.♗xa8 罝xa8 24.罝xb1±, and 21...罝ad8 22.罝xb7 罝xd6 (22...♕a5 23.♗xd8 罝xd8 24.罝d1+-) 23.♗xd6 罝xe2 24.罝b8† ♗f8 25.♗xe2 ♘xf1 26.♗xf8 h5 27.♗c5† ♔g7 28.♗d4†+- are obviously very bad for Black.

22.♕xf3 ♗f8 23.罝xb7 a5 24.h4± a4

24...♕e6 25.罝d1 ♗e7? 26.罝xe7 ♕f5 27.d7, and 24...♗xe7 25.罝xe7± don't help matters.

25.罝d1

White protects d6 with a view to retreating the e7-bishop to safety, and then advancing the d-pawn.

25...♕e6 26.♗g5! h6

26...♗xd6 27.罝xd6 and 26...a3 27.d7 are both terrible for Black.

27.d7 hxg5 28.dxe8♕ 罝xe8 29.hxg5 a3 30.g3! a2 31.♔g2

White is much better and should win this position, however Black's a-pawn coordinates well with his bishop and could potentially cause White some problems. In anticipation of this

Kramnik removes his king from the back rank, so that the a-pawn can never queen with check.
31...♖d8

Less accurate is 31...♗g7 32.♖e1! a1♕ 33.♖xe6+–, which illustrates the importance of having the king on g2, and 31...♖c8 32.♖a7 ♕c4 33.♖c1+– is another nice point to White's king position.
32.♖e1

Kramnik does not assign an assessment to this move, however GM Curt Hansen considers it a serious inaccuracy, awarding it a question mark. By way of improvements Kramnik notes that 32.♖xd8 a1♕ 33.♖bb8 ♕e7 is slightly better for White, however Hansen points out that White has a far stronger resource in 32.♖a7!, e.g. 32...♖xd1 33.♕xd1 ♕e4† (33...♗g7? 34.♖a8† ♔h7 35.♕h1†+– is rather cute) 34.♕f3 ♕e6 35.♕a8+–.
32...♕c4 33.♖a7 ♖d3! 34.♕a8 ♖d2! 35.♕f3 ♖d3 36.♕a8 ♖d2 37.♖a4?

37.♖e4! ♕d3 (37...♕b3 38.♖f4 ♕e6 39.♖a6! ♕b3 40.♖xg6† wins for White, as does 37...♕c5 38.♖f4.) 38.♖f4 ♖d1 39.♖xa2 ♕f1† 40.♔h2 ♕g1† 41.♔h3 ♕f1† 42.♔g2 would have won according to Kramnik.
37...♕c5 38.♖f1 ♕c2 39.♖a7 ♕b3! 40.♕f3?

40.♖c7 ♕a3 41.♖c8 ♕xa8† 42.♖xa8+– – Kramnik.

40...♕xf3† 41.♔xf3 ♗c5=

Now Topalov should be able to hold this ending because Kramnik can only win the a2-pawn if he gives up the f2-pawn. Once this has transpired White will struggle to make use of the extra exchange, because the g5-pawn remains vulnerable to Black's rook and bishop.
42.♖a8† ♔g7 43.♖a1 ♖xf2† 44.♔g4 ♖d2 45.♖a4 ♗b6 46.♖1xa2 ♖d5 47.♔h4 ♗d8 48.♖g4 ♖d1 49.♖h2 ♔g8 50.♖e4 ♖d5 51.♖e8† ♔g7 52.♔g4 ♗xg5 53.♖b2 ♖d4† 54.♔f3
½–½

Game 31 Conclusions: Black is having some trouble holding the balance after 13.♗e3 ♘c6 14.d5 ♗xf3 (14...♘e5, by analogy with 13.♗g5 h6 14.♗e3 ♘c6! 15.d5! ♘e5, is very bad here because White can make use of the g5-square to play ♗e3-g5 at some timely moment, possibly harassing a rook on d8.) 15.♗xf3 ♘e5 16.♗e2! ♘c4 17.♗g5. White has managed to demonstrate an edge in all lines other than McShane's recent discovery 17...♖fb8!?, which requires further tests but held up well in its only outing.

Game 32
Lautier – Shipov
FIDE World Ch Moscow 2001

1.d4 ♘f6 2.c4 g6 3.♘c3 d5 4.cxd5 ♘xd5 5.e4 ♘xc3 6.bxc3 ♗g7 7.♘f3 c5 8.♖b1 0–0 9.♗e2 cxd4 10.cxd4 ♕a5† 11.♗d2 ♕xa2 12.0–0 ♗g4 13.♗e3 ♘c6 14.d5 ♘a5 15.♗g5

Currently this is regarded as White's most challenging treatment of the 14.♘a5 line. By analogy with the positions reached after 13.♗g5 h6 14.♗e3 ♘c6 15.d5 ♘a5 16.♗c5, White should also consider 15.♗c5. However the more secure position of the h-pawn ensures that Black can maintain equality: 15.♗c5 ♘f6 16.e5 ♘xe5 17.♖b4 ♗xf3 18.♗xf3 ♖ae8 19.♗xa7 (In the 13.♗g5 h6 14.♗e3 variation White could now play 19.♗e3, hitting the h6-pawn and threatening 20.♖b4, however here White must satisfy himself with the rather less rewarding capture of the a7-

pawn. Also note that 19.♖a4? is bad on account of 19...♕b3 20.♖xa5 ♕xd1 21.♖xd1 b6∓.) 19...b5! 20.♖xb5 (20.♕e2 ♕xe2 21.♗xe2 ♘c4= as in van Wely – Leko, Fontys 1998, and 20.♗d4 ♗xd4 21.♕xd4 ♘c4 22.♖a1 ♕c2 (22...♕d2? 23.♖xc4!+-) 23.♗e4 ♕e2 24.♗f3 ♕c2 were equal according to Leko.) 20...♘c4 21.♕e2?! (21.♗c5 ♘d2 (21...♘d6!?) 22.♖e1 ♘xf3† 23.♕xf3 ♕c4=) 21...♕xa7 22.♕xc4 ♖c8∓ Krasenkow – Leko, Madrid 1998.

15...♕a3

Practice has also focussed on 15...♗xf3 16.♗xf3, after which Black has tried two moves:

a) Svidler once played 16...♖fe8? against Kramnik, however he ran into some devastating home prep: 17.e5!!

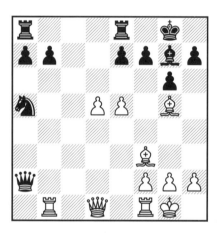

17...♘c4 (17...♗xe5 is obviously critical, however Kramnik seems to have everything covered: 18.d6 (Krasenkow analyses 18.♖e1 which may also be good, e.g. 18...♘c4 (18...♘d6? 19.♖a1 picks up the a5-knight, and 18...f6? 19.d6 ♔h8 20.d7 ♖ed8 21.♖xe5 fxe5 22.♗xe7 ♖xd7 23.♗f6† ♖g7 24.♗xg7† ♔xg7 25.♖a1 is also winning for White. Black could try 18...♗c3 however simply 19.♖xe7 guarantees White the better chances.) 19.♖xb7 f6 20.d6! e6 21.♖xe5! ♘xe5 22.♗xf6±) 18...exd6 (18...♗xd6 19.♖a1 ♕c4 20.♖xa5 ♗xh2† 21.♔h1 is clearly better for White, as is 18...♗e6 19.♗xe7, e.g. 19...♗xd6? 20.♗xd6 ♖ad8 21.♕a4+-)

19.♗d5 ♕a3 20.♗d2! ♘c6 (20...♗c3? 21.♕f3 and 20...♕c5 21.♕f3! ♖f8 22.♖fc1 are both terrible for Black.) 21.♖xb7 ♖ec8 22.♖xf7 ♔h8 23.♕g4 ♗g7 24.♗h6 ♗xh6 25.♕d7+-) 18.d6 ♘xe5 (18...exd6 19.exd6 ♕a5 20.d7 ♕xg5 21.dxe8♕† ♖xe8 22.♕a4!+-) 19.♗d5! ♕a3 (19...♕a5 20.♗xe7 ♗f8 21.♖e1! ♗xe7 22.♖xe5+-) 20.♗xe7 ♗f8 21.♗xb7 ♗xe7 22.♗xa8 ♗xd6 23.♗d5± Kramnik – Svidler, Linares 1999. The comments here are based on Kramnik's annotations for *Informant 75*.

b) 16...♕a3!?

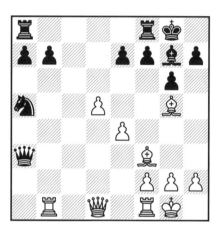

was suggested by Kramnik by way of an improvement over his game with Svidler. 17.♗d2 (17.♕e2!?) 17...♗c3 18.♗c1 (18.♖e1 intending 19.e5 makes more sense.) 18...♗d6 19.♗d2 ♗xd2 20.♕xd2 b6= Jelen – Votava, Pardubice 1999.

16.♖e1!

This logical novelty seems stronger than the established mainline with 16.♗d2 ♗c3 17.♗c1 ♕d6 (17...♕c5 18.♕a4! is strong according to Shirov) 18.e5 ♕c7 19.d6 exd6 20.exd6 ♕d7 21.♗f4 ♖fe8 22.h3 ♗f5 23.♗b5 (23.♖c1 ♖ac8) 23...♘c6 24.♖c1 ♗f6 25.♕d2 (25.♖e1 ♖xe1† 26.♕xe1 ♖e8 27.♕d2 ♖e4 seemed fine for Black in Xu Jun – Harikrishna, Tripoli 2004.) 25...a6 (25...♗e4 26.♘g5!) 26.♗xc6 bxc6 27.♘d4 ♗e4 28.♘b3 ♗d5 29.♘c5 ♕a7 30.♕a5 ♗d4 31.d7 ♖ed8 32.♗c7 ♗xc5 33.♗xd8 ♗d6 34.♗f6 ♕xd7

35.♗b2 ♖f8 36.♖fe1 ½–½ Kramnik – Kasparov, Frankfurt 1999.

16...♗xf3

The immediate 16...♗c3?! runs into 17.♕d3 when 17...♗b4 18.♕xa3 ♗xa3 19.♖a1 ♗b4 20.♖eb1 ♗c3 21.♖a3 f6 22.♗e3 leaves White better, and 16...♖fc8 17.e5 ♗f5 18.♖a1 ♕c5 19.♗e3 was also better for White in Maetzig – Kruse, e-mail 1999.

17.♗xf3 ♕d6 18.♕e2 ♗e5 19.g3 b6 20.♗g4 ♘b7

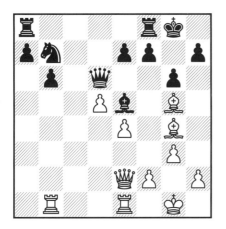

21.f4

The game we are presently considering was a tie-break game between Lautier and Shipov in the 2001 FIDE World Championship qualifying stages. In an earlier game in that match Lautier had tried 21.♖bd1 but achieved little: 21...a5 22.♕c2?! (22.f4 ♗f6 or 22...♗c3 23.♖f1 a4 are both unclear according to Krasenkow.) 22...a4 23.f4 ♗g7 24.e5 ♕b4 25.♕c7 f6! 26.exf6 exf6 27.♕xb7 fxg5 was better for Black in Lautier – Shipov, Moscow 2001, although the game was eventually drawn.

21...♗f6 22.♗xf6

22.♗h6 ♗g7 23.♗xg7 ♔xg7 24.♗f3 intending 25.e5 also merits consideration according to Krasenkow.

22...exf6 23.♗f3 ♘c5 24.e5 fxe5 25 fxe5±/±

25...♕d7 26.♖b4 a5 27.♖f4 a4 28.d6 a3

Krasenkow suggests that it may have been better to play 28...♖a5!? with a view to discouraging 29.♗d5.

29.♗d5 ♘e6 30.♖f6 ♕a4 31.♕a2 ♕d4† 32.♔g2 ♖ae8 33.♖e2?!

33.♖ef1! is stronger according to Krasenkow, e.g. 33...♕xe5? 34.d7+-.

33...♘d8 34.♖f4 ♕d3?! 35.♖a4 ♘e6 36.♖xa3 ♕d4 37.♖a7 b5 38.♖e7 ♕g4 39.♖e4 ♕f5 40.♕a7 ♖xe7 41.dxe7 ♖e8 42.♗c6 ♘g5 43.♖e2 ♕g4 44.♖f2 ♕e6 45.♗xe8 ♕d5† 46.♔g1 ♘h3† 47.♔f1

1–0

Game 32 Conclusions: 13.♗e3 ♘c6 14.d5 ♘a5 seems a bit better for White after 15.♗g5 ♕a3 16.♖e1!. Black's position remains solid of course, but it is quite clear that it is White who will dictate the pace at which the game develops.

Conclusions on 12...♗g4!:

12...♗g4 is definitely a highly resilient system, and currently represents Black's most popular method of meeting the Modern Exchange Variation, as well as the most reliable. In terms of specifics, Black should meet 13.♗g5! with 13...h6!, as retreating with 13...♕e6 gives White time to convert his development and space advantages into a substantial initiative (see Game 21). Following 13...h6 Black has no reason to fear 14.♗xe7 as Kasparov has demonstrated a forcing route to equality (see Game 22). For some time White was able to maintain an advantage with 14.♗h4!?, when Black's primary attempts to generate counterplay with 14...♖d8, 14...♕e6 (Game 23) and 14...g5 15.♗g3 ♘c6 16.d5 ♖ad8 (Game 24) all failed to equalize. However in time solutions were found, and it is now clear that 14...a5!? (Game 25) gives Black excellent counterplay. Indeed it is currently questionable whether White can achieve anything more than a draw in this line with best play.

White's main weapon against the 12...♗g4 system currently seems to be 13.♗g5 h6 14.♗e3!? (at least this was Bacrot's choice when he recently used this line against English GM Luke McShane). Black has had no success with 14...b6 (Game 26), which leaves the queenside light squares rather vulnerable. Black's traditional response has been 14...♘c6 15.d5 ♘e5 (Game 27) 16.♖xb7 e6 17.d6 ♖fd8 18.♖e1 ♗xf3 19.gxf3 ♕a5!? however the continuation 20.♖f1! ♗f8 21.d7! ♕a2! 22.♗b5 a6 23.♗a4! is presently posing serious problems, and is better for White on existing evidence. More resilient is 14...♘c6 15.d5 ♘a5 (Game 28), however the continuation 16.♗c5! ♗f6 17.e5! ♗xe5 18.♖b4! also appears to be better for White.

That only leaves 14...♘c6 15.d5 ♗xf3 (Game 29), which is fine for Black after 16.♗xf3, but more tricky after 16.gxf3. I wouldn't go so far as to assert that White is definitely better after 16.gxf3 (especially given that I think Black will eventually find a way to neutralise this little move), however results have been positive so far, and Black has yet to demonstrate a clean method of equalizing.

White's last attempt in this line is 13.♗e3!? (Games 30-32). In Game 30 Black tried 13...b6, however this was just as bad here as against 13.♗g5 h6 14.♗e3 (Game 26), and these games should be considered in conjunction with one another. In Game 31 Black tries 13.♗e3 ♘c6 14.d5 ♗xf3 15.♗xf3 ♘e5 however after 16.♗e2! ♘c4 17.♗g5 Black comes under some serious pressure. In this instance Black's best chance of equalizing presently lies in McShane's 17...♖fb8!?, although there is very little practical experience of this move upon which to found solid conclusions.

Finally, in Game 32 Black tries 13.♗e3 ♘c6 14.d5 ♘a5, the point being that 15.♗c5 is less good here than when Black has played h7-h6 (the specific details of why are discussed in the notes to the game). However after 15.♗g5 ♕a3 16.♖e1! Black never quite managed to neutralise White's initiative, and Lautier went on to win in convincing fashion.

Chapter 5: Rare 12th Move Alternatives and 11.♕d2!?

Game 33
Gelfand – Kamsky
Belgrade 1991

1.d4 ♘f6 2.c4 g6 3.♘c3 d5 4.cxd5 ♘xd5 5.e4 ♘xc3 6.bxc3 ♗g7 7.♘f3 c5 8.♖b1 0–0 9.♗e2 cxd4 10.cxd4 ♕a5† 11.♗d2 ♕xa2 12.0–0 ♕e6

Although 12...♕e6 received some attention in the eighties, nowadays it is a rare guest in tournament play, primarily because retreating the queen gives White the time and manoeuvring space necessary to build a powerful initiative. Before proceeding with the game, it may be worth noting that 12...♘c6!? should be met by 13.d5 with the following options:

a) 13...♘a5 14.♗b4 ♗d7 15.e5!? (15.♗xe7 ♖fe8 16.d6 looked a little better for White in Andeer – Dziel, e-mail 2001.) 15...♗a4 16.♕e1 ♘b3 17.♗xe7 ♖fe8 Ramirez – Dorner, corr. 1996, and now 18.d6 looks clearly better for White.

b) 13...♘d4 14.♘xd4 ♗xd4 15.♗h6 (15.♗b4!?) 15...♗g7 16.♗xg7 ♔xg7 17.♕d4† f6± Gehring – Ferrari, e-mail 1999.

c) 13...♘e5 14.♘d4! ♗g4 15.f3 ♘c4 16.♗g5

♘d2 17.♗xd2 ♗xd4† 18.♔h1± -Korchnoi, *Informant 41*.

13.♕c2 ♕c6
Alternatives:
a) 13...b6 14.♗c4 ♕d7 15.♕a2!

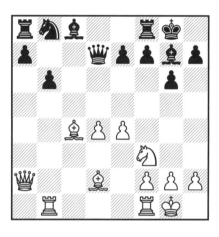

15...♘c6! (15...♗b7 16.♘g5 ♕e8 17.♖b3! gives White a clear advantage and an attack according to Lars Bo Hansen (*Informant 51*)) 16.♗b5 ♕b7 (16...a6? 17.d5 axb5 18.♕xa8 ♘a7 (18...♘a5 19.♗xa5 ♗b7 20.♕a7+-) 19.♕b8+-) was L.B. Hansen – Brinck Claussen, Naestved 1991, and now Hansen suggests that 17.d5! should be better for White, e.g. 17...♘e5 (17...♘b8 18.♗e3 (18.♗f4 ♗d7 19.♘c4± J. Watson – Mont Reynaud, USA 1996) 18...a6!? 19.♗c6 ♘xc6 20.♖xb6 ♘b4!? 21.♕c4 ♕d7 22.♖xb4 a5 23.♕a3±) 18.♘xe5 ♗xe5 19.♗c6 ♗a6! 20.♖a1! ♕xa2! (20...♗xa1 21.♖xa1 ♕xa2 22.♖xa2 ♖b8 23.♖xa7±) 21.♖xa2 ♖b8 22.♖xa7 ♗d6 23.♖b1 f5! 24.♗e3 fxe4 25.h3!±.

b) 13...♕d7 14.d5 b6 15.♕a2 ♕d8 16.♗e3 (16.♖fc1 ♗g4 17.♗f4 ♘d7 18.♗c7 ♕e8 19.♗b5 ♕c8 20.♗a6 ♕e8 21.♗b7± Sokolin – Fedorowicz, New York 1993) 16...♘d7 was Conquest –

Korchnoi, Lugano 1986, which Black ultimately won after 17.♘d4. However, in his annotations for *Informant 41*, Viktor Korchnoi suggests that 17.♗b5!? (intending 18.♗c6) 17...a5 18.♗xd7 (18.♗c6!?) 18...♕xd7 19.♖xb6 guarantees White a small but definite advantage.

c) 13...♕d6 14.♗b4! ♕d8 15.d5 ♗g4 16.♖fc1 ♘a6? The question mark was assigned to this move by Gelfand and Kapengut in *Informant 49*. As a general rule, a knight will be badly placed on a6 in the 8.♖b1 Grünfeld unless it is able to occupy c5 or b4 in the near future. Nevertheless, White seems to be better in any case: 16...♘d7 17.♕c7 leaves the b7 and e7-pawns weak, whereas 16...♗h6?! 17.♖d1± and 16...♗xf3 17.♗xf3 (17. gxf3!?±) 17...♘a6 18.♗a3 b6± both leave White better according to Gelfand and Kapengut.

17.♗a3 ♗xf3 (17...♖c8 18.♕a4±) 18.gxf3! ♕d7 (18...♗h6 19.♖xb7! ♗xc1 20.♕xc1!?±) 19.♗xa6 bxa6 20.♕c7!± Gelfand – Kindermann, Dortmund 1990.

14.♕d3

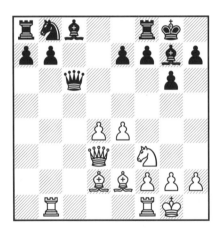

14...♕d6

These types of positions have been reached a vast number of times, despite the fact that the conclusion is consistently favourable to White. A couple of alternatives:

a) 14...b6 15.♖fc1 ♕d7 (15...♕d6 16.♗b4 ♕d8 17.♕a3 ♖e8 18.d5 gave White good

compensation in Selin – Karavaev, Tula 1998, according to Krasenkow.) 16.♕a3 (Also good is 16.♕e3 ♗a6 17.d5 ♖c8 (17...♗xe2 18.♕xe2 a5 19.♗c3 ♗xc3 20.♖xc3 a4 21.♕e3 ♖c8 22.♕h6 f6 23.♖xc8† ♕xc8 24.♘d4 ♕f8 25.♕c1± Komarov – Karasev, Leningrad 1989) 18.♗d1 ♖xc1 19.♖xc1 ♗b7 20.♗c3 ♗xc3 21.♖xc3 ♘a6 22.♕h6 ♕g4 23.♗e2 ♕h5 24.♕f4± Schulte – Iatrino, Cattolica 1993) 16...♗b7 (16...e6 17.♗b5! ♕b7 18.♗b4 ♖d8 19.♗e7 ♗f8 20.♗xf8 ♖xf8 21.♘d2, intending 22.♘d2-c4-d6, is clearly better for White – Krasenkow.) 17.d5 ♖c8 (17...e6 18.♗b5 ♕d8 19.♗g5 f6 20.dxe6! gives White a decisive advantage, and 17...♕d8 18.♗f4 ♘d7 19.♖c7 ♘c5 20.♖xc5 bxc5 21.♖xb7 was also winning for White in Steinmacher – Schmitt, Zell 1993.) 18.♖xc8† ♗xc8 19.♗b4 ♗f8 20.♘e5 ♕b7 21.♕f3 f6 22.♗c4± Correa – Matsuura, Curitiba 1992.

b) 14...♗g4 15.d5 (15.♗f4 ♕d7 16.d5 a5 17.♕a3 e6 18.♗b5 ♕d8 19.♘e5 g5 20.♗g3 ♗h5 21.dxe6 fxe6 22.♗c4± Arkhipov – Ruzhkovich, Novokuznetsk 1999) 15...♕d7 16.♕a3

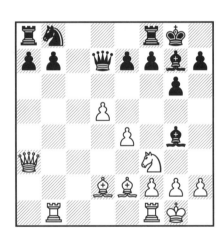

16...♗xf3 (16...♖c8 17.♗b5 ♕d8 18.♗b4 ♗f8 19.♘e5± Touzane – Kasantsev, Budapest 1995) 17.♗xf3 ♘a6 18.♗g5 ♖fe8 19.♗e2 ♕d6 20.♕e3 e6 21.dxe6 ♕xe6 22.♖xb7 h6 23.♗f4 ♕xe4 24.♗xa6 ♕c6 25.♕b3 1–0 Sakaev – Albrecht, Biel 1994.

15.♗b4

My own preference is for the text, however Lautier recently scored a convincing victory with 15.d5.

15...♕d8 16.d5!

In an earlier game with Kamsky, Gelfand had tried 16.♕a3 however the American No.1 managed to hold the balance with some resourceful tactical gymnastics: 16...♘c6 17.♗c5 ♗xd4! 18.♘xd4 ♘xd4 19.♗xe7 ♘xe2† 20.♔h1 ♕e8 21.♗xf8 ♕xf8 22.♕e3 a5! when it was White who had to think about equalising! In the present game Gelfand just expands his centre, taking the c6-square away from the b8-knight and securing an enduring positional advantage.

16...♘a6

Again, Black has tried alternatives:

a) 16...♗g4 17.♕a3 ♖e8 18.♗b5 ♘d7 (18...♗d7 19.♗a5 b6 20.♗xb6 ♕c8 21.♗e2±) 19.♗a5 b6 20.♗d2 a6 21.♗c6 ♖a7 22.♘g5! ♖f8 (22...h6 23.♘xf7 ♔xf7 24.f3 ♗h5 25.g4±) 23.h3 ♗e2 (23...♘e5? 24.hxg4 ♘xc6 25.♗e3 ♘d4 26.♗xd4 ♗xd4 27.♕h3+-) 24.♖fe1 ♗c4 25.♗e3 was clearly better for White in Shneider – Urban, Berlin 1992, according to Krasenkow.

b) 16...a5 17.♕a3 ♖e8

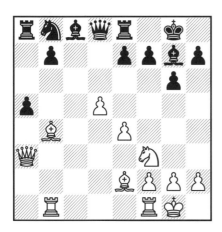

18.♖fc1 (18.♗b5!? ♗d7 19.♗c3±) 18...b6 19.♗b5!? (I am not sure about this one; 19.♗xe7! ♖xe7 20.♖xc8 ♕xc8 21.♕xe7± appears stronger for White.) 19...♗d7 20.♗d2 ♗xb5 21.♖xb5

♘d7 22.♗e3 ♖c8 23.♘d4 ♘e5 24.♖xc8 ♕xc8 25.♕b3 ♕c4 gave Black a good position in Se. Ivanov – Grimm, Cologne 1993.

17.♗a3 b6 18.♕e3! ♘c5 19.♖fd1 ♗g4 20.e5 ♖c8

This works out badly, however in a subsequent game (albeit a somewhat less elite encounter) Black managed to hold the balance with 20...♕c7 21.d6 exd6 22.exd6 ♘d7 23.♗xc5 bxc5 24.♕xc5 ♖fc8 25.♕a5 ♖ab8 26.♖xb8 ♖xb8 27.♘e5 ♗xe5 28.♕xe5 ♕e6= Ebner – Klocker, Austria 1993, although no doubt White's play can be improved.

21.h3 ♗xf3 22.♗xf3

22...♕c7?!

22...f6 23.d6! fxe5 24.d7 ♖c7 25.♗xc5 ♖xc5 26.♗g4 intending 27.♖bc1, is clearly better for White according to Kamsky. Kamsky does however suggest that 22...♖e8!? may merit attention.

23.d6 exd6 24.exd6 ♕d8

24...♕d7? 25.♗g4 f5 26.♗e2 intending 27.♗b5 is clearly better for White.

25.♗e2! ♖e8 26.♕f3± ♖e6!? 27.d7 ♖c7

27...♘xd7 28.♗b5 ♖c7 29.♕d5+- - Ftacnik.

28.♗b5 28...♖e7!

Black's best chance is to sacrifice an exchange to pick up the invasive d7-pawn, and then rely on the extra queenside pawns to hold the balance. Trying to undermine the d-pawn's support with 28...a6?! quickly leads to problems: 29.♗xc5 (29.♗c4 is also strong according to Ftacnik, e.g. 29...♖e7 30.♖xb6 ♖cxd7 31.♖xd7 ♖xd7 32.♗xc5 ♖d1† 33.♗f1+-) 29...axb5 (29...bxc5? 30.♗c4 intending 31.♖b8 is winning for White.) 30.♖a8! ♗f6 (30...♕xa8?? 31.d8♕† ♖e8 32.♕xc7 bxc5 33.♕xc5+-) 31.♕xd8† ♗xd8 32.♗e3±.

29.♖d2 ♖exd7 30.♗xd7 ♖xd7 31.♖xd7 ♕xd7

31...♘xd7?! 32.♖d1±.

32.♕a8†

32.♗xc5 bxc5 33.♖b7 ♕e6 34.♖xa7± - Ftacnik.

32...♗f8 33.♖e1!± h5! 34.h4 ♕d4! 35.♖e8?

An unfortunate error that lets the advantage slip. According to Kamsky 35.g3 ♔g7 36.♕xa7± was stronger, when 36...♗d6?! 37.♗xc5 ♗xc5 38.♕a1 guarantees White a clear advantage in the endgame.

35...♔g7!∞ 36.♕xa7??

36.g3 was forced, when the position remains unclear.

36...♗d6 37.♔f1 ♘d3 38.♔e2 ♘f4† 39.♔f3 ♕d1†

0–1

The comments to this game are based on Kamsky's annotations for *Informant 53*.

Game 33 Conclusions: Retreating with 12...♕e6 has been tried from time to time at GM level, but has never fully established itself as a reliable defence. Although White is unlikely to be able to whip up a winning attack in the next few moves, it should be remembered that a significant element of White's compensation is positional. Rather than trying to land any knock-out blows White should simply develop his pieces to sensible squares, try to play d4-d5 at an appropriate moment to remove the c6-square from Black's knight, and then either blast through in the centre with e5-e6 or d5-d6, or gradually strangle Black by restricting the mobility of his minor pieces with the advanced pawn centre.

Game 34
Shipov – V. Ivanov
Moscow 1995

1.d4 ♘f6 2.♘f3 g6 3.c4 ♗g7 4.♘c3 d5 5.cxd5 ♘xd5 6.e4 ♘xc3 7.bxc3 c5 8.♖b1 0–0 9.♗e2 cxd4 10.cxd4 ♕a5† 11.♗d2 ♕xa2 12.0–0 ♗d7!?

Like 12...♕e6, this is another one of those moves that has been played by decent players from time to time (GM Dvoirys for one), but has never really acquired any widespread popularity. That 12...♗d7 remains in the chapter on minor alternatives is hardly surprising, as it does nothing to challenge White's centre, and d7 is certainly not an optimal outpost for the bishop. Black does have some ideas involving ♗d7-a4 to disrupt White's coordination, and there is also the vague trick of meeting ♖xb7 with ♗c6, when Black may be able to pick up the e4-pawn, but this is all a bit speculative. I have complete confidence that White should be able to prove an advantage with a few accurate moves.

13.♖xb7!

A plethora of alternatives have been tried, but the text is the most obvious way to punish Black for relinquishing the defence of the b7-pawn. Moreover, I like the notion of challenging the 12...♗d7 concept head on!

13...♖c8

After the more obvious 13...♗c6 White has three options:

a) 14.♖b4 ♗xe4 15.♗c4 ♕c2! 16.♕xc2 ♗xc2 17.♖c1 (17.♗d5 ♘a6 18.♖b2 ♗d3 19.♗xa8 ♗xf1 20.♗b7∓ Brodsky – Odeev, USSR 1991) 17...a5 18.♖xb8 ♖fxb8 19.♖xc2 ♖b1† 20.♗f1 a4∓ Solozhenkin – Kleinplatz, Hyeres Open 1992.

b) 14.♖c7 ♗xe4 15.♗c4 ♕a3 16.♘g5 ♕d6! 17.♗xf7† ♔h8! (17...♖xf7 18.♖c8† ♖f8 19.♘xe4 ♕d5 20.♖xf8† ♔xf8?! (20...♗xf8 21.♘c3 ♕b7 22.♕e2 ♘d7 23.♕c4† ♔h8 24.♖b1 ♘b6=) 21.♕f3† ♔f5 22.♗f4 ♘c6 23.♘d6! exd6 24.♕xc6± Kakageldyev – Odeev, USSR 1991) 18.♖c3 ♗f5 19.♕f3 (19.g4 ♗d7 20.♖h3 h6 21.♕f3 ♘c6 22.♕e4 ♘xd4 23.♗c3 e5∓) 19...♘a6 20.♗d5 ♖ad8 21.♘f7† ♖xf7 22.♗xf7 ♕xd4 23.♗e1 ♗d3∓ -Odeev, Informant 52.

c) 14.♖xe7! ♕a3 (14...♗f6 15.♖c7 ♗xe4 16.♗c4± -S. Shipov, Informant 63.) 15.♗g5 h6 (15...f6 16.♗c4† ♔h8 17.♖xg7 ♔xg7 18.d5 ♕c3 was Petkov – Lalev, Bulgarian Championship 1992, and now 19.♕c1 ♕xc1 20.♗xc1! gives White compensation (Informant 54, anonymous)) 16.♕c1 ♕b4 17.♕d2 ♕a3 18.♗h4! g5

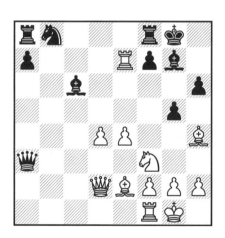

19.♗xg5!! hxg5 20.♕xg5 with a very strong attack:

c1) Ftacnik analyses 20...♕d6 in some depth: 21.♘h4! ♕f6 (21...♖e8? 22.♖xf7 ♔xf7 23.♗c4†

♖e6 24.♕g6† is winning for White, and 21...♕h6 22.♕g3 ♗d7 23.♗c4 ♗e6 24.d5 ♖c8 25.e5 gives White an ongoing attack. Finally 21...♕xd4 22.e5 ♕e4 23.♗d3! (23.♘f5 ♕xg2†! limits White to a slight edge) 23...♕xd3 24.♘f5 ♕xf5 25.♕xf5 is clearly better for White.) 22.♕g4 ♗d7 (22...♕xe7? 23.♘f5 ♕f6 24.e5, and 22...♖e8 23.♖xe8† ♗xe8 24.e5 ♕e7 25.♕xg7†! are both winning for White, and 22...♘d7 23.e5 leaves Black considerably worse for wear.) 23.♖xd7 ♘xd7 24.♗b5!± Lavrov – Chkurkin, Nagykanisza 1993.

c2) 20...♖e8 21.♖xf7! ♔xf7 22.♗c4† ♔f8 23.♘h4! ♗xe4 24.♕f4†+-.

c3) 20...♘d7 21.♘h4± ♕d6 22.♘f5 ♕f6 23.♕g4 ♖ae8 24.e5 ♕xf5 25.♕xf5 ♖xe7 26.♖c1 ♗d5 27.♖c7 ♗e6 28.♕g5 ♖fe8 (28...f6 29.♕h4) 29.f4+- Chernin – Fernandez Garcia, Pamplona 1991. The notes here are based on Chernin's annotations for Informant 53 unless indicated otherwise.

14.♗g5

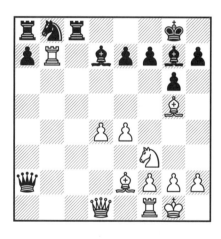

A novelty, although White had previously been successful with 14.♗f4 e6?! (Better is 14...♗c6!? 15.♖xe7 ♗f8 with an unclear position: Shipov.) 15.♘e5! ♗xe5?! 16.♗xe5 ♗c6 17.♖e7 ♗xe4 18.♗b5!± Khalifman – Dvoirys, Podolsk 1992. 14.♕a1 has also proved popular in practice, however White has never managed to really prove much by simplifying so early.

14...h6!

14...♘c6? 15.♖xe7 ♗f8 16.d5 ♗xe7 17.♖xe7 ♗a4 18.♕d3±.

15.♗h4

15.♗xe7?! ♕e6! 16.♗c5 ♕xe4∓.

15...♗c6?!

An inaccuracy according to Shipov, who notes that 15...♕c2 16.♕xc2 ♖xc2 17.♗d1! ♖c8 18.♗b3 limits White to a slight edge, and 15...a5!? 16.♕d3 e6 is unclear.

16.♖xe7 ♗f8 17.d5! ♗a4 18.♕d3 g5?

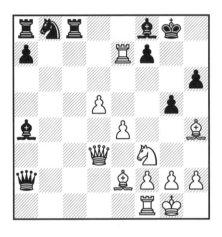

This just invites bad news, however 18...♗xe7 19.♗xe7 ♘d7 20.e5! gives White a powerful initiative according to Shipov, whereas Ftacnik notes that 20.♘d4 may also be strong.

19.♗xg5!

Absolutely essential if White is to prove his advantage. The tempting 19.♖xf7 ♔xf7 20.♘e5† ♔g7 21.♕f3 fails to 21...♗e8!∓, whereas preserving the rook with 19.♖b7 lets the initiative slip after 19...♘d7! when Black threatens 20...♘c5, forking White's queen and rook.

19...hxg5 20.♖xf7!! ♔xf7

Unsurprisingly Black has to just munch the material and hope. Shipov notes that 20...♕a3 21.♕xa3 ♗xa3 22.♘xg5 is winning for White, and that 20...♗c2 21.♕e3 ♔xf7 22.♕xg5 gives White a strong attack. Building on these

comments, Ftacnik observed that 20...♕c2 21.♘xg5 ♕xd3 22.♗xd3 ♗h6 23.♖f5 also gives White a strong initiative.

21.♘xg5† ♔e7

21...♔g8 22.♕h3! ♖c7 23.♗g4+-, or 21...♔f6 22.e5† ♔xg5 (22...♔xe5 23.♕e4† ♔d6 24.♕e6†+-) 23.♕g3† ♔h6 (23...♔f5 24.♗d3 mate) 24.♗d3+-. Mate cannot be far off in either case.

22.e5!+- ♗c2

22...♕c2 23.d6† ♔d8 (23...♔d7 24.♕h3†) 24.♘e6† ♔d7 25.♕h3, and 22...♔d8 23.♘e6† ♔d7 24.♗g4 ♖c4 25.♘xf8† are also pretty fatal for Black.

23.♕f3

1–0

Black resigned as 23.♕f3 ♔d7 24.♕f7† ♗e7 25.♗g4† is the end of the road.

A genuinely beautiful game, and a powerful demonstration by Shipov of how significant and dangerous White's opening lead in development can be - note that the b8-knight and the a8-rook still haven't moved! The comments to this game are based on Shipov's notes for *Chessbase Magazine 46* and *Informant 63*, unless otherwise indicated.

Game 34 Conclusions: There is still much uncharted territory in the 12...♗d7!? line, and it is quite possible that it may one day establish itself as a major mainline – but I doubt it. To my mind 12...♗d7!? is little more than a bag of tricks (albeit a bag that includes a few clever and dangerous tricks!) and I suspect that White should be clearly better with accurate play.

Game 35
Jelen – Naumann
Baden 1999

1.d4 ♘f6 2.c4 g6 3.♘c3 d5 4.cxd5 ♘xd5 5.e4 ♘xc3 6.bxc3 ♗g7 7.♘f3 c5 8.♖b1 0–0 9.♗e2 cxd4 10.cxd4 ♕a5† 11.♗d2 ♕xa2 12.0–0 ♘a6!?

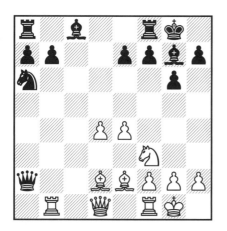

This little move was successfully introduced by GM Atalik in a game against GM Lembit Oll in 1997, however it has since failed to gather any popularity whatsoever, and consequently fallen into obscurity. Opinions of 12...♘a6 vary widely. Atalik himself describes the move as interesting in *Informant 71* (although notably he has never repeated it since!), and Ftacnik (in *Chessbase Magazine*) enthusiastically exclaims that "It is hard to believe this move was not tried before." However Krasenkow describes 12...♘a6 as "suspicious", noting that its only quality is to control b4 and c7, but that it does so at the cost of accepting prolonged inactivity. Rowson goes even further, observing "I can see little or no merit in this idea; in fact I doubt there is an idea." Rowson then goes on to relate a charming story of some relevance to avant-gardes of the 8.♖b1 variation.

Apparently GM Suat Atalik only played this move as a symbolic "thank you" gesture to a friend who had given him a D85 (the ECO code for the 8.♖b1 variation) computer disk. The disk showed that 12...♘a6 was the only non-losing move which, at that time, had not yet been played in this position! I have no idea if this is true, but it would be cool if it was, and you can't help but respect Atalik for playing 12...♘a6 against 2650 opposition! Anyway... back to the

merits of 12...♘a6. There probably aren't many, and I certainly wouldn't play it as Black, but in practice Black has scored reasonably, so it helps to have something prepared.

13.♕c1!?

White can justifiably play more or less any normal 8.♖b1 move here (except 13.♗b4 of course), however this seems convincing so I won't spend too much time on alternatives.

a) 13.♗e3 ♖d8 14.♖e1 ♘c5 15.♖a1 ♕b3! 16.♕xb3 ♘xb3 17.♖a4 ♗g4 18.♖d1 a5 19.e5 ♗f5 20.♘e1 ♗e4∓ is a line given by Atalik in *Informant 71*.

b) 13.♗g5 h6 14.♗h4 (14.♗xe7 ♖e8 15.♖a1 ♕e6 16.♗h4 (16.♗a3 ♕xe4 17.♗xa6 bxa6 18.♖e1 ♕c6∓ - Ftacnik) 16...♕xe4 17.♗xa6 (17.♖e1 ♗g4 18.♗xa6 ♕xe1† 19.♕xe1 ♖xe1† 20.♘xe1 bxa6 is winning for Black, and 17.♗b5 ♖f8! 18.♖e1 ♕d5 gives Black a clear advantage.) 17...bxa6 18.♖e1 ♕c6∓ -Atalik) 14...g5 15.♗g3 was Oll – Atalik, Maroczy Memorial 1997, and now rather than 15...♖d8?, which could have left f7 feeling very vulnerable after 16.♘e5!, Atalik proposes that Black should play 15...♗g4!, when he gives the following variation: 16.♖xb7 ♖fd8 17.d5 ♘c5 18.♖xe7 ♗f6 19.♖c7 ♘xe4 20.♗c4 (20.d6 ♕a5 21.♕b3 ♗e6 22.♗c4 ♘xd6 23.♗xd6 ♖xd6∓) 20...♕a5 (20...♕a3 is also supposed to be good for Black) 21.d6 ♕xc7 22.dxc7 ♖xd1 23.♖xd1 ♘xg3 24.h3!! (24.hxg3 ♖c8–+) 24...♗f5 25.fxg3 ♖c8 26.♖d6 ♗c3!! (26...♔g7? loses to another long line) 27.♗d3 ♗e6∓. Exciting stuff, although probably of little consequence as Black is worse in most of White's other lines!

13...♕e6 14.♖e1! ♕d6

This much is given by Atalik in his annotations for *Informant 71*, but without a concluding assessment. White's pieces seem well mobilized whereas Black's are still contemplating where they would be best placed, so I feel that there should be a concrete route to an advantage here.

15.♗f4 ♕d8 16.♖d1

16.♗xa6!? bxa6 17.d5 with the idea of 18.♕c6 is given by Rowson with the conclusion that Black's position is unpleasant, which it is!

16...♘b8

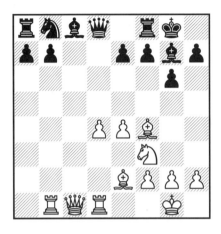

What on earth am I going to write about this move? I mean, Black's opening has been a complete disaster, he hasn't got any pieces out, and now he is setting them up for the next game!! Well, at least he hasn't created any new weaknesses for White to strike at, and I suppose the queen is safer on d8 than it was on a2, and we mustn't forget Black's extra pawn, must we?

17.d5 b6 18.♗c7

This may be a slight error according to Krasenkow, who instead proposes 18.d6 ♗b7 (18...♖e8 19.♗g5!) 19.dxe7 ♕xe7 20.♗d6 ♕xe4 21.♗xf8 ♗xf8 22.♗c4!, or 18.♘e5! ♗xe5 19.♗xe5 ♗a6 20.♗g4 in either case with a clear advantage to White.

18...♕d7 19.♗b5 ♕g4 20.♕e3 ♗a6 21.♗a4 b5 22.♗xb5?!

White grabs the pawn but allows Black to instigate a series of tactics leading to mass simplification. Instead 22.♗b3!? would have maintained the tension and preserved White's advantage.

22...♗xb5 23.♖xb5 ♕d7!

Now Black should be fine.

24.♖xb8

24.♖b7 ♘a6 25.♖c1 ♖fc8 26.♕f4 ♘xc7 27.♖cxc7 ♖xc7 28.♖xc7 ♕d6 is equal according to Krasenkow.

24...♖fxb8 25.♗xb8 ♖xb8= 26.h3 a5 27.e5 a4 28.♖d4 ♖b3 29.♕f4?! a3 30.e6 fxe6 31.dxe6 ♕e8 32.♖a4 h6 33.♕e4 ♔h7 34.♘h4? ♗f6! 35.♖a8 ♕xa8?

Black has fought back to a winning position and now 35...♖b4! was the way to make it all count: 36.♕c2 (36.♕xb4 ♕xa8 37.♕g4 ♗g5–+; 36.♕f3 ♖b1†! 37.♔h2 ♖b8) 36...♖c4! 37.♕d3 a2!–+.

36.♕xa8 ♗xh4 37.♕a4 ♖b1† 38.♔h2 ♗xf2 39.♕xa3 ♗h4 40.♕a4 ♗f6 41.♕e8 g5?! 42.♕f7† ♔h8 43.♕g6 ♖b4 44.♕xh6† ♔g8 45.♕g6† ♔h8 46.♔g3 ♖f4 47.♔h2 ♖d4 48.♔g1 ♖d6 49.♕f7 ♖d2 50.♔f1 ♖d4 51.♔e2 ♖c4 52.g4 ♖c5 53.♔d2 ♖d5† 54.♔c2 ♖c5† 55.♔b1 ♖e5 56.♔c2 ♖c5† 57.♔d3 ♖e5 58.♔c4 ♖e4† 59.♔c5 ♖e3 60.♔d5 ♖xh3 61.♔e4 ♖h1 62.♔f5 ♖h6 63.♔e4 ♖h1 64.♔f5

½–½

Game 35 Conclusions: It is usually not a good idea to put the knight on a6 in these lines – well, that is unless there is some specific purpose such as bringing it to c5 next move, but that is certainly not the case here! Nevertheless, in master-level practice 12...♘a6 has scored fairly well. I can't think why, because it is obviously completely pants! Best advice: play over the notes to this game and bash the next person who has the audacity to punt it.

Game 36
Krivoshey – Ruck
Oberwart Open 2000

1.d4 ♘f6 2.c4 g6 3.♘c3 d5 4.cxd5 ♘xd5 5.e4 ♘xc3 6.bxc3 ♗g7 7.♘f3 c5 8.♖b1 0–0 9.♗e2 cxd4 10.cxd4 ♕a5† 11.♕d2

There was a period when 11.♕d2 was considered the standard response to 10...♕a5†, and even after the power of 11.♗d2 began to emerge many players remained loyal to the 11.♕d2 line. White's plan is to play a zero-risk game: exchange queens and reach an endgame where the strong centre and slight lead in development will ensure that Black must suffer long and hard before reaching a draw. Unfortunately things are never this simple, and Black has now more or less solved all his problems in the 11.♕d2 variation, thereby relegating it to the category of minor alternatives.

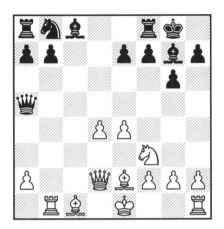

11...♕xd2† 12.♗xd2 b6!

12...e6 is also playable, but the text seems superior.

13 0–0

The obvious choice, however White has alternatives:

a) 13.♖c1 ♗b7! when White has a choice of two moves:

a1) 14.♗d3 ♖d8 15.♗e3 (15.♖c7 ♖d7 16.♖xd7 ♘xd7 17.♔e2 ♖c8 18.♗f4 e6 19.h3 f5! gave Black good play in Gaprindashvili – Roesch, Germany 1990) 15...♘c6 16.d5 ♘b4 17.♗b1 ♗a6 as in Petursson – Conquest, Hastings 1986, was slightly better for Black according to Conquest (*Informant 43*).

a2) 14.d5 ♘a6 15.♗g5 (15.♗e3 ♖fc8 16 0–0 ♘b4! 17 a3 ♘c2 18.♗d2?! ♗b2 19.♖b1 ♖xa3∓ Kiriakov – Vorobiov, Moscow 1996) 15...♖fc8 16 0–0 (16.♖xc8† ♖xc8 17.♗xe7 ♖c2! is fine for Black) 16...♔f8 17.e5 h6 18.♗h4 g5 19.♗g3 ♖xc1 20.♖xc1 ♘c5 21.d6 ♖d8= Pavlovic – Mikhalchishin, Trnava 1988.

b) 13.d5 ♘a6 with the following possibilities:

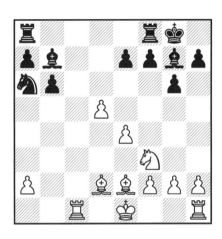

b1) 14.♗e3 f5!? (Rowson gives the line 14...♗c3† 15.♗d2 ♗xd2† 16.♘xd2 ♘c5 17.f3 e6 as promising for Black.) 15.e5 f4! 16.♗d4 ♗f5 17.♖c1 b4 18.♗c4 ♘d3† 19.♔d2 (The obvious 19.♗xd3 ♗xd3 is also bad for White.) 19...♘xc1 20.♖xc1 ♖fc8 21.d6† ♔f8 22.♘g5 exd6 23.♘xh7† ♔e8 24.♗b5† ♔d8 25.♖d1 dxe5 26.♗c3 ♖xc3 27.♔xc3† ♔e7 28.♘g5 ♖c8† 29.♔b3 ♗c2† 0–1 Hertneck – Kasparov, Munich 1994. A very powerful handling of the endgame indeed!

b2) 14.♗b5 ♗b7 15 0–0 ♘c5 (15...♖fc8 16.♖bc1?! ♘c5 17.♖fe1 e6 18.♗c4 exd5 19.exd5 b5! 20.♗xb5 ♖xd5 was at least equal for Black in Recoulat – Pierrot, Buenos Aires 1998) 16.♖fe1 ♖fc8! 17.♗b4 ♗c7 18.a4 (18.♖bc1 ♖ac8=) 18...f5! 19.exf5 (19.♗xc5 ♖xc5 20.exf5 ♗xd5 (20...gxf5 21.♖xe7 ♗xd5 looks fun) 21.fxg6 hxg6 22.♖xe7 ♗xf3 23.gxf3=) 19...♗xd5 20.fxg6 hxg6 21.♖bd1 (21.♗xc5?! bxc5 22.♘e5 ♖xe5 23.♖xe5 e6 24.♗d3 (24.♖c1?! c4∓) 24...♔g7∓ -Nadanian, *Informant 54*) 21...♗b3 22.♖c1 ♖ac8= Zimmerman – Nadanian, Katowice 1992.

13...♗b7 14.d5 ♖c8!

This move became popular after Judit Polgar used it to defeat Piket in convincing fashion.

15.♖fc1

The game that originally sparked the widespread popularity of 14...♖c8 continued 15.♗b4 ♔f8

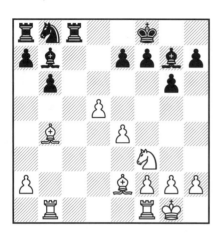

16.♖fd1?! (16.♖fc1 ♘d7=) 16...♘a6 17.♗xa6 (17.♗a3 ♖c2∓) 17...♖xa6 18.e5 (18.♖d2 ♗h6∓) 18...♗e2 19.d6? (19.♖e1 ♗xf3 20.gxf3 ♖c2 21 a4 ♖a2∓) 19...♗xd1 20.dxe7† ♔e8 21.♖xd1 ♗h6!–+ Piket – J. Polgar, Madrid 1997.

15...♘d7 16.♗e3

In a recent internet game Shipov tried 16.♗b4, after which 16...♔f8 (immediately exploding the centre with 16...f5!? is also possible) 17.♔f1 ♘e5 18.♘xe5 ♗xe5 19.h3 ♗f4 20.♖xc8† ♖xc8 21.♗d3 f5 22.exf5 ♗xd5 23.fxg6 hxg6 was about equal in Shipov – G.Shahade, Internet 2000, although White went on to win after some inaccurate play by Black.

16...♘f6

16...♔f8!? 17.♘d4 ♘c5 18.♗g4 ♖e8 19.♘b5?! (19.f3!±) 19...♘xe4! 20.♘c7 ♘c3 21.♖b3 ♘xd5 22.♘xe8 ♔xe8∓ Hanko – Jelen, Bled 1999.

17.♘d2 e6 18.dxe6 ♘xe4 19.♗f3

19.exf7† ♔xf7 20.♗c4† ♔f8 21.♘xe4 ♗xe4 22.♖b3 ♖c6! 23.♗b5 ♖xc1† 24.♗xc1 ♗d5∓ Starke – Seger, Hessen 2000.

19...♘d6!?

19...f5!?

20.exf7† ♔xf7 21.♘c4 ♖xc4 22.♗xb7 ♖xc1†

23.♖xc1 ♘xb7 24.♖c7† ♔e6 25.♖xg7 ♖d8 26.♔f1 ♖d7 27.♖xd7 ♔xd7 28.♔e2 ♔e6 29.♔d3
½–½

Game 36 Conclusions: 11.♕d2 really doesn't promise White any advantage whatsoever. Provided Black knows what he is doing White can't make much of this ending, and I certainly would not consider playing the White side of it!

Chapter 5 Conclusions: 12...♕e6 (Game 33) is passive but solid. In order to play the White side of these positions well one really has to develop a feel for exploiting the positional aspects of White's compensation. In Game 33 Gelfand increases his advantage by gradually suppressing all of Kamsky's counterplay. This is a highly instructive example, and well worth playing over in full.

In Game 34 we examined 12...♗d7!? in some detail. In general I don't feel that this system should guarantee Black equality – partly because the bishop feels misplaced on d7, and partly because Black immediately returns the pawn but does little (if anything) to challenge White's central dominance.

Game 35 was devoted to Atalik's wonderful 12...♘a6!?. Logic dictates that this move should be bad for Black, however for some reason it scores reasonably in practice. The notes to the main game indicate several methods by which White should be able to obtain a definite advantage.

Finally, there is the 'endgame' system, with 11.♕d2, which we examined in Game 36. This system once contained some venom, so those defending the Black side would be well advised to learn the theory on it. However, provided Black treats 11.♕d2 with respect and develops sensibly along the lines we considered in Game 36, White should not have any chance of an advantage.

Chapter 6: The Provocative 9...♘c6

There are many players who love the Grünfeld Defence, but would rather not go chasing pawns on a2 and then scurrying around the board with their queens, trying to placate White's raging initiative. In general, the mainline positions are more difficult for Black to handle than White, and even if Black is thoroughly "booked-up", well-prepared exponents of the Modern Exchange Variation will rarely find themselves under pressure from the opening.

An inevitable consequence of the difficulties associated with the mainlines is that it can be hard to win with Black, and for this reason some strong players have looked to sidelines as a way of avoiding theory and preserving winning chances. For a period the most popular of Black's alternatives was to meet 1.d4 ♘f6 2.c4 g6 3.♘c3 d5 4.cxd5 ♘xd5 5.e4 ♘xc3 6.bxc3 ♗g7 7.♘f3 c5 8.♖b1 0–0 9.♗e2 with 9...♘c6!? (At present most of those defending the Black pieces have switched their attention to the rather unassuming 9...b6, which will be discussed in Chapter 8. Black's more rare 9th move alternatives will be discussed in Chapter 9.) After 9...♘c6!? White almost inevitably plays 10.d5, offering to sacrifice the pawn on c3. In this chapter we will discuss those lines in which Black decides to capture on c3 and attempts to weather the tempest, and in Chapter 7 we will examine the more stalwart lines, where Black avoids 10...♗xc3† in favour of 10...♘e5!?.

Game 37
Kasparov – Natsis
Malta 1980

1.d4 ♘f6 2.c4 g6 3.♘c3 d5 4.cxd5 ♘xd5 5.e4 ♘xc3 6.bxc3 ♗g7 7.♘f3 c5 8.♖b1 0–0

8...♘c6 is similar to the game, but less accurate: 9.d5 ♗xc3† 10.♗d2 ♗xd2† 11.♕xd2 ♘d4 (11...♘a5? is similar to 12...♘a5 in Game 38, but with the significant difference that now White can play 12.♗b5†, as 12...♗d7 13.♗xd7† ♕xd7? drops a knight to 14.♕xa5) 12.♘xd4 cxd4 13.♗b5†!? (13.♕xd4 also makes sense, but I am slightly concerned that after 13...♕a5† 14.♕d2 ♕xd2† 15.♔xd2 Black may have an improved version of the main game, as the king is slightly closer to the centre and White is a couple of moves away from finishing development. Nevertheless, White is probably marginally better here in any case.) 13...♗d7 14.0–0 0–0 15.♕xd4 (In a recent game at the 2004 Olympiad in Calvia I tried to preserve the queens with 15.♗e2!?, however after 15...♖b8! 16.♕xd4 ♕a5 Black seemed to be fine (although I eventually won a complicated rook ending): Dearing – A. Corke, Calvia, Spain 2004.) 15...♗xb5 16.♖xb5 ♕d7 (After 16...b6 White can play 17.a4 intending 18.a5 bxa5 19.♖fa1 followed by 20.♖bxa5 when it is likely that Black's a-pawn will be captured. The pivotal question in these types of positions is very often whether White will be able to win an ensuing rook endgame with an extra pawn on the kingside (4 pawns v 3 is most common, although 5 v 4 is also possible).) 17.♖c5! ♖fc8 18.♖fc1 ♖xc5 19.♕xc5 b6 20.♕c7 ♖d8 21.g3± Shishkin – Kovchan, Alushta 2000. White will gradually improve his position, eventually exchange queens, and hopefully emerge with a superior endgame that can be converted into a win.

9 ♗e2 ♘c6!?

There is quite a lot to be said about this little move. The first thing to note is that 9...♘c6 is quite logical: Black attack's White's centre head-on, and forces White to take immediate defensive action or lose the d4-pawn. If White limits the scope of the g7-bishop by 10.e5, play will continue 10...cxd4 11.cxd4 when the d4-pawn is left slightly weak, but the real problem is that White cannot then advance the d-pawn without dropping the e5-pawn. Alternatively, if White plays 10.♗e3, Black will play 10...cxd4 11.cxd4 ♕a5† forcing an exchange of queens and reaching an endgame similar to the one we examined in Game 36. That only leaves White with one option: to advance the d-pawn and risk dropping the c3-pawn with check.

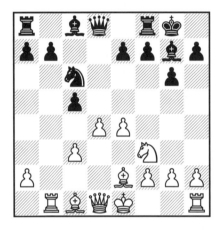

10.d5! ♗xc3†

With this move Black bags a pawn at the cost of accepting eternal weaknesses on the dark squares. The mainline with 10...♘e5 will be considered in Games 40–43.

11.♗d2 ♗xd2† 12.♕xd2 ♘d4!?

This gives back the pawn and forces a transition into the endgame, however the alternatives all leave Black vulnerable to a kingside attack.

a) 12...♘a5 is Black's most challenging follow-up to 10...♗xc3†, and this will be considered in Games 38 and 39.

b) 12...♘b4?! is rather misguided, e.g. 13.a3 ♘a6 14.h4 h5 15.♕h6 ♕a5† 16.♔f1 ♕c3 17.e5 ♕c2 18.♖c1 ♕b2 19.♖e1 f6 20.♕xg6† ♔h8 21.♗d3 1–0 Markos – Harris, Litohoto 1999.

c) 12...♘b8?! looks as though it should be complete rubbish, and I suspect it is! 13.h4 e6 (13...f6 14.h5 g5 (14...gxh5 15.e5 fxe5 16.♕g5† ♔h8 17.♗d3 ♗g4 18.♖xh5 ♖f7 19.♕xe5† ♔g8 20.♖g5† 1–0 Z. Szabo – Bognar, Budapest

1993) 15.♘xg5!? (15.h6 is more restrained, and gives White a slight edge.) 15...fxg5 16.♕xg5† ♔f7 (16...♔h8 17.h6 ♕a5† 18.♔f1 ♕c3 19.e5 ♖g8 20.♕xe7 ♘d7 21.♖h5 ♕c2 22.♖d1, ♕g6? 23.♗d3!+- Cooper – Knott, Chester 1979) 17.h6 ♔e8 18 0–0± Halkias – Dovramadjiev, Calicut 1998) 14.h5 (14.d6!? and 14.♗c4 exd5 15.♗xd5 ♘c6 16.h5 ♕a5 17.♕xa5 ♘xa5 18.hxg6 hxg6 19.♖b5 ♘c6 20.♖xc5± Azizian – Martsvalashvili, Yerevan 1996 also look good for White.) 14...♕f6 15.hxg6 (15.e5 ♕g7 16.h6 ♕h8 17.♗c4!? exd5 18.♕xd5 (18.♗xd5±) 18...♘c6 19.♖h4 ♗e6 20.♕xc5 ♖fe8 21.♗xe6 ♖xe6 22.♖e4 ♖ae8 23.♖xb7 ♘xe5 24.♘xe5 ♖xe5 25.♕xe5! ♕xe5 26.♖xe5 ♖xe5† 27.♔d2± Cvitan – Grushka, Mexico 1981, but both sides' play could have been improved at various points.) 15...hxg6 16.e5 ♕g7 17.dxe6 ♗xe6 18.♖xb7 ♘c6 19.♕d6± B. Christensen – Jorgensen, Aarhus 1990.

13.♘xd4 cxd4 14.♕xd4 ♕a5† 15.♕d2 ♕xd2† 16.♔xd2

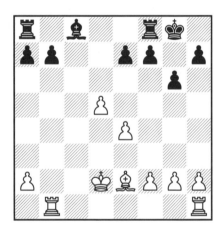

This type of endgame is similar in appearance to the typical Exchange Grünfeld endings that are reached in the 7.♗e3 or 8.♗e3 variations (these variations are beyond the scope of this text, however Game 36 offers a reasonable comparison in terms of form), but with the critical differences that White is ahead in development and will play ♖hc1 next (taking control of the c-file), and that the absence of the extra minor pieces (the g7-bishop and the b8-knight) emphasises the limited scope of Black's light-squared bishop. Black will have to be very careful here if he is to avoid a clearly worse endgame.

16...♖d8

This is probably Black's most challenging approach, exploiting the pin on White's king to prepare 17...e6. Alternatively 16...f5 is premature because 17.e5 ♖d8 18.♔e3 is good for White, and 16...e6 has also scored badly. A couple of examples: 17.♗c4 (17.d6 e5 18.♖hd1 b6 19.♔e3 ♖d8 20.f4 exf4† 21.♔xf4 ♗e6 22.♖bc1 ♗xa2 23.♗a6 ♗e6 24.♖c7 ♖ab8 25.♔e5 b5 26.♔f6 ♖b6 27.♔e7 ♖db8 28.♖xa7 ♗b3 29.♖c1 ♔g7 30.♗c8 b4 31.d7 ♔g8 32.d8♕† ♔g7 33.♕d4† 1–0 Yrjola – Holmsten, Helsinki 1996) 17...b6 18.d6 ♗d7 19.♖hc1 ♖fb8 20.e5 a6 21.♗d3 b5 22.♗e4 ♖a7 23.♖c7 ♖xc7 24.dxc7 ♖b6 25.♔c3 f5 26.♖d1 1–0 Ftacnik – Gollasch, Hamburg 1993.

17.♔e3! b6

Alternatives:

a) 17...e6 18.♗c4 b6 (18...exd5 19.♗xd5 ♖b8 20.♖hc1 ♖d7 21.♖c3± Hebert – Mirza, Thessaloniki 1984) 19.♖hd1 ♔f8 20.♖bc1 ♗e7 21.e5 exd5 22.♗xd5 ♖b8 23.♖c7† ♖d7 24.♖dc1 ♗b7 25.♗xf7 ♗xg2 26.♖xd7† ♔xd7 27.♔f4 ♖b7 28.e6† ♔d6 29.♔g5 ♔e7 30.♖c8 ♗d5 31.♖e8† ♔d6 32.♖d8† 1–0 Eingorn – Sideif Sade, Tashkent 1980.

b) 17...♖b8 18.♖hc1 ♔f8 19.♖c7 ♖d7 20.♖bc1 ♖xc7 21.♖xc7 ♔e8 22.d6 ♗d7 23.dxe7 a6 24.♗c4 f6 25.♗d5±/+- Pein – M.Broom, Sheffield 1991.

c) 17...f5 18.f3!? (18.e5) 18...♔f7 19.♖hc1 a6?! 20.♖b6± Kolev – Serrano, Barbera 1993.

d) 17...♔f8 18.♖hc1 ♔e8!? 19.♔d4!? (19.♖c7) 19...b6 20.♖c7 ♗d7 21.♗a6 ♗c8 22.♗b5† ♗d7 23.♔c4 f5 24.f3 ♗xb5† 25.♔xb5 ♖d7 26.♖bc1 fxe4 27.fxe4 ♔d8 was Lesiege – Fernandes, Istanbul 2000, and now GM Ernst gives the line 28.♖xd7† ♔xd7 29.♔a6 ♖f8 30.♖c2 ♖f4 31.♖e2±.

18.♖bc1!

An interesting idea. Most players seem to automatically play 18.♖hc1, presumably on the

basis that it appears more 'natural'. However a young Kasparov acknowledges that the b1–rook has achieved everything it could hope for on b1 (temporarily tying the c8-bishop to the protection of the b7-pawn and forcing Black to play b7-b6, thereby weakening the queenside light squares) and consequently shifts it over to the c-file. By using the b-rook instead of the h-rook Kasparov preserves the option of playing ♖hd1 at some point, so that the d-pawn can be promptly supported if the need should arise.

18...e6 19.♗c4 e5

a) 19...♗d7 20.♖hd1 ♗a4 (20...♖dc8 21.d6 ♖c5 22.♗a6 ♖xc1 23.♖xc1 e5 24.f4 exf4† 25.♔xf4 ♗e6 26.e5 ♖d8 27.a3 ♔g7 28.♖c7 ♖d7 29.♖c8 h6 30.♖e8 g5† 31.♔e3 ♗d5 32.♗c8 1–0 Chloupek – A.Peters, Mlada Boleslav 1992) 21.♖d2 exd5 22.♗xd5 ♖ac8 23.♗b7!? ♖xc1 24.♖xd8† ♔g7 25.♗d5 ♖c7 26.♖a8 ♗d7 27.♔d4 ♔f6 28.f4± Vaisser – Roski, Berlin-West 1988.

b) 19...♖b8 20.♖hd1 exd5 21.♖xd5 ♗b7 22.♗xf7† ♔xf7 23.♖xd8 ♖xd8 24.♖c7† ♔f6 25.♖xb7 h5 26.♖xa7 1–0 Miladinovic – Mandic, Cetinje 1991.

20.♗b3 ♗d7 21.♖c7 a5 22.d6 b5 23.f4!

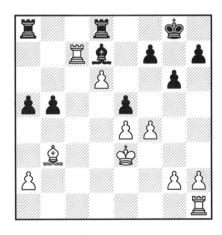

23...exf4† 24.♔xf4 ♖a6 25.e5 a4 26.♗d5 a3 27.♖f1 ♖a4† 28.♔e3 ♗e6 29.♗xe6 fxe6 30.♖ff7 ♖h4 31.♖g7† ♔h8 32.♖ge7

1–0

Game 37 Conclusions: The endgames that occur after 10.d5 &xc3† 11.&d2 &xd2† 12.Wxd2 ♘d4!? 13.♘xd4 cxd4 14.Wxd4 Wa5† 15.Wd2 Wxd2† 16.&xd2 should be better for White. However White's advantage at move 16 is somewhat embryonic: White enjoys slightly more space, a better bishop, a more centralized king, and some pressure down the b-file, but of themselves these factors will not prove decisive. White's advantage needs to be nurtured by playing accurately for the next ten moves or so. Depending upon how Black proceeds, White may have to seize control of the c-file, prevent the freeing break e7-e6 (&d2-e3! is often an important move in this respect), expand on the queenside with a4-a5, or advance in the centre with e4-e5 and d5-d6. The actual 'theory' in this line is less important than developing a good understanding of these endings.

Game 38
Halkias – Lputian
Yerevan 2000

1.d4 ♘f6 2.c4 g6 3.♘c3 d5 4.cxd5 ♘xd5 5.e4 ♘xc3 6.bxc3 &g7 7.♘f3 c5 8.Bb1 0–0 9.&e2 ♘c6 10.d5 &xc3† 11.&d2 &xd2† 12.Wxd2 ♘a5

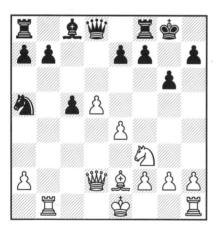

13.h4!
This is White's most challenging approach; the alternatives tend to be less promising:

a) 13.Wh6 f6 14.h4 Bf7 15.h5 g5 16.e5 b6 17.Bd1 &b7∓ Gretzinger – Steck, Wattens 2000.

b) 13.Wc3 b6 14.Bd1 (Solozhenkin has tried 14.h4 successfully, however after 14...e6 15.Bd1 exd5 16.Bxd5 We7 17.h5 &b7 (17...Wxe4!?) 18.Be5 Wf6 it was questionable whether he was really better: Solozhenkin – El Kher, Montecatini Terme 1999.) 14...f6 (14...&g4 15.e5∞ - Ftacnik) 15.h4 &g4 16.♘g5?! (16.h5 &xh5 17.e5 gives White an attack according to Ftacnik, although Black does not appear to be in any immediate danger.) 16...Wd7 was at least slightly better for Black in Iashvili – Ilincic, Belgrade 1992.

c) 13 0–0 &g4 (13...b6!? 14.e5 (14.Wh6?! f6 intending 15...e5 secures Black's position.) 14...&b7 15.Bbd1 e6 16.d6 f6 17.Wh6 Wd7 intending 18...&d5 and 19...♘c6 is slightly better for Black according to Stohl.) 14.h3!? (14.e5 e6!? (Less good is 14...&xf3 15.&xf3 ♘c6 16.We3 ♘d4 17.Bxb7 Wa5 18.e6 fxe6 19.&g4± Petursson – Jansa, Biel izt 1985 although 14...f6!? certainly deserves consideration.) 15.d6 ♘c6 16.We3 b6∞) 14...&xf3 15.&xf3 b6 (15...e5 16.Wc3 Be8 17.Wxc5 b6 18.Wb4 ♘b7 19.&e2 gives White the initiative, whereas 15...♘c6 16.Bxb7 ♘d4 17.Bc1 Wd6 intending 18...e6 is unclear.) 16.Wf4 Wd7 17.Bfe1! Bad8 18.e5 e6 was Lobron – Stohl, Manila 1990, and now rather than 19.Wf6? Stohl proposes that White should have played 19.d6! ♘c6 (19...f6 20.Bbd1 fxe5 21.Wxe5 ♘c4 22.Wxe6† Wxe6 23.Bxe6±) 20.&xc6 Wxc6 21.Bbd1!?± The comments here are based on Stohl's annotations for *Chessbase Magazine 19*.

13...&g4!
Exchanging the light-squared bishop for White's knight is Black's most logical defence: White's remaining knight plays a key role in the kingside attack, whereas Black's c8-bishop contributes little to the defensive cause. In the past attention briefly focussed on 13...f6, however this is now widely acknowledged to be bad for Black: 13...f6 14.h5 g5 15.Wc3! (15.♘xg5 is dangerous for Black, but has ultimately proved insufficient for an advantage.)

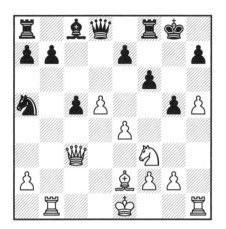

15...b6 (15...g4 16.♘h2!±) 16.h6 ♖f7 17.♖d1! ♕d6! (17...♘b7 18.e5 fxe5 19.♘xe5 ♖f6 20.d6! ♘xd6 (20...♖xd6 21.♖xd6 ♘xd6 22.♘g6+–) 21.♗c4† ♔f8 22.♘f7+–) 18.e5 (according to Novik 18.♖h5! is even stronger, e.g. 18...♗g4 19.e5! ♕b8 20.♘xg5 ♗xh5 21.♗xh5 ♖f8 22.d6!+–) 18...fxe5 19.♘xg5 ♖f5! (19...♖f4 20.♕g3 ♕g6 21.♗h5+–) 20.♘e6! ♖f6! 21.♗h5 e4 22.♕e3! ♖f5! (22....♕e5 23.f4+–) 23.♗g4! ♖f6 24.♗h5 ♖f5 25.♗g4 ♖f6 26.♖h5! ♗xe6 27.dxe6 ♕f4 was Novik – Arbakov, Bratislava 1991, and now Novik gives the line 28.♕xf4 ♖xf4 29.♗f5! ♖f8 (29...♘c6 30.g3 ♖f3 31.♗xe4+–) 30.♖g5† ♔h8 31.g4 ♘c6 32.♖g7 ♘d4 33.♖xh7† ♔g8 34.♖xd4 cxd4 35.♖xe7 ♖c8 36.♖g7† ♔h8 37.e7 ♖e8 38.♖f7 ♔g8 39.♖f8† ♖xf8 40.h7†+–. The comments here are based on Novik's annotations for *Informant 52*.

14.h5

14.♘g5!? is considered in Game 39.

14...♗xf3 15.gxf3 e5!

This excellent move halts the advance of White's centre and consolidates Black's control of the dark squares. It will now become increasingly difficult for White's light-squared bishop to play a role in the attack.

16.hxg6

Capturing on g6 and opening the h-file makes a lot of sense, however there have been various attempts to gain an edge by delaying this capture until a more opportune moment:

a) 16.♕c3?! seems misguided; the white queen should probably be focussing on the kingside attack rather than chasing pawns on the queenside: 16...♖e8 17.hxg6 fxg6 18.♕xc5 (18.♗b5 ♖e7 19.d6 ♖e6 20.♖d1 ♕b6 21 a4 ♖d8 22.f4 ♖exd6 23.♖b1 ♖d4 –+ B.Lalic – Ubilava, Varna 1985) 18...b6 19.♕e3 ♖c8 20.♖c1?! (20.♗a6 is stronger according to Timman) 20...♖xc1† 21.♕xc1 was Kamsky – Timman, Linares 1991 and now Timman, in his annotations for *Informant 51*, claims that 21...♘b7 intending 22...♘c5 would be clearly better for Black.

b) 16.f4 exf4 17.♕xf4 ♕e7 (17...g5 18.♖g1 f6 also looks quite solid and has scored well for Black in practice.) 18.f3 (18.♖b5 b6 19.hxg6 fxg6 20.♕h2 ♖ad8 21.♔f1 ♖d6 22.♖b2 ♖f7 23.♗g4 ♘c4 24.♖e2 ♘e5∓ Ulko – van Wely, Moscow 2002) 18...♖ae8 19.♗b5 ♕e5 20.♕xe5 ♖xe5 21.♗d3 ♖fe8 22.♔f2 g5 23.♖bg1 ♔f8 24.h6 c4 25.♗b1 f6 ½–½ Tyomkin – Vydeslaver, Rishon le Zion 1995.

c) 16.♕h6!? is a logical continuation of the kingside attack, but one that also carries a secondary idea:

16.♕h6 provokes 16...g5, weakening Black on the light squares, and giving White the possibility of playing f3-f4 and ♗e2-g4, when the light-squared bishop is suddenly promoted to being a key attacking piece. Play has continued 16...g5 17.♖g1 f6 18.f4 exf4 19.e5! ♕e7 (Fritz is very fond of 19...♔h8!? which it assesses as clearly better for Black.) 20.exf6 ♕xf6 21.♖xg5† ♔h8 22.♕xf6† ♖xf6 23.♔d2 was Karason – Rytshagov, Gausdal 1991. Krasenkow, in his annotations for *Chessbase Magazine*, seems enthusiastic about this idea and suggests that it has some future, however I don't see any advantage for White in any of these lines.

16...fxg6 17.d6!

17.♕c3   ♖e8   18.♕xc5   b6   19.♕e3   ♖c8 transposes to Kamsky – Timman, Linares 1991, considered above.

17...b6

17...♖f6 18.♕d5† ♔h8 19.♕xe5 b6 (19...♕xd6 20.♕c3) 20.♖d1 ♘c6 21.♕d5 ♘d4 22.e5 ♖f5 23.♖xd4! cxd4 24.♗d3 ♖c8 25.♗xf5 ♖c1† 26.♔e2 ♖xh1 27.e6+- Novikov – Danailov, Poznan 1985.

18.♕d5† ♔g7 19.♕xe5† ♕f6 20.♕h2!?

The text has the idea of provoking h7-h5, thereby weakening Black's kingside structure. In the game this does not turn out to be enough, so alternatives must be considered: 20.♕xf6†? ♖xf6 21.e5 ♖f5 22.f4 ♖xf4 as in Comas Fabrego – Sion Castro, Alicante 1989, was good for Black, however Agrest's 20.♕g3!? deserves attention,

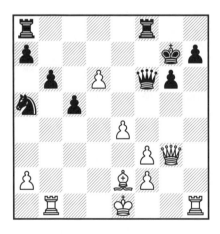

e.g. 20...♖ad8?! (20...♘c6? is bad because 21.♕h3! simultaneously threatens 22.♕xh7 mate

as well as 22.♕d7† and 23.♕xc6, when Black must jettison material. On the other hand 20...♖ae8!?, with the idea of 21.♖d1 ♖e5! intending 22...♖g5, looks sensible and quite awkward for White.) 21.e5 ♕f5 22.♖d1 ♘c6 23.f4 ♘d4 24.♖xd4 cxd4 25.♗d3 ♕f7 26.f5 ♖fe8 27.♖xh7†! 1–0 Agrest – Tella, Italy 1998.

20...h5 21.♖d1

21.♕g3 has also been played, but is perhaps academic in view of 21...♘c6!? when White should transpose to the game with 22.♖d1 as 22.♖xh5?! ♖h8 23.e5 ♕e6 24.♖g5? (24.f4!?∓) 24...♖h1† 25.♗f1 ♘d4 26.d7 ♖g1 0–1 Kornev – Kalantarian, Kstovo Open 1994, is clearly inferior.

21...♘c6!

An important moment: Black must go backward in order to go forward! Trying to force the issue with 21...♘c4?! seems to be bad for Black: 22.♗xc4 ♕c3† 23.♔f1 ♕xc4† 24.♔g2

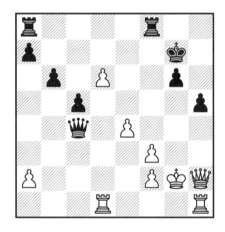

24...♖xf3 (24...♖ad8 25.♕e5† ♔g8 26.♖d5 ♖f7 27.♖h3 ♖dd7 28.♖g3 ♖g7 29.♕e6† 1–0 was Kramnik – Ivanchuk, Paris PCA-Intel GP 1995) 25.♔xf3 ♖f8† 26.♔e3 ♕c3† 27.♖d3 ♖f3† 28.♔xf3 ♕xd3† 29.♔f4? (After 29.♔g2! ♕e4† 30.f3 ♕e2† 31.♔g3 ♕e5† 32.f4 ♕c3† 33.♔h4 ♕f6† 34.♔h3 ♕f5† 35.♔g3+- ♕d3† (or 35...♕g4† 36.♔f2) 36.♔h4 Black will run out of checks and White will emerge a rook up!)

29...♕xd6† 30.e5 ♕d4† 31.♔f3 ♕d3† 32.♔g2 ♕e4† 33.♔g1 ♕e1† 34.♔g2 ♕e4† 35.♔f1 ♕b1† 36.♔e2 ♕e4† 37.♔f1 ♕b1† 38.♔g2 ♕e4† ½–½ Kiriakov – Panzalovic, Internet 2003. The continuation in the main game is far more logical: if Black can re-route the a5-knight to d4 it will become vastly superior to the e2-bishop, and will also obstruct the d1-rook.

22.♕g3

22.♖d5!? ♘d4 (When I first analysed this position my main concern was how White would meet 22...♕a1†!? and even after analysing the position with Fritz I am still not sure what is going on: 23.♗d1 (after 23.♖d1 Black has 23...♕f6 with a repetition, at the very least) 23...♖ad8 (23...♘b4 24.♖xh5!! gxh5 25.♕xh5±) 24.♕g3 ♘d4!

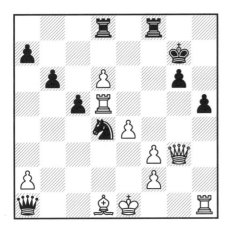

(24...♖f6 25.♖dxh5 ♖fxd6 26.♖h7† ♔g8 27.♖h8† ♕xh8 28.♗b3†! ♔g7 29.♖xh8 ♔xh8 30.e5±) 25.♖dxh5 (25 0–0!?) 25...♘xf3† 26.♔e2 (26.♔f1? ♕xd1† 27.♔g2 ♘e1†! 28.♖xe1 ♕xh5–+) with an unclear position in which Black can force a draw via 26...♘d4† 27.♔e1 ♘f3†) 23.♕g3 ♘xf3† 24.♔f1 ♕c3 25.♔g2 ♘e1† 26.♔h2 ♕xg3† 27.♔xg3 ♘c2 28.e5?! (The text looks sensible but turns out badly; perhaps White could try and make use of Black's weakened kingside structure with something like 28.♖g5!? ♘d4 (28...♔h7?

29.♗xh5, and 28...♔h6? 29.f4 ♖xf4 30.♔xf4 ♖f8† 31.♖f5 gxf5 32.♖xh5† are winning for White. White also maintains a definite advantage after both 28...♖ae8 29.♗xh5 ♖e6 30.e5, and 28...♔f6 29.f4) 29.♗xh5±) 28...♘d4 29.♖xd4 cxd4 30.e6 ♖fd8 31.d7 ♔f6–+ Bu Xiangzhi – Kalantarian, New York Open 2000.

22...♘d4!

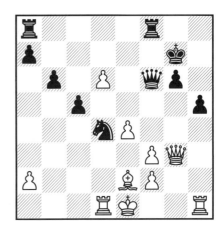

A very important discovery by Lputian that largely resuscitates this variation from Black's perspective. Previously play had focussed on the following alternatives:

a) 22...♕c3†?! 23.♔f1 ♘d4 24.♖xh5+- - Gelfand, *Informant 56*.

b) 22...♖ae8 23.♖xh5 ♕c3† (23...♖h8 24.d7! ♖d8 (24...♖xh5 25.dxe8♘†!) 25.♖d6+- Gelfand) 24.♔f1 ♖xe4 25.♗d3 ♖e6 26.♖h7†! ♔xh7 27.♕h3† ♔g7 28.♕xe6 ♘e5 29.d7 ♘xd3 30.♕e7† ♖f7 31.d8♕ 1–0 Etchegaray – Milesi, Cannes Open 1997.

c) 22...♔h6 23.♖d5 when the following options must be considered:

c1) 23...♘d4 24.f4 (24.♕g4! threatening 25.♖dxh5 with mate to follow, looks even stronger) 24...♘xe2 25.♕g5†± - Gelfand, *Informant 56*.

c2) 23...♖ae8 24.f4 ♕a1† (24...♖xe4 25.♖dxh5† ♔g7 26.♖h7† ♔g8 27.♕b3† c4 28.♕xc4†! ♖xc4 29.♗xc4† ♖f7 30.♖h8† ♕xh8 31.♗xf7† ♔g7

32.♖xh8 ♔xh8 33.♗xg6+–) 25.♖d1 ♕f6 26.♖d5 ♕a1† 27.♖d1 ♕f6 28.f3! ♘d4 29.f5 gxf5!? (29...g5?? 30.♖xh5† 1–0 was Gelfand – Stohl, Tilburg 1992, and 29...♖d8 is bad on account of 30.♔f2 ♕xd6 31.f4, when White threatens 32.♗xh5) 30.d7! ♖e6 31.f4!! 31...♘xe2 32.♔xe2 ♕b2† (32...♖xe4† 33.♔f2 ♕b2† 34.♔g1 ♕f6 35.♖d6 ♖e1† 36.♔f2+–) 33.♔f1 ♕b5† 34.♕d3! ♕xd3† 35.♖xd3 ♖d8 36.e5 intending 37.♖dh3 is winning for White according to Boris Gelfand. The notes here are based on Gelfand's annotations for *Informant 56*.

c3) 23...♘b4 24.♖e5! with the following possibilities:

c31) Chernin notes that 24...♖ae8 is best met by 25.f4.

c32) 24...♕f4 loses to 25.♖hxh5† gxh5 26.♖e6† ♔h7 27.♕g6† ♔h8 28.♕xh5† ♔g7 29.♖g6† ♔f7 30.♖h6†+–.

c33) 24...♘c6 deserves particular attention. Play should continue: 25.♖exh5†! (25.f4! ♘xe5 26.fxe5 ♕f4 (26...♕f7 27.♖g1!) 27.♕xf4† ♖xf4 28.f3 is also winning according to Gelfand) 25...gxh5 26.f4 ♕a1† 27.♗d1 ♖f5!. Thus far we have been following Gelfand's annotations for *Informant 56*, however now Gelfand concludes that White's best is 28.d7. In fact, as Chernin reveals in *Informant 58*, White has a much stronger follow-up in the form of 28.♖g1!

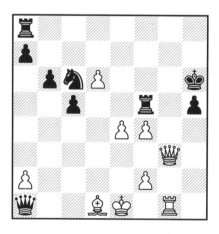

28...♕f6 29.exf5 ♘d4 (29...♖e8† 30.♔f1 ♘d4 31.♗xh5 ♘xf5 32.♕h3 ♖d8 33.♖g6† ♕xg6 34.♗xg6† ♔xg6 35.♕g4† ♔f6 36.♕g5† ♔e6 37.♕g6†) 30.♕g5†! ♕xg5 31.fxg5† ♔g7 32.f6† ♔g6 33.f4 ♖d8 34.♖h1+–.

c34) 24...♘c2† 25.♔f1 ♘d4 26.f4 ♘xe2 (26...♕xf4 27.♖exh5† ♔g7 28.♖h7† ♔g8 29.♖8h8† ♔g7 30.♖1h7†+–) 27.♔xe2 ♖ad8 (27...♕xf4 28.♖hxh5†! gxh5 29.♖e6† wins for White. 27...♖ae8 28.♔e3! ♖xe5 29.fxe5 ♕e6 30.♖g1! intending f4-f5 is also winning according to Chernin.) was Chernin – Stohl, Pardubice 1993. White now played 28.♕g4 and was ultimately victorious, however Chernin suggests that White's strongest line of attack was 28.f5! ♖xd6 (28...♕xd6 29.♕e3† ♔h7 30.♖e6 ♕d4 31.♕h6†! ♔xh6 32.♖xg6† ♔h7 33.♖xh5 mate.) 29.fxg6 ♔g7 30.♖hxh5 ♖fd8 31.♖hf5+–. The comments here are based on Chernin's annotations for *Informant 58*.

23.♖xh5 ♖h8 24.♖d5! ♘e6!

An excellent move, seizing control of the d8, f4 and g5 squares, and opening up the h8-a1 diagonal for the black queen, thereby making 25...♖h1† a real threat. Note that the immediate 24...♖h1†? 25.♔d2 is fine for White, because Black has no active follow-up.

25.e5 ♕f4! 26.♕g4

26.♕xf4?! ♘xf4 is fine for Black, who will pick up an exchange as 27.♖5d2? ♖h1† 28.♗f1 ♖ah8 is winning for Black!

**26...♖h1† 27.♗f1 ♔f7 28.d7 ♖d8 29.♕xf4†
♘xf4 30.♖d6 ♔e7 31.♗d2 ♖h4 32.♔c3 ♖h5
33.♖f6 ♖f5 34.♖xf5 gxf5 35.♗b5 ♔e6 36.♖e1
♘d5† 37.♔b3 ♘f4**
½–½

It feels as though White should have been better in this endgame, however Black's pieces always seemed to get where they needed to be in the nick of time.

Game 38 Conclusions: In the line with 1.d4 ♘f6 2.c4 g6 3.♘c3 d5 4.cxd5 ♘xd5 5.e4 ♘xc3 6.bxc3 ♗g7 7.♘f3 c5 8.♖b1 0–0 9.♗e2 ♘c6 10.d5 ♗xc3† 11.♗d2 ♗xd2† 12.♕xd2 ♘a5 13.h4 ♗g4 14.h5 Black is definitely playing with fire. For a long time this variation was thought to be practically winning for White, however now this assessment is very much in doubt. Certainly White is close to winning at every turn, however 21...♘c6! and GM Smbat Lputian's excellent discovery 22...♘c6! is keeping Black afloat for the time being. At various points in this game I suggested alternatives for White, and although some of my suggestions create new chances, none of them seem to promise White an indisputable edge. This rather invites the question: 'If the mainline is a draw, then what should White play?'. Well, two years later 8.♖b1 expert GM Etienne Bacrot switched to 14.♘g5!?, and this is examined in the next illustrative game.

Game 39
Bacrot – Popovic
European Cup Halkidiki 2002

**1.d4 ♘f6 2.c4 g6 3.♘c3 d5 4.cxd5 ♘xd5 5.e4
♘xc3 6.bxc3 ♗g7 7.♘f3 c5 8.♖b1 0–0 9.♗e2
♘c6 10.d5 ♗xc3† 11.♗d2 ♗xd2† 12.♕xd2
♘a5 13.h4 ♗g4 14.♘g5!?**

Given that White has recently been encountering difficulties proving an advantage with 14.h5, it is possible that attention will shift to this ambitious lunge. I fell quite in love with this move when I saw an old game by Chernin in which he managed to sacrifice the knight on g5 and then whip up a furious attack that began on the h-file but then spread across much of the board before Black could even mobilize his forces.

14...♗xe2 15.♔xe2 e6!

Definitely best; previously practice had seen two other continuations:

a) 15...e5 16.h5 ♕f6 (16...h6? 17.♘h7! g5 18.♘xf8 ♔xf8 19.♕c3+– Kargoll – Chabanon, Germany 1991) 17.♘xh7 (17.hxg6 fxg6 18.f3!? has been suggested by N.Gaprindashvili & E.Ubilava, and appears to be slightly better for White (*Informant 40*)) 17...♔xh7 18.♕xa5 b6 19.hxg6† ♔g7 (19...♔xg6 20.♕c3±) 20.♕d2 fxg6 (20...♔xg6 is better, when White is only slightly better according to Krasenkow.) 21.♕h6† ♔f7 22.♕h7† ♔g7 23.♖b3± Gaprindashvili – Kouatly, Albena 1985.

b) 15...h6 16.♘h3 ♔h7 (16...e6? 17.♕xh6 ♕f6 18.♘g5 ♖fe8 19.h5 exd5 20.hxg6 fxg6 21.♕h7† ♔f8 22.♕c7 ♔g8 23.♖h8† 1–0 Gladischev – Szeberenyi, Budapest 1997) 17.♕c3 with two possibilities:

b1) 17...e5?! 18.dxe6 ♕d4! (18...fxe6? 19.♘g5†
hxg5 20.hxg5† ♔g8 21.♖h8† ♔f7 22.♖h7† ♔e8
23.♕g7!+– Susan Polgar, *Informant 53*) 19.♕xd4
cxd4 20.exf7 (Susan Polgar also mentions the line
20.♖b5 b6 21.exf7 ♖ad8 (2...♖xf7? 22.♖d5 ♘c6
23.♖d6+–) 22.♖d5 ♖xd5 23.exd5 ♖xf7 24.♖d1
♖d7 25.♖xd4 ♘c6 26.♖d2 ♘e7 27.♘f4 g5±)
20...♖xf7 was Su. Polgar – De la Villa Garcia,
Pamplona 1991, and now Susan Polgar gives
the continuation 21.♖hc1! ♖e8 22.♔d3 ♖fe7
23.♘f4! ♖xe4 (23...♖f7 24.♘d5 ♖xf2 25.♖c7†
♔h8 26.♖b5 b6 27.♖xa7±) 24.♘d5 with a
decisive advantage for White.

b2) 17...b6 18.♘g5† (18.f4!?) 18...♔g8
19.h5!!

19...hxg5 20.hxg6 fxg6 (20...f6 21.♕h3+–)
21.♖h8†! ♔f7 22.♖h7† ♔e8 23.♕g7 ♔d7
(Chernin notes the lines 23...♘c4?! 24.♕xg6†
♔d7 25.♕c6 mate, 23...♕d6 24.e5+–,
23...♘b7? 24.♕xg6†+– and 23...♕d7!?±) 24.d6!
♕e8 (24...♘c6 25.dxe7 ♘xe7 26.♖d1†+–)
25.dxe7 ♖g8 (25...♖f4 26.♖h8!! ♕xe7
(26...♕xh8 27.e8♕†) 27.♖xa8! ♖xe4† 28.♔f1
♕xg7 29.♖xa7†± or 25...♖h8 26.♖xh8 ♕xh8
27.e8♕†+–) 26.♕e5 ♘c6 27.♖d1† ♘d4†
28.♖xd4†! cxd4 29.♕d5† ♔c7 30.♕xa8! ♕b5†
31.♔f3± Chernin – Stohl, Austria 1993. The
comments here are based on Alex Chernin's
annotations for *Informant 56*.

16.h5

Krasenkow notes the line 16.dxe6!? ♕xd2†
17.♔xd2 fxe6 18.♔e2 when White has some
pressure against the e6-pawn and can consider
19.h5, pressurising the kingside. Nevertheless, I
doubt White has much (if any) advantage in this
position.

16...♘c4!

An important discovery by GM Petar Popovic,
and one which challenges the validity of White's
attack. The alternatives are known to be dangerous
for Black:

a) 16...h6? is powerfully answered by
17.♘h7!!

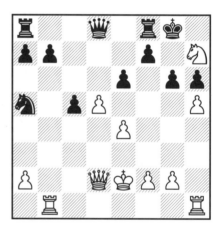

17...g5 18.♘xf8 ♔xf8 19.♕c3+– Ermenkov
– Mrdja, Baden-Baden 1985.

b) 16...exd5 17.hxg6 (17.♘xh7!? ♖e8 (17...
dxe4 18.♘xf8 ♕xd2† 19.♔xd2 ♖xf8 20.♔e3±)
18.hxg6 ♖xe4† 19.♔f1 fxg6 20.♕h6 ♕d6
21.♘g5+– A. Zadrima, *Informant 53*) 17...hxg6
18.♕f4!? (18.♕c3 d4 19.♕h3 ♔g7 20.♕h6†
♔f6 21.♘h7†±) 18...dxe4 19.♖bd1 ♕e7 20.♕h4
♔g7 21.♕h6† ♔f6 22.♖d6†! ♕xd6 (22...♔e5
23.♕h2† ♔f5 24.♕h3† ♔e5 25.♕g3† ♔f5
26.♖d5† ♔f6 27.♕c3†+– Ljungberg) 23.♘xe4†
♔e5 24.♘xd6 ♔xd6 25.♕d2† ♔c7 26.♕xa5†
1–0 Sjödin – Hjelm, corr. 1990.

17.♕c1 exd5 18.♘xh7

18.hxg6 fxg6 19.♖xb7 ♕f6 20.f4 h5∓.

[Editor's note: Soon after Eddie had completed the book and gone on holiday to Thailand two vitally relevant games were played: Avrukh – Sutovsky, Israel 2004, continued 18.hxg6 fxg6 19.♖xh7! ♕f6 20.f4 b6 21.♖b3 ♖ae8 22.♖bh3 ♖e7 23.♖7h6 ♘d6 24.♕d2 d4 25.♕d3 ♘f7 (A couple of weeks later, on New Year's Day 2005, Belov – Knott, Hastings 2004/5, reached this position and instead continued 25...♖fe8 but after 26.♔d1!, threatening e4-e5, White was soon winning: 26...♖xe4 27.♘xe4 ♖xe4 28.f5! ♕xf5 29.♖xg6! ♕xg6 30.♖g3) 26.♕c4 (Fritz suggests that 26.♕b3! is clearer. The clever point is that if 26...d3† White can now play 27.♔e1! winning.) 26...d3† 27.♖xd3 and, despite the complications, White won quickly.]

18...♖e8 19.hxg6 ♖xe4† 20.♔f1 ♖h4 21.♖xh4 ♕xh4 22.♔g1 ♘e5!

It is clear that White's attack has failed and Black now holds the advantage. White still has some tricks however, and Bacrot is quick to show that he is no push-over!

23.gxf7†

Krasenkow notes that 23.♕c3 d4! 24.♕xc5 ♕xf2†! 25.♔xf2 ♘d3†, and 23.g3 ♕e7 24.♕h6 ♘xg6 are both clearly better for Black.

23...♘xh7 24.♕xc5 ♔g7 25.♖b3?

25.♖xb7 ♖f8 26.♕xd5 ♕f6! gives White better drawing chances, but Black should still be winning in any case.

25...♕c4??

An awful blunder that just loses! Simply 25...♕e4 or 25...♕f6 would have been completely winning!

26.f8♕†! ♖xf8 27.♕e7†

1–0

Black resigned as White will pick up the e5-knight, restoring material equality with a decisive attack on the black king in full swing.

Game 39 Conclusions: 14.♘g5!? is definitely dangerous, however 14...♗xe2 15.♔xe2 e6! 16.h5 ♘c4! presently looks very satisfactory for Black, which may mean that White has to consider Krasenkow's suggestion 16.dxe6!?, although I doubt this holds much promise. Notably, since

this game there have been no other GM-level games with 14.♘g5!?.

Conclusions on 9...♘c6!?:

In Game 37 we saw Black force an immediate transition from opening to endgame with 1.d4 ♘f6 2.c4 g6 3.♘c3 d5 4.cxd5 ♘xd5 5.e4 ♘xc3 6.bxc3 ♗g7 7.♘f3 c5 8.♖b1 0–0 9.♗e2 ♘c6!? 10.d5 ♗xc3† 11.♗d2 ♗xd2† 12.♕xd2 ♘d4! 13.♘xd4 cxd4 14.♕xd4 ♕a5† 15.♕d2 ♕xd2† 16.♔xd2. Although material remains level in this ending, White enjoys certain advantages in terms of greater space, a superior minor piece, a more centralized king position and more active rooks. Individually these factors don't amount to much, however in cumulative terms they can pose Black serious problems, and White should be very happy to play these endings.

In Games 38 and 39 we considered the ultra-sharp 12.♕xd2 ♘a5 13.h4 ♗g4 and now 14.h5 was discussed in Game 38, whereas 14.♘g5!? was examined in Game 39. On present evidence neither of these promises White an advantage (the notes to both games include routes to satisfactory positions for Black), but after 14.h5 (the mainline) Black has to endure prolonged defence against a vigorous attack, with the sole reward of reaching a drawn ending if everything goes right. Obviously this isn't everyone's cup of tea, however I can't help but wonder why there has not been more attention in this line since Halkias – Lputian 2000 (Game 38). Indeed, over the last four years there has been hardly any GM interest in the line whatsoever, whereas many of the world's top players continue to reel out 8.♖b1 on a regular basis. The obvious conclusion is that White has a big improvement that is yet to be unveiled, and I can only apologise that I am not aware of it to share it with you.

[Editor's note: No need to apologise Eddie, we have you covered! The big improvement seems to be over Game 39: Avrukh – Sutovsky, Israel 2004 and Belov – Knott, Hastings 2005 in the notes to White's 18th move may supply the answer. This is a vivid example of the volatile nature of Grünfeld theory.]

Chapter 7: The Insidious 10...♘e5

In terms of avoiding mainline theory, but still obtaining a reasonable position from the opening, 10...♘e5 is undoubtedly one of Black's most reliable options.

1.d4 ♘f6 2.c4 g6 3.♘c3 d5 4.cxd5 ♘xd5 5.e4 ♘xc3 6.bxc3 ♗g7 7.♘f3 0–0 8 ♗e2 c5 9 ♖b1 ♘c6 10.d5 ♘e5

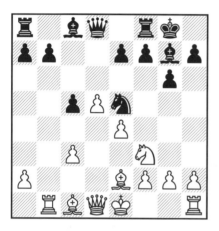

By playing the knight to e5 Black hopes to exchange White's only active piece (the f3-knight) and then strike back at White's central pawn mass before he has time to complete development and play c3-c4 and f2-f4. The downside to this plan is that White is permitted to establish a potentially dynamic pawn centre that restricts the movement of Black's pieces and can cause Black no end of long-term problems. All this leads to tense and highly intricate positions, which offer excellent chances to fight for the full point.

Game 40
Mozetic – Vujacic
Yugoslavia 1995

1.d4 ♘f6 2.c4 g6 3.♘c3 d5 4.cxd5 ♘xd5 5.e4

♘xc3 6.bxc3 ♗g7 7.♘f3 0–0 8 ♗e2 c5 9 ♖b1 ♘c6 10.d5 ♘e5 11.♘xe5 ♗xe5 12.♕c2

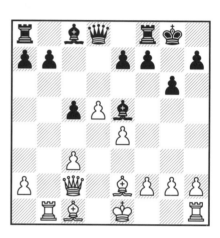

From a purely superficial perspective, the text is perhaps White's most natural response, although on present evidence it does not promise any advantage whatsoever. The mainline is 12.♕d2, and this will be discussed in Games 41 and 42, and the extravagant 12.♖b3 will be considered in Game 43.

White has one other common line which runs: 12.c4 ♕c7! (As we shall see in the main game, it is very important for Black to contest the dark squares at every turn. In this instance Black is fighting for control of the f4-square. The alternative 12...♕d6!? pursues a similar aim: 13.♕d2 ♗d4 14.♗b2 ♗xb2 15.♖xb2 e5 16 0–0 b6 17.♖b3 was Gelfand – Ghinda, Halle 1987, and now Ghinda, in *Informant 45*, claims that Black should have played 17...f5 with an unclear position.) 13.♕d2 ♗d4 14 0–0 (14.♗b2 e5 15 0–0 f5 16.♗d3 is unclear according to Ftacnik, although notably White did well in the only practical outing of this line: 16...f4 17.♗xd4 exd4 18.♖fe1 ♕e5 19.f3 ♖f7

20.♕a5!± b6?? 21.♖xb6+- Shirov – Carlhammar, Budapest 1989) 14...e5 15.♖b3!? f5 16.exf5 ♗xf5 (16...gxf5 17.♖g3† ♔h8 18.♕h6± - Haba) 17.♕g5 ♗f7 18.♕h4 ♖e8 (18...b6!?± - Ftacnik) 19.♗g4 ♕a5 20.♖f3 Black now has the following possibilities:

a) 20...♕xa2? 21.♗xf5 gxf5 22.♖xf5+- was Haba – Pribyl, Lazne Bohdanec 1994.

b) 20...♗xg4? 21.♖xf7 ♔xf7 22.♕xh7† ♔f6 23.♗h6+-.

c) 20...e4 21.♖xf5 (21.♗xf5 exf3 22.♗e6 ♖ef8 23.♗h6 ♗g7 leads to equality according to Ftacnik) 21...gxf5 22.♗h5 ♖ef8 23.♗xf7† ♖xf7 24.♕g3† ♗g7 25.♗b2±.

d) 20...♖ef8! seems best: 21.♗xf5 (21.♗h6 ♗xg4 22.♖xf7 ♖xf7 23.♕xg4 ♗xf2†! 24.♔h1 ♖f5∓) 21...♖xf5 22.♖xf5 ♖xf5 23.♗h6 (23.♗e3=) 23...♕c7 (23...♖h5? 24.♕e7 ♖xh6 25.d6, and 23...♖xf2? 24.♕xf2 ♗xf2† 25.♖xf2 ♕d8 26.♔f1 are obviously bad for Black, however 23...♖f7!?

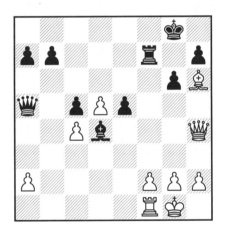

is interesting according to Haba) 24.♕e4 with an equal position. Unless otherwise indicated the comments here are based on GM Petr Haba's annotations for *Informant 60*.

12...♕d6!

The text represents the critical test of White's set-up. 12...f5, 12...♕c7 and 12...e6 have all either been analysed or tried in practice, however none seem quite as convincing as the text.

13.g3

13.♕d2 has been played, but makes very little sense given that White has just played 12.♕c2. Play has continued 13...e6 (13...♗g7 14 0–0 b6 15.f4 e5 16.dxe6 ♕xe6 17.♗b2 ♗b7 18.f5 ♕e7 19.♖be1 ♖ad8 20.♕c1 ♗e5 was very comfortable for Black in Ubilava – Smejkal, Trencianske Teplice 1985) 14.♗c4 exd5 15.♗xd5 ♕f6 16.♗b2 ♗e6 17 0–0 ♗xd5 18.exd5 c4!

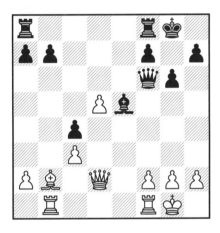

19.♗a3 ♖fd8 20.♖xb7 ♕a6 21.♖e7 ♘f6 22.♗b4 ♗xe7 23.♗xe7 ♖d7 24.d6 ♖e8 25.♖e1 ½–½ Jankovic – Palac, Croatia 2003.

13...e6!

In this instance Black is best advised to hit the pawn chain at its head. It may be tempting to strike at the base of the pawn chain with 13...f5!?, however 14.f4 ♗g7 15.e5! ♕xd5 16 0–0 ♖b8 17.♖d1 ♕c6 18.♗b5 ♕c7 19.♕b3† ♔h8 (19...e6?! 20.♗e3 intending 21.♖d6 is clearly better for White according to Dzhanoev, *Informant 59*) 20.♗e3 b6 21.♕d5 ♗b7 (21...a6 22.♗e2 ♗b7 23.♕d7± - Dzhanoev) 22.♕d7 ♖fc8 23.♖d2 ♕xd7 24.♖xd7 ♗f8 as in Bagaturov – Smejkal, Mlada Boleslav 1993, was much more comfortable for White, and Dzhanoev points out that 25.♗c4! would have secured White a clear advantage. It is never a psychologically easy task to give up a pawn and then simplify into an endgame, however, as GM

Bogdan Lalic points out in his text *The Grünfeld for the Attacking Player*, "the control of the d-file is the (most) important factor" in the position.

14.f4

14.c4!? exd5 15.cxd5 ♓h3! 16.♜xb7 ♜fe8 gives Black good compensation according to Vujacic.

14...♙g7 15.c4 exd5 16.cxd5 ♜e8

Black now threatens to tear White's pawn chain to pieces with 17...♜xe4 18.♕xe4 ♗f5!∓.

17.♜b3 ♗d7

17...♗d4!?

18.e5

Vujacic notes the variations: 18.♜xb7? ♗f5!!∓, and 18.♜a3 b5 19 0–0 c4 (19...♗d4† also looks good, e.g. 20.♔g2 f5 21.e5 ♕xd5† 22.♗f3 ♕e6 23.♗xa8 ♜xa8 when Black's dominant control of the light squares provides excellent compensation for the sacrificed exchange.) 20.♗f3 ♕c5†! 21.♔g2 b4 22.♜e3 ♗d4 23.♜ee1 a5 intending 24...a4 with a clear advantage to Black.

18...♕xd5 19.♗f3 ♕e6 20.♜xb7 ♗c6 21.♜b3 c4! 22.♜c3 ♗xf3 23.♜xf3 f6∓ 24 0–0 fxe5 25.f5 gxf5 26.♜xf5 ♜f8 27.♗b2? ♕b6†! 28.♔g2 ♕c6† 29.♔h3

29.♔g1 ♕c5† 30.♔g2 ♕d5† 31.♔g1 ♕d3–+.

29...♜xf5 30.♜xf5 ♜e8 31.♕d2 ♕e6 32.g4 h6 33.♕e3? ♜d8 34.♕e4 ♜d3† –+ 35.♔h4 ♗f6† 36.g5 ♗xg5† 37.♔g4 ♗e7! 38.♕xe5 ♕g6† 39.♔f4 ♗d6 0–1

Game 40 Conclusions: This was a good game by Black, and an excellent demonstration of how important it is to establish control over the central dark squares at an early stage in this system. In this encounter White ultimately recaptured control of the f4 and e5 squares, but achieved this only at the cost of his development, and it was not long before Black managed to bring serious pressure to bear on White's centre.

Game 41
Khalifman – Greenfeld
St Petersburg 1999

1.d4 ♘f6 2 ♘f3 g6 3.c4 ♗g7 4 ♘c3 d5 5.cxd5 ♘xd5 6.e4 ♘xc3 7.bxc3 c5 8.♜b1 0–0 9.♗e2 ♘c6 10.d5 ♘e5 11.♘xe5 ♗xe5 12.♕d2

When the defects surrounding 12.♕c4 and 12.c4 became clear, 12.♕d2 emerged as White's primary line of attack against 9...♘c6 and 10...♘e5. As we saw in Game 40, the battle for the advantage revolved around who could successfully seize control of the f4 and e5-squares, and at what cost. By playing 12.♕d2 White acknowledges that it is necessary to enhance control of the f4-square immediately, even at the cost of obstructing the path of the c1–bishop. White's reward for disrupting his coordination is an immediate threat of 13.f4 that cannot be prevented.

12...e6

The text is now the mainline of this variation, however three other moves have also attracted their followers over the years and have enjoyed varying degrees of popularity:

a) 12...♗g7 13.f4 e5?! (better is 13...e6 14.c4 with a transposition to the main game) 14 0–0 exf4 15.♕xf4

Black has now tried two possibilities:

a1) 15...f5? has only been tried once, and is now known to be bad for Black: 16.e5! ♗xe5?! (16...♖e8 17.e6 ♕xd5 18.♗c4 ♕e5 19.e7† ♔h8 20.♕xe5 ♗xe5 21.♗g5 h6 22.♗f7 ♗e6 23.♗xe8 ♖xe8 24.♗h4± - Avrukh) 17.♕xe5 ♖e8 18.♕g3 ♖xe2 19.♖e1! ♕e8 (19...♖xe1† 20.♕xe1 b6 21.♕e5! is very good for White - just look at those dark squares!) 20.♗h6 ♗d7 21.♖xe2 ♕xe2 22.h3!? (22.♕d6 is also strong) 22...b6 23.♕c7 ♕e8 24.c4 ♔f7 (24...♕f7 25.♕b7 ♕e8 26.d6 ♕c8 27.♕d5† ♗e6 28.d7!+-) 25.♗g5 h6 was Avrukh – Greenfeld, Tel Aviv 2002, and now Avrukh notes that White should have played 26.♗xh6 ♕e7 (26...♕d8 27.♕g3 ♕f6 28.♗g5 ♕d4† 29.♔h1) 27.♕b7 ♕d8 28.d6 ♕c8 29.♕d5† ♗e6 30.♕f3±. The comments here are based on GM Boris Avrukh's annotations for *Chessbase Magazine 93*.

a2) 15...♕e7 16.♗c4 ♗e5 (16...♗xc3 17.d6 ♗d4† 18.♔h1 ♕e8 19.♗d5 ♖b8 20.♕f3 gives

White compensation for his sacrificed pawn according to Ftacnik.) 17.♕g5 ♕d6 (17...♕xg5!? 18.♗xg5 f6 (18...♗xc3 19.♗e7±) 19.♗e3 (Avrukh notes that 19.♗h6!? is interesting, but another interesting idea would be 19.d6†!? with the point that 19...♗g7 can be met by 20.d7! ♗xd7 21.♖xb7) 19...b6 is unclear according to Avrukh) 18.♗f4! f6 (Ftacnik notes the line 18...♗xf4 19.♕xf4 ♕xf4 20.♖xf4 b6 21.♖bf1±, and 18...♖e8 19.♗xe5 ♖xe5 20.♕f4 is also clearly better for White according to Israeli GM Boris Avrukh) 19.♗xe5 fxe5 (19...♕xe5 20.♕xe5 fxe5 21.d6† ♔g7 22.♖xf8 ♔xf8 23.♖f1†+-) 20.h4!

20...h5 21.♖xf8† ♔xf8 22.♕h6† ♔g8 23.g4! b5 (23...♗xg4? 24.♖xb7 ♗d7 25.♖xd7 ♕xd7 26.d6†, and 23...hxg4 24.h5 b5 25.hxg6 ♕d7 26.♗xb5 are both winning for White) 24.g5!? ♗h3 25.♖xb5 ♖d8 26.♖b7 ♗d7 (26...♖d7 27.♖b8†! ♕xb8 28.d6† ♖f7 29.♗xf7† ♔xf7 30.♕h7† ♔f8 31.♕h8†+-) 27.b5 c4 was Wells – Rowson, London 1997 and now rather than 28.♖xd7?, which gave Black a perpetual check draw after 28...♕b6† 29.♔g2 ♖xd7 30.♗xd7 ♕b2†, Ftacnik notes that 28.♔g2! a6 29.♗xd7 ♖xd7 30.♖xd7 ♕xd7 31.♕xg6† would have concluded the game in White's favour. It is a real shame that Peter Wells blundered at the end, as this was truly a beautiful game. The comments here are based on Ftacnik's notes for *CBM*.

b) 12...♕a5 is best met by 13.♖b3 when White intends to play 14.c4, exchange queens, and then expand his centre with f2-f4 and e4-e5. 13...a6 14.f4 ♗g7 15.c4 ♕xd2† (15...♕c7 16.♗b2 (16. e5!?±) 16...b5 17.♗xg7 ♔xg7 18 0–0± Meduna – Atanasov, Varna 1983) 16.♗xd2 (16.♔xd2!? ♖b8 17.♗a3 ♗d4 18.♗b2 ♗xb2 19.♖xb2 ♗d7 20.♖b6± Franco Alonso – Romero, Madrid 1999) 16...♗d4 17.a4 ♖b8 18.a5 ♗d7 19.♖b6± Agrest – Sarwinski, Mikolajki 1991.

c) 12...b6 has proved a more challenging alternative in practice. White has two reasonable ways to approach the position:

c1) 13.f4 ♗g7 14.c4 e5 15 0–0 (15.♗b2 exf4 (15...♕d6!? has also been played, but the text is a simpler route to equality) 16.♕xf4 (16.♗xg7? ♕h4† 17.g3 fxg3 18.♕h6 g2† 19.♕xh4 gxh1♕† 20.♔f2 (20.♔d2 ♕xb1 21.♗f6 ♕xa2† 22.♔e1 ♕b1† 23.♔d2 ♕g1! 24.♕h6 ♕d4† 25.♗xd4 cxd4∓) 20...♕xb1 21.♗f6 ♕c1–+ Stohl, *Informant 48*) 16...♕e7 17 0–0 ♗d7 18.♗d3 ♗xb2 19.♖xb2 f6 20.♗c2!? ♖ae8! 21.♖e1 ♕e5 22.♕xe5 ♖xe5 23.a4 f5 24 a5 fxe4 25.axb6 axb6 26.♖xe4 ♖xe4 27.♗xe4 ♖f6 28.♖a2 b5!= Sakaev – Ftacnik, Dortmund 1992). And now:
c11) 15...exf4 16.♕xf4 (16.♗b2?! g5!? 17.♗xg7 (17.e5? ♖e8∓) 17...♔xg7 18.a4 (18. e5 f6 19.♕c3 (19.e6? ♗xe6) 19...fxe5 20.♕xe5† ♕f6∓ - Ftacnik) 18...♕d6 was very comfortable

for Black in Topalov – Mohr, Altensteig 1990) 16...♗d4† 17.♗e3 ♗xe3† 18.♕xe3 ♕e7 19.♕f4 (In *Informant 46* Vladimir Epishin gives the line 19.e5! ♖e8 20.e6 fxe6 21.♗f3 ♖b8 (On 21...♗b7 Epishin proposes 22.d6 ♕d7 23.♗xb7 ♕xb7 24.♕e5, intending 25.♖f6 with a clear advantage to White.) 22.♕e5 ♗d7 23.♖be1 ♕g7 24.♕c7±) 19...f6 20.a4!± Epishin – Ftacnik, Belgrade 1988.
c12) 15...f5!? 16.♗b2 ♕d6 17.♕c3

17...♖e8 18.♗d3 fxe4 (18...♖e7 19.exf5 gxf5 (19...e4 20.f6!) 20.fxe5! ♗xe5 21.♕d2 ♗xh2† 22.♔h1 ♗e5 23.♕g5† ♕g6 (23...♗g7 24.♗xe5 ♕xe5 25.♕d8† ♔f7 26.♖be1+-) 24.♕xe7 ♕h6† 25.♔g1 ♕e3† 26.♔h1 ♕h6† 27.♔g1 ♕e3† 28.♖f2! ♗h2† 29.♔xh2 ♕xe7 30.♖f3! ♕d6† 31.♖g3† ♔f7 32.♖f1± Gelfand – Ftacnik, Debrecen 1989) 19.♗xe4 ♖e7 20.f5! (Originally recommended by GM Dimitri Komarov in his annotations for *Informant 48*, where he also opines that after 20.fxe5 ♗xe5 21.♕f3 Black should be able to maintain the balance with 21...♗xh2†! 22.♔h1 ♗a6 23.♖be1 ♗e5! 24.♗xe5 ♖xe5 25.♗xg6 hxg6 26.♕f7† ♔h8 27.♖xe5 ♕xe5 28.♖f3 ♕e1† 29.♔h2 ♕e5†=) 20...gxf5 21.♗xf5 e4 22.♕h3 ♗xf5 23.♖xf5 is slightly better for White according to Komarov, however Kirchanov – Kibalnichenko, corr. 1990, continued 23...♕g6 (Kibalnichenko and Ivannikov, in their annotations for *Informant 54*, give the line 23...♗d4† 24.♗xd4 cxd4 25.♕g4† ♔h8 26.♖bf1 ♕g6 as being Black's route to equality, however they only mention 27.♖f8†, when in fact 27.♖g5 appears to be very strong for White, e.g. 27...♕d6 28.♕f5 and White threatens 29.♕f8 mate, so Black is in serious trouble.) 24.♗xg7 ♕xg7 25.♖bf1 e3 26.d6 (26.♖5f4!? threatening 27.♖g4 may be an improvement) 26...e2 27.dxe7 exf1♕† 28.♖xf1 ♕xe7 29.♕f5 ♖e8=.

c2) 13 0–0! e6 14.♗c4!?

A new idea for this chapter, but a common idea in practice. White improves the position of the light-squared bishop, pressurising the e6-pawn and hoping to force 14...exd5 15.♗xd5, when the d5-bishop will be a dominant force. Play has continued as follows:

c21) 14...♖b8?! 15.f4 ♗g7 16.d6 e5 17.f5 ♗b7 18.♕d3 ♕h4 19.♗d5± -Yermolinsky, *Informant 59*.

c22) 14...♗b7!? 15.dxe6 fxe6 (forced as 15...♗xe4? 16.exf7† ♔h8 17.♕e3 ♕h4 18.f4+- (Krasenkow) and 15...♕xd2? 16.exf7† ♔g7 17.♗xd2 ♖ad8 18.♗g5 ♖d7 19.♖bd1+- (Sapis) are both losing for Black) 16.♗xe6† ♔h8 17.♗d5 ♗xd5 18.exd5 ♕d6! 19.f4 ♗g7 20.c4 ♖ae8 21.♕d3 (21.♖e1? ♕xf4!!∓) 21...♖f7 22.♗d2 ♖fe7 23.f5 ♗d4† 24.♔h1 ♔g7! 25.a4 ♖e2 26 a5 gxf5! 27.♖xf5 ♕g6! (27...bxa5? 28.♖f7†!! ♔xf7 29.♕xh7† ♔g7 30.♖f1† ♔e7

31.♕xg7† ♔d8 32.♕xa7+- - Sapis) 28.♖g5 ♕xg5 29.♗xg5 ♖e1† 30.♕f1 ♖xf1† 31.♖xf1± Sapis – S. Larsen, corr. 1995.

c23) 14...♗g7

This is Black's most common approach, in answer to which White has tried three moves:

c231) 15.♖e1 ♖b8 16.e5 exd5 17.♗xd5 ♕c7 18.c4 ♗e6 19.♕e2 ♖bd8 20.♗g5 was good for White in Galliamova – Qin Kanying, Kishinev 1995, however Black's play was rather obliging.

c232) 15.f4 is also of interest, however Ftacnik's trademark line with 15...♗b7! seems to be holding the balance for Black, e.g. 16.dxe6 ♗xe4 17.exf7† ♔h8 18.♗b2 ♕xd2 19.♗xd2 (19.♖xd2 ♗xc3, as in Sadler – Stohl, Isle of Man 1994, leads to equality) 19...♖ad8 20.♖e1 ♗d3! (20...♗d5!? should also lead to a drawn ending according to Krasenkow, however note that 20...♖xd2? 21.♖xd2 ♗xc3 22.♖d8 ♖xd8 23.♖xe4 ♖f8 24.♖e7 was clearly better for White in Wells – Krasenkow, Politiken Cup 1996.) 21.♗xd3 ♖xd3 22.♖e7 ♗xc3 23.♗xc3† ♖xc3 24.♖xa7 ♔g7 25.♖xb6 ♖xf7 26.♖bb7 ♖xb7 27.♖xb7† ♔g8 was van Wely – Holzke, Germany 1999. Obviously White can try and create some chances here, however the rook ending should be drawn, and the players signed the peace eleven moves later.

c233) 15.♕c2!? is a slightly unusual try for the advantage.

Play has continued 15...♕f6 16.♗d2 (16.♗b2 e5 17.♗b5 ♕d6 18.c4 f5 gives Black counterplay) 16...exd5? (16...e5! 17.a4 ♕d6 18.f4 f5!∞) 17.♗xd5 ♖b8 18.♕a4! a6 19.c4 b5 20.♕a3!± Ehlvest – Yermolinsky, Rakvere 1993. The comments here are based on Yermolinsky's annotations for *Informant 59*.

13.f4 ♗g7

From time to time those defending the Black side have experimented with 13...♗h8!?, however the results have rarely been positive: 14.c4 ♖e8 15.e5! f6 16.f5!! Black now has three options:

a) 16...gxf5 17.♖b3 ♖e7 (17...fxe5 18 0–0! exd5 (18...f4 19.d6 gives White good compensation according to GM John Nunn) 19.cxd5! f4 20.d6 ♖b8 21.d7! ♗xd7 22.♖d3 ♖e7 23.♖d6 (23.♖d1!? also looks sensible) 23...♕e8 24.♗c4† ♔f8 25.♕d5 ♗e6 26.♖xe6 ♖xe6 27.♕xe6 ♕xe6 28.♗xe6 is slightly better for White according to Nunn) 18.d6 ♖g7 19.exf6 ♕xf6 20.♗b2 e5 was McCambridge – Hjartarson, Grindavik 1984, and now 21.♗xe5!? worked out well in the game, however Belov (in his annotations for *Informant 37*) notes that 21.♖e3!? ♖xg2 22.♗xe5 is clearly better for White.

b) 16...fxe5 17.fxg6 hxg6 18 0–0 exd5 19.cxd5 ♕d6 20.♕g5 ♗g7 21.♖b3 ♖e7 22.♗c4 ♖c7 23.♖bf3 ♗f5 24.g4 ♗f6 25.♕xf6 ♕xf6 26.d6† ♔g7 27.dxc7 ♕d6 28.♗b2 ♗xg4 29.♖g3 b5?!

(29...♗e6±) 30.♖f7† ♔h6 31.♗d3+- Alterman – Odeev, Jurmala 1989.

c) 16...exd5 17.fxg6 hxg6 18.cxd5 ♖xe5 19 0–0 b6 20.d6 (20.♗c4!? ♕d6 21.♕h6 deserves attention.) 20...♗e6 21.♗f3 ♖c8 22.♗b2 f5?! 23.♕h6 ♗f7 was Agzamov – Pribyl, Sochi 1984 and now 24.♗d5!! would have given White an immediate attack that appears to be completely winning.

14.c4 b6

The text is a good move that alleviates the b1–rook's pressure on the b-file and creates possibilities of developing the c8-bishop on b7 or a6, however Black also has a wide range of alternatives:

a) 14...exd5 15.cxd5 ♗d4! (The only way for Black to compensate for permitting White to establish such a dominant centre is to disrupt White's development immediately. More hesitant attempts are convincingly dispatched: 15...♖e8 16.e5 ♗f5 (16...b6 17.♗b2 ♗f5 18.♖d1 ♕d7 19 0–0± Stoeber – Radecke, Porz 1990) 17.♖xb7 ♗e4 18.♗c4 ♕h4† (18...♗h6 19 0–0 ♖xe5 20.♗b2 ♗xd5 21.♖d1+-Andrianov–Yandemirov, USSR 1982) 19.♕f2 ♕g4 20 0–0± S.Pedersen – Mendeiros, Cappelle 1995) 16.♗b2

Black has now tried the following possibilities:
a1) 16...♕e7 17.♗xd4 ♕xe4 18.♔f2 ♕xd4† 19.♕xd4 cxd4 20.♖hd1 b6 21.♖xd4 occurred in

Cebalo – Sibarevic, Mendrisio 1988. This ending looks slightly better for White to me, however notably Jansa gives 21...♗f5 as equal in *Informant 41*.

a2) 16...f5 17.♗xd4 cxd4 18.♕xd4 fxe4 19 0–0 ♕d6 20.♕e5 ♕a3 21.d6 ♕xa2 22.♖fc1! b5 23.♗xb5 ♗e6 24.♖b2 ♕d5 25.♗c4+- Andrianov – Tseitlin, Severodonetsk 1982.

a3) 16...♕h4† 17.g3 ♕e7 18.e5 ♗f5 19.♖c1 ♕d8 20.♗f3 ♗xb2 21.♕xb2 ♕b6 22.♕b3! 22...♖fe8 (22...♖fc8 23.g4 ♗d7 24.♕c3 a5 25.♖g1 c4 26.♖g2 ♕b4 27.f5 ♕xc3† 28.♖xc3 b5 29.e6 fxe6 30.fxe6±/+- M. Gurevich – Ehlvest, Sverdlovsk 1984) 23.g4 ♗d7 24.h4 ♗b5 25.♕c3 c4 26.♔f1 ♕c5 27.h5 ♖ad8 28.♖d1 g5 29.h6 gxf4 30.e6 f6 31.♕xf6 ♕e7 32.♕e5 c3† 33.♔g2 c2 34.♖h5 1–0 Psakhis – Lechtynsky, Banja Luka 1985.

a4) 16...♕b6 17.♗d3 c4 18.♗xc4! ♖e8 19.♕xd4 (19.e5!?) 19...♕xd4 20.♗xd4 ♖xe4† 21.♔d2 ♖xd4† 22.♔c3 ♖xf4 23.d6!

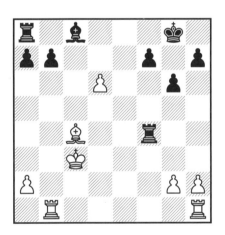

This endgame has been reached a number of times and is widely believed to be bad for Black. Practice has seen:

a41) 23...♔g7 24.♖hf1 ♖xf1 25.♖xf1 ♗f5 26.g4 ♗xg4 27.♖xf7† ♔h6 28.♔d4 ♖c8 29.♗d5 ♔g5 30.♔e5 h5 31.d7 ♖d8 32.♗e6 ♗h4 33.♗xg4 ♔xg4 34.♔d6 ♔h3 35.♔c7 1–0 Khalifman – Ivanchuk, Tilburg 1994.

a42) 23...♖f6!? 24.♖hd1 ♗e6 25.♖xb7 ♖d8 (25...♖c8 26.♖c7) 26.♗xe6 ♖xe6 27.♖xa7 ♖exd6 28.♖xd6 ♖xd6 29.a4 ♔f8 30.♖b7 ♖d1 31.♖b2 ♖a1 was Cebalo – Ilincic, Yugoslavian Championship 1989, and now instead of 32.♔b4?! White should have put his rook behind the a-pawn as quickly as possible. In *Informant 47* Cebalo gives the line 32.♔b3! ♔e7 33.♖a2 ♖xa2 (33...♖b1† 34.♔c4+-) 34.♔xa2 ♔d6 35.♔b3 ♔c5 (35...♔d5 36.♔b4) 36.♔c3+-.

a43) 23...b6 24.♗d5! ♖b8 25.♖hf1 ♖f5 (25...♖xf1?! 26.♖xf1 ♗e6 27.♔d4!± -Arakelian, *Informant 67*) 26.♔d4 ♔f8 was Arakelian – Nadanian, Armenia 1996, and now Arakelian gives 27.g4! with a clear advantage to White, one point being the line 27...♖xd5† 28.♔xd5 ♗b7† (28...♖xg4 29.♖bc1 ♗e6† 30.♔c6 ♖c8† 31.♔b7+-) 29.♔e5 ♖e8† 30.♔f4+-.

b) 14...♖e8 15.e5 f6 16.d6 fxe5 17.♗b2

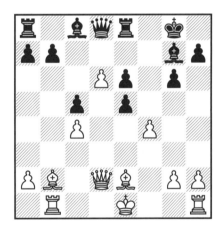

We have now reached a rather critical position for the 9...♘c6 variation, upon which much Grandmaster attention has been focussed over the years. Black has tried the following possibilities:

b1) 17...e4 18.♗xg7 ♔xg7 19.h4 h5 (19...b6 20.h5 ♖f8 21.hxg6 hxg6 22.♖b3 ♕f6 23.♖bh3 ♕d4 24.♖h7† ♔f6 25.g4 ♕xd2† 26.♔xd2 e5 27.♖f1! ♖d8 28.g5† ♔e6 29.♔e3 was clearly better for White in Wells – Gruenberg, Lloyds Bank Open 1984, and 19...e3 20.♕c3† ♕f6

21.♕e5! as in Kouatly-Cocozza, Thessaloniki 1984 was also better for White.) 20.♖d1 (20. g4!? is given as clearly better for White by *NCO*) 20...♗d7 21.♕b2† ♕f6 22.♕xb7 ♖c3† 23.♔f1 ♖ad8 24.♕xa7 ♕e3 25.♖h3 ♖xf4† 26.♔g1 e5 27.♖b3± K. Georgiev – Kouatly, Bulgaria – France Match 1984)

b2) 17...exf4 18.♗xg7 ♔xg7 19.0–0 with a further division:

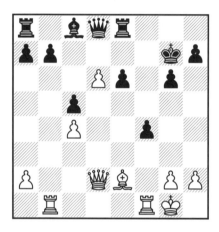

b21) 19...e5 20.d7 ♕xd7 21.♕xd7† ♗xd7 22.♖xb7 ♖e7 23.♖d1 ♖d8 24.♗g4 ♗xg4 25.♖xe7† ♔f6 26.♖xd8 ♔xe7 27.♖d5±/± Doering – Fliegner, Dortmund 1992.

b22) 19...♖f8 20.♖xf4 ♖xf4 21.♕xf4 ♕f6 22.♕e4 ♖b8 23.♖f1 ♕d4† 24.♕xd4† cxd4 25.♖b1 ♗d7 (25...♔f6 26.c5 ♗d7 27.♗f3 d3 28.♔f2±/+- van der Sterren – van Voorthuijsen, Roosendaal 1983) 26.♗f3 b6 27.c5 ♖c8 28.c6! ♗xc6 29.♖c1 ♗d7 30.♖xc8 ♗xc8 31.♗c6 ♔f6 32.d7 ♗xd7 33.♗xd7 e5 34.♔f2 e4 35.♗c6 ♔e5 36.h4!+- Novikov – Tukmakov, Lvov 1984.

b23) 19...b6 20.♕xf4! e5 21.♕f7† ♔h8 22.♖f6 ♕d7 (22...♗f5 23.♖f1 ♖g8 24.g4! ♗g7 25.♕d5 ♕xf6 26.♕xa8† ♖g8 27.♕d5± Rodriguez – Lambers, e-mail 1999) 23.♖d1 ♕xf7 24.♖xf7 ♗e6 25.♖c7 ♔g8 26.h3 ♖f8 27.d7 ♖ad8 28.♖d6 ♔f7 29.♖xa7 ♗e7 30.♖xb6 ♗f4 31.♖c7 ♖e4 32.♗d3 ♖d4 33.♗f1 ♗c4 34.♖xc5 ♗xf1 35.♖xe5† ♔xd7 36.♔xf1± Yusupov – Malaniuk, Moscow 1983.

c) 14...♕e8 15 0–0 exd5 16.exd5 b6

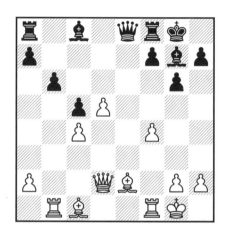

17.♗d3 (17.♗b2!? ♗f5 18.♗xg7 ♔xg7 19.♗d3 ♕d7 20.♖be1 ♖fe8 21.♖e5 f6 22.♗xf5 gxf5 23.♖xe8 ♖xe8 24.♖e1 was Se. Ivanov–Yandemirov, St Petersburg 1993, and now 24...♔f7?! 25.♖xe8 ♔xe8 26.♕d3 was clearly better for White, however 24...b5!? has been given as equal by IM Maksim Notkin) 17...♕e7 (17...♗f5?! 18.♗xf5 gxf5 19.♗b2 ♕d7 20.♗xg7 ♔xg7 21.♖fe1± Cebalo – Yandemirov, Djakovo 1994) 18.♕c2 (White also has a couple of reasonable alternatives: 18.a4!? ♖e8 19.a5 ♖b8 20.♕c2 was given as slightly better for White by Notkin in *Informant 66*, and 18.f5 ♗d7 19.♕f4 ♗xf5 20.♗xf5 gxf5 21.♕xf5 ♖ae8 22.♗f4 ♗d4† 23.♔h1 f6 24.♗h6 ♖f7± was Osokin – Yandemirov, Kstovo 1998) 18...♗d7 19.f5 ♖ae8 20.♗f4 ♗e5 21.♗xe5 ♕xe5 22.♖bd1 g5!? (22...♕d4†!? 23.♔h1 ♕h4! 24.♕d2 ♖e5 is unclear according to Notkin) 23.f6 h6 24.♖f2 ♕d6? (Notkin gives the line 24...♔h8! 25.♗f1 ♕e3 as equal, however 26.♖d3! ♕e5 27.♖a3 leaves Black under some pressure.) 25.♖df1 ♖e3 26.♕d1! ♖fe8 27.♗b1 ♖c3?! (27...♖8e5 28.♕c2 ♖5e4 29.♕xe4 ♖xe4 30.♗xe4 ♕e5 31.♗d3 ♕c3± - Notkin) 28.♕h5 ♕f8 29.♗f5 ♗a4? (29...♗xf5±) 30.♗e6!+- Notkin – Yandemirov, Minsk 1996. The threat is 31.♕g6† and 32.♗xf7.

d) 14...♖b8 15.♗b2 e5 16 0–0 ♕d6 17.♕c3! ♖e8 (17...f6 18.fxe5 fxe5 19.♖xf8† ♕xf8

20.♕a5±) 18.f5! ♗d7 (18...g5 19.f6! ♗xf6 20.♗h5! gives White an attack) 19.♕f3 a6 20.f6 ♗h6 21.♗c1 ♗xc1 22.♖bxc1 b5 23.♕e3 ♔h8 24.h4! bxc4 25.♗xc4 ♗b5 26.♗xb5 ♖xb5 27.a4 ♖b2 28.♖xc5± Agrest – Muse, Berlin 1993. The comments here are based on Agrest's notes for *Chessbase Magazine 40*.

15.♗b2! ♗xb2

16.♖xb2

The text represents White's traditional treatment of this position, however some strong players have also experimented with 16.♕xb2. Play has continued 16...exd5 (16...♕h4†?! is less accurate, e.g. 17.g3 ♕h3 18.♗f3 ♗a6 19.♖c1 ♖ae8 (19...exd5 20.cxd5 ♖ae8 21.♔f2 ♗d3 22.♗g2 ♕h5 23.♖he1± – Greenfeld, *Informant 69*) 20.♗g2 ♕h5 21.♕a3 ♗c8 22 0–0± exd5 23.cxd5 ♗h3 as in Greenfeld – Liss, Israel 1997. GM Alon Greenfeld now recommends 24.♗xh3 ♕xh3 25.e5 with a clear advantage to White.) 17.cxd5 ♖e8 18.e5 ♕xd5! (The Canadian GM Dimitri Tyomkin notes the lines 18...f6? 19 0–0, and 18...♗b7 19.♖d1 ♗xd5 20 0–0, in either case with a substantial advantage for White: *Chessbase Magazine 71*). Black is playing with fire and sacrificing a rook in the process! Unfortunately such measures are already very much a necessity if Black is to avoid being positionally crushed. 19.♗f3 ♕c4 20.♗xa8

♕xf4 21.♗f3 ♖xe5† 22.♔f1! ♕e3 (Black now threatens 23...♗a6–+. By way of alternatives, Krasenkow notes that 22...♗b7 23.♖e1! ♖xe1† 24.♔xe1 ♗xf3 25.gxf3 ♕xf3 26.♖f1 should be winning for White.) 23.♕e2 ♕c3 (23...♕d4 24.♖d1 ♖xe2 25.♖xd4 ♖xa2 26.♖d8† ♔g7 27.♔e1! intending 28.♖f1 and 29.♖f2 is better for White according to Tyomkin, e.g. 27...♗a6! 28.g3 ♗b5 29.♖d2 ♖a3 30.♗e2±) 24.♗b3! ♕a1† (24...♖xe2 25.♖xc3 ♖xa2 26.♔e1! is similar to the ending considered above, and 24...♕d4 25.♖d3 ♗a6 26.♖xd4 ♗xe2† 27.♔xe2 cxd4 28.♔f2 is also good for White) 25.♕d1

and now 25...♕xa2? 26.h4! h5 27.♔g1 ♔g7 28.♖c3! ♗f5 29.♕c1! ♕a4 30.♖c4 ♕e8 31.♕c3 ♔h7 32.♔f2 ♕e7 33.♖e1±/+- was Huzman – Sutovsky, Tel Aviv 1999. However, there is a suggestion by Krasenkow and/or Tyomkin (it is not clear which) in *Chessbase Magazine 71* that Black may be able to save his bacon with 25...♗a6†! 26.♔f2 ♕xa2† 27.♔g1 (27.♔g3?! ♖g5† is dangerous for White, e.g. 28.♔h3 ♗c8† 29.g4 h5 30.♔h4 ♖xg4†!! 31.♗xg4 ♕f2†∓/–+) 27...♖e2!! 28.♗xe2 (28.♕b1? ♕d2–+) 28...♖xe2 29.♖g3 ♖d2 30.♕e1 ♖e2 31.♕d1=.

16...♗a6

Alternatives:

a) 16...e5 17 0–0 f6 (17...♕d6 18.f5 gxf5 19.exf5 f6 was at least slightly better for White in

Muehlebach – Moor, Pontresina 2000, although Black's position remains solid.) 18.fxe5 fxe5 19.♖bb1 ♖xf1† 20.♖xf1 ♕h4 21.♕c3 ♕xe4 22.♗f3! ♕f4 (22...♖d4† 23.♕xd4 cxd4 24.d6 ♖b8 25.♗d5† ♔g7 26.♖f7† ♔h6 27.♖f8+- - Krasenkow) 23.g3 ♕f5 24.♗g2 ♕d7 25.d6 ♗b7 26.♗xb7 ♕xb7 27.♕xe5 1–0 Sherbakov – Aronian, Decin 1996.

b) 16...♖e8 17.e5 ♗b7 18 0–0 exd5 19.♗f3 f6 20.♖e1 fxe5

21.fxe5! ♕c7 22.♗xd5† ♗xd5 23.♕xd5† ♔g7 (23...♔h8 24.e6 ♕g7 25.♖d2 ♕f6 26.e7 ♖ac8 27.♕d7 ♔g7 28.♕xa7 ♕h4 29.♖f2 ♕xc4 30.♕xb6 ♕d5 31.♕f6† ♔g8 32.h4 1–0 Cosma – Iashvili, Moscow 1991) 24.e6 ♖ad8 25.♕f3 ♖e7 (25...♕e7 26.♖f2±) 26.♖f2 ♕d6 27.♕f6† ♔g8 28.♕g5!± Khalifman – Khenkin, Leningrad 1989.

c) 16...exd5 17.cxd5 ♕h4† 18.g3 ♕e7 (18...♕h3 19.♔f2 ♗b7 20.♗f3 ♖ac8 21.♗g2 ♕d7 22.♖d1 c4 23.♕c3± Worek – Karavade, Greece 2002) 19.e5 ♗b7 20 0–0± 1–0 Malakhatko – Shishkin, Ukraine 2003.

17.♖b3!?

The text is a novel idea of Khalifman's that was introduced in this very game. White intends to swing the b-rook over to the centre or the kingside and begin advancing the pawns immediately. There are also a variety of 17th move alternatives:

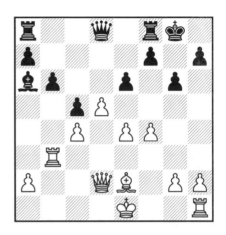

a) 17 0–0 exd5 18.cxd5 (18.exd5 has also scored well, e.g. 18...f5 (18...♖e8 19.f5 ♕h4 20.♖f4 ♕g5 21.♗f1 ♖ad8 22.♕f2 ♖e1?! 23.♖b3± Ricardi – L. Bronstein, San Fernando 1993) 19.♖b3 ♕f6 20.♖a3! ♗b7 21.♖e1 ♖fe8 22.♖e3! ♖e4? 23.♖xe4 fxe4 24.♗g4!+- Agrest – Berebora, Austria 1993) 18...♗xe2 19.♕xe2 f5! 20.♖d2 fxe4 21.d6 21...♕d7 (21...♕f6 22.♕xe4 was slightly better for White in Sakaev – Kharlov, URS-chJ Kherson 1991, however 21...♕e8! 22.♕c4† ♔g7 23.♕c3† ♔g8 is equal according to GM Konstantin Sakaev) 22.♕xe4 ♖ae8 23.♕d5† ♕e6 was balanced in Kiriakov – Sutovsky, Internet 2003.

b) 17.h4?! deserves a mention only because it was used by Israeli super-GM Boris Gelfand in 1999, however Black has nothing to fear from this audacious pawn thrust: 17...exd5 18.cxd5 ♗xe2 19.♔xe2 (19.♕xe2 f5!) 19...♕d7 20.♔f2 ♖ad8 21.♖d1 ♕g4 22.♖b3?! (22.g3 ♖fe8 23.♖e1 f6!? intending to break open White's king position with 24...g5, is unclear according to Krasenkow) 22...♖fe8 23.♖e1 ♕xh4† 24.♔f1 ♕h1† 25.♔f2 ♕h4† 26.♔f1 g5! (26...♕h1† was agreed drawn in Gelfand – Liss, Tel Aviv 1999, however Krasenkow noted that Black is clearly better here.) 27.f5 (27.fxg5 ♖xe4 28.♖xe4 ♕xe4 29.d6 ♕c4†!–+) 27...g4 28.♖be3 (28.♕f4 ♖xd5! 29.♖h3 ♖xf5!) 28...♕f6!∓.

c) 17.e5

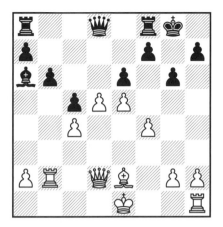

17...exd5 (GM Sergey Ivanov, in *Informant 71*, notes the variations 17...f6!? 18 0–0 exd5 19.♕xd5† ♔g7∞ and 17...♕h4† 18.g3 ♕h3 19.♗f1 ♕f5 20.♗d3 ♕h3 21.d6±) 18.cxd5 ♗xe2 19.♔xe2 f6 was Se. Ivanov – Berebora, Benasque 1997, and now Ivanov notes the line 20.d6!? fxe5 21.♕d5† ♔g7 (21...♔h8 22.fxe5 ♕h4 23.♖f1! ♖xf1?? 24.♕xa8†+–) 22.fxe5 ♕h4 23.♔d1±.

17...♖e8?!

Krasenkow suggests that Black should open up the position immediately with 17...exd5 18.cxd5 (18.exd5 ♖e8 19 0–0 ♕f6) 18...♗xe2 19.♔xe2 ♕h4 when White's loose king position gives Black counterplay. By giving White time to play 18.♖e3 Black loses the option of forcing White's king to remain in the centre.

18.♖e3! exd5! 19.cxd5 ♗xe2 20.♖xe2! ♕h4†

Black can also try to advance the c-pawn with 20...c4 21 0–0 ♖c8 22.e5 (22.♖c1 b5) 22...c3 however after 23.♕d4! it is clear that Black will have some difficulty involving the rest of his pieces in the attack, and the advanced c-pawn may ultimately prove to be a liability.

21.g3 ♕h3 22.♖f1 b5 23.f5!

Black has managed to keep White's king in the centre at the cost of maintaining the queen on h3, however now we see that there is more to Khalifman's idea than meets the eye! White's rooks aren't just there to support the central pawns, they are also getting ready to launch a kingside attack.

23...♕h5 24.♖f4

White now threatens 25.♖h4 ♕f3 26. ♕h6, when Black is in serious trouble.

24...g5 25.♖ff2 f6 26.e5! ♖xe5 27.♖xe5 fxe5 28.d6

28...♖d8

Krasenkow suggested that 28...♖c8!? was better, e.g. 29.♕d5† ♔f7 30.♕e6 ♖e8 31.d7 ♖d8 32.♖d2 when White has compensation for his sacrificed pawn, but things are still very unclear. However, surprisingly Krasenkow does not mention the more obvious 29.d7!, which just seems to be good for White, e.g. 29...♖d8 30.g4! ♕xg4 (30...♔f7 31.♕xg5† picks up the d8-rook) 31.♕d5† ♔g7 32.♕xe5† ♔h6 33.♕e6† ♔h5 34.h3!! (34.♕e8† ♔h6 35.♕xd8 ♕e4† gives Black a perpetual check) 34...♕g1† (34...♕c4 loses to 35.♕xc4 bxc4 36 f6, and 34...♕xh3 can be met with 35.♕e2†) 35.♔e2 ♕b1 36.f6±.

29.♕d5† ♕f7 30.♕xc5 ♕c4?!

Black had a more resilient defence in 30...♕f6 31.♕d5† ♔g7 32.d7 although White's chances remain preferable.

31.♕xe5 ♕c1† 32.♔e2 ♕c2† 33.♔f1 ♕c1† 34.♔e2 ♕c4† 35.♔e3 ♕c1† 36.♔f3 ♕c6† 37.♔g4 ♖xd6

37...♕xd6 38.♕xd6 ♖xd6 39.♔xg5+–

38.♔xg5 ♖d5 39.♕f6 ♕xf6†?!

39...♖d6 40.♕e5 ♖d5 41.♖c2!+–

40.♔xf6 b4?! 41.♖c2 1–0

Game 41 Conclusions: Black has a relatively solid line in 10...♘e5 11.♘xe5 ♗xe5 12.♕d2 e6 13.f4 ♗g7, and White must play well in order to really test Black's defences. Clearly 12.♕d2 is superior to 12.♕c2, and in the mainline Khalifman's 16.♖xb2 should probably be preferred to Huzman's 16.♕xb2!?, although such assertions may be premature because there is still very little experience with the latter of these. Khalifman's novelty 17.♖b3!?, intending to swing the rook across the third rank to support the advancing pawns or participate in a kingside attack, is certainly a noteworthy idea that produces fantastic results in this encounter, and if Black is to continue playing this line then improvements must be found. A good starting point is probably Krasenkow's suggestion, 17...exd5!?.

Game 42
Khalifman – Tseitlin
St Petersburg 1999

1.d4 ♘f6 2.c4 g6 3.♘c3 d5 4.♘f3 ♗g7 5.cxd5 ♘xd5 6.e4 ♘xc3 7.bxc3 c5 8.♖b1 0–0 9.♗e2 ♘c6 10.d5 ♘e5 11.♘xe5 ♗xe5 12.♕d2 e6 13.f4 ♗c7!?

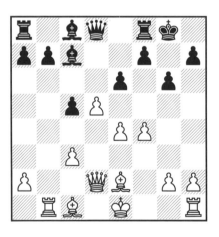

This unusual move enjoyed a brief spell of popularity in the late 1990s, but has now been largely abandoned, perhaps undeservedly. Strong players still play 13...♗c7 from time to time

(GMs Ftacnik and Avrukh to name but two), however it is no longer a regular guest in GM competition.

14.0–0

The text is now established as the mainline, however for a long time 14.♗c4 was equally popular. Play then continues: 14...a6 15.a4 (15. dxe6!? ♕xd2† 16.♗xd2 fxe6 17.♖f1 b5 18.♗b3 ♗d7 19.♖d1 c4 20.♗c2 ♗c6 21.♔e2 g5! 22.g3 ♗e8! was already better for Black in Neuman – Ftacnik, Czech Republic 2004) 15...b5 (15...♖e8!? threatening 16...♕xa4 has also been played quite frequently, however Ftacnik's preference is for the text.) 16.axb5 axb5 17.♗xb5 (17.♖xb5? ♗a6 18.♖xc5 ♗b6 19.♖c6 ♗b7 20.♖xb6 ♕xb6 21.dxe6 fxe6= - Neven, *Informant 67*) 17...exd5 18.♗c6 ♕h4†!? (Also not bad is 18...♖a6 19.♗xd5 ♖d6 20.0–0 ♗f5! 21.♕c2 ♖xd5 22.exf5 ♖xf5 23.c4 as in Smirin – Neven, Calgary 1996, when Smirin gives 23...♖f6 24.f5 ♕d7 as equal (*Informant 67*)).

19.g3 ♕h5 20.♕xd5 (Ftacnik has given 20.♗xa8 ♕f3 21.♖g1 ♕xe4† 22.♔f2 ♕xb1 23.♗xd5 as equal, however now 23...c4! looks good for Black. Ftacnik also mentions the line 20.♗xd5 ♗a6!? 21.♗xa8 ♖xa8 22.♕e3 (22.♕g2 ♗d3 23.♖b7 ♖a4!) 22...♖d8 23.♗d2 ♖d3 24.♕f2 (24.♕e2! may be stronger) 24...♖xg3! when Black has excellent counterplay. Finally, I would add that 20 0–0, just getting the king to safety, may merit attention.) 20...♕f3 21.♖f1 (21.e5 ♕xc3†!? 22.♗d2 ♕a3 23.♗xa8 ♗e6 24.♕c6 (24.♕f3! forcing an exchange of queens, looks more challenging.) 24...♗a5 25.♗xa5 ♕xa5† 26.♔f1 ♖xa8 gives Black good counterplay according to Ftacnik.) 21...♕xc3† 22.♗d2 ♕c2 23.♖c1 ♕b2 24.♗xa8 ♖d8 25.♖xc5 ♖xd5 26.♗xd5 ♕a1† 27.♔f2 ♕d4† 28.♗e3 ♕b2† 29.♔g1 ♗h3 30.♖f2 ♕a3! 31.♖xc7 (31.♗xf7† ♔f8 32.♖xc7 ♕xe3 33.♗c4 ♕xe4 34.♖xh7 ♕xc4 35.♖xh3 ♕c1† 36.♔g2 ♕c6† 37.♖f3 ♕c2†=) 31...♕xe3 32.♗xf7† ♔h8 ½–½ Hracek – Ftacnik, Germany 1998. The comments here are based on Ftacnik's annotations for *Informant 74*.

14...exd5 15.exd5 ♗a5

15...♗f5?! 16.♖xb7 ♗b6 17.d6 ♕f6 18.♖d1 ♖ae8 19.♗b5 c4† 20.♔h1 ♖e3 21.♗xc4 ♗g4 22.♖e1 ♕xf4 23.♖xb6 ♖xe1† 24.♕xe1 ♕xc4 25.♖b4+- van Wely – Timman, Breda 1998.

16.d6!

The text is currently considered to be White's most challenging line of attack. Practice has seen White experimenting with a number of alternatives, however one in particular captured my interest for a time. In *Understanding the Grünfeld* Rowson recommends the line 16.♗a3 b6 17.♖b5 intending 18.♖xa5 and 19.c4, a continuation originally suggested to him by GM Bogdan Lalic. The reason this line has not caught

on in practice is probably because White does not need to play 16.♗a3 at all. In fact 16.♖b5!? achieves the same end, but with the additional possibility of saving a tempo, e.g. 16...b6 (If Black attempts to preserve his pawn structure with 16...a6? then 17.♖xa5! ♕xa5 18.f5! f6 (18...♗xf5? 19.♖xf5!±) 19.fxg6 hxg6 20.♕h6 gives White a strong attack against the black king.) 17.♖xa5 bxa5 18.c4

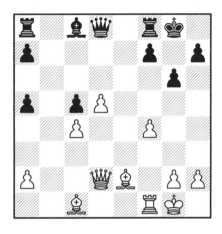

18...♕d6 (Given that the b-file is now open, it may be more logical to try 18...♖b8!? 19.♗b2 (19.♗a3?! ♖b4! 20.♗xb4 axb4 gave Black a comfortable position in S. Ernst – van Beek, Groningen 1999) 19...♕e7 20.♗f3 ♗a6 was Selin – Nikolenko, Tula 2000, and now White could have tried 21.d6 ♖xb2 (21...♕d7 22.♗d5!±) 22.♕xb2 ♕xd6 23.♗d5! although after 23...♗c8 it is questionable whether White really holds any advantage.) 19.♗b2 f6 20.g4!? ♗d7 (20...♖b8 21.♗a1! (preserving the dark-squared bishop against counter exchange sacrifices) 21...♖e8 22.♗f3 ♖b4 23.♖c1 ♗a6 24.g5 ♖xc4 25.♖xc4 ♗xc4 26.♗xf6 a4 27.♔f2 ♕d7 28.♔g3 a3 29.♗a1! ♗f1 30.♗g4 ♕b5 31.d6 ♕d3† 32.♕xd3 ♗xd3 33.d7+- Kiriakov – Sowray, Hastings Challengers 1998) 21.g5 ♖ae8! 22.♗xf6 ♖xf6! 23.gxf6 ♕xf6 24.♗f3 a4 is slightly better for Black according to Krasenkow (*CBM 76*): Selin – Yandemirov, St Petersburg 2000.

In conclusion, it would appear that even with an extra tempo the exchange-sac idea of 16.♖b5 b6 17.♖xa5 bxa5 18.c4 should not suffice for an advantage.

[Editors' note: Another interesting line is 16.f5!? ♗xf5 17.♖xb7 ♕f6 18.♖f3.

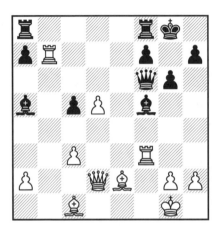

Here 18...h5!? was played in Kiriakov-Smikovsky, Borovoye 2004. Now Smikovsky gives 19.♕h6! ♕e5 20.c4 ♗c3 21.♖xc3 ♕xe2 22.♖f3 "with advantage for White". The extent of this advantage is probably quite significant, because White's attack looks rather dangerous. However 18...c4 as played in Chernin – Tseitlin, Beersheba 1992 looks inferior for Black after the computer's suggestion 19.g4! ♕a6 20.gxf5 ♕xb7 21.♕h6 and now:

a) 21...♗b6† 22.♔f1 f6 23.fxg6 hxg6 24.♕xg6†! (24.♗xc4 ♖ac8 25.♗a3 ♕g7 26.♗xf8 ♕xh6 27.♗xh6 ♖xc4 28.♖xf6 ♖xc3 29.♗f4 might only be a draw.) 24...♕g7 25.♕xg7† ♔xg7 26.♖g3† ♔h8 27.♗xc4±

b) 21...♔h8 22.f6 ♖g8 23.♕xh7†!+–.

c) 21...f6 (22.fxg6 hxg6 23.♗xc4 ♖ac8 24.♗a6! ♕g7 25.♗xc8 ♖xc8 26.♕h3±.]

16...b6
Alternatives:

a) 16...♕f6 17.d7 ♗xc3 18.dxc8♕ ♖axc8 19.♕c2+– Peter – Finkel, Budapest 1999.

b) 16...♖b8 17.♗a3 (17.g4!? ♗d7 18.f5 gxf5

19.♗d3 ♔h8 20.♗xf5 ♖g8 21.♗xd7 ♕xd7 22.h3 f5 23.♗b2 c4 24.♕d4† ♖g7 25.♗c1 b5 26.♕f6± Wells – Huzman, Antwerp 1993) 17...♗f5 (17...b6!?) 18.♖bd1 b6 19.h3 ♕f6 20.♗b2 ♖bd8 21.♗b5 ♗d7 22.c4 ♕f5 23.♗xd7 ♖xd7 24.♕e2 ♕e6 25.♕xe6 fxe6 26.♗e5± Khalifman – Roos, Germany 1998.

c) 16...♗f5!? 17.♖xb7 ♕f6 18.♗b2 ♖fb8 19.♖xb8† ♖xb8 20.♖d1 ♗e6 21.♗f3 h5 22.♖c1 ♗f5 23.♗a3 c4 was slightly better for White in Sakaev – Tseitlin, St Petersburg 1992, according to van Wely & Cifuentes.

17.♗f3 ♗f5!
Less accurate is 17...♖b8 18.♗b2 (18.♗a3!? was used with success in Solozhenkin – Schuil, Haarlem 2000, but seems less natural) 18...♗f5 19.♖bd1±.

18.♗xa8 ♗xb1 19.♗c6!

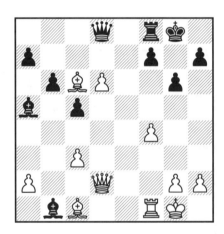

This excellent move at once restricts the mobility of Black's rook and queen, and also prepares the advance of the d-pawn. It is not clear that White is now guaranteed an advantage, however Black certainly can be made to suffer for some time to come, and the fact that the 13...♗c7 variation suddenly plummeted in popularity after this game speaks volumes.

19...♗f5!
19...♕f6 20.♗b2 ♗xa2?! (20...♖d8? 21.♖xb1 ♖xd6 22.♕e3 ♖xc6 23.♕e8† ♔g7 24.c4! ♗c3

25.♗xc3 ♕xc3 26.♕xc6 is obviously losing for Black, however 20...♗f5 21.♖e1 may be an improvement) 21.c4!

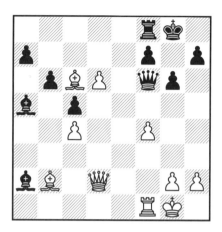

21...♗xd2 (Trying to avoid the queen exchange with 21...♕e6 is also difficult for Black: 22.f5!! ♗xd2 (22...gxf5 23.♕f4 (23.♕g5† also looks strong) 23...h6 (23...♗xc4 24.♗d7+-) 24.♗d5+-) 23.fxe6 fxe6 24.♖xf8† ♔xf8 25.♗f6! ♗e3† 26.♔h1 d4 27.♗g5 ♗e5 28.d7 ♗c7 29.♗b5!+- Schandorff – Borge, Aarhus 1999) 22.♗xf6 ♗xc4 23.♖f3! ♗e6 (Van Wely and Cifuentes note the lines 23...♗e2 24.♖a3 ♗c1 25.♖xa7 ♗e3† 26.♔h1 ♗xf4 27.d7+- and 23...b5 24.d7 ♗a5 25.♗e7 ♖b8 26.♗xc5 a6 27.♖e3 ♔g7 28.♖e8 ♗d8 29.♗a7+-) 24.d7 ♗xd7 25.♗xd7 a6 26.♔f1 b5 27.♔e2 ♗a5 28.♖a3 ♗d8 29.♗e5 ♗e7 30.♖xa6+- van Wely – van der Werf, Holland 1999.

20.♖e1 ♕f6 21.♗b2 ♖d8

The text leads to a simplified middlegame/endgame in which each side has two bishops and a queen, but Black is under constant pressure because of White's advanced d-pawn. Alternatives have been tried, however Black has yet to discover a satisfactory route to a comfortable game:

a) Forcing White into a queenless endgame with 21...♕d4† also leads to difficulties: 22.cxd4 ♗xd2 23.♖e7 (23.♖e2 ♗xf4 24.d7! cxd4 25.♗xd4 ♗e6 26.♗f6 ♗c7 27.♗e7 ♖b8 28.♖d2 ♗d8 29.♗d6+-) 23...♗xf4 24.dxc5 bxc5 25.d7+- - Krasenkow.

b) 21...♗e6 22.a4 ♕d4†? (22...♖d8 23.d7 is clearly better for White according to Krasenkow, who notes that 23...♕d4†? 24.cxd4 ♗xd2 25.♖e2 ♗xf4 26.d5 is winning for White) 23.cxd4 ♗xd2 24.♖e2 ♗xf4 25.d5 ♗xd5 26.♗xd5 ♗xd6 27.♖f2 ♗e7 28.♔f1 ♗g5 29.♗e5 h5 30.♗c4 ♗e3 31.♖f3 ♗d4 32.♗d6 1–0 Schandorff – Borge, Gentofte 1999.

22.♖e8† ♖xe8 23.♗xe8 c4?!

White now plays 24.♗b5 and 25.♗xc4 picking up a pawn. In a subsequent game Khalifman faced sterner resistance from Mikhalevski, who circumvented this manoeuvre by first playing 23...a6!. Black now threatens to play 24...b5 and 25...c4, blocking in the b2-bishop and freeing the a5-bishop, which can then come to b6 with check and simultaneously guard the d8-queening square. Play continued 24.a4 ♕d4†! (24...♕d8 25.♗c6 ♗d7 26.♗xd7 ♕xd7 27.f5 (27.♕d5!?± Koster – Profit, e-mail 2000) 27...c4 28.f6 ♕d8 29.d7 b5 30.♗a3± Sutton – Profit, e-mail 2001) 25.♕xd4 cxd4 26.d7 b5 27.cxd4 b4.

Black should now be able to hold this endgame, however Khalifman keeps pressing and eventually secures the full point: 28.d5 ♔f8 29.♗f6 b3 30.d6 ♗d8!? 31.♗b2 (31.♗xd8 ♗xd7!) 31...♗e4?! (31...♗e6! would hold the draw according to Krasenkow) 32.♔f2 f5 33.♔e3!? ♗c6 34.♔d3 ♗xa4 35.♔c4 ♗c6 36.g3 ♗f3 37.♔xb3 ♗d5† 38.♔b4 ♗f7?? 39.♗xf7 ♔xf7 40.♔c5 ♔e6 41.♔c6 a5 42.♗a3 a4 43.♗b4 h6 44.h4 h5 45.♗a3 1–0 Khalifman – Mikhalevski, St Petersburg 1999. Black resigned as White has forced him into zugzwang, e.g. 45... ♗a5 46.♗c5 ♗d8 47.♗b4+-. There is no doubt that Black should have been able to draw this ending (he is, after all, an experienced grandmaster), however the point is really that White cannot lose, and yet retains reasonable chances of pressing for the full point.

24.♗b5 ♕d8 25.♗xc4 b5 26.♗b3 ♗b6† 27.♔h1 ♕e8 28.♗d5?!

An unfortunate slip. Instead 28.c4! would have guaranteed White a clear advantage.

28...♗e4! 29.♗xe4 ♕xe4 30.d7 ♕b1† 31.♗c1

♔g7 32.h3 h5 33.♔h2 ♔h7 34.♔g3 ♕e4 35.♔h2 ♕b1 36.♕d1 ♗c7 37.♕e1?! ♗b6?

This allows White more chances to press for the full point. Instead 37...♕d3? 38.♕e7 ♔g7 39.♗e3 ♕xc3 40.♗xa7 ♗xf4† 41.♔h1 is winning for White, however Krasenkow notes that 37...♕xa2! 38.♕e7 ♕d5 should have enabled Black to hold a draw.

38.♕d2 ♗c7 39.♗a3 ♗b6 40.♗c1
1–0

Black lost on time at this point. Although it is clear that White is better, it is by no means obvious that White possesses enough of an edge to win this position.

Game 42 Conclusions: The positions after 10.d5 ♘e5 11.♘xe5 ♗xe5 12.♕d2 e6 13.f4 ♗c7!? are complex and potentially dangerous for both sides. I was amused to read GM Igor Stohl's comments on the 9...♘c6 line generally: "The line ... was still fairly popular in the mid-1990s, but it has lately come upon hard times. The fact that Black has more often than not felt it necessary to resort to the extravagant 13...♗c7!? is enough in itself to scare off many a staunch Grünfeld supporter, not to mention that this move does not solve all Black's problems in any case." (*Instructive Modern Chess Masterpieces*). Indeed it does seem somehow counterintuitive to bring the bishop to g7, placing it on the optimum diagonal, but then to reposition it on a5 (via e5 and c7), where it appears less active and leaves the kingside dark squares potentially weak.

However matters are more complicated: as we saw in Game 41, very often White clears all the pieces off of the long-diagonal, leaving the g7-bishop striking at thin air; by comparison, on a5 the bishop puts pressure on the c3-pawn and, if White plays c3-c4, the bishop then disrupts White's coordination by controlling the d2 and e1-squares, making it difficult for White to organise his major pieces to any effect. Alternatively, if White does not play c4, then the d5 pawn may become weak and Black may disrupt White's development by playing c5-c4 himself at some

stage, temporarily fracturing White's queenside pawn structure and opening up the a7-g1 diagonal for the dark-squared bishop. So things really aren't so bad for Black after all.

Anyway, getting back to our discussion of the theory on 13...♗c7!?, Khalifman's 16.d6! followed by 16...b6 17.♗f3 ♗f5! 18.♗xa8 ♖xb1 19.♘c6! promises White excellent practical chances, although with best play Black should probably be able to hold a draw with Mikhalevski's 23...a6! – albeit after a thousand moves of miserable suffering!

Game 43
Se. Ivanov – Mikhalevski
St Petersburg 1999

1.d4 ♘f6 2.c4 g6 3.♘c3 d5 4.cxd5 ♘xd5 5.e4 ♘xc3 6.bxc3 ♗g7 7.♘f3 c5 8.♖b1 0–0 9.♗e2 ♘c6 10.d5 ♘e5 11.♘xe5 ♗xe5 12.♖b3!?

An excellent multi-purpose move that I am sure we shall be seeing more of in the future. White protects the c3-pawn, preparing c4, 0–0, f4 and e5, but also avoids the obstruction of the c1-bishop (unlike after 12.♕d2) and opens up the possibility of swinging the b-rook over to a central or kingside file where it can participate in an attack (a theme reminiscent of Game 41, Khalifman – Greenfeld).

12...e6

Natural, but possibly not best. Given that White has not enhanced his grip over the f4-square, it seems logical to borrow an idea from Game 40: With 12...♕c7!

Black takes the f4-square under control, prevents White castling, and prepares ...c5-c4 at the same time. In practice White has tried two moves:

a) 13.c4 ♗d7 (13...f5 14.exf5 ♗xf5 15.h3 ♗d7 16.♖a3 ♗d4 17 0–0 ♗e8 18.♗e3 was better for White in Kakageldyev – Mikhalchishin, Ivano Frankovsk 1982, but 13...e6!? deserves attention) 14.♕d2 ♖ab8 15.f4 ♗d4 16.e5 a6 17.♗b2 ♗xb2 18.♕xb2 b5 19 0–0 ♖b6 20.♗d3 ♖fb8 21.♖b1± Mah – van der Meijden, Hengelo 1999.

b) 13.♕d2 is White's most common response. Play has continued 13...e6 (13...♗d7 14.f4 c4 (14...♗g7 15.c4 e5 16.♗b2± Gavrish – Pelagejchenko, Kharkov 2000) 15.♖b4 ♗g7 16.♖xc4 ♕a5 17 0–0 ♗b5 18.♖b4 ♗xe2 19.♕xe2 b6 20.♖b3± Popov - Okrugin, Russian Championship Knockout 1999) 14.f4 c4! 15.♖b4! (15.♖b1?! ♗g7 16.d6 ♕c6 as in Nilssen – Hracek, Bled 2002, was already better for Black. Note that if White protects e4 with 17.♗f3 then 17...e5! leaves White's pawn structure in a real mess.) 15...♗d6 16.♖xc4 ♕b6 17.e5!

We must now consider two moves:

b1) 17...exd5? 18.♖xc8! ♖axc8 19.exd6 ♕xd6

was at least slightly better for White in Hillarp Persson – Golod, Copenhagen 2000.

b2) 17...♗c5 is better. After 18.d6 ♗d7 (Krasenkow notes the line 18...f6 19.d7 (19.♗f3 ♗d7 20.a4 ♖ac8 looks fine for Black, but 19.f5!? deserves consideration) 19...xd7 (19...♖d8 20.dxc8♕ ♖axc8 21.♗d3) 20.♖xc5 ♕xc5 21.♕xd7 which he assesses as unclear, although if anyone is better here it should be White.) 19.a4 ♗c6 (19...♖ac8!?) 20.♗f3 ♗xf3 21.gxf3 f6 Krasenkow believes that Black has good compensation for his sacrificed pawn. The way to test this assessment seems to be 22.♕b2! because, after Black recovers his pawn with 22...fxe5 23.♕xb6 ♗xb6 24.fxe5 ♖xf3, White can then try 25.♖f1! when White's protected passed d-pawn may give Black problems in the endgame.

13.f4 ♗g7 14.c4

14.d6 is less effective here: e.g. 14...♗d7 15.♕d2 ♗c6 16.♗f3 e5 17 0–0 exf4 18.♕xf4 ♕e8 19.♕g3 c4 20.♖b1 ♗xc3 21.♗h6 ♗e5 22.♕e1 ♕e6 23.♗xf8 ♖xf8∓ Bagirov – Yermolinsky, USSR 1982.

14...♖e8 15.e5! f6 16.f5!!

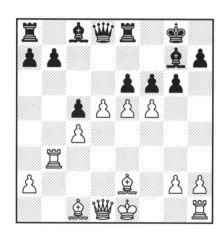

16...gxf5 17.♗h5 ♖e7?!

Krasenkow notes the line 17...♖f8 18.♖g3 ♔h8 19.♗b2 fxe5 20.♖xg7! ♔xg7 21.♗xe5† ♔g8 22 0–0 when White's position has excellent attacking potential based on the active bishop pair, the passed d-pawn, and the weak dark squares surrounding the black king.

18.d6! ♖d7 19.♖g3! fxe5 20.♗b2
20...♔h8

Krasenkow observed that 20...♖xd6? loses to a beautiful queen sacrifice: 21.♖xg7† ♔h8 22.♗xe5 ♖xd1† 23.♗xd1 ♕a5† 24.♔f1 h5 (24...h6 25.♗h5+-) 25.♖e7† ♔g8 26.♖e8† ♔h7 27.♖h8† ♔g6 28.♗xh5† ♔g5 29.h4 mate.

21 0–0! ♖xd6 22.♕e2 ♖d4 23.♖xg7! ♔xg7 24.♕xe5† ♔g8 25.♖f4! ♕g5 26.♖xd4 cxd4 27.♕xd4 ♔f8 28.♕h8† ♔e7 29.♗a3† ♔d7 30.♕d4†
1–0

Game 43 Conclusions: White has a cogent alternative in 12.♖b3!?, and in practice this line has reached excellent positions. However it is perhaps a shade premature to start drawing conclusions, especially given that Black has rarely found the most testing continuations in over-the-board play. GM Vitali Golod's 12...♗c7! seems like Black's best line of defence, and then provided Black avoids 17...exd5? in favour of 17...♗c5 he should be able to obtain a playable position, although in general matters remain unclear.

Conclusions on 10...♘e5!?:

In this chapter we considered the systems that have developed out of the line 1.d4 ♘f6 2.c4 g6 3.♘c3 d5 4.cxd5 ♘xd5 5.e4 ♘xc3 6.bxc3 ♗g7 7.♘f3 0–0 8.♗e2 c5 9.♖b1 ♘c6 10.d5 ♘e5 11.♘xe5 ♗xe5, and now 12.♕c2?! is examined in Game 40. I included this primarily as an illustrative example of some of the ideas upon which Black's counterplay is based and, in particular, as a vehicle for emphasising the importance of the battle for control of the f4 and e5 squares. In Game 40 White spends much of the

game battling for control of those squares, however this is achieved at the cost of his development and Black rapidly develops a initiative with powerful play against White's centre.

Game 41 is the first of two games in this chapter dealing with 12.♕d2, in this case addressing the line 10.d5 ♘e5 11.♘xe5 ♗xe5 12.♕d2 e6 13.f4 ♗g7, which is the old mainline of the 9...♘c6 variation. On present evidence White is doing well here, and although Black's play can be improved in a number of the various sub-variations that are discussed, 13...♗g7 has become quite rare at GM-level in recent years.

Game 42 discusses the modern interpretation of the 9...♘c6 variation, namely 10.d5 ♘e5 11.♘xe5 ♗xe5 12.♕d2 e6 13.f4 ♗c7!?. I have never fully trusted this move, and I would not play it as Black, but that is based on intuition rather than solid evidence of a refutation. Indeed in practice Black has scored quite well with 13...♗c7, and thus far White has not been able to demonstrate an entirely convincing strategy against Black's audacious bishop retreat. That said, although a definite path to an advantage does not exist, a path to superior practical chances certainly does. Khalifman's treatment of 13...♗c7 in Game 42 offers Black a miserable defensive task, and is possibly responsible for the widespread decline in popularity of the 13...♗c7 variation.

Finally, Game 43 sees White experimenting with 12.♖b3!?, a very unusual way of defending the c3-pawn. In general White's results have been good here, and there is still a lot of unexplored territory that may well hold challenging new ideas. However, on the limited material available, with careful play Black should be able to hold the balance here.

Chapter 8: The Indubitable 9...b6!?

1.d4 ♘f6 2.c4 g6 3 ♘f3 ♗g7 4 ♘c3 d5 5.cxd5 ♘xd5 6.e4 ♘xc3 7.bxc3 c5 8.♖b1 0–0 9.♗e2 b6!?

With this move Black declines the a2-pawn and delays the development of the b8-knight until it is clear whether d7 or c6 is the appropriate square for the beast. Although 9...b6 may appear unassuming, White should not be fooled into thinking that obtaining an advantage will be easy; quite the contrary in fact. 9...b6 became popular in the mid-nineties, and has retained its popularity throughout the 'noughties' for the simple reason that Black's set-up is solid, flexible, low-risk and exceptionally resilient. Indeed those who have relied on the Black side include the likes of Leko, Harikrishna, Avrukh, Tseitlin and even Kasparov – so 9...b6 is definitely a line to be taken seriously!

Game 44
Bacrot – J. Horvath
Balatonbereny 1996

1.d4 ♘f6 2.c4 g6 3 ♘f3 ♗g7 4 ♘c3 d5 5.cxd5 ♘xd5 6.e4 ♘xc3 7.bxc3 c5 8.♖b1 0–0 9.♗e2 b6!? 10 0–0 ♗b7 11.♕d3 e6!?

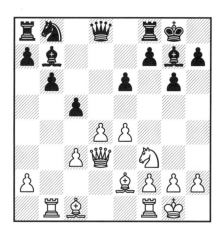

Traditionally Black has tried to simplify the position with 11...♗a6 and 12...♗xe2 (considered in Games 45-47), however increasingly those defending the Black side are realising the merits of maintaining the tension, and consequently are turning to moves such as 11...e6 to preserve winning chances. Alternatives often lead to similar types of positions, but do enjoy some independent value:

a) 11...♘d7 12.♗g5 ♕c7 13.♕e3 e5 (13...♖ac8 14.d5 ♘f6 15.♘d2 e6 16.♗f4± Bets – Eljanov, Alushta 2000; 13...♖fe8 14.♖fd1 (14.♗b5!?) 14...♗c6 15.d5 ♗a4 16.♖d2 ♘e5 17.♘e1 f6 18.♗h4 ♖ad8 19.c4 ♘f7± Poluljahov – Gunnarsson, Gausdal 1994) 14.d5 ♘f6 15.♘d2 ♘e8 16.♗h6 ♘d6 17.♗xg7 ♔xg7 18.f4 ♖ae8 19.f5 gxf5 (19...f6 20.fxg6 hxg6 21.♗g4 ♕e7 22.♕g3 ♗c8 23.♗xc8 ♖xc8 24.♖be1 ♖h8 25.♖e3 ♖h5 26.♕e1 ♖ch8 27.h3 ♖h4 28.♖ef3± Bets – Eljanov, Alushta 2000) 20.♕g5† ♔h8 21.♕f6† ♔g8 22.♕g5† ♔h8 23.♕f6† ♔g8 24.♘c4 ♘xe4 25.♕xf5 ♗xd5 26.♘e3 ♗c6 27.♗d3 ♕b7 28.♘g4 f6 29.♖be1 ♘d6 30.♘xf6† ♔h8 31.♕g5 ♕g7 32.♕xg7† ♔xg7 33.♘xe8† ♖xe8 34.♖e3± Sherbakov – Eljanov, Polanica Zdroj 1996.

b) 11...♕c7 12.d5!? (12.♗g5 ♘d7 13.♕e3 is likely to transpose to established channels) 12...♘d7 13.♗g5 13...e6 (13...♖fe8 14.♖bd1 ♘e5 15.♗f4?! ♘xd3 16.♗xc7 c4 17.♘d2 ♘b2 18.♖c1 ♖ac8 19.♗g3 b5∓ Handke – Timofeev, Chalkidiki 2000) 14.♖bd1 ♘e5 15.♕d2 ♘xf3† 16.♗xf3 ♕e5 17.♗e7 ♖fe8 18.d6 ♕xc3 19.♕g5 h6 20.♕h4 g5 21.♕h5 was Lesiege – Turov, Montreal 2001, and now instead of 21...♗f6, when 22.♖d3! would have been strong, Black should have played Krasenkow's suggestion 21...♕e5!?, intending to march the c-pawn, with an unclear position.

12.♗g5

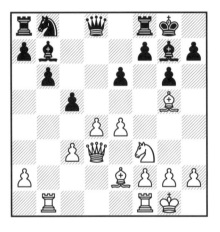

a) 12.dxc5?! ♕xd3 13.♗xd3 ♘d7 gives Black excellent structural compensation according to Korchnoi.

b) 12.♗f4?!, taking the c7 and d6-squares away from the black queen, is perhaps the most natural approach. Unfortunately this fails tactically to 12...cxd4 13.cxd4 ♘c6! 14.♖fd1 (14.d5 exd5 15.exd5 ♘e7 16.d6 ♘d5 17.♗g3 ♖c8 18.♖bc1 ♘c3 19.♗d1 ♖c5 20.♗b3 ♗e4∓ M. Andersson – Heinola, Sweden 2003) 14...♘xd4!? 15.♘xd4 e5 16.♗e3 exd4 17.♗xd4 ♗xd4 18.♕xd4 ♕xd4 19.♖xd4 ♖fd8 20.♖bd1 (20.♖xd8† ♖xd8 21.f3 ♗c8 22.♗c4 ♔f8 was at least equal for Black in Shipov – Dvoirys, Cappelle la Grande 1995) 20...♖xd4 21.♖xd4 ♔f8∓ Gretarsson – Dvoirys, Leeuwarden Open 1995.

c) 12.♖d1!? is seen surprisingly rarely in practice, but is an entirely standard move.

Play has continued 12...cxd4 (Maintaining the tension with 12...♘d7!? 13.♗g5 ♕c7 seems better, when positions similar to those in the main game are likely to arise.) 13.cxd4 ♕d7 14.♗f4 ♕a4 15.♕e3 ♗a6 16.♗xa6 ♕xa6 17.h4 ♘d7 18.h5 ♘f6 19.hxg6 hxg6 20.♘g5 gave White good attacking chances in Salov – Mikhalchishin, Ivano Frankovsk 1982.

12...♕c7

Deploying the queen on c7 has proved both Black's most popular and most reliable formation, however two other postings merit a mention:

a) 12...♕d6!? 13.♕e3 (13.e5 ♕d5 was played in Radziewicz – Tseitlin, Rethymnon 2003. Although White is not yet worse, it is suddenly difficult to achieve much progress now that Black has control of the d5-square, and eventually Black managed to grind White down. In general, therefore, White should not commit the e-pawn to e5 until his other pieces are suitably coordinated to effect a follow-up.) 13...♖c8 (13...cxd4!? 14.cxd4 ♖c8 (14...♘c6 15.♖fd1 ♖fc8 16.♗h6 ♖d8?! 17.♗xg7 ♔xg7 18.h4 h5 19.♖b5! ♘a5 20.♖g5 ♕c6 21.d5 exd5 22.♘d4! ♕a4 23.e5 ♘c6 24.♖xh5!! gxh5 25.♘f5† ♔f8 26.♕h6† ♔e8 27.e6! 1–0

Chuchelov – Stone, Hamburg 1993) 15.♗f4 ♕f8 16.♖bc1 ♘d7 17.♗c4 ♘f6 18.♘d2 a6 19.♖fe1 b5 20.♗d3 ♖xc1 21.♖xc1 ♖c8 saw Black force a simplification and obtain equality in Genova – Krupkova, Ostrava 1999) 14.♖fd1 (14.♗h6 ♘d7 (14...♔h8!?) 15.♗xg7 ♔xg7 16.♗b5 cxd4 17.cxd4 ♖c7 18.♗xd7 ♖xd7 19.h4 h5 20.♖fc1± Moiseenko – L'Ami, Dieren 2001). Black has now tried two approaches:

a1) 14...♘d7 15.♗b5 ♗c6 gives White a choice of three options:

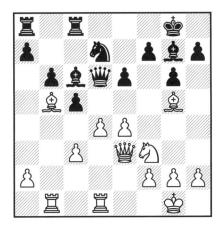

a11) 16.♗xc6 ♕xc6 17.d5 exd5 18.♖xd5 b5 19.♖bd1 ♘b6 20.♖d6 ♕e8 21.♕f4 was Zontakh – Colovic, Lazarevac 1999, and now Krasenkow's 21...♘a4! gives Black good play.

a12) 16.♗f4!? ♕f8 (16...♕e7 17.♗xc6 ♖xc6 18.d5 exd5 19.exd5 ♕xe3 20.♗xe3 ♖cc8 21.c4± Vera – Valdes, St Vincent 2001) 17.♗xc6 ♖xc6 18.d5 exd5 19.exd5 was slightly better for White in Peek – Delafargue, Amsterdam 2001, but Black's position remains very solid.

a13) 16.♗a6! seems best; play has continued: 16...♖e8 17.♗f4 ♕e7 18.e5 ♗d5 19.♖b2 (19.♗b5!?±) 19...♘b8 20.♗b5 ♖c8 21.♘d2 (21.c4!? cxd4 22.♖xd4 intending 23.♖bd2 looks good for White) 21...cxd4 22.cxd4 ♕b7 23.f3 a6 24.♗d3 ♘d7 25.♘e4 ♖c6 26.♘d6 ♕c7 27.♗e4± Eriksson – Colovic, Paide 1999.

a2) 14...cxd4 15.cxd4

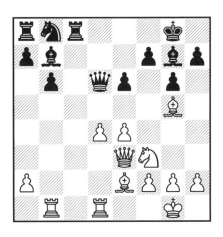

15...♘d7 (An interesting idea that attempts to at once remove the queen from the line of fire and enhance Black's control of the kingside dark squares is 15...♕f8!?, e.g. 16.h4 h6 17.♗f4 ♘d7 18.e5 (Now that Black has committed the knight to d7, White plays e4-e5, taking away the f6-square and making it difficult for the knight to reach its optimum position on d5.) 18...a6 (18...♗d5 19.a4 ♖c7 20.♘d2 ♖ac8 21.♘e4 ♗xe4 22.♕xe4 ♕e7 23.♗d2 f5 24.exf6 (24.♕f4!?±) 24...♕xf6± Gofshtein – Spiekermann, Lausanne 2000) 19.a4 ♗c6 20.♖dc1± Kohlweyer – Coenen, Germany 1999) 16.♗b5 (16.h4 ♕f8 17.e5 ♖c7 was a little better for White in Haba – Jansa, Czech Championship 1996) 16...♗c2 (16...♘f8 17.♗a4!? (17.♗f4 ♕e7 18.a4!?±) 17...♗c6 18.♗b3 ♘d7 19.d5 exd5 20.exd5 ♗b7 21.♗e7 ♕c7 22.d6 ♕c5 23.♕f4 1–0 Gormally – Moore, Scarborough 2001) 17.♗a4 (17.e5 ♕c7 (17...♕d5 18.♗a4!±) 18.♗a4 ♖c4 19.♖bc1 ♘f8 20.♗b5 ♖c2 21.♘e1 ♖xc1 22.♖xc1 ♕b8 23.♗e7± Dobrev – Gross, Elenite 1986) 17...♖xa2 18.e5 ♕d5 19.♗b3± Yevseev – Coenen, Groningen 1998.

b) 12...♕c8!? 13.♖fd1 ♗a6 14.♕e3 ♗xe2 15.♕xe2 ♕a6 16.♕d2 ♘d7 17.h4 (17.♗h6!? may be an improvement) 17...♕a5 18.♖bc1 cxd4 19.cxd4 ♕xd2 20.♘xd2 ♖fc8 21.♘c4 ♗f8 22.♗f4 ♗e7 23.♘d6 ♗xd6 24.♗xd6 f5! 25.exf5 exf5= Browne – Ehlvest, San Francisco 2000.

13.♕e3

13.d5!? exd5 14.exd5 ♕d6 (14...♘d7!? 15.c4 ♖fe8 16.♕d2 ♘f6 17.♗d3 ♘e4 18.♕f4 ♕xf4 19.♗xf4 ♘c3! 20.♖b3 ♘xa2∓ Palsson – Tseitlin, Canada 2004) 15.c4 ♘d7 16.♕d2 ♖ae8 17.♖fe1 ♗c8 18.h3 ♘e5 19.♘xe5 ♗xe5 20.♗h6 ½–½ Haba – Navara, Luhacovice 2003.

13...♖c8?!

The text works out well for Black , however White's play is open to improvement (see below) and recent practice has instead focussed on 13...♘d7.

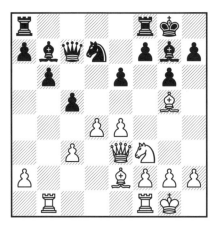

Play has now continued:

a) 14.♗d3?! Although there is nothing obviously wrong with this move, I still consider it to be inaccurate. It makes more sense to play 14.e5! immediately, because White will need to play e4-e5 some time soon in order to prevent ♘d7-f6, so why not now? Black is not in a position to exploit the weakening of the d5-square, and it is not yet clear where White will want his minor pieces or his rooks, so there is a certain logic to delaying their deployment. A good example of this logic in practice was seen in the game Moiseenko – Eljanov, Kharkov Russia 2001, which continued 14...♖ac8 15.e5 (so this proved necessary anyway) 15...♗d5 16.♗a6 (a third bishop move) 16...♖ce8 17.a4 f6! 18.exf6 ♘xf6.

Consider the position above. White's position has not changed much since move 12, but just look at the dynamic activity inherent in Black's formation. In my opinion the latent ability for Black's position to transform itself from 'solid' to 'dynamic' in a relatively short space of time really embodies the attractiveness of the 9...b6 system. Let's consider some more of this game: 19.♗f4 (19.♘e5 ♘e4!) 19...♕d8 20.♗g5 (20.♘e5 ♗xg2! 21.♔xg2 ♘d5–+ - Krasenkow) 20...♘g4 21.♗xd8 ♘xe3 22.fxe3 ♖xd8 23.♗d3 ♗h6!∓ 24.♔f2? (24.♖be1 was necessary) 24...cxd4 25.cxd4 (25.exd4? ♗d2∓) 25...e5! 26.e4 ♗a2! 27.♖b2 ♖xd4 28.♖xa2 ♖xd3∓/–+, Moiseenko – Eljanov, Kharkov, Russia 2001.

b) 14.e5! 14...♖ac8 (Although it seems 'natural' to place the rook on c8, recently Eljanov questioned the logic of this, instead placing the rook on e8 and setting about cracking open the centre with f7-f6: 14...♖ae8 15.♗b5 (15.♘d2!?) 15...♗c6 16.♗xc6 (16.a4!? looks stronger) 16...♕xc6 17.h4?! f6 18.exf6 ♘xf6 19.♘e5 ♕c7 20.♖be1 ♘d5 21.♕g3 ♖f5 was at least equal for Black in Halkias – Eljanov, Ohrid 2001.) 15.♘d2! (White begins re-routing the f3-knight to the vulnerable d6-square. This is the start of a very important plan, of which anyone playing either side of this system should be aware.) 15...cxd4 16.cxd4 ♕c3 17.♗b5! (suddenly the d7-knight is under fire) 17...♕xe3 18.fxe3 ♖c2 19.♖f2 ♘b8 20.♘c4 ♖xf2 21.♔xf2 f6 22.exf6 ♗xf6 23.♗xf6 ♖xf6† 24.♔g3

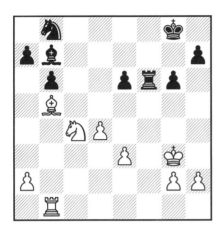

24...♗c6 25.a4 ♗xb5 26.axb5 ♖f7 27.♘e5±: Yusupov – Brinck-Claussen, Plovdiv 1983. Yusupov went on to win the game in convincing fashion. Before returning to the main game, note how Yusupov's handling of the position differed from, for example, Halkias': whereas Halkias tried to attack Black, Yusupov simply utilised his space advantage to restrict Black. Black was allowed to achieve his freeing breaks, but only at the cost of incurring slight but enduring structural weaknesses.

14.♖fd1 cxd4

14...♘d7!? 15.e5 (15.♗f4!?) 15...cxd4 16.cxd4 ♕c3 17.♕f4 (17.♗b5!) 17...♕a3 18.♗h6 ♗xh6 19.♕xh6 ♕f8 20.♕e3 ♖c7 gave Black good counterplay in Plachkinova – Genova, Plovdiv 2001, according to Krasenkow, however I rather prefer White's position here after 21.♘d2!.

15.cxd4 ♘d7 16.♗b5

The text is Bacrot's attempt to incrementally improve his position without relying on aggressive tactics. An earlier game in this variation had continued: 16.d5!? exd5 17.exd5 ♕c5 (17...♖e8 18.♕d2 (18.d6!?) 18...♖ac8 19.d6± - Ftacnik) 18.d6 ♕xe3 19.♗xe3 ♖c2 20.♗d3. The game we are following is Se. Ivanov – Dvoirys,

Elista, Russian Championship 1995, which now continued 20...♖c3 21.♗b5 when White held the superior chances. However Ftacnik suggests that the improvement 20...♖xa2!? is good for Black, e.g. 21.♗c4 (21.♗b5!?) 21...♖a3 22.♘g5 ♘e5 23.d7 (23.♗b3 h6 24.f4 hxg5 25.fxe5 ♗xe5 26.♗xg5 ♗e4 27.♗d5 ♗xd5 28.♖xd5 ♖a5 29.♖bd1 f6∓) 23...♗f6 24.♗d5 ♗xd5 25.♖xd5 ♖d8∓.

16...♘f6   17.♖bc1   ♕b8   18.♖xc8†   ♕xc8 19.♖c1±

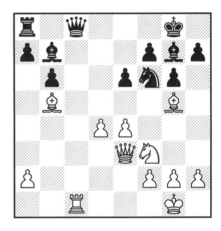

White controls the centre, his minor pieces are all superbly placed, he is ahead in development and his rook occupies the only open file. White is definitely better at this stage, however it is noteworthy that most commentators agree that White's advantage is only slight, despite superiority in terms of space, development and central control. Indeed, the fact that Black goes on to win this game is further testimony to the enduring resilience of Black's set-up.

19...♕b8

The queen may look out of place on b8, but the alternatives favour White:

a) 19...♕d8 20.e5 ♘d5 21.♗xd8 ♘xe3 22.fxe3 ♖xd8 23.♖c7 ♗xf3 (23...♖b8 24.♘g5 ♗h6 25.h4) 24.gxf3 is clearly better for White according to Korchnoi.

b) 19...♕f8? 20.♖c7 ♕b8 21.♗f4 ♗h6!? 22.♖xb7 (22.♕c1!? ♗xf4 23.♕xf4 a6 (23...♗xe4

24.♘g5±) 24.♗d3 ♗xe4 (24...♖a7 25.♘g5)
25.♗xe4 ♖a7 26.♕xf6 ♖xc7 27.g3±) 22...♕xf4
(22...♕xb7 23.♗xh6 ♘g4 24.♕f4 ♘xh6
25.♕xh6 ♕xe4 26.♘g5 ♕e1† 27.♗f1+-)
23.♕xf4 ♗xf4 24.e5 ♘d5 25.g3 ♗h6 26.a4 is
also substantially better for White according to
GM Lev Psakhis.

20.♗f4?!

20.♗d3!?± - Korchnoi.

20...♕f8 21.♖c7?!

Another inaccuracy. 21.♗c6 ♕e7 is still slightly
better for White according to Korchnoi.

21...♗xe4 22.♘g5 ♕b4

22...♘d5? 23.♕xe4 ♘xc7 24.♗xc7 ♖c8
25.♗e5±.

23.♗f1 ♗f5 24.♖xf7 h6

24...♘d5? 25.♗e5!! ♘xe3 26.♖xg7† ♔f8
27.♘xh7† ♔e8 28.♘f6† ♔f8 (28...♔d8?
29.♗c7† ♔c8 30.♗a6 mate.) 29.fxe3! ♖d8
30.e4±.

25.♕f3 hxg5! 26.♕b7?

A further error by Bacrot. Instead 26.♖xf6!
♖d8 27.♗xg5 ♘d5 (27...♗xf6 28.♗xf6⩱) 28.♕e3
♕xd4 29.♖xe6 ♗xe6 30.♕xe6† ♔h7 31.♕h3†
would have held the balance.

**26...gxf4–+ 27.♖xg7† ♔h8 28.♖e7 ♖d8
29.♕xa7 ♕xd4 30.h3 g5 31.♖f7 ♗g6**
0–1

Game 44 Conclusions: In this game we examined
the plans which involve Black maintaining a
bishop on b7 (in the mainlines Black forces an
exchange of bishops with ♗b7-a6) and developing
his pieces to sensible squares. In general White
should be slightly better in these lines, however
Black's position remains solid and highly resilient,
and it is for this reason that an outright attack
is unlikely to succeed (see, for example, Halkias
– Eljanov, in the notes to Black's 13th move).
Instead White should employ a strategy of patient
restriction: if Black is to generate counterplay it
will usually be necessary to initiate a pawn break,
which may lead to structural weaknesses. White's
strategy should therefore be to anticipate these
transformations in the pawn structure and ensure

that they only ever come at the cost of permanent
structural weaknesses that can be exploited. A
model game in this respect is Yusupov – Brinck-
Claussen, Plovdiv 1983, which is also examined
in the notes to Black's 13th move.

Those defending the Black side would be well
advised to study GM Pavel Eljanov's games in
this line.

Game 45
Avrukh – Harikrishna
36th Olympiad, Calvia 2004

**1.d4 ♘f6 2.c4 g6 3.♘c3 d5 4.cxd5 ♘xd5 5.e4
♘xc3 6.bxc3 ♗g7 7.♘f3 c5 8.♖b1 0–0 9.♗e2
b6 10 0–0 ♗b7 11.♕d3**

This is well-established as the mainline of 9...
b6, however White does try alternatives from
time to time:

a) Advancing in the centre with 11.d5 is an
idea somewhat reminiscent of the variation
with 9...♘c6 10.d5 ♗xc3† which we examined
in Chapter 6, however in this instance Black
is better developed and so should not have
many problems. 11...♗xc3 (11...e6 12.c4 ♘d7
is slightly better for White. In one game Black
declined the c3-pawn with 11...♕d6, but
quickly found himself under serious pressure:
12.♕c2 ♘d7 13.♘d2! ♖ad8 14.f4 e6 15.c4 ♕e7

16.♘f3 g5 17.e5 exd5 18.cxd5 ♗a6 19.♕f5! gxf4?! 20.♗e4 ♖fe8 21.♕xh7† ♔f8 22.♖xf4 ♘xe5 23.♖b3 ♗b7 24.♖g3+- Avrukh – Berndt, Halkidiki 2002) 12.♗c4 (Probably best. 12.♗g5 ♗g7 13.♕b3 ♔h8 14.♖bd1 f6?! 15.♗f4 ♘d7 16.♖fe1 was better for White in Ripari – Recoulat, Buenos Aires 1999, however Black's play was hardly perfect, and 12.♕b3 ♗g7 13.♗f4 ♕c8!? 14.♖fe1 ♗a6 15.e5 (15.♗xa6 ♕xa6 16.e5 ♘d7 17.♗g5 ♖ae8 18.♖bd1 c4 19.♕c2 ♘c5 20.d6 exd6 21.exd6 ♖xe1† 22.♘xe1 ♖e8∓ Dobrov – Eljanov, Internet 2003 (Dobrov, *Informant 89*)) 15...♗xe2 16.♖xe2 e6 17.♘g5 h6 18.dxe6 hxg5 19.exf7† ♖xf7 20.e6 ♖e7 21.♗xg5 ♘c6 22.♗xe7 ♘xe7 was good for Black in Belov – Eljanov, Internet 2003).

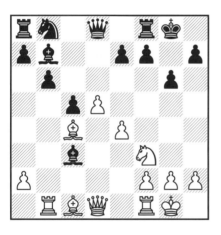

Black has now tried two possibilities:

a1) 12...♘d7 13.♗f4 ♗g7 14.♖e1 ♘f6 (14...♕c8 15.♕d3±) 15.♕b3!? (An important idea, enhancing White's control over the a2-g8 diagonal: if White hesitates then Black will have time to re-route the f6-knight to a better square, e.g. 15.h3 ♘e8 16.a4! (16.e5 ♘c7 17.d6 exd6 18.exd6 ♘e6 19.♗xe6 fxe6∓ - Ruck) 16...♘d6 17.♗a2 ♖c8 18.e5 ♘f5 19.♗c4 ♔h8! (19...♘d4?! 20.♘xd4 cxd4 21.♕xd4 ♕d7?! (21...♖c5 22.♖bd1 ♕a8∞ - Beliavsky, *Informant 69*) 22.♗b3 ♖fd8 23.♖bd1 ♖c5 24.♗d2!± Beliavsky – Ruck, Ajka 1997) 20.g4

♘d4 21.♘xd4 cxd4 22.♕xd4 ♕d7 23.♗a2 ♖c5! was already preferable for Black in Jagodzinski – Ruck, Gyula 1998. The comments here are based on GM Robert Ruck's annotations in *Informant 72*) 15...♘e8 (According to Krasenkow 15...♘h5 16.♗d2 leaves Black with nothing better than 16...♘f6 when White can continue to build his position with 17.♖bd1.) 16.e5

16...♘c7 (16...b5!? 17.♕xb5 ♗xd5 18.♖ed1! ♘c7 (18...e6 19.♗xd5 exd5 20.♕xc5 ♘c7 21.♕d6±) 19.♕xc5 e6 20.♖bc1!± White now threatens 21.♗e2, when Black will have real problems with the c7-knight – Krasenkow.) 17.d6 exd6 18.exd6 ♘e6 19.♗xe6 fxe6 20.♕xe6† ♔h8 21.♗g5 ♗f6 22.♗h6 ♗g7 was Krasenkow – Mikhalevski, Ohrid 2001 and now Krasenkow, *Chessbase Magazine 84*, recommends the line 23.♗xg7† ♔xg7 24.♘e5!± on the basis that after 24...♖f6 25.♕c4 the d6-pawn is immune from capture, e.g. 25...♕xd6? (25...♖xd6? 26.♕f7†+-) 26.♖bd1+-.

a2) 12...♗g7! 13.♕d3 (13.♕e2 ♕c8 14.♗g5 (14.♗b2!?) 14...f6!? 15.♗h4 as in Avrukh – Sutovsky, Israel 2002, also looked reasonable for White) 13...♕c8 14.♗g5 ♘e8 15.e5 ♗a6 16.♖bd1! ♗xc4 17.♕xc4.

There are now three moves that merit consideration:

a21) 17...♘d7!? 18.♖fe1 e6 19.d6 h6 (19...♕c6 20.♕f4) 20.♗e7 ♕c6 21.h4 b5 22.♕f4 c4 23.h5 gives White compensation according to GM Petr Haba.

a22) Another alternative is 17...♕f5 18.♖fe1 ♘d7 as in Hebert – Barbeau, Montreal 2001, and now White played 19.♗f4?! but was quickly worse after 19...b5! 20.♕c1 f6 21.e6 ♘b6 22.♗c7 ♘c4∓. Instead White should have played 19.e6, with reasonable compensation for the sacrificed pawn.

a23) 17...♕a6 18.♕h4 ♕b7 19.♗h6! ♘d7 20.e6 fxe6 21.♘g5!

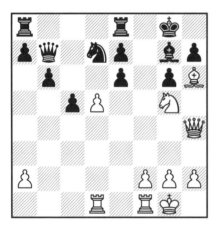

21...♘f8 (21...♗f6? 22.dxe6 ♘e5 23.f4 ♘c4 24.♗g7!! ♗xg5 25.fxg5 ♘e3 26.♖f2!! ♕c6 (26...♘xd1 27.♕f4! ♔xg7 28.♕e5† ♔g8 29.♖f7+-) 27.♖a1! ♖ed8 28.♖e1 ♕xe6 29.♕h6 ♘f5 30.♖xe6 ♘xh6 31.gxh6 is winning for White.) 22.dxe6 ♗xh6 (22...♖ad8? 23.♗xg7 ♔xg7 (23...♖xd1 loses to 24.♕f4!! ♖xf1† 25.♔xf1 ♔xg7 26.♕e5† ♔g8 27.♘f7+-) 24.♕f4 ♕b8 25.♕f7† ♔h8 26.♖d7 ♖xd7 27.exd7 ♖d8 28.♖d1 leaves Black clearly worse.) 23.♕xh6 ♖ed8 24.f4 ♖xd1 25.♖xd1 c4 (25...♕a6!? 26.f5 ♕e2 27.♖f1 ♕e3† 28.♔h1 gxf5 29.♕h5 deserves attention, although White retains decent compensation.) 26.f5 gxf5 27.♕h5 ♕c7? (27...c3! gives Black better chances of holding the balance.) 28.♖d5! ♕f4 29.♕f7† ♔h8 30.♕xe7!

♕c1† 31.♔f2 ♕b2† was Haba – Banas, Austria 1997, and now Petr Haba proposes the line 32.♔g3! ♕c3† 33.♘f3 ♕g7† (33...♘g6 34.♖d8† ♖xd8 35.♕xd8† ♔g7 36.e7+-) 34.♕xg7† ♔xg7 35.e7 ♘e6 36.♘g5! ♖f6 37.♘xe6 ♔xe7 38.♘d4 when White should win. The comments here are based on Petr Haba's very detailed notes in *Informant 71*.

b) 11.♗d3!? cxd4 (GM Glenn Flear notes that 11...♕d6 12.♗a3 ♘d7 13.♕e2 e6 14.♖fd1 ♖fd8 15.h3 was slightly better for White in Gual Pascual – Jerez Perez, Sitges 2000, as was 11...♕c7 12.♗e3 ♘d7 13.♕d2 e5 14.d5 c4 15.♗c2 f5 16.♕e2 f4 17.♗c1 ♖f6 18.♗a3 ♗f8 19.♗xf8 ♖axf8 20.♗a4 in Gamarra Caceres – L. Bronstein, Corientes zt 1985). 12.cxd4

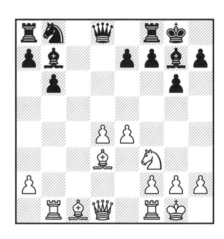

12...e6 (Black can, of course, take the plunge with 12...♗xd4, which wins a pawn at the cost of accepting permanent vulnerability on the dark squares. 13.♘xd4 ♕xd4 14.♗b2 ♕d7 15.♕b3 ♘c6 16.♗b5 ♖ad8 17.♖bd1 ♕c7 18.♕c3 e5 19.♖c1 ♖c8 20.f4± gave White a dangerous initiative in Mietus – Vokarev, Poland 1999) 13.♗a3 ♖e8 14.♖c1 a6 15.e5 h6 (15...♘c6 16.♗e4 gives Black some problems on the light squares, so Glenn Flear proposes 15...♗d5!? as an improvement, intending to follow up with 16...♘c6 next. This certainly looks like a sensible approach.) 16.♖c3 b5 17.♗d6 ♘c6 18.a4! b4

19.♖c5 ♗f8 20.♗xf8 ♖xf8 21.♗e4 ♘a5 22.♗xb7
♘xb7 23.♖c4 b3 (23...a5 secures the queenside
structure, but then the question arises of what
to do with the b7-knight.) 24.♕d2 ♔g7 25.♖c3
♘a5 26.♘g5 ♖b8 27.♘xh7!± Bergez – Vallejo
Pons, France 2004.

11...♗a6

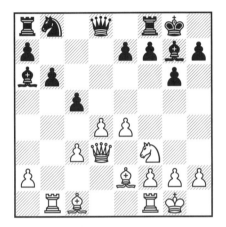

This has traditionally been Black's standard
treatment of the 9...b6 system: by moving the
light-squared bishop a second time Black forces
an exchange of bishops. The time it takes to
achieve this simplification is mirrored in the time
White must take moving the queen around.

12.♕e3

The text is the mainline, however recently
some attention has been focussed on 12.♕c2,
when Black has the following options:

a) 12...cxd4 13.♗xa6 (13.cxd4 ♕c8!) 13...♘xa6
14.cxd4 ♕d7 15.♗a3 (15.♗g5 ♖ac8 16.♕e2 ♘c7
17.♖fd1 ♘e6 18.♗e3 ♕a4 19.d5 ♖c2 20.♖d2
♖xd2 21.♕xd2 ♘c5= Lautier – Svidler, France
2003). Black has now tried two moves:

a1) 15...♖ac8?! 16.♕e2 ♕a4?! (16...♘c7 17.d5
f5 18.♖fd1 ♖fd8 limits White to a slight edge
according to Krasenkow.) 17.♗xe7 ♖fe8 was
Sasikiran – Goloshchapov, Calcutta 2002, and
now instead of 18.♗d6?!, Krasenkow proposed
that 18.♗g5! should be strategically winning
for White, e.g. 18...♖c2 19.♕d3 ♖xa2 20.e5

♘b4 21.♕e4 ♕c6 22.♕xc6 ♘xc6 23.♖fc1 ♘e7
24.♗xe7 ♖xe7 25.♖c8† ♗f8 26.d5±/+-.

a2) 15...♖fe8 is better according to Krasenkow,
e.g. 16.♖fd1 (16.♕c4 ♕b7 17.♗a4 ♖ac8 18.d5
e6 19.d6 ♘b8 looked better for White in Lautier
– Shipov, Internet 2004, but Black's position
remains solid and in the game Lautier failed to
prove an edge, so perhaps matters are less clear
than they would appear.) 16...♖ac8 17.♕b3 e6
18.h4 ♕b7 19.d5 exd5 20.♖xd5 ♖cd8 21.♖bd1
♖xd5 22.exd5 h6 23.d6 ♕d7 24.♕d5 ♖e6 25.g3
♘c5? (This hands White the game; instead
something solid such as 25...♗f6!? puts the
question to White of how he intends to break
through.) 26.♗xc5 bxc5 27.♕xc5 ♗f8 28.♕c7
1–0 B. Lalic – Tomescu, Italy 2004.

b) 12...♕d7 13.♗xa6 (13.♗g5!?) 13...♘xa6
14.d5 is slightly better for White according to
Bacrot.

Bacrot – Smirin, Biel 2003 continued 14...c4
(14...♕a4!?) 15.♗a3 ♖fc8 16.♘d4 ♗xd4 (16...♘c5
17.♘c6†) 17.cxd4 b5 (17...c3 18.♕d3±) 18.f4!
e6 19.dxe6 ♕xd4† 20.♔h1 fxe6 21.♖xb5 ♕d3
(21...♘c5 22.♖xc5!! ♖xc5 23.♖d1 ♕e3 24.♗c1)
22.♕xd3 cxd3 23.♖d1 ♖c4 24.♖xd3 ♖xe4 25.h3
♖xf4 26.♖b7 1–0.

c) 12...♕c8 13.d5 ♗xe2 14.♕xe2 transposes to
the line with 12.♕e3 ♕c8, considered in Game
46.

12...♕d7

The alternative 12...♕c8 will be considered in Game 46, and 12...cxd4 will be discussed in Game 47. However Black does have another option in 12...e6!? which should be met with 13.♗xa6! ♘xa6 14.♕e2! when Black is forced to retreat the knight or displace his queen. Play has then continued:

14...♘b8 (14...♕c8 15.a4 (15.♗f4 ♖d8 16.♖fd1 ♕b7 17.♘e5 ♘b8 18.d5 ♗xe5 19.♗xe5 ♘d7 20.♗g3 e5 21.♗h4± Huzman – Kudrin, Canada 2004) 15...♘b8 16.♗a3 ♘d7 17.e5 ♕c6 18.♕b5 ♖fc8 19.♖fd1 ♖c7 20.♕xc6 ♖xc6 21.d5 exd5 22.♖xd5 ♘f8 23.c4 ♘e6 24.♗b2 ♖d8 25.♖bd1 gave White a slight but enduring advantage in Pelletier – Banas, Mitropa Cup 1995, and he eventually secured the full point on move 62.) 15.♖d1 cxd4 16.cxd4 ♕d7 17.h4 ♕a4 18.♗g5 ♘c6 19.♕d2 ♖ac8 20.h5±/± Barus – Dineley, Bled 2002.

13.d5

The text is currently considered to be one of White's most challenging ways to play against Black's set-up. However 13.d5 is only just beginning to gather the recognition it deserves, and practice has focussed on a number of alternatives:

a) 13.♖b2!? is a very new idea. At first glance it seems illogical to place the rook back on the a1–h8 diagonal, however White's plan is to shift the rook to d2 and then play ♖fd1 and march the d-pawn down the board. The only practical example I am aware of continued: 13...e6 14.h4 ♖d8 15.♖d1 cxd4 16.cxd4 ♕a4 17.♖bd2 ♘c6 18.♗xa6 ♕xa6 19.h5 ♖ac8 (the immediate 19...♘a5!? may be better) 20.d5 exd5 21.exd5 ♘a5 22.hxg6 hxg6 23.♗g5! ♘c4 24.♕h3 ♕a4 25.♖d3+- ♘d6 26.♗a3 ♖c5 27.♗xc5 bxc5 28.♕h7† ♔f8 29.♘e6† fxe6 30.dxe6 1–0 Lesiege – Tseitlin, Canada 2004.

b) 13.♗xa6 ♘xa6 with the following possibilities:

b1) There is a good argument that White's best here may be 14.d5 ♕a4 15.♕e2! which transposes to the main game, but with the additional benefit of avoiding the line 13.d5 ♕a4 14.♗xa6 ♕xa6 which has so far scored better for Black than the more normal 14...♘xa6.

b2) 14.♕d3 ♕a4 15.♗g5 ♖fe8 16.d5 c4 17.♕e3 ♘c5 18.♘d4 e6 gave Black good play in Hummel – Gormally, Oakham 2000.

b3) 14.h4. I don't really believe this move, but with the centre under control it makes some sense. Play has continued 14...♕a4 (14...cxd4 15.cxd4 ♖fd8 16.♗b2, and 14...♖fd8 15.d5 c4 16.♘d4 are both a little better for White according to GM Vitali Golod.)

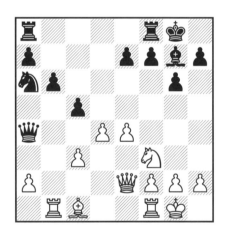

15.♖b3 (This looks unnatural, however 15.a3 cxd4 16.cxd4 ♖fd8 17.♗b2 ♖ac8 18.h5 ♖c2

gives Black counterplay according to Golod.) 15...♘c7! (15...♕xa2? 16.♖a3 ♕c4 17.♘d2 is good for White) 16.d5? (Better was 16.dxc5 ♕xa2 17.♖b2 ♕c4 18.cxb6 axb6 19.♖xb6 ♕xc3 (19...♘e6!?⩲) 20.♕xc3 ♗xc3 when the position is somewhere between equal and slightly better for White according to Golod.) 16...♕xa2 17.c4 ♕c2! 18.♘d2 ♗d4! 19.♕f4 ♘e8 20.♖h3 ♘g7 21.g4 f6 22.♕h6 ♖f7∓ Lev – Golod, Israel 2002.

b4) 14.♕e2 is the mainline, after which Black has a choice of two moves:

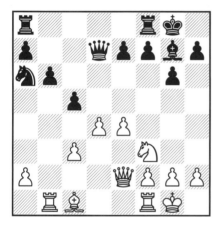

b41) 14...♕a4 15.♗g5 (15.♖b3!? cxd4 (15...c4 16.♖b1 is slightly better for White according to GM Yuri Shulman, *Chessbase Magazine 44*, whereas 15...♘c7 16.d5 is clearly better for White.) 16.cxd4 ♘b4 17.♗a3 ♘c6 18.d5 ♘a5 19.♖d3 ♖fe8 20.e5 ♘c4 21.♗c1± is some analysis by Avrukh in *Chessbase Magazine 77*. 15.d5 transposes to the note to Black's 13th move in the main game) 15...e6 (15...♖fe8 16.d5 ♗xc3 17.e5 gives White compensation) 16.e5 cxd4 17.cxd4 ♖fc8 18.♕e4?! (18.♖fc1!?=) 18...♘c7 19.♕h4 ♘d5 20.♗h6 was J. Lopez Martinez – J. Fernandez Garcia, Elgoibar 2000, and now Krasenkow gives 20...♖c2! 21.♘g5 ♗xe5 (21...♘h8!?) 22.♘xe6 ♖e8 23.♕g5 ♗xh2† 24.♔xh2 fxe6 25.♕e5 ♕d7 ∓/∓.

b42) 14...♘c7! 15.♖d1 with a further division:

b421) 15...♖ad8 16.♗e3 ♕a4!

17.♖dc1 (17.h4 cxd4 18.cxd4 was Plachkinova – Jovkova Draganova, Bulgaria 2001, and now 18...♘e6 19.d5 was good for White, but Krasenkow suggests that Black's play can be improved by 18...f5!) 17...♖d7 18.♕c2 (18. dxc5 bxc5! 19.♗xc5 ♘e6 20.♗b4 ♖fd8 intending 21...a5 gives Black good compensation.) 18...♕xc2 19.♖xc2 cxd4 20.cxd4 f5! 21.♖bc1 ♘b5 (21...♘e6 22.d5 ♘c5 23.exf5 ♗xf5 24.♗xc5 bxc5 25.♖xc5 ♖fxd5= – Krasenkow) 22.e5 (22. exf5 gxf5 23.g3 ♘xd4 24.♗xd4 ♗xd4 25.♖d2 ♖fd8 26.♖cd1 e5 27.♔g2 ♖d6 28.♘h4 ♖f8 29.♘f3= - Avrukh) 22...f4 23.a4! fxe3 24.axb5 (24.fxe3? ♗h6−+) 24...♗h6 25.♖a1! was Avrukh – Kasparov, Ramat Aviv 2000, and now Avrukh notes that Kasparov should have played 25... exf2† 26.♔xf2 ♖xd4 27.♖xa7 ♖d5 (27...♗g5 28.♖b7 ♖e4 29.♖e2) 28.♖xe7 ♗g5 29.♖b7 ♖xe5 30.♖cc7 ♗f6!! 31.♖xh7 (31.♖xb6? ♗d8−+) 31...♖xb5, with equality.

b422) 15...♕a4! The text is Avrukh's improvement over his earlier game with Kasparov - on the White side! 16.♗g5 ♖fe8 17.♕d2?! (17. d5 ♗xc3 18.e5 f6 is fine for Black, however 17.♕e3!? ♕xa2 18.d5 deserves consideration.) 17...♖ad8 18.♗h6 e5! 19.♗xg7 ♔xg7 20.♕g5? (20.♖e1 exd4 21.cxd4 cxd4 22.♖b4 ♕a5 23.♖xd4

(23.♘xd4 ♘b5!∓) 23...♕xd2 24.♖xd2 ♖xd2 25.♘xd2 ♘e6∓ - Krasenkow) 20...exd4 21.e5 (21.cxd4 ♘b5) 21...♗e6! 22.♕f6† ♔g8 23.♕h4 ♕xa2 24.cxd4 ♕d5∓ Ulko – Avrukh, Moscow 2002.

　　c) 13.dxc5!?

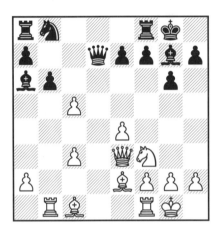

13.dxc5 was popular for a while, however Black now seems to have solved his problems in this line. 13...♗xe2 (13...bxc5? 14.♖xb8 ♖axb8 15.♗xa6±/+- Gelfand – I. Sokolov, Oakham 1988) 14.♕xe2 bxc5 15.♕c4 ♕c6 16.e5 (16.♖d1 ♘d7 17.♗g5 ♘b6 18.♕d3 ♖fe8 19.♕e3 ♕a4 20.♕xc5 ♕e4 21.♖e1 ♕c2 22.♖bc1 ♕xa2 23.♖xe7 h6 24.♖xe8† ♖xe8 25.♗e3 ♖c8= /∓ Elsness – Avrukh, Istanbul 2000) 16...♘d7 17.♖e1 e6! 18.♗g5 (18.♕h4 ♖fb8 19.♖a1 (19.♗h6? ♘xe5! - Se. Ivanov) 19...♕c7 20.♗h6 ♘xe5 21.♘g5 ♗xh6 22.♕xh6 f6 23.♘xe6 ♕e7 24.♘f4 ♕f7 25.♖ad1 ♖d8 was fine for Black in Murdzia – Kovchan, Cappelle la Grande 2003.) 18...♖fb8 (18...h6!? 19.♗e7 ♖fc8 20.♗d6 ♘b6 also led to a reasonable position for Black in Se. Ivanov – Urban, Poland 2001.) 19.♖bd1 ♘b6 20.♕e2 ♕a4 21.♖d6 ♘d5 (21...♘c4!? 22.♕e4 ♕xa2 23.♖d7 ♘b6 24.♖c7 ♕a5 is given by Krasenkow without an assessment, although Black looks at least equal here.) was Markos – Greenfeld, Leon 2001, and now Krasenkow gives 22.♖a6! (22.c4?! ♘c3 23.♕d3 ♘xa2 24.♖d1

♘b4∓/∓ is what was actually played.) 22...♕d7 23.c4 ♘b4 24.♖d6 ♕a4 25.♖d2 with an unclear position.

　　d) 13.♖d1

13...cxd4 (13...♕a4 14.♖d2 ♗xe2 15.♖xe2 ♖c8 16.d5 ♘d7 17.♕d3 c4 18.♕d2 ♘c5 19.♖b4 ♕a6∞ Shulman) 14.cxd4 ♕a4 15.♗d2 ♗xe2 16.♕xe2 ♖c8 17.e5 ♘a6 18.e6!? f6 19.d5 ♕c4 20.♕xc4 ♖xc4 21.♖bc1 ♖xc1 was Lputian – Zilberstein, Blagoveshchensk 1988, which has been given by Krasenkow as slightly better for Black. Shulman queries this, instead proposing 22.♗xc1, which he assesses as slightly better for White. In *Chessbase Magazine 77* Avrukh then builds on this dispute by adding the analysis 22...♖d8 23.♗f4! g5 (23...♘c5 24.♖d2; 23...♘b4 24.d6) 24.♗g3 ♘c5 25.♖d2 ♘e4! when Black has counterplay.

　　e) [editors' note: Just before this book's printing Informant 91 was published, in which Xu Jun annotated a game of his, which we include here. 13.h4!? ♗xe2 (13...♖c8!? Xu Jun.) 14.♕xe2 ♘c6 15.dxc5 bxc5 16.♕c4 Here Krasenkow writes in Megabase 2005: "Comparing to one of the "theoretical" lines, the white pawn is on h4 (instead of h2) and the black knight is on c6 (instead of b8). This should favour Black." However Xu Jun's annotation seems to suggest an advantage for

White. 16...♘d8 "Anti-development is certainly out of place" - Krasenkow. (16...♖ac8 17.♖b5 ♖fd8 18.♖xc5 ♘a5 19.♕b4 ♖xc5 20.♕xc5 ♘c6 21.♗e3±; 16...♕g4!? 17.♖b5 ♘e5 18.♘xe5 ♗xe5 19.♖xc5 ♖ac8 20.♗g5±) 17.♗e3 ♕e6 18.♕d5! ♖c8 19.♖b5!± Xu Jun – Harikrishna, Tripoli (rapid) 2004. All lines by Xu Jun.]

13...♗xe2

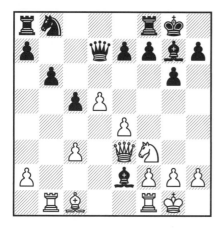

13...♕a4 14.♗xa6 (In a recent game in this line Mikhalevski tried to improve with 14.♖b3!?. That encounter continued 14...♗xe2 15.♕xe2 e6 16.c4 ♖e8 17.e5 ♘d7 18.♖a3 ♕b4 19.♖e3± b5?! 20.dxe6 fxe6 21.cxb5 ♖ab8 22.♖d1 ♘b6 23.♗a3 ♕a4 24.♗xc5± Mikhalevski – Tseitlin, Canada 2004). Black has now tried two approaches:

a) 14...♕xa6 15.♖b2 (Krasenkow's suggestion of 15.e5!? ♕xa2 16.♕e4 with initiative looks like an improvement, as does the simple 15.a3 ♕c4 16.♗b2 intending 17.♘d2 followed by f4 and c4.) 15...♕c4! 16.♖b3 ♘d7 17.♘d2 ♕a4 18.♖a3 ♕c2 19.c4 e6 20.♕b3 (20.♕h3 ♗d4 21.♕h6 ♖fe8 22.♖h3 ♘f8 23.♘f3 ♗g7 24.♕f4 ♕xc4 25.d6 e5∓ Pogorelov – Avrukh, Andorra 2001) 20...♕xb3 21.axb3 exd5 22.exd5 ♖fe8 23.♘f3 ♖e2 24.♖e1= Comas Fabrego – Avrukh, Ubeda 2001.

b) 14...♘xa6!? 15.♕e2! (Less accurate is 15.e5?! as 15...♘c7 16.♕d3 c4 17.♕d2 ♕a5

leaves White's d-pawn in trouble.) 15...♘c7 (15...♗xc3? 16.♖b3 ♗b4 17.♘e5 ♖ac8 18.♖h3 c4 19.♕e3 1–0 Najer – Yuferov, St Petersburg 2000. Black resigned as 20.♕h6 will give White an irresistible attack. However 15...c4 should be considered.) 16.c4 e5 17.♖b3 (17.♘d2!? ♘e8 (17...♕xa2 18.♗b2 f6 19.♗c3) 18.♗b2 ♘d6 19.f4 ♖ae8 20.♕d3±) 17...♘e8 18.♗b2 f6 19.♖a3 ♕d7 20.♘d2 ♘d6= gave Black a solid position in Diu – Shomoev, Krasnodar 2002, so Krasenkow suggests that White should try 19.♕e3!? intending f2-f4 and/or ♕h3 with a view to invading on the h3-c8 diagonal.

14.♕xe2 ♗xc3

14...e6 15.c4 ♖e8 16.♗b2 ♗xb2 17.♕xb2 exd5 18.exd5 ♕d6 19.♖fe1 ♘d7 20.a4 ♖ab8 21.g3 a6 22.♘g5 ♖xe1† 23.♖xe1±

23...b5? 24.axb5 axb5 25.♕h8†! ♔xh8 26.♘xf7† ♔g8 27.♘xd6 bxc4 28.♘xc4+- Vera – Ripari, Malaga 2001.

15.♗h6

15.♖d1!? ♗g7 16.♗b2 (16.e5 e6 17.d6 ♘c6 as in Notkin – Shomoev, Internet 2004 was less good because White will struggle to make further progress, whereas Black can gradually complete his development and then undermine White's centre with f7-f6 at some timely moment.) 16...♕a4 17.♗xg7 ♔xg7 18.♖bc1 ♘d7 19.♖c4 ♕a6 20.e5 b5?! 21.♖h4 h6 22.♕e3 ♖h8

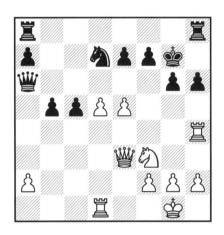

23.e6! fxe6 24.d6 ♕xa2 25.♘e5 exd6 26.♘xd7 ♖ae8 27.♕f4 e5 28.♕f6† ♔h7 29.♕xd6 ♖e6 30.♘f8† 1–0 Pein – T. Newman, USA 2003.

15...♖e8

15...♗g7 16.♗xg7 ♔xg7 17.♖fd1 leaves Black with some serious problems to address concerning the development of that b8-knight. Play has continued: 17...♔g8 18.♖b3 ♖c8 19.e5 c4 20.e6 fxe6 21.♘e5 ♕e8 (21...♕c7 22.♖g3+-) 22.♘xc4 ♘a6 23.♕xe6†± Moiseenko – Kovchan, Kharkov 2002.

16.♖b3! ♗h8

16...♗g7 17.♗xg7 ♔xg7 is similar to 15...♗g7, as considered above.

17.♘g5!? e5

Harikrishna is trying to reach the structure that Black achieved in Diu – Shomoev, Krasnodar 2002 (considered above in the notes to Black's 13th move), however in this position Black is much further behind in development and quickly comes under serious pressure. Notwithstanding the course of the main game, superior alternatives are not obvious. For example, 17...♕d6 18.♖h3 ♘d7 19.♘xh7! may not be entirely clear, but it is certainly much scarier for Black than White!

18.f4 f6

18...exf4 19.♖xf4 ♗d4† 20.♔h1 f6 21.♘f3 may be an improvement, however Black still

has some problems to solve before he is out of the woods. Note that the tempting 21.♘e6?! is actually bad on account of 21...♘c6! (21...♖xe6!?∓) 22.♘g7 ♕xd5!/!? which looks good for Black.

19.fxe5 ♖xe5

19...fxg5 20.e6 ♗d4† 21.♔h1 ♕d6 22.♕f3 (22.♖bf3 ♘c6!?) looks good for White, e.g. 22...♕f4 23.g3 ♕xf3† 24.♖bxf3 ♗g7 (24...♘a6 25.d6+-) 25.♗xg7 ♔xg7 26.♖f7† ♔g8 27.♖b7+-.

20.♘f3 ♖e8 21.♕c4! ♗g7

Trying to develop the queenside bits with 21...♕d6 runs into 22.e5! fxe5 23.♘g5 ♘d7? (23...e4 24.♘xe4 (24.♘f7!?+-) 24...♖xe4 25.♕xe4±/+-) 24.♘e4 ♕e7 25.♗g5! is winning for White.

22.♗xg7 ♕xg7

22...♔xg7 23.e5! is similar to the note above.

23.e5± ♘d7 24.e6 b5 25.♖xb5 ♘b6 26.♖xb6!?

26.♕xc5+-.

26...axb6 27.d6 ♔h8 28.♕d5!?

28.e7!? should also win, but the text is risk-free and leaves Black entirely paralysed for the rest of the game.

28...♖ad8 29.d7 ♖e7 30.♕d6 g5 31.♖b1 ♕f8 32.a4 ♔g8 33.♖xb6 ♖g7 34.♕c7 g4 35.♘h4 ♖g5 36.♖f1 ♕e7 37.♘f5 ♖xf5 38.♖xf5 ♔g7 39.♖f1 ♔g6 40.♖d1

1–0

Game 45 Conclusions: The line examined in this game with 11...♗a6 12.♕e3 ♕d7 is currently very popular and has a reputation as being ultra-solid, although the fact that Kasparov once played it probably contributed to this. Particular attention should be played to GM Boris Avrukh's experiences in this line, as he has employed this system with success from both sides, and indeed my own preference is for the pawn sacrifice 13.d5!? ♗xe2 14.♕xe2 ♗xc3 which Avrukh used with persuasive success in the main game. In terms of improvements from Black's perspective, special attention should be paid to 13...♕a4 14.♗xa6 ♘xa6 (14...♕xa6 also looks respectable on the basis of existing games, however some of the improvements discussed may prove problematic for Black in the future) which currently looks quite solid for Black. On this basis White may wish to consider trying Mikhalevski's idea 14.♖b3!?, which was very successful in its debut appearance.

Game 46
Cebalo – Sarno
Italy 2002

1.d4 ♘f6 2.c4 g6 3.♘c3 d5 4.♘f3 ♗g7 5.cxd5 ♘xd5 6.e4 ♘xc3 7.bxc3 c5 8.♖b1 0–0 9.♗e2 b6 10.0–0 ♗b7 11.♕d3 ♗a6 12.♕e3 ♕c8!?

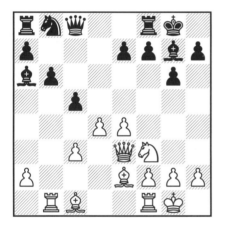

This line is obviously quite similar to 12...♕d7, which we examined in Game 45. The essential differences are that Black keeps the d7-square free for the knight, and creates the option of recapturing on a6 with the queen. Against these benefits is the observation that the queen is somewhat misplaced on c8, and inevitably enjoys less activity than on d7 (♕d7-a4 is ruled out, and Black's pressure on the d-pawn is reduced).

13.d5 e6

The text sees Black attacking White's centre immediately, however it is also possible to

capture on e2 and then pursue other options:

a) 13...c4?! 14.♗a3 ♖e8 15.♘d4 e6 16.dxe6 fxe6 17.e5 ♘d7 18.f4 ♗f8 19.♗xf8 ♘xf8 20.h4 ♕c7 21.h5± Muse – Kindl, Germany 1993.

b) 13...♗xe2 14.♕xe2 with the following possibilities:

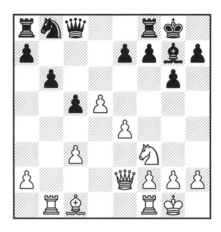

b1) 14...e5!? gives rise to a quasi-King's Indian structure, but one in which Black has a bad bishop and White enjoys a passed d-pawn and a target on b6 to take aim against. Play has continued 15.a4 ♘d7 16.♘d2! ♖e8 17.♘c4 ♕a6 18.♕a2 ♖ab8 19.♕b3 ♗f8 20.f4 exf4 21.♗xf4± Gelfand – Cyborowski, Rethymnon 2003.

b2) 14...♖e8 15.c4 e6 16.e5 (16.♕c2 ♘d7 17.♖e1 ♕a6 18.♗f4 ♖ac8 19.a4 ♕b7 20.♖bd1 was also better for White in Flumbort – Jeremic, Hungary 2001.) 16...exd5 17.cxd5 ♕f5 18.♗b2 ♘d7 19.♖fe1 ♖ac8 20.♖bd1 c4 21.♗c3 b5 22.♕b2, White is better, Halkias – Karagiannis, Athens 2000.

b3) 14...c4 15.♖b4 (15.♘d4!?) 15...♘d7 16.♖xc4 ♕a6 17.♖e1 ♘c5 18.♗g5 (18.♗e3 ♖ac8 19.♗xc5 ♖xc5 20.♖xc5 ♕xe2 21.♖xe2 bxc5 22.e5± Fritz – Recoulat, e-mail 2000) 18...♖fe8 19.e5 ♖ad8 20.♖d4 ♕xe2 21.♖xe2± Whitehead – Fernandez Garcia, New York Open 1987.

b4) 14...♗xc3 15.e5 with a further division:

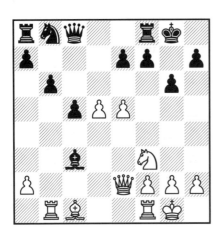

b41) 15...♘a6!? 16.♗h6 (16.♗g5!? and 16.♕c4 also merit attention) 16...♖d8 17.♖bc1 ♗a5 18.♖fd1 ♘c7 19.d6 ♘e6 20.♘g5 exd6 was Belotti – Honfi, Budapest 1987, and now GM Yuri Shulman suggests that 21.♘e4 is strong, the point being that 21...dxe5?! 22.♘f6† ♔h8 23.♕xe5 ♕c7 (23...♖xd1† 24.♖xd1 ♕b8 looks better, although after 25.♕e3 White maintains a strong initiative) 24.♗g7†! is winning for White.

b42) 15...♕f5 16.♖b3 ♗d4 (16...♗a5 17.♘h4 ♕d7 18.♗h6 ♕xd5 19.♗xf8 ♔xf8 20.♖d3+– Khalifman – Lau, Rotterdam 1988) 17.♘xd4 cxd4 18.♖f3 ♕d7 19.♕e4 f5 20.exf6 exf6 21.♗a3 ♖f7 22.♖d1± Sakaev – Maslov, Leningrad 1989.

b43) 15...f6 16.♗h6 ♖e8 17.♖fc1 ♗a5 18.♘d4!? ♕d7 19.♘b3 ♕xd5?! (19...♗b4!?) 20.♘xa5 bxa5 was Sokolin – Fortado, Chicago 1997, and now instead of 21.♕b5 (which also turned out well for White) the strongest seems to be 21.exf6 ♕f7 (21...♘c6 22.♖xc5! ♘d4 23.♕xe7!!+–) 22.♖b7±.

b44) 15...♖d8 16.♗g5 ♕f5 (16...♖xd5?? 17.♕c4 is winning for White, as is 16...f6? 17.d6! fxg5 (17...♗xe5 18.♕c4† ♔g7 19.♘xe5 fxe5 20.dxe7+–) 18.♕c4† ♔g7 19.♕xc3 exd6 20.exd6† ♔h6 (20...♔g8 21.♕c4† ♔g7 22.♘xg5 ♖xd6 23.♕f7† ♔h6 24.f4 ♕h8

25.♖b3+–) 21.♕f6+–, according to Sokolin) 17.♖b3!

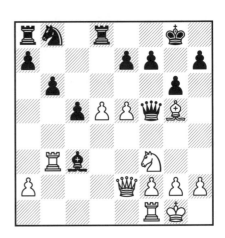

17...♗xe5? (17...♗d4!? 18.♘xd4 cxd4 19.f4! ♖xd5 20.♕f3 ♕e6 (Sokolin notes the lines 20...e6 21.g4! ♕c2 22.f5 with a promising attack, and 20...♕d7 21.f5 with compensation.) 21.♗xe7 ♘d7!?) 18.♘xe5 ♕xg5 19.♖g3! ♕h6? (19...♕f4 20.♖f3 is clearly better for White according to Sokolin, who also observes that 19...♕h4 20.♖h3 ♕g5 (20...♕b4? 21.♘xf7! ♔xf7 22.♖xh7† ♔g8 23.♕xe7+–) 21.f4 ♕f6 22.f5! gives White an attack.) 20.d6! ♕g7 (20...♖xd6 21.♕f3, and 20...exd6 21.♘xf7! ♔xf7 22.♖f3† are both very good for White) 21.dxe7± Sokolin – Kudrin, USA 1996.

14.c4!

Capturing on a6 immediately complicates White's task by activating the black queen: 14.♗xa6 ♕xa6! 15.dxe6 ♕xa2! 16.exf7† ♖xf7 17.♖b2 ♕c4 18.♘g5 (18.e5 ♘c6 19.♘g5 (19.e6? ♖e7 20.♘g5 ♕xc3†) 19...♗h6 20.♕e2 ♕xe2 21.♖xe2 ♖e7 22.♘f3 is equal according to Shulman) 18...♖e7!? (18...♗h6 is also good according to Shulman's annotations in *Chessbase Magazine 42*) 19.♕h3 h6 20.♕c8† ♗f8 21.f4!? (21.♖d2!?) 21...♕a6! 22.♕g4 (22.♕d8? ♕b7 23.f5 ♘d7–+) 22...hxg5 23.♕xg5 ♕c4 was good for Black in Shulman – Yandemirov, Minsk 1994.

14...exd5

14...Re8 15.&b2 has received a couple of outings.

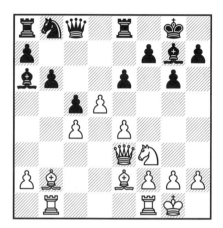

Play has continued:

a) 15.exd5 16.&xg7 &xg7 17.cxd5 &xe2 18.Wxe2 f6 19.e5! fxe5 20.Dg5 (20.Dxe5!? intending 21.f4 deserves attention) 20...&g8 21.f4?! (21.Wc4! looks stronger, e.g. 21...Wf5 22.De6 threatening 23.Dc7 and planning Rb3-f3, when Black is under serious pressure.) 21...exf4 22.Wc4 Wf5 23.d6† &h8 24.Wc3† &g8 25.Wc4† &h8 26.Wc3† &g8 27.Wc4† ½–½ Wells – Ruck, Honved 1997.

b) 15...Dd7 16.&xg7 &xg7 17.Wc3† f6 18.&d3 exd5 19.exd5! De5 20.Dxe5 Rxe5 21.f4 Re3 22.Rbe1 Rxe1 23.Rxe1 looked much better for White, but Black managed to hold things together after 23...Rf8 24.Wa3 Re8! 25.Rxe8 Wxe8 26.&f2 Wc8 27.&e2 (27.d6!?) 27...&f7. Cebalo – Tomescu, Italy 2003. The game was eventually drawn in 45 moves.

15.cxd5 &xe2 16.Wxe2 Wa6 17.Wc2!

White's space advantage and advanced pawn centre can be put to better use with the queens on the board. An exchange of queens would not only give Black more manoeuvring space, but also make it easier for Black to make use of his queenside pawn majority in the ensuing middle/endgame. An example: 17.Re1 Re8 18.&f4 Wxe2 19.Rxe2 Dd7 20.&c7 Rac8 21.d6 &f6 22.&f1

&d8 23.&xd8 Rcxd8 24.e5 f6 25.e6 De5 26.Dxe5 fxe5 27.Rxe5 Rxd6 28.Rbe1 &f8 29.R1e3 &e7 30.g4 Rf8 31.Rh3 Rh8 32.Ra3 a5 33.Rae3 Rf8 34.Rh3 ½–½ Shipov – Yandemirov, Minsk 1997. Although the players agreed to a draw, Black could certainly have considered pressing for more in this endgame.

17...Dd7

18.&g5!

An important moment. It may seem more natural for White to try and maintain control of the e5-square via 18.&f4, however in practice Black has managed to hold his own here: 18...Rfe8 19.Rfe1 b5 20.e5 (White is already clearly better according to Yuri Shulman, however this seems incorrect.) 20...c4 21.Wd2 (21.Wb2 Dc5 22.Wxb5 Wxb5 23.Rxb5 Dd3 24.Re4 c3 is a line noted by Krasenkow, with the assessment that Black has good counterplay.) 21...Dc5 22.Dd4 Dd3! 23.Dxb5! Dxe1 24.Dc7 c3! 25.Dxe1 (25.Wxc3?! Wa4∓) 25...Wc4 26.Dxe8 Rxe8 27.g3 was agreed drawn in Moiseenko – Yandemirov, St Petersburg 2000 as 27...Wxd5 28.Wxc3 &xe5 29.Rxe5 Wxe5 leads to a dead level endgame.

18...Rfe8 19.d6!

Previously play had continued 19.Rbd1 c4 (19...b5 20.Rfe1 c4 21.h4 Dc5 22.d6 Dd3? (22...Wb7! is better, when the position remains unclear) 23.Rxd3! cxd3 24.Wxd3 Wxa2 25.d7

Ｒed8 26.Ｂxd8 Ｒxd8 27.Ｗxb5 Ｗe6 28.Ｒd1±/+-
Vera – Morovic Fernandez, Linares 1994) 20.d6
b5 21.Ｒfe1 b4 22.e5 Ｗb5 (22...Ｂxe5!? 23.Ｎxe5
Ｎxe5 24.d7? Ｎxd7!∓) 23.e6 fxe6 (23...Ｒxe6!?)
24.Ｂe7 b3 25.Ｗe2 bxa2 26.Ｗxe6† Ｋh8, which
was unclear in Vera – Sarno, Saint Vincent 2001.
White eventually won this game, but I suspect
Black may be better at this stage. Perhaps this
is why Cebalo chose to press on with 19.d6
immediately.

19...c4

Theory has also considered two other moves:

a) 19...b5 20.Ｂe7 Ｂf8 21.Ｂxf8 Ｋxf8 22.Ｒbd1
Ｒe6 23.e5! Ｎxe5 24.Ｎg5 Ｒxd6 25.Ｗxc5 Ｎc4
26.Ｗc7 Ｒf6 27.Ｎxh7†+- is a line given by Sakaev
and Nesis in *Informant 64*.

b) 19...Ｒe6 20.Ｂe7 Ｒe8?! (20...Ｂf6 21.Ｂxf6
Ｎxf6 22.e5 Ｎd7 23.Ｒfe1 is given by Sakaev and
Nesis as clearly better for White, the point being
that 23...Ｒae8 can be met by 24.Ｒe3! f6 25.exf6
Ｒxe3 26.fxe3 Ｎxf6 27.e4! Ｒxe4 28.d7+-) 21.Ｎg5
Ｒ6xe7 22.dxe7 Ｒxe7 23.f4 Ｂd4† 24.Ｋh1 Ｎf6
25.e5 Ｎd5 26.Ｎe4! Ｎe3 27.Ｎf6† Ｋg7 28.Ｗe4
Ｗb7 (28...Ｎxf1 29.Ｗa8 Ｂxe5 30.fxe5 Ｗd3
31.Ｒe1!+-) 29.Ｗxb7 Ｒxb7 30.Ｒf3 and White was
better in Sakaev – Zilberstein, St Petersburg Open
1995.

20.Ｂe7 b5 21.Ｒfe1 Ｎc5 22.e5±

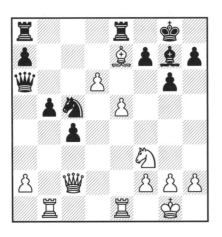

22...b4?

22...Ｒab8 looks more sensible, when one
possible continuation is 23.Ｒbd1 Ｎd3 24.Ｒxd3
cxd3 25.Ｗxd3 Ｗxa2 26.Ｂg5! when the position
is unclear, but White definitely has good
compensation for the exchange, and the threat
of 27.d7 poses Black serious problems. After the
text White quickly gains a decisive advantage.

**23.Ｒxb4! Ｎd3 24.Ｒeb1 Ｎxb4 25.Ｒxb4 Ｂf8
26.Ｂxf8 Ｒxf8 27.h4!?**

27.Ｒa4 Ｗb7 28.Ｒxc4 Ｒac8 29.h4± looks like a
more sensible way to maintain the advantage.

27...Ｒac8 28.Ｗc3 Ｗxa2 29.e6!

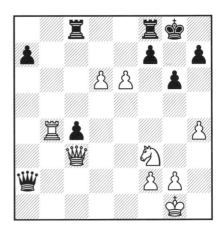

29...fxe6 30.Ｒb7 Ｒf7 31.Ｒxf7 Ｗb1†??

An awful blunder. Instead 31...Ｋxf7 32.Ｎg5†
Ｋg8 33.d7 Ｒf8 34.Ｎxe6! (The attempt to press for
more with 34.Ｗe3? Ｗb1† 35.Ｋh2 Ｗb6 is winning
for Black.) 34...Ｗxf2† 35.Ｋh2 Ｗxh4† is a draw.

32.Ｋh2 Ｋxf7 33.Ｎg5† Ｋg8 34.Ｗf6! Ｗf5

34...Ｒf8 35.Ｗe7+-.

35.Ｗe7

1–0

Game 46 Conclusions: 12...Ｗc8!? has always
seemed somewhat unnatural to me, and it would
appear that at present Black is having trouble
maintaining the balance in this line. A move
that is of particular importance in this context
is Sakaev's 18.Ｂg5!, which poses Black serious
problems which as yet remain unresolved.

Game 47
Gelfand – Groszpeter
Palma de Mallorca 1989

1.d4 ♘f6 2.c4 g6 3.♘c3 d5 4.cxd5 ♘xd5 5.e4 ♘xc3 6.bxc3 ♗g7 7.♘f3 c5 8.♖b1 0–0 9.♗e2 b6 10.0–0 ♗b7 11.♕d3 cxd4 12.cxd4

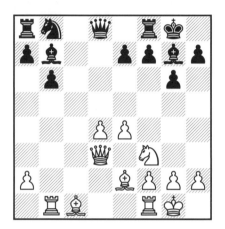

Relieving the central tension immediately avoids White establishing a powerful advanced pawn centre (i.e. with pawns on c4, d5 and e4), but does so at the cost of enhancing the mobility of White's forces.

12...♗a6

The text is consistent with the plans we examined in Games 44-46, however Black has also tried alternative plans:

a) After 12...♕d7 White has several good moves:

a1) 13.♗a3 ♖d8 (13...♘c6 14.♖fd1 ♖ac8 15.♕b5!? ♖fd8 16.d5 ♘a5 17.♗b4 ♖c5 18.♖bc1 ♖dc8 19.♖xc5 ♖xc5 20.♕b1 ♖c7? 21.♖xe7± was Laurent – Cools, Belgium 2004) 14.d5!? ♘a6 15.♕e3 ♘c7 16.♖fc1 ♖ac8 17.♕f4± was Fyllingen – Myrvold, Norway 1994.

a2) 13.♗g5 e6 14.♕e3 ♖c8 (14...♗a6 15.♗xa6 ♘xa6 16.♖fd1 ♖ac8 17.♖d3!? (17.♘e5!) 17...♖c2 18.♖a3 ♘b8 19.♗h6 ♖fc8 20.h4 ♘c6 21.♖d1 ♘a5 22.♗xg7 ♔xg7 23.♘e5 ♕e7 was unclear in J. Watson – Trammell, Philadelphia 1996)

15.♗b5 ♗c6 16.♘e5! ♕b7 17.♗d3 f6 18.♘xc6 ♘xc6 19.♗h4 f5 20.d5! exd5 21.exf5 ♕f7 22.fxg6 hxg6 23.♗g3 was at least slightly better for White in Bacrot – Ganguly, St Lorenzo 1995.

a3) 13.♗f4! ♕a4 (13...e6 14.♘e5 ♕a4 15.♕e3 ♗a6 16.♗xa6 ♘xa6 17.♖b3! ♖fc8 18.♖a3 ♕b5 19.♗h6 ♘b4?! 20.♕f4 ♕e8 21.♖h3 ♕f8 22.♘d7 1–0 Correa – Low Pe Yeow, Novi Sad 1990. Alternatively 13...♖c8 14.♕e3 ♕a4 15.a3 was slightly better for White in Hernandez – Fedder, Luzern 1982) 14.♖fc1! e6 (14...♕xa2 15.♖a1 ♕e6 16.d5 ♕g4 (16...♕d7 17.♘e5⩲)) 17.♗e5 gives White good compensation according to GM Ivan Sokolov (*Informant 42*)) 15.♗d1! ♕a6 16.♕e3 ♘c6 17.d5!

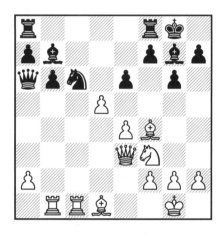

17...exd5 18.exd5 ♖ae8 (18...♖fe8? 19.dxc6! ♖xe3 20.cxb7 ♕xb7 21.fxe3 is clearly better for White according to I.Sokolov, who observes that White's plan is to play ♗b3, ♖c7 and ♘g5 with considerable pressure against the vulnerable f7-pawn.) 19.♕d2 ♖d8 20.♗h6 (20.♘c7!? ♖d7 21.♗e2 ♕a3 22.d6 looks at least slightly better for White.) 20...♘e7 21.♗xg7 ♔xg7 22.d6! ♘d5 (22...♘f5 23.d7) 23.♗b3 ♕a5 (23...♖xd6 24.♘g5 intending 25.♘e4 and 26.♕d4† is good for White according to I.Sokolov, however I am not so sure about this after 24...♕a3!? 25.♘e4 ♖d7.) 24.♕d4† ♔g8 (24...f6? 25.♘g5 ♖xd6 26.♖c7† ♘xc7 27.♕xd6 ♕e5 28.♕xc7†+-)

25.♘g5 ♘c3? (25...♖xd6 26.♘e4 ♖e6 27.f3! is winning for White according to I.Sokolov, however he does not offer any explanation as to how White should meet 27...♘f4 28.♘f6† ♖xf6 29.♕xf6 ♘e2† 30.♔h1 ♖xc1 31.♖xc1 ♗d5 which appears to be good for Black.) 26.♕h4+- ♘e2† 27.♔h1 h5 28.♖e1 ♖de8 29.♘xf7! ♗g3† (29...♖xf7 30.d7) 30.hxg3 ♖xe1† 31.♖xe1 ♕xe1† 32.♔h2 ♗c8 33.♘e5† 1–0 I. Sokolov – van Mil, Budapest 1986.

b) 12...e6

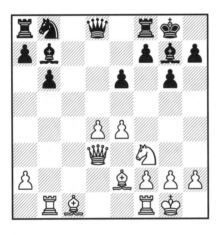

13.♗g5 (also good is 13.♖d1!? ♕d7 14.♗f4 (14.♗g5 f5 15.exf5 ♖xf5 16.♕e3 ♗d5 17.♘e5 ♕b7 18.♗g4! ♖f8 19.♖b5!? ♖e8 20.♖xd5 exd5 21.♕h3 h5 22.♗e6† ♔h7 23.♘xg6+- Wells – A. Ledger, Oakham 1993) 14...♕a4 15.♕e3 ♗a6 16.♗xa6 ♕xa6 17.h4 ♘d7 18.h5± Salov – Mikhalchishin, USSR 1982) 13...♕d6 14.♖fd1 (14.♕e3!? ♘d7 15.♖fd1 ♖fc8 16.♗b5 ♖c2 17.♗a4 ♖xa2 18.e5 ♕d5 19.♗b3 ♕a5 20.d5!± Eingorn – Malaniuk, USSR 1979) 14...♘c6 15.♕e3 ♖fe8 (15...♘a5 16.♗h6 ♖ac8 17.♗xg7 ♔xg7 18.♘e5± Savchenko – Turov, St Petersburg 1993; 15...♖ac8 16.h4 ♘a5 17.h5± Psakhis – Birnboim, Israel 1995) 16.♗b5! (16.h4!? h5?! 17.♗b5 a6 18.e5 ♕d5 19.♗xc6 ♕xc6 20.♗f6† Pelletier – Rowson, Duisburg 1992). 16...a6 17.♗f4 ♕d8 18.♗f1 ♘a5 19.♘e5 ♖c8 20.h4 h5 21.♕f3± Beliavsky – Popovic, Sarajevo 1982.

c) 12...♘d7!? 13.♗g5 (The text is the most popular, however in this position I rather like the idea of developing the bishop on a3: 13.♗a3 ♘f6 14.d5 ♘h5 15.♕e3 ♖c8 16.♖bc1 ♕d7 17.♘d4!

17...♘f6?! (17...♘f4!±) 18.♗b5! ♕g4 19.♘c6 ♗xc6 20.♗xc6 ♕xe4 21.♕xe4 ♘xe4 22.♗xe7+- Sharavdorj - Fedorowicz, Philadelphia USA 2004) 13...h6 14.♗h4 ♘f6 15.d5 ♘h5 16.♕e3 ♕d6 17.♖fd1 e5?! 18.♕d2! ♘f4 19.♗b5 g5 20.♗g3 ♖ac8 21.♖bc1 ♕g6 22.♔h1 ♖fd8 23.♕a3 a6 24.♕e7!± Wells – Knott, Edinburgh 1985.

13.♕e3 ♕d7

13...♕xe2 14.♕xe2 ♘c6 (14...e6 15.♗g5 ♕d7 16.♖fd1 h6 17.♗e3 ♕a4 18.h4 h5 was B. Lalic – Morris, Andorra 1991, and now 19.e5 ♘c6 was certainly better for White, but perhaps it would be even better to play 19.♖dc1 ♘d7 20.e5 when the d7-knight and g7-bishop are both very restricted.) 15.d5 (15.♖d1 ♘xd4? 16.♘xd4 ♗xd4 17.e5+- was Haba – Hlavac, Ceske Budejovice 1994) 15...♘d4 16.♘xd4 ♗xd4 17.♖d1 ♗g7 18.♗a3 ♕d7 19.e5±/± Browne – Martz, Chicago 1982.

14.♗a3

a) 14.♗xa6 ♘xa6 15.♕a3 ♘c7 (15...♕b7 16.♗g5 e6 17.♖bd1 ♖ac8 Sandström – Winge, Swedish Championship 1989) 16.♖d1!? ♖fc8 (16...♖fd8 17.♗g5± Meister – Kyas, Germany 1993) 17.♗b2 ♘b5∞ Khalifman – Epishin USSR 1988.

b) 14.d5 ♕a4 15.♗xa6 ♘xa6 16.♗a3 ♘c5 17.♗xc5 bxc5 18.♕xc5 ♕xa2 19.♖b7 ♖fe8 20.e5 a5, as in Lobron - Miralles, France 1990, was given as equal in *Informant 50*.

14...♗xe2

The most principled approach, however Black has also delayed this exchange in favour of various rook moves:

a) 14...♖e8 15.♖fc1 e6 16.♗xa6 (16.♘e5 ♕b7 17.♗d1!? (17.♘c4 and 17.♗f3 also look good) 17...♘d7 18.♘c6 ♘b8 was Dudas - Talla, Pardubice 1991, and now 19.♗a4 was clearly better for White, however 19.♘a5! ♕d7 20.e5 leaves Black's position practically crippled, and the threat of 21.♗f3 will ensure that White wins material.) 16...♘xa6 17.h4 ♖ac8 18.h5 ♘c7 19.h6! ♗h8 20.♘e5± Komarov - Tomescu, Montecatini Terme 1999.

b) 14...♖d8 15.d5 e6 16.♖fd1 exd5 17.♖xd5 ♕e8 18.♕d2 ♖c8 19.♖c1 ♖xc1† 20.♗xc1 ♗f6 21.♗b2±/+- Solozhenkin - Piankov, Avoine 1995.

c) In terms of results, probably best is 14...♖c8

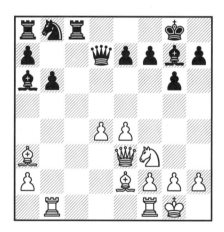

15.♖fd1! (15.♗xa6 ♘xa6 16.♕e2 ♕b7 17.♖fd1 e6 18.h4 ♘c7 was a little better for White in Polak - Gross, Czech Republic 2003, although the game was eventually drawn. The most popular move thus far has been 15.♖fc1!?, but it seems to

me that acquiescing in such simplification can only really benefit Black. Play has continued: 15...♗xe2 16.♖xc8† ♕xc8 17.♕xe2 ♕a6 18.♕xa6 ♘xa6 19.♖c1 ♔f8 with an equal ending in Chernin - Ehlvest, Pamplona 1991, and subsequently San Segundo - Leko, Mancha Real 1998.) 15...e6 16.♘e5 ♕b7 17.♗f3! (Suddenly the a6-bishop is misplaced and Black is critically behind in development.) 17...♗c4 18.♘xc4 ♖xc4 19.e5 ♘c6 20.♖dc1 ♖xc1† 21.♖xc1 ♖c8 22.♕c3 1–0 Navara - Jaracz, Pardubice 2004.

15.♕xe2

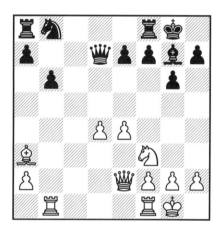

15...♘c6

15...♖e8 16.♖fc1 e6 17.♖c3 (The Hungarian GM Robert Ruck has twice faced the move 17.♕c4!?, in both cases with some success: 17...♕b7 18.e5 (18.d5 exd5 19.exd5 ♘d7 20.♕c7? (20.♕c6!) 20...♕xd5 21.♗d6 ♘f8 22.♖d1 ♕xa2∓/–+ Jelen - Ruck, Zagreb 1997.) 18...♘a6 19.♕c6 (19.♗d6!?) 19...♕xc6 20.♖xc6 ♖ec8 21.♖bc1 ♖xc6 22.♖xc6 ♗f8 23.♗xf8 ♔xf8 24.a3 ♔e7 25.♔f1 h6 26.♔e2 ♔d7 27.♖d6† ♔e7 28.♖c6 ♔d7 29.♖d6† ♔e7 ½–½ Gladyszev - Ruck, Oberwart 1999) 17...♖c8 18.♖xc8† ♕xc8 19.♖c1 ♕b7 (19...♕a6!? 20.♕e3 (20.♕xa6!? ♘xa6 21.♔f1± -Pribyl, *Informant 48*) 20...♘d7 21.♖c7 ♘f6 22.♘e5 ♖c8! 23.♖xf7 ♕b5 24.g3 ♕b1† 25.♔g2 ♕xe4† 26.♕xe4 ♘xe4 27.♖xa7 ♗e5 28.dxe5 ♖c2= Janjgava - Malisauskas, Uzhgorod 1988) 20.♕c4 ♘a6

21.h4 ♖d8 22.e5 h6 23.h5 gxh5 24.♖c3 b5! 25.♕c6 ♕xc6 26.♖xc6 ♘b8 27.♖c7 ♗f8 28.♗xf8 ♔xf8 29.d5! exd5 30.♘d4 gave White excellent positional compensation for his sacrificed pawns in Khalifman - Pribyl, Leningrad 1989.

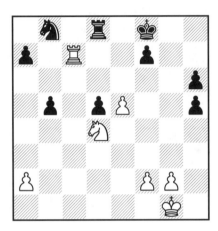

White ultimately lost this ending, so we should probably have a quick look at where things went wrong: 30...♖e8 31.f4 ♖e7 32.♖c5 ♘a6 33.♖xd5 ♘c7 34.♖d6!? (34.♖c5!? may be stronger, as 34...♘e6 35.♘xe6† ♖xe6 36.♖xb5 would leave Black under enduring pressure in the rook ending.) 34...♘e6 35.♘c6 ♖c7 36.f5 ♘g5?! (36...♘c5!) and now instead of 37.f6?!, 37.♖xh6! would have guaranteed White the advantage.

16.d5 ♘e5

16...♘a5!? 17.♖fd1!? (17.♗b4 ♖fc8±) 17...♖fc8 18.e5 gives White an initiative according to Gelfand.

17.♘xe5 ♗xe5 18.f4 ♗d6

18...♗g7 19.♖bd1 ♖ac8 20.e5±.

19.♗b2 e6 20.♖bd1

20.♕g4!? f5 (20...♖ad8 21.♗f6 ♗e7 (21...exd5 22.♕g5+-) 22.dxe6 fxe6 23.♖bd1+-) 21.♕h3 exd5 22.exd5 ♗e7 23.♕b3 ♗f6 24.♗e5±.

20...♖ae8 21.♕g4!

White exploits the pin on the h3-c8 diagonal to force an opening of the position. The alternative was 21.♕f3 however 21...e5 limits White to a slight advantage (albeit a comfortable one).

21...f5!?

21...♕b5 22.♗f6 exd5 23.♕g5 ♖e6 24.f5 ♖xf6 (24...h6 25.♕h4) 25.♕xf6 ♗c5† 26.♔h1 dxe4 27.fxg6 hxg6 28.♖f4 ♕a4 29.♖df1 ♕d4± - Gelfand.

22.♕g3!? ♕b5

22...fxe4 23.dxe6 ♖xe6 24.♕c3 ♖ff6 (24...♖ef6 25.♕b3† ♖e6 26.♗a3+-) 25.♔h1! is clearly better for White according to Gelfand, although after 25...♕b5! White will still have to prove this.

23.♗e5 ♗xe5 24.fxe5 fxe4 25.d6±

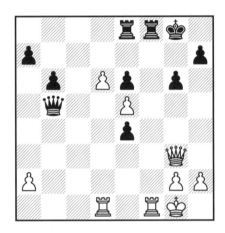

25...♕c5† 26.♔h1 e3?!

26...♖f5 27.♖xf5 exf5 28.e6 is winning for White, however 26...♕b5!? targeting f1 and e5, and keeping an eye on the d7-square keeps things complicated.

27.♖fe1 ♖f5 28.♖xe3 ♖ef8 29.h3 ♖f1† ?! 30.♖xf1 ♖xf1† 31.♔h2+- ♕c1 32.♕g5 ♖h1†

32...♖f5 33.d7!

33.♔g3 ♕g1 34.d7
1–0

Game 47 Conclusions: Implementing the thematic idea of 13...♗a6 and 14...♗xe2 seems less effective after Black has permanently defined the nature of the pawn structure with 12...cxd4. Once the pawns are exchanged White no longer has to worry about the c3-pawn, and enjoys more manoeuvring space for his forces, as well as easy access to the c-file for his rooks. Overall I believe that White's chances of an advantage after the central pawn exchange are superior to the systems that we considered in Games 44-46.

Conclusions on 9...b6!?:

I really like the 9...b6 systems: they are dynamic and flexible on the one hand, and yet solid and reliable on the other. Those studying the Black side of these lines would be well advised to study the games of GMs such as Pavel Eljanov, Boris Avrukh and Robert Ruck.

However, although I clearly have a soft spot for this system, with accurate handling of the opening and middlegame White should be able to prove an advantage. Game 44 deals with 10. 0–0 ♗b7 11.♕d3 e6!? and similar lines where Black maintains the bishop on b7 rather than exchanging it on a6. In these systems Black is very often just a little worse, but with excellent chances of counterplay if White commits a slight inaccuracy. In this context I am rather fond of Eljanov's ideas in the 13...♘d7 line (considered as a 13th move alternative in Game 44 on page 168) from the Black perspective, and from the White perspective I believe it is very important to be familiar with the game Yusupov – Brinck-Claussen, Plovdiv 1983, which illustrates some important plans.

Game 45 addresses the line 9.♗e2 b6 10.0–0 ♗b7 11.♕d3 ♗a6 12.♕e3 ♕d7!? which is currently very popular. Much about this variation remains unclear, however I am rather fond of the gambit with 13.d5!?, which Avrukh employs with devastating effect in the illustrative game. There has been relatively little experience with this move to date, however so far results have been positive. The resulting positions are fun to play as White, but rather difficult to handle as Black, making it an excellent practical weapon (as Harikrishna discovered!).

Game 46 sees Black employing the conceptually similar idea 12...♕c8!?, however in this case Black's queen is less active on c8, and White achieves an easy game with 12.d5. Of particular importance in this context is Sakaev's 18.♗g5!, which currently poses Black serious problems.

In Game 47 we examined lines where Black clarifies the position in the centre with 12...cxd4 13.cxd4. Although I don't object to this idea in principle, I do believe that this exchange is premature as White then enjoys more manoeuvring space for his forces, as well as easy access to the c-file for his rooks. In general this line is less popular than the alternatives, and I believe that White should be able to establish a stable opening edge without too much trouble.

In this chapter we are going to have a brief look at some of Black's sidelines. In objective terms none of these lines should constitute a real challenge to the Modern Exchange Variation, however they do have a certain surprise value, and can be tricky when encountered over the board.

Chapter 9: Early Alternatives and Miscellany

Game 48
Beliavsky - I. Sokolov
Groningen 1994

1.d4 ♘f6 2.c4 g6 3.♘c3 d5 4.cxd5 ♘xd5 5.e4 ♘xc3 6.bxc3 ♗g7 7.♘f3 c5 8.♖b1 0–0 9.♗e2 ♕a5!?

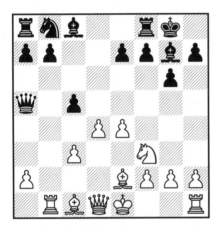

This line is similar in appearance to the mainline with 10...♕a5†, examined in Chapters 1–5, the obvious differences being that White does not have to play ♗d2 (and can consequently develop the bishop more actively), but that Black can capture a more central pawn on c3, instead of the less relevant pawn on a2. There are other differences, but we shall deal with them as they arise.

10 0–0 ♕xc3?!

The most principled way to try and justify 9...♕a5, but also the most risky. The more standard 10...♕xa2 is discussed in Game 49.

11.♗d2!

11.d5 and 11.♖b3 have also been played, however the text seems best.

11...♕a3 12.♕c2 ♗d7

12...♘c6 13.d5 (13.♖b3 ♕a4 14.d5 was Haag - Howell, corr. 1986, and now the line 14...♘d4

15.♘xd4 cxd4 16.♗b5 d3 17.♗xd3± is given by Sa.Velickovic in *ECO D*) 13...♘a5 14.♗c1 (14.♖fe1!?±) 14...♕c3 15.♕a4 b6 16.♗g5 ♖d8 17.♗xe7 (17.♖fc1 ♗d7 18.♗b5 ♗xb5 19.♖xb5 ♕d3 20.♗xe7±) 17...♗d7 18.♗b5 ♗xb5 19.♕xb5 ♖e8 20.d6 ♕c4 21.♕xc4 ♘xc4 22.♖fd1 ♗f8= 23.d7 ♖xe7 24.d8♕ ♖xd8 25.♖xd8 ♖xe4∓ Andrianov - Elianov, USSR 1982.

13.♖xb7

Alternatives:

a) 13.dxc5 ♗c6 (13...♗e6?! 14.♖xb7 ♘c6 15.♗b5 ♖fc8 16.♕a4! ♕xa4 17.♗xa4 ♗xa2 18.♖c1± Vaiser - Konopka, Frunze 1987) 14.♗b5 ♘a6 15.♖fc1 ♘c7 (15...♗xb5 16.♖xb5 ♖fc8 17.♖a5 ♕b2 18.♕xb2 ♗xb2 19.♖c2 ♗g7 20.c6 ♖ab8 21.♘e1 ♘c7 22.cxb7 ♖xb7 23.♖ac5 ♗d4 24.♖5c4± Sakaev - Zagorskis, Frunze Open 1989) 16.♖b3 ♕xb3 17.♕xb3 ♘xb5 18.♕e3 ♖ad8 19.♗a5 ♖d7 20.e5 e6 21.h4 ♗xf3 22.♕xf3 ♘d4 23.♕e3 ♘c6 24.♗c3 was perhaps a little better for White in Beliavsky - Tukmakov, USSR Championship 1983, although the game was eventually drawn.

b) 13.d5 ♗a4 14.♕c4 b5 15.♖xb5 ♗xb5 16.♕xb5

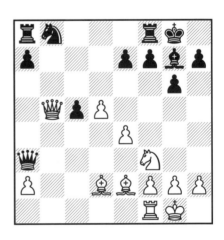

16...♖d8 17.♗g5 c4 18.e5 ♘d7 19.d6 was equal in Lerner - Veingold, USSR 1983.

13...cxd4

13...♗c6 14.♖b3!? (14.♖c7 ♗a4?! (14...cxd4 may be better, although I still prefer White) 15.♕xc5 ♕xa2 16.♗c4 ♗b3 17.♗xb3 ♕xb3 18.♖xa7 ♖xa7 19.♕xa7± was Swinkels - Burer, Soest 1995, and 14.♖xe7 cxd4 15.♖c7 ♕d6 16.♗a5 also looks good for White) 14...♗a4 15.♖xa3 ♗xc2 16.dxc5 ♗xe4 was equal in Miniboeck - Konopka, Eger 1985.

14.♖c1!?

The text seems best, as thus far White has been unable to demonstrate much of an edge with 14.♗b4, e.g. 14...♗a4 15.♕xa4 ♗xa4 16.♗xe7 ♖c8 17.e5 ♘c6 18.♗d6 ♗c2 19.♗c4 (19.♖b2?! d3 20.♗d1 ♘a5 was better for Black in Brglez - Sax, Radenci 1998) 19...♘d8 20.♖e7 ♗f8 21.♖e8 ♘c6 22.♖xc8 (22.♖xf8†! ♖xf8 23.♗xf8 ♔xf8 24.♖c1 preserves some advantage, e.g. 24...d3 25.♗xd3 ♗xd3 26.♖xc6 ♗e4 27.♖c7±) 22...♖xc8 23.♗a6 ♖d8 24.♗b5 ♗xd6 25.exd6 ♖xd6 26.♗xc6 ♖xc6 27.♘xd4= Fomichenko - Beshukov, Krasnodar 1999.

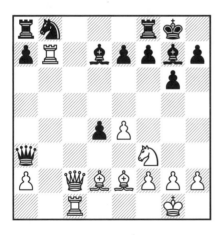

14...♗a4

By way of improvement Ftacnik notes the line 14...♗c6 15.♖b3 (15.♗b4 runs into 15...♕xc1†! 16.♕xc1 ♗xb7 17.♗xe7 ♖e8 18.♕c7 ♗a6∓. Ftacnik also notes the line 15.♖c7 ♖d8 16.♗d3

which he assesses as slightly better for Black. In my opinion this assessment is highly questionable, but in any case it strikes me that 16.♗d3 is not critical. Instead Black must present a suitable answer to 16.♖xc6 winning two pieces for a rook and a pawn. Play might continue: 16...♘xc6 17.♕xc6 d3 18.♗f1 ♗b2 (18...♕xa2 19.♗xd3) 19.♖c5 ♕xa2 (19...♖ac8 20.♕xc8 ♖xc8 21.♖xc8† ♔g7 22.♘e1±) 20.♖d5±. Finally, there is one other move that deserves consideration: 15.♖xb8!? e.g. 15...♖axb8 16.♕xc6 ♖b2 17.♖d1 ♕xa2 18.e5 when the position is tense and unclear.) 15...♕d6 (15...♕a4 16.♗f4 ♗d7 17.♕d2±) 16.♖xb8 ♖axb8 17.♕xc6 ♕xc6 18.♖xc6 ♖fc8 (18...♖b1†!? 19.♗f1 ♖a1 looks stronger) 19.♖xc8† ♖xc8 20.♗d3 with an unclear position, although I must admit that I would prefer to have White here.

15.♕b1

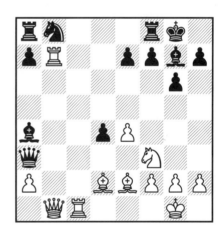

15...a5

The alternative 15...♘c6 16.h4 ♖ab8!? 17.♖xc6 ♖xb7 18.♕xb7 ♗xc6 19.♕xc6 ♕xa2 20.♕b5 gives White an initiative according to GM Alexander Beliavsky (*Informant 62*), as does 15...♗c6 16.♖c7 (16.♗b4 ♕xc1† 17.♕xc1 ♗xb7 18.♗xe7 ♖c8 19.♕f4 ♘d7 is better for Black) 16...♕d6 17.♗a5.

16.♖c4 ♗c6

16...♘c6 reveals the point of White's last move: 17.♗c1! ♕d6 18.♖xa4+-.

17.罝b6 豐d6

17...e5 18.豐c2!? 罝c8 19.h4 gives White good compensation according to Beliavsky.

18.豐c1 罝c8 19.e5±

19...豐c7

19...鱼xe5 20.匂xe5 豐xe5 21.鱼f3 豐c7 22.鱼xc6 豐xb6 23.鱼xa8 罝xc4 24.豐xc4 豐b1† 25.豐f1 豐xa2 26.豐c1+-.

20.罝b2 匂d7?!

The text is bad, however Beliavsky also notes that Black is losing after 20...豐d7 21.匂xd4 鱼xe5 22.罝xb8 鱼xb8 (22...罝cxb8 23.匂xc6+-) 23.匂xc6 鱼d6 24.鱼h6 e6 (24...f6 25.鱼g4 e6 26.豐c3 f5 27.匂e7†+-) 25.豐c3 鱼f8 26.匂e7† 豐xe7 27.罝xc8+-. Ftacnik observes that 20...鱼xe5 is equally bad because of 21.匂xe5 豐xe5 22.鱼f4 豐f5 23.鱼xb8 罝axb8 24.罝xc6+-.

21.罝bc2+- 匂xe5 22.匂xe5 豐xe5 23.鱼d3 1-0

Black resigned because there is no way to avoid the loss of material.

Game 48 Conclusions: 9...豐a5!? is definitely quite sharp, and it is easy to see why White might worry about dropping the c3-pawn. However, boldly calling Black's bluff with 10.0-0 is the strongest continuation, and should Black try to justify his play with 10...豐xc3?! then 11.鱼d2! 豐a3 12.豐c2 鱼d7 13.罝xb7! looks good for White. By way of

improving Black's play, Ftacnik has suggested 14...鱼c6!?, which may well be superior to the game continuation, however on closer inspection I believe that White should be able to retain the better chances in this line also.

Game 49
Petursson – Kouatly
Iceland 1993

1.d4 匂f6 2.c4 g6 3.匂c3 d5 4.cxd5 匂xd5 5.e4 匂xc3 6.bxc3 鱼g7 7.匂f3 c5 8.罝b1 0-0 9.鱼e2 豐a5 10.0-0 豐xa2 11.鱼g5!

The text is of course very similar to the variation with 9...cxd4 10.cxd4 豐a5† 11.鱼d2 豐xa2, however in this case the bishop is developed more actively on g5, a factor that should favour White.

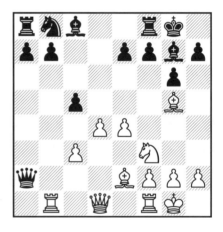

11...cxd4

Black has also tried a variety of alternatives:

a) 11...豐e6 with the following possibilities:

a1) 12.罝e1 has never received much GM attention, but has scored excellently in practice so perhaps deserves consideration.

a2) 12.豐c2 b6 (12...匂d7 13.e5 匂b6 14.罝b5 cxd4 15.匂xd4 豐d7 16.罝a1 豐c7 17.罝aa5 鱼d7 18.罝c5 鱼c6 19.e6 f5 20.鱼b5 鱼xd4 21.cxd4 罝fc8 22.鱼xc6 bxc6± Jeschonnek - Bogdanovic, Baden Baden Open 1988) 13.d5 豐d6 14.e5!? 豐xd5

(14...♗xe5 15.♘xe5 ♕xe5 16.♕d2! transposes to 12.♕d3) 15.♗xe7 ♗f5 16.♕a4 ♖c8 (16...♗xb1?! 17.♗xf8 ♗xf8 18.♖xb1 ♕d7 19.♕b5! ♗f5 20.♖d1 a6 21.♗c4 gives White good compensation according to Susan Polgar (*Informant 64*).) 17.♖bd1 was Su. Polgar - Hort, Prague 1995, and now instead of 17...♕b7?!, Susan Polgar proposes that Black's best was 17...♕e4! 18.♕xe4 (18.♕a2 ♗xe5! 19.♖fe1 ♗xc3 20.c4 ♕c2! 21.♗xf7† ♔g7–+) 18...♗xe4 19.♘g5 ♗f5! 20.♗c4 ♘c6! 21.♗xf7† ♔h8 22.♗d6 ♗xe5 23.♗xe5† ♘xe5 24.♗d5 ♖ab8 25.♖fe1 h6! 26.♖xe5 (26.♘e4 ♖d8 27.♘xc5 ♘d3! 28.♘xd3 ♖xd5∓) 26...hxg5 27.♖e7 a5∓.

a3) 12.♕d3! b6 (12...♗d7 13.♕e3 cxd4 (13...♕c7 14.♗f4 ♕d8 15.d5 b6 16.♖bd1 ♗a6 17.c4 ♕e8 18.e5± Miniboeck - Banas, Austria 2000) 14.cxd4 b6 15.♗b5 ♕d8 16.♖fd1 ♗d7 17.♗e2 f6 18.♗f4 ♕e8 19.♗c4† ♔h8 20.e5 ♗a4 21.♖e1 ♕d8 22.d5± Notkin - Beshukov, Groningen 1994) 13.d5! ♕d6 14.e5!

14...♗xe5 15.♘xe5 ♕xe5 16.♕d2! ♕d6 (Shirov notes the line 16...♘d7!? 17.♗f3 ♕d6 18.♖fe1 f6 (18...♘e5?! 19.♖xe5! ♕xe5 (19...f6 20.♖e6! ♗xe6 21.♗f4 ♕d7 22.dxe6 ♕xd2 23.♗xd2±) 20.♖e1 ♕f5 21.d6 ♗d7 22.dxe7 ♖fe8 23.♗xa8 ♖xa8 24.h3±) 19.♖e6 fxg5 20.♖xd6 exd6 21.♖e1 (21.♕xg5!?) 21...a5! which he assesses as unclear, although I have to admit that I would rather

have the queen in this position!) 17.♕e3! ♖e8 18.♗f3 ♘d7 19.♗f4 (19.♖fe1 ♘f6 20.c4!? ♗f5 was Epishin - Khenkin, Barnaul 1988, and now GM Khenkin recommends 21.♖bd1! with the following analysis: 21...♗g4!! (21...♘g4? 22.♗xg4 ♗xg4 23.f3 intending 24.♗xe7±) 22.♗xf6 ♗xf3 23.♗e5 ♗xd1! 24.♗xd6 exd6 25.♕c3 ♗e2 26.f3 b5! 27.cxb5 ♗xb5 28.♖xe8† ♖xe8 29.♕f6 ♖e1† 30.♔f2 ♖e2† 31.♔g3 c4 32.♕xd6 a6±) 19...♕f6 20.d6 ♖b8 21.♖bd1.

There are now three possibilities of which White should be aware:

a31) 21...♗b7? 22.dxe7 ♖xe7 (22...♗xf3 23.♖xd7 ♗g4 24.♖xa7±) 23.♖xd7! ♖xe3 24.fxe3 ♗xf3 (24...♖d8 25.♖xb7 ♕xc3 26.♗g5+-) 25.♗xb8 ♕xc3 26.♖xf3 ♕e1† 27.♖f1 ♕xe3† 28.♔h1 ♕e8 29.♖fd1+- - Shirov, *Informant 47*.

a32) 21...e5? 22.♗g5 ♕g7 (22...♕f5!?) 23.♗h6 ♕f6 24.♗c6± Shirov - Akopian, Tbilisi 1989.

a33) 21...e6! 22.♗c6 ♕d8 23.♖fe1 ♗b7 (23...f6?! 24.♕h3! ♗b7 25.♗b5 a6 26.♗c4 ♗d5 27.♗xd5 exd5 28.♖e7 ♖xe7 29.dxe7 ♕xe7 30.♗xb8 ♘xb8 31.♕c8† ♔f8 32.♕e6†±) 24.♗g5 f6 25.♗xd7 ♕xd7 26.♗xf6 ♗d5 27.♗e5∞ - Shirov, *Informant 47*.

b) 11...♘d7 12.♗xe7 ♖e8 13.♗d6 cxd4 14.♘xd4 ♘f6 15.f3 ♘d5 16.♕d3 b6 (In *CBM* Ftacnik notes the lines 16...♖d8 17.♖a1 ♕b2 18.exd5 ♗xd4† 19.♕xd4 ♖xd6 20.♗c4± and

16...♘xc3 17.♕xc3 ♗xd4† 18.♕xd4 ♕xe2 19.♗e5! f5 20.♗h8 ♖e7 21.♕d8† ♔f7 22.♖fe1 ♕c4 23.exf5±) 17.♔h1 ♗d7? (17...♗b7 18.♖fc1!?, and 17...♘xc3 18.♕xc3 ♗xd4 19.♕xd4 ♕xe2 20.♗e5 are both better for White.) 18.♖fe1 ♖ac8 (18...♘f6 19.♖a1 ♕b2 20.♖eb1+-) 19.exd5 ♗xd4 20.♖a1! ♕b2? (The text is bad, however Ftacnik notes that 20...♗f5! 21.♕b5! ♖xe2 22.♕xe2 ♕xd5 23.cxd4 ♕xd6±, and 20...♖xe2 21.♕xe2 ♕xe2 22.♖xe2 ♖c3 23.♖e7+- are also good for White.) 21.cxd4 ♖c3 (21...♗f5 22.♕b5+-) 22.♕a6 ♖ce3 23.♗e5!+- Sadler - Tseitlin, Ischia 1996.

c) 11...♖e8 12.♗b5 ♗d7 13.♗xd7 ♘xd7 14.♖xb7 ♘f6 15.♗xf6 ♗xf6 16.e5 ♗g7 17.♕a1 ♕xa1 18.♖xa1 cxd4 19.cxd4± Chuchelov - Mohandesi, Belgium 1997.

d) 11...♘f6 12.♗h6 ♖d8 13.d5 ♘d7 14.♗f4 ♘b6 15.♗c7 ♖d7 16.♖a1 ♕b2 17.♗e5 c4 18.♖b1 ♕a3 19.♕d2 ♖d8 20.♕f4± Sherbakov - Fominyh, Perm 1997.

12.cxd4

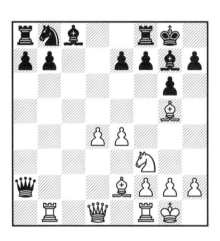

12...♖e8

a) 12...♕e6 13.♕d3 b6 14.d5 ♕d6 15.e5 ♗xe5 16.♘xe5 ♕xe5 17.♕d2 ♗f5 18.♖be1 ♕d6 19.♗f3 ♖c8 20.♗xe7 ♕d7 21.d6 ♘c6 22.♗f6 ♘d8 23.♖e7 1–0 Jelen - Skok, Pula 1998.

b) 12...♘d7 13.♗xe7 (13.♖e1!?±) 13...♖e8 14.♖a1 ♕e6 15.♗b4 ♕xe4

(15...a5 16.e5 ♕d5 17.♕c1 b5 18.♖xa5 ♖xa5 19.♗xa5± Brenninkmeijer - Kouatly, Wijk aan Zee 1988) 16.♗c4 ♕f4 17.♖e1 ♘f6 18.♕b3 ♗e6 19.♗xe6 fxe6 20.♖xe6 ♖xe6 21.♕xe6† ♔h8 22.♘e5 ♖e8 23.♗e7±/+- Lobron - Steinbacher, Germany 1990.

13.d5!

13.♗b5 ♗d7 14.♗d3!? (14.♗xd7 ♘xd7 15.♖xb7 ♘f6 is also playable, however Black seems to be holding his own here.) 14...♗g4 (IM Yuri Zimmerman, in *Informant 68*, notes the line 14...b6 15.♕c1 ♖c8 (15...♘c6?! 16.♗c4 ♕a4 17.♗b3 ♕a5 18.♕f4 e6 19.♕d6 ♘b8 20.♖fc1±) 16.♕f4 f6 (16...e6 17.♗h6⩲) 17.♖bc1 fxg5? (17...♖xc1 looks better) 18.♖xc8† ♖xc8 19.♕c7 ♗a6 20.♕d8†! ♗f8 21.♖xa6 ♕xa6 22.♕d5†+-) 15.♖xb7 ♗xd4 (15...♘c6!? 16.♕c1!) 16.♗b5 ♖d8 17.♕c1! ♗xf3 18.gxf3 ♘a6 19.♗c4 ♕a4 20.♗b3 ♕a5 21.♗xf7†! ♔xf7 22.♗xe7!! ♖dc8 23.♗c5†± Zimmerman - Mansurov, Budapest 1996.

13...b6 14.e5

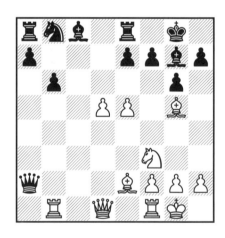

14...♗a6

14...e6 15.d6 h6 16.♗e3 ♗a6 17.♗xa6 ♘xa6? 18.♖a1 ♕c4 19.♖a4 ♘b4 20.♗d2 a5 21.♗xb4+- Sakaev - Kouatly, Doha 1993.

15.♖e1 ♘d7 16.♗xa6

GM Margeir Petursson mentioned the alternative 16.♖a1!? ♗xe2 17.♖xe2 ♕c4 18.♖c1 ♕b5 19.e6, with compensation for the sacrificed pawn.

16...♛xa6 17.e6 fxe6 18.♖xe6 ♝f6 19.d6 ♛c4 20.♛e1 ♞c5 21.♖e3 ♝xg5?

Black had to try 21...♛f7 22.dxe7 h6 23.♝xf6 ♛xf6 24.♛d2, which looks a little better for White, but much remains undecided.

22.♞xg5 e5

22...e6? runs into 23.♞xh7! ♚xh7 24.♖h3† ♚g8 25.♛e5+-.

23.♖xe5 ♖xe5 24.♛xe5 h6 25.♛f6! hxg5 26.♛xg6† ♚f8 27.♛h6† ♚g8

27...♚f7? 28.♖e1!

28.♛xg5† ♚h8 29.♛h5†

According to GM Petursson, at this point he missed a chance to decide matters immediately via 29.♛h6†! ♚g8 30.♖e1 ♛g4 (Upon 30...♖f8, 31.♖e7 is strong, and 30...♛d4 31.h3! and 30...♛c3 31.♛g5† ♚h8 32.♛h5† ♚g8 33.♛d5† ♚g7 34.♖e7† should also be winning for White.) 31.h3! ♛g7 32.♛h5! ♖f8 33.♖e5!+-.

29...♚g8 30.♖e1?! ♞e6! 31.h4?

31.d7! ♞g7! 32.♛g5 ♛d4 33.♛e7! ♖f8 34.♚h1! a5 35.h3 a4 (35...♛d2 36.♖e3!+-) 36.♖e4!+- was White's last chance to secure the full point. After the text it is White who suddenly has to fight to equalise.

31...♞g7 32.♛g5 ♛c5!∓ 33.♛h6 ♖f8 34.♖e3 ♛f5! 35.♖e2 ♛f6 36.♛d2 ♖d8 37.♛d5† ♛f7 38.♛c6 ♛d7 39.♛d5† ♛f7 40.♛c6 ♛d7 41.♛c4†! ♛f7 42.♛c6

½-½

Game 49 Conclusions: I have always regarded 9...♛a5 10.0-0 ♛xa2 11.♝g5! as an inferior version for Black of the mainline Modern Exchange Variation, and nothing we have looked at here has changed that opinion. Obviously Black's position is playable, and White must still exercise due care in his handling of the initiative, however in this variation White enjoys both the superior practical chances, and the superior position from an objective theoretical standpoint.

Game 50
Haba - Oral
Czech Republic 2001

1.d4 ♞f6 2.c4 g6 3.♞c3 d5 4.cxd5 ♞xd5 5.e4 ♞xc3 6.bxc3 ♝g7 7.♞f3 c5

In an attempt to avoid mainline theory, those defending the Black side sometimes delay or forgo c7-c5 in favour of more reserved measures. Such play shouldn't really challenge White too much, but there is nothing especially wrong them. A couple of examples:

a) 7...b6 8.♝b5†! c6 (8...♝d7 should be met by 9.♝e2 when 7...b6 has weakened Black's queenside light squares, and the d7-bishop is rather misplaced.) 9.♝c4 (9.♝e2 is also playable.) 9...0-0 10.0-0 ♝a6 11.♝xa6 ♞xa6

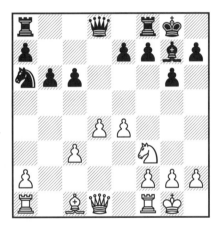

12.♛a4 (12.♝g5 ♛d7 13.♛d2± is suggested as superior in *Garry Kasparov's Fighting Chess*.) 12...♛c8 13.♝g5 ♛b7 14.♖fe1 e6 15.♖ab1 c5 16.d5! ♝xc3 17.♖ed1 exd5 18.exd5 ♝g7 19.d6 f6 20.d7! fxg5 21.♛c4† ♚h8 22.♞xg5 ♝f6 23.♞e6 ♞c7 24.♞xf8 ♖xf8 25.♖d6 ♝e7 26.d8♛! ♝xd8 27.♛c3† ♚g8 28.♖d7 ♝f6 29.♛c4† ♚h8 30.♛f4 ♛a6? (If 30...♝g7 then 31.♛xc7 ♛xc7 32.♖xc7 ♝d4 33.♖f1 wins.) 31.♛h6 1-0 Kasparov - Pribyl, Skara 1980.

b) 7...0-0 8.♝e2 b6 9.0-0 ♝b7 10.♛d3 (10.♛c2 c5 11.d5 ♞d7 12.♝g5± f6?! 13.♝e3±

Solozhenkin – Maslov, St Petersburg 1992) 10...♕d7 (10...c5 11.♖b1 transposes to the lines considered in Chapter 8, although White could also consider 11.♗g5!? with an improved version of the Chapter 8 lines, (White will play 12.♖ad1, thereby saving a move on ♖b1) and indeed this was Gelfand's choice when faced with this position.) 11.♗f4 (11.♖b1!? ♕c6 12.e5 ♖d8 13.♕e3 ♘e4 14.♗a3 c5 15.dxc5! ♕xe3 16.fxe3 ♗h6 17.♔f2 is better for White).

Black has now tried the following options:

a) 11...♘c6 12.♖ad1 ♘a5 13.d5!? (13.♘e5) 13...e6 14.c4 ♖fe8 15.♗e5 f5 16.exf5 exf5 17.♗xg7 ♕xg7 18.♖fe1± Petursson - Conquest, Reykjavik 1992.

b) 11...♗a6 12.♕e3 ♗xe2 13.♕xe2 ♘c6 14.♖ad1 e6 15.h4 h6 16.♖fe1 ♖ad8 17.♕d2 ♔h7 18.♕c2 f6 19.♗c1 ♕f7 20.c4 e5 21.d5 ♘a5 22.c5± Kramnik - Ljubojevic, Monte Carlo 1997.

c) 11...c5 12.♖ad1 cxd4 13.cxd4 ♕a4 14.♕b1±/± Mohandesi - Atalik, Cappelle la Grande 2001.

d) 11...♕c6! 12.d5 ♕a4 13.♗e5 (13.♕e3 c6 14.♗d1 (14.♗h6!? ♘d7 15.♗xg7 ♔xg7 16.♘d4!±) 14...♕a5 15.♗b3 cxd5 16.exd5 ♖xd5 17.♗xd5 ♕xd5 18.♕xe7 ♘c6∓ Alburt - Kuzmin, Kiev 1978) 13...♘d7 14.♗xg7 ♔xg7 15.♕d4† (15. c4!? ♘c5 16.♕d4† ♔g8 17.♖fc1 ♖fd8 18.♕e3±

Li Wenliang - Zhu Dinglong, PRC-chT 1987) 15...♕xd4 16.cxd4 c6 17.dxc6 ♗xc6 18.d5 ♗a4 19.♘d4 ♘c5 20.f3 ♖fd8 21.♘b5 ½–½ Dorfman - Kuzmin, USSR Championship 1981.

8 ♖b1 0–0 9.♗e2

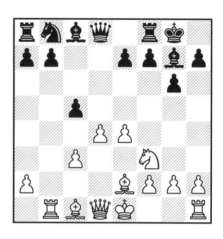

9...♘d7!?

9...♗g4 10.0–0

Black has now tried the following possibilities:

a1) 10...♘c6 11.d5 ♘a5 12.♘d2!? ♗xe2 13.♕xe2 ♗xc3 (13...e6 14.c4±) 14.♘c4! b6 (14...♘xc4 15.♕xc4 ♗d4 16.♖xb7±) 15.♘xa5! ♗xa5 (15...bxa5 16.♗e3±) 16.♗h6 ♖e8 17.♕b2 f6 18.f4! c4 (18...e6 19.♖fd1! exd5 20.♖xd5 gives White good compensation, and 18...e5 19.♖f3 intending 20.♖bf1, should be better for White.) 19.f5! gxf5! (19...g5 20.h4! gives White an attack, and 19...c3 20.♕c2 ♕d6 21.fxg6 hxg6 22.e5! fxe5 23.♖f3 is clearly better for White.) 20.♖xf5 ♔h8 was Khalifman - Tseshkovsky, USSR Championship 1986, and now instead of 21.♕c2, best was 21.♖d1 intending 22.e5 with advantage to White. The comments here are based on Khalifman's annotations for *Informant 41*.

a2) 10...cxd4 11.cxd4 ♘c6?! 12.d5 ♘a5 13.♕a4 (Krasenkow suggested that 13.♗e3!? deserves attention, the idea being to place pressure on a7, thereby provoking the weakening move 13...b6.) 13...♖c8 14.♗d2 ♗c3 15.♗h6 ♗g7 (15...♗xf3 16.♗xf3 ♖c4 17.♕a3 ♗g7 18.♗xg7 ♔xg7

19.e5±) 16.♗xg7 ♚xg7 17.♕d4† ♚g8 18.♕xa7 ♖c2 19.♗d3 ♖xa2 was Sasikiran - Tseshkovsky, Hastings 2003, and now GM Michal Krasenkow, in his annotations for *Chessbase Magazine 93*, suggests 20.♘e5 ♗e2 21.♗xe2 ♖xe2 22.♕d4 with a clear advantage to White.

a3) 10...♗xf3 11.♗xf3 cxd4 12.cxd4 with a further division:

a31) 12...♕xd4 13.♖xb7 ♘c6 14.♕xd4 (14.♗e3 ♕d1 (14...♕c3 15.♕a4 ♖fc8 16.♖c1 ♕f6 17.♗g4± Shneider - Gunnarson, Reykjavik 1994) 15.♖xd1 e5 (15...♖fc8 16.♗e2 a5 17.a4± Lerner-Vakhidov, USSR 1983) 16.♖dd7 ♖ab8 17.♗e2 a5 18.♗c4 ♖xb7 19.♖xb7+- Hoffmeyer - Gazi, Bratislava 1990.) 14...♗xd4 15.♗a3 ♖ac8 (15...♖fb8 16.♖c7 ♖c8 17.♖xc8† ♖xc8 18.♖c1 e6 19.♖c2± ♗b6? 20.e5+- Nogueiras - Donchev, Varna 1982. 15...♖ab8 16.♖c7 ♖b6 17.♗e2 ♖d8 18.♖d1 (18.♖c1!?) 18...e6 19.g3 was just marginally better for White in Polovodin - Semeniuk, USSR 1982) 16.♗d1 ♖b8 17.♖c7 ♖fc8 18.♖xc8† ♖xc8 19.♗a4± Ornstein - Kirov, Eksjö 1982.

a32) 12...♗xd4 13.♖xb7 ♘c6 14.♕a4 ♕d6 (14...♖c8 15.♗a3! ♖e8 16.♖d1 e5 17.♗g4 ♗xf2† (17...♖c7 18.♖xc7 ♕xc7 19.♖c1, and 17...♕h4 18.♗xc8 ♕xf2† 19.♚h1 ♖xc8 20.♕c4 intending 21.♖f1, are both winning for White.) 18.♚h1! ♗d4 19.♖c1! ♕f6 20.♗xc8 ♖xc8 21.♕c4 Popovic

- Gershkovich, Vrnjacka Banja 1990) 15.♖b5 ♗e5 (15...♖ac8 16.♖d5 ♕f6 17.♗g5 ♕g7 18.♖c1+- Hoffmann - Zakic, Budapest 1991) 16.♖d5 ♕f6 17.♗e3 ♖ab8 (17...♖fc8 18.♗e2! ♗d6 19.♖c1± Khalifman – T. Vakhidov, Tashkent 1987) 18.♖c1 ♘b4 19.♖dd1 ♗d6 20.♖c4 ♕e6 21.♗e2 ♖fc8 22.♖dc1 ♖xc4 23.♖xc4 ♕e5 24.g3 a5± Damljanovic - Kouatly, Sainte Maxime 1983.

b) 9...♕c7 10.0–0 ♗g4 11.d5 a6 12.c4 b5 13.cxb5 axb5 14.♕c2 c4 15.♖xb5± Yusupov - Kouatly, Toluca 1982.

10.0–0

10...♘f6

Black has a popular alternative in 10...♕c7!? when I have found two continuations to be of interest:

a) 11.♕b3!? is an appealing idea. If Black proceeds with the traditional plans with 11...b6 then White can exert pressure on Black's queenside with a2-a4-a5. Play has continued: 11...b6 (11...♖b8 12.a4 b6 13.e5 e6 14.♗g5 ♖e8 15.♕a2 ♗b7 16.♕d2 ♖bc8 17.♖fc1 f6 18.exf6 ♘xf6 19.♗f4 ♕e7 20.a5 was better for White in Pogorelov - Conquest, Cordoba 1994, and 11...♘f6 can be met by 12.e5!±. Finally, Krasenkow suggested that 11...e5!? may deserve attention, however I tend to prefer White after 12.♗a3 b6 13.♗c4.) 12.d5!? (12.e5 forfeits control of the d5-square, but makes some sense here as the d7-knight is then rather restricted.) 12...c4?! 13.♕xc4 ♕xc4 14.♗xc4 ♗xc3 15.♗a3 ♘c5 16.♖bc1 ♗g7 17.♗b5± Hetey - Heinrich, Berlin 1995.

b) 11.♗g5 ♘f6 12.♗d3 b6 (12...h6 13.♗h4!? (13.♗e3!?) 13...♘h5 14.e5 b6 15.♗e4 ♖b8 16.♕d2!? (16.♕d3! would rule out Black's f7-f5 plan) 16...♔h7 17.♖fe1 f5 18.exf6 exf6 19.d5 (19.dxc5!?) 19...♕d6 gave rise to a dynamically balanced position in De Villiers – Sisniega, Manila 1992.) 13.♕e2 h6 14.♗d2 e6 15.e5 ♘d5 16.c4 ♘e7 17.♗e4 ♗b7 18.♗xb7 ♕xb7 19.dxc5 ♖fc8 20.cxb6 axb6± Bacrot - McShane, Lausanne 2003.

11.♗d3 b6 12.h3 ♕c7 13.♕e2

13.♗g5!? e6 14.♕d2 ♗b7 15.♖fe1 ♖ac8 16.♗f4 ♕d8 17.a4 ♘e8 18.a5 ♘d6 19.axb6 axb6 20.♕b2± Kiriakov - Sergienko, St Petersburg 2000.

13...♗b7 14.d5 ♖ae8 15.c4 e5

The structure is now transformed into something similar to a King's Indian formation. Ordinarily White would attack on the queenside, however here the absence of the b-pawn will make it difficult for White to force the issue at present. Taking this into account GM Haba implements a clever plan of restricting Black on the kingside, gradually suppressing all counterplay.

16.g4!? ♗c8 17.♗c2 ♕d6 18.♖b3 ♔h8 19.♘h2 ♘g8 20.♖g3

20...f5 21.gxf5 gxf5 22.exf5 e4 23.♖xg7!! ♔xg7 24.♗b2† ♘f6 25.♕h5! ♖e5 26.♕g5† ♔h8 27.♕g3!+- ♖fe8 28.♘g4 ♘xg4 29.hxg4 ♔g8 30.♖e1 ♕e7 31.f4
1–0

Game 50 Conclusions: There is really not much to say about these lines. In general White should be able to maintain a stable edge with sensible moves, and it is for this reason that these lines are encountered quite rarely at GM-level.

Index of variations

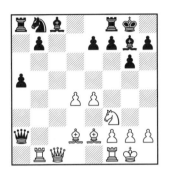
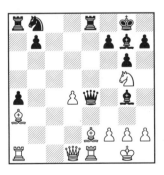

Chapter 2 (Games 9-14) (Pages 41-61)
1.d4 ♘f6 2.c4 g6 3.♘c3 d5 4.cxd5 ♘xd5 5.e4 ♘xc3 6.bxc3 ♗g7 7.♘f3 c5 8.♖b1 0–0 9.♗e2 cxd4 10.cxd4 ♕a5† 11.♗d2 ♕xa2 12.0–0 b6!?

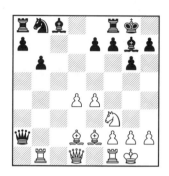

A 13. ♗g5 *41* **13...♗b7!** *43*
         13...♖e8?! *41*
                14. ♖c1 *43* **♗xe4!** =/± *44*
B 13.♕c1 *45* **13...♕e6!** *45*
         13...♗b7!? *51* 14.♗c4 ♕a4 15.♗b5 ♕a2 16.♗c4 ♕a4 17.♗b5 ♕a2 18.♖e1 ♖c8
         19.♕d1 ♕c2 (19...e6! 20.h4!? ∞ *56;* 20.♕e2= *57;* 20. ♗a4 ♘a6!= *59*) 20.♕e2
         ♘c6 *52* (20...♕c7!?= *52*) 21.♗d3!± *55*
             14.♗c4 *46*
         14.♖e1!? *49* 14...♗b7 *49*
                14...♕xe4 *46* **15.♖e1!** = *46*
                  15.♗xf7=/∓ *46*

Chapter 3 (Games 15-20) (Pages 62-84)
1.d4 ♘f6 2.c4 g6 3.♘c3 d5 4.cxd5 ♘xd5 5.e4 ♘xc3 6.bxc3 ♗g7 7.♘f3 c5 8.♖b1 0–0 9.♗e2 cxd4 10.cxd4 ♕a5† 11.♗d2 ♕xa2 12.0–0 ♘d7!?

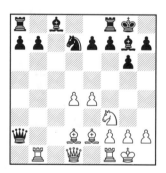

13.♗b4!
13.♖e1 *81* 13...♘b6 14.♖a1 ♕b2! 15.h3 f5!? (15...♗d7!? *82* 16.♗d3!⊠) 16.♖b1= (16.♗d3± *82*)
         13...♘b6! *66*
         13...a5!? *63* 14.♖a1! ♕e6 15.♕c2 ♘f6 16.♘e5!±/± *64*

Chapter 4 (Games 21-32) (Pages 85-124)

1.d4 ♘f6 2.c4 g6 3.♘c3 d5 4.cxd5 ♘xd5 5.e4 ♘xc3 6.bxc3 ♗g7 7.♘f3 c5 8.♖b1 0–0 9.♗e2 cxd4 10.cxd4 ♕a5† 11.♗d2 ♕xa2 12.0–0 ♗g4!

a) 15...♘e5 *103* 16.♖xb7 e6 17.d6

        17.♖e1= *103*

           17...♖fd8 18.♖e1 ♗xf3

                18...♘c4= *104*

                      19.gxf3 ♕a5 *104* 20.♖f1! ♗f8

20...♕a3± *105*

21.d7! ♕a2! 22.♗b5 a6 23.♗a4! *105* 23...♘xf3† 24.♔g2 ♘e5

                   24...♘h4† 25. ♔h3!⩱ *106*

                 25.♗b6±/+− *106*

b) 15...♘a5 16.♗c5! ♗f6

        16...b6!? 17.♗xe7 ♖fe8 18.d6± *108*

            17.e5! ♗xe5 18.♖b4! ♗xf3 19.♗xf3 ♖ae8 20.♗e5 ♘c4 21.♗xh6 ♘d6

22.♗xf8 *104*

22.h4!?± *109*

22...♖xf8 23.h4! ♕a5±

23...a5∞ *110*

c) 15...♗xf3 16.gxf3

        16.♗xf3 = *111*

           16...♘d4

           16...♖fd8 17.♖xb7± *112*

               17.♗d3 ♕a3!?

               17...b6± *112*

               17...a5± *112*

                    18.f4 ♕d6 19.♖xb7± *113*

B 13.♗e3 *114* 13...♘c6

        13...♖c8± *115*

        13...b6 14.♕d3 (14.♖a1⩱ *115*) 14...♗xf3 (14...♖c8 15.♖fc1!± *115*) 15.♗xf3 e5 16.♖a1± *116*

           14.d5

           14.♖xb7= *117*

               14...♗xf3

               14...♘e5 ±/± *117*

               14...♖fd8± *118*

               14...♘a5 *121* 15.♗g5 (15.♗c5= *121*) 15...♕a3 (15...♗xf3± *122*)

               16.♖e1!±/± (16.♗d2= *122*)

                   15.♗xf3 ♘e5 16.♗e2! *118* 16...♘c4 17.♗g5 ♘d6

                      17...♖fe8±/± *119*

                      17...♖fb8!?∞ *119*

                         18.♗xe7! ±/± *120*

Chapter 5 (Games 33-36) (Pages 125-134)
1.d4 ♘f6 2.c4 g6 3.♘c3 d5 4.cxd5 ♘xd5 5.e4 ♘xc3 6.bxc3 ♗g7 7.♘f3 c5 8.♖b1 0–0 9.♗e2 cxd4
10.cxd4 ♕a5† 11.♗d2

11.♕d2 ♕xd2 12.♗xd2 b6!= *133*

    11...♕xa2 12.0–0 ♕e6

13.♕c2 ♕c6

Chapter 6 (Games 37-39) (Pages 135-145)
1.d4 ♘f6 2.c4 g6 3.♘c3 d5 4.cxd5 ♘xd5 5.e4 ♘xc3 6.bxc3 ♗g7 7.♘f3 c5 8.♖b1 0–0 9.♗e2 ♘c6
10.d5! ♗xc3† 11.♗d2 ♗xd2† 12.♕xd2

12...♘a5

Chapter 7 (Games 40-43)   (Pages 146-164)
1.d4 ♘f6 2.c4 g6 3.♘c3 d5 4.cxd5 ♘xd5 5.e4 ♘xc3 6.bxc3 ♗g7 7.♘f3 c5 8.♖b1 0–0 9.♗e2 ♘c6
10.d5! ♘e5 11.♘xe5 ♗xe5

12.♕d2
12.♕c2?!= *146*
12.♖b3!? e6 (12...♕c7!? ∞ *163*) 13.f4 ♗g7 14.c4 ♖e8 15.e5! f6 16.f5!!± *163*
    12...e6
    12...♕a5 13.♖b3± *150*
    12...♗g7 13.f4 e5?!± *149*
    12...b6 13.f4± *150*; 13.0-0! e6 14.♗c4!?± *151*
        13.f4 ♗g7
        13...♗h8!?± *152*
        13...♗c7!? *158* 14.0-0 (14.♗c4= *158*) 14...exd5 15.exd5 ♗a5 16.d6!
        (16.♖b5!?= *159*; 16.f5!?± *160*) 16...b6 17.♗f3 ♗f5!= *160*)
            14.c4 b6
            14...exd5± *152*
            14...♖e8 15.e5 f6 16.d6 fxe5 17.♗b2 ±/± *153*; 14...♕e8± *154*
            14...♖b8± *154*
                15.♗b2! ♗xb2 16.♖xb2
                16.♕xb2= *155*
                   16...♗a6
                16...e5± *155*
                16...♖e8± *156*
                16...exd5± *156*
                    17.♖b3!?
                  17.0-0= *156*
                  17.h4?!∞ *156*
                  17.e5∞ *156*
                    17...exd5∞ *157*
                  17...♖e8?!± *157*
                       18.cxd5 ♗xe2 19.♔xe2 ♕h4∞ *157*

Chapter 9 (Games 48-50) (Pages 188-196)
1.d4 ♘f6 2.c4 g6 3.♘c3 d5 4.cxd5 ♘xd5 5.e4 ♘xc3 6.bxc3 ♗g7 7.♘f3 c5 8.♖b1 0–0 9.♗e2 ♛a5!?

10.0-0 ♛xa2
    10...♛xc3?!± *189*
         11.♗g5! cxd4
            11...♛e6 12.♛d3!∞ *191*
            11...♘d7± *191*
                12.cxd4 ♖e8 13.d5!± *192*

Early alternatives:
1.d4 ♘f6 2.c4 g6 3.♘c3 d5 4.cxd5 ♘xd5 5.e4 ♘xc3 6.bxc3 ♗g7 7.♘f3

7...c5 *193*
7...b6 8.♗b5†!± *193*
7...0-0 8.♗e2 b6 9.0-0 ♗b7 10.♛d3± *194*
    8 ♖b1 0–0 9.♗e2 ♘d7!?
        9...♗g4 ± *194*
        10.0-0 ♘f6
            10...♛c7 ± *195*
                11.♗d3± *196*

Forthcoming titles April-May 2005

Rogozenko – *The Sicilian Sveshnikov Reloaded*

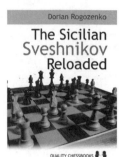

In 2003 Dorian Rogozenko was hired by World Champion Ruslan Ponomariov to advise on the Sicilian Sveshnikov for his championship match with Garry Kasparov. The match was cancelled, but now you can enjoy tutoring worthy of a World Champion in this highly topical opening.

Rogozenko is an experienced grandmaster and is well known in chess circles for his ability to explain opening theory to players of all levels.

About 304 pages.   Europe: €24.99. UK: £16.99. US: $25.95.

Tiger Hillarp Persson – *Tiger's Modern*

The Swedish Grandmaster explains his own original and highly combative ideas in the Modern Defence, an opening he has used to defeat world class grandmasters. Tiger has played his version of the Modern Defence for more than a decade, usually starting with the moves 1...g6, 2...Bg7, 3...d6 and 4...a6.

About 224 pages. Europe: € 23.99. UK: £ 15.99. US: $24.95.

Esben Lund – *Rook vs. Two Minor Pieces*

Some years ago Esben Lund co-authored *Meeting 1.d4* with IM Jacob Aagaard. Now he is back with his debut as sole author and he does not disappoint. This examination of material imbalance and dynamic equality, which is so rarely comprehended well even by strong grandmasters, is a sensational first effort for a young writer.

About 144 pages. Europe: € 21.99. UK: £ 14.99. US: $22.95.

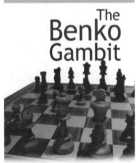

Jan Pinski – *The Benko Gambit*

Though still in his 20s IM Jan Pinski is already a renowned author and opening expert. Here he combines his usual high level of theoretical insight with a wonderful introduction on the typical decisions every player faces in this opening.

About 160 pages. Europe: € 19.99. UK: £ 13.99. US: $20.95.

All books are available at www.qualitychessbooks.com